Diehard Rebels

Diehard Rebels

The Confederate Culture
of Invincibility

JASON PHILLIPS

The University of Georgia Press
Athens and London

Paperback edition, 2010

© 2007 by the University of Georgia Press

Athens, Georgia 30602

www.ugapress.org

Set in 10/13 New Caledonia by BookComp, Inc.

Printed digitally in the United States of America

The Library of Congress has cataloged the hardcover
edition of this book as follows:

Phillips, Jason, 1973–
Diehard rebels : the Confederate culture of invincibility / Jason Phillips.
x, 257 p. : ill. ; 24 cm.
Includes bibliographical references (p. 231–249) and index.
ISBN-13: 978-0-8203-2836-2 (hardcover : alk. paper)
ISBN-10: 0-8203-2836-7 (hardcover : alk. paper)
1. Confederate States of America. Army—Military life.
2. Soldiers—Confederate States of America—Attitudes.
3. Soldiers—Confederate States of America—Social conditions.
4. Soldiers—Confederate States of America—Psychology.
5. Soldiers—Confederate States of America—Biography.
6. Confederate States of America—Social conditions.
7. Confederate States of America—Politics and government.
8. United States—History—Civil War, 1861–1865—Social aspects.
9. United States—History—Civil War, 1861–1865—Psychological aspects.
I. Title
E607.P48 2007
973.7'42—dc22   2007010378

Paperback ISBN-13: 978-0-8203-3433-2
           ISBN-10: 0-8203-3433-2

British Library Cataloging-in-Publication Data available

To my mother and father,
Nancy H. Phillips
and
Frederick H. Phillips

Contents

Acknowledgments

I am grateful for the generosity of many people who made this book possible. Chief among them is John B. Boles, who encouraged me to pursue this topic as a dissertation and helped me every step of the way. He has been an unfailing mentor, teacher, editor, and friend. The other members of my dissertation committee, Ira D. Gruber and Michael Emerson, provided fresh perspectives and criticism that enriched the final product in innumerable ways. At the University of Georgia Press, Andrew Berzanskis first showed interest in this book, but more than that he reminded me to be a writer as well as a historian. I also thank the press's anonymous readers for their careful analyses, which spotted many shortcomings and mistakes. Whatever deficiencies remain are mine alone.

My research and writing benefited from the financial generosity of the Pew Foundation, the Mellon Foundation, Rice University, and Mississippi State University. I am also grateful to Mississippi State for attractive teaching assignments that helped me finish this book. The archivists and librarians at every library listed in the bibliography made my research trips productive and fun. I also thank the staffs at the libraries of Rice University and Mississippi State University for their help. Scholars, colleagues, and friends not formally connected to this project have been generous with their time and insights. My past mentors, Paul Escott and Robert Kenzer, continue to offer advice and encouragement. I am also grateful to Bob for giving me a place to stay while I worked at the Virginia Historical Society. Since our meeting at the Pew Younger Scholars Program at Notre Dame University, Orville Vernon Burton has been an enthusiastic supporter. My fellow Pew Scholars, especially Charles Irons, Kent McConnell, and Randall Stephens, inspired me to dig deeper into Civil War religion. In numerous conversations at Rice, Allison Sneider helped me to see the greater implications of my work. Many friends in graduate school took the time to critique early drafts. I am especially grateful for the help of Jim Good, Charles Israel, Bethany Johnson, and Scott Marler. Lynda Crist at the Papers of Jefferson Davis encouraged my work and shared some excellent points at my dissertation defense.

Panel and audience members at meetings of the Southern Intellectual Historians' Circle and the Southern Historical Association asked important questions that I have tried to answer. John Coski, David Dillard, Aaron Sheehan-Dean, and Joan Waugh were especially helpful in this regard. Colleagues at Mississippi State critiqued my work throughout the revision process. In particular, I thank Peter Messer for his sharp criticism, Matthew Hale for his probing questions, and Anne Marshall for her help at the very end.

I gratefully acknowledge permission to reprint portions of this book that first appeared in other publications: Peter Wallenstein and Bertram Wyatt-Brown, eds., *Virginia's Civil War* (Charlottesville: University of Virginia Press, 2005); Aaron Sheehan-Dean, ed., *The View from the Ground: The Experiences of Civil War Soldiers* (Lexington: University Press of Kentucky, 2006); *Journal of Southern History* 72 (November 2006); Paul Cimbala and Randall M. Miller, eds., *Reconstruction: The Civil War's Unfinished Business* (New York: Fordham University Press, 2007). All of the editors of these publications deserve thanks for their insightful critiques. I especially thank Randal Hall for making my work on rumors more relevant.

My family supported my passion for this book for more years than I care to remember. If my mother and father had not encouraged me to pursue what I love, I would most likely be an unhappy lawyer or some such thing. I dedicate this book to them as a testament to their parenting. My brother has cheered for my academic achievements just as loudly as I hollered for him when he dominated college water polo as an All-American. Despite our different talents and the miles between us, I know he is always there. From my earliest days, my grandparents told me I was their favorite writer and artist. This mattered more than they will ever know. Finally, there is Trisha, my river runner and wife. Her intelligence and understanding saw me through the final years of this book. She is my smartest critic, my closest friend, and my favorite philosopher. For her, my love and gratitude knows no bounds.

Diehard Rebels

For every southern boy fourteen years old, not
once but whenever he wants it, there is the
instant when it's still not yet two oclock on that
July afternoon in 1863.
—William Faulkner, *Intruder in the Dust*

Introduction

Southern Invincibility and Confederate Defeat

The guns were ready, the flags unfurled at Seminary Ridge. Summer's afternoon
sun passed through the leaves, beating on the shoulders of thousands waiting for
the order. For William Faulkner, Gettysburg just before Pickett's Charge, "the
instant when it's still not yet two oclock on that July afternoon," called white
southerners because "it's all in the balance; it hasn't happened yet, it hasn't even
begun yet." For Faulkner, that moment, that ridge, represents the fulcrum on
which history pivots. He imagined being there just before the event not to stop
the charge but to savor the possibilities before it failed. Replaying the instant in
a dream, the writer and his fellow southerners "think *This time. Maybe this time*
with all this much to lose and all this much to gain."[1]

Unlike Faulkner, General Pickett's men did not know that they faced a turning point in the war on July 3, 1863. Their perspective lacked the imminent doom
that colors our view of the Confederacy. During the final twenty-two months of
the war (July 1863–April 1865), many Confederates remained confident despite
Gettysburg and other major defeats. In January 1864, Sergeant Rawleigh Downman thought, "There is a great deal of useless and uncalled for despondency in
the country." He admitted that "we have met with some serious reverses" but
nevertheless saw the glass as half full: "We have survived the mightiest efforts
of one of the most powerful nations in the world." The trooper saw "no reason
why, if we are but true to ourselves, we cannot resist them another year equally as
well." His only requirements for victory were "nerve to stand up amid difficulties
and a determination to succeed and by the help of God we shall succeed." In
March 1864, Louisiana sergeant Reuben Pierson thought the health and morale
of the Army of Northern Virginia were "unsurpassed by any band of soldiers that

history either modern or ancient give an account of." He told his sister that the veterans were "eager for the opening of the spring campaign in the full belief that we will be blessed with some grand and glorious victories." When Atlanta fell in September 1864, Georgian J. Frederick Waring considered it "a trifling success" for the enemy because "we shall as certainly win our independence as the sun shines in heaven." In January 1865, Mississippian William Nugent believed "it is not now too late to remedy our losses" and hoped "the day star of our Independence will soon dawn." A month later, South Carolinian John McLure expected "renewed zeal . . . throughout the country." According to McLure, "a victory or two on our part would change the [face] of things very much, and perhaps open the eyes of the Yankees a little."[2] Hopeful statements such as these, however dissonant they seem today, pervaded soldiers' diaries and letters.

These soldiers expressed a resilient ethos or culture of invincibility. Throughout the war, diehard Rebels knew they were not conquered, but even more, they thought they were unconquerable. Such men did not stick it out because of peer pressure, military authority, inertia, or even Confederate nationalism. They submitted to unending carnage and squalor because they expected to win. Their convictions combined with other factors, including weaponry that favored the defensive, the vast expanse of the southern nation, and Rebel generalship, to prolong the war. Unlike these other elements, however, the soldiers' ethos survived defeat and shaped the New South. Defiant southerners transformed their wartime culture into the Lost Cause. Like the Rebel yell, invincibility echoed through generations of southern life, stirring the hearts of some and chilling the souls of others.

Terms such as *ethos* and *culture* are used to describe many things, so some clarifications are in order. Confederates combined a host of ideas, assumptions, and fears into a system of beliefs that affirmed the indomitable nature of the South and its people. The elements of this ethos predated the Confederacy, but the war forged them into a cohesive culture that diehards espoused. Faith in Rebel invincibility strengthened military morale, but ethos is different from esprit de corps. As military theorist Carl von Clausewitz warned nearly two centuries ago, "We should take care never to confuse the real spirit of an army with its mood."[3] Faith in invincibility ran deeper than morale; for many Rebels, it was an undercurrent that retained its pull despite the ebb and flow of war. Diehards felt gloom and elation like everyone else, but their spirit and conviction sustained them in spite of vicissitudes. Similarly, notions of invincibility boosted Confederate nationalism, but the two are not the same. Diehard assumptions of innate courage, noble lineage, and divine blessing adorned the Confederacy for four years, but thoughts of southern superiority predated and outlasted the rebellion. With or without independence, diehard Rebels believed they were superior to Yankees and unbeatable in a fair fight. Southern or Confederate nationalism, a unifying ideology meant to attach southerners to the Confederacy, failed. The ethos of invincibility, a fierce faith in southern superiority, prevailed. Despite the war's outcome, this conviction survived to shape southern culture and postwar life.[4]

Exploring the ethos of invincibility builds on recent work on Confederate persistence. Since the mid-1990s, historians have explained troop determination by pointing to ideology, camaraderie, masculinity, vengeance, faith in General Robert E. Lee, and the generational values of the final slave owners.[5] Most Civil War historians ask "what they fought for" when exploring motivations, and most agree that Confederates struggled for their people and principles. But explaining why thousands of men continued to fight for cause and comrades despite the long odds of 1864 and 1865 requires a different approach. Instead of asking what they fought for, we must explain why they fought on.[6] Thousands of soldiers protracted the war not in spite of their knowledge of imminent doom but because they still anticipated independence. War tests all its participants, and some expend faith in victory before others. In the Confederate ranks, those who lost all hope most likely deserted—and thousands did so in the last months of the war. Those who remained to the end of the conflict often exhibited an undying faith in their success and even a sense that they and their country were unconquerable. This mentality helps to explain why wars seldom end when the outcome seems inevitable in hindsight: some of war's momentum lives in the hearts and minds of eventual losers who cannot fathom defeat.[7]

Explaining how people remained hopeful through trying circumstances requires a firm understanding of how they constructed reality within the flux of war. Diehard Rebels, like all the war's participants, pieced together disparate events to make sense of revolutionary times.[8] Their reluctance to accept the implications of major setbacks was more than stubborn partisanship. Elements that supported Confederate notions of invincibility—religion, stereotypes, combat, rumors, camaraderie, and more—formed the fabric of the diehard experience. For stalwart Confederates, grasping the full meaning of losses like Atlanta meant divorcing themselves from their private war, refuting fundamental beliefs and formative actions, and assuming a new consciousness. But by continuing to fight from their peculiar vantage, defiant Rebels created friction against the course of events. Their actions and beliefs countered the trajectory of history. In the process, they altered the conflict's meaning and planted the seeds of the Lost Cause.

Though this book concentrates on Confederate soldiers, its explanations and conclusions touch southern history writ large. A quest for meaning, both emotional and cognitive, fostered Rebels' sense of invincibility. Explaining this wartime ethos requires a backward glance into antebellum cultural influences and a forward gaze into its postwar effects. The soldiers' perspectives, like many aspects of the Civil War, lack relevance unless they are examined beyond the traditional boundaries of military history. Raimondo Luraghi puts it best when he argues that "military problems, if studied in a vacuum, do not make much sense. War is the hardest test to which a given society is subjected. Every society meets this challenging strain in a way that is directly linked to its social, moral, ethical—in other words, its cultural—scale of values." Because war demands so much from a culture, "any society wages its own peculiar kind of warfare." Confederates not only defended a "peculiar institution" but fought and thought of warfare in unique ways. This Rebel way of war used southern culture to delineate war's gory ethnography, the reckoning of "us" and "them" through blood. For diehards, certain elements of southern life combined with the war to form an impassable gulf between North and South, black and white. Their ethos stemmed from more than slavery. Many slave owners believed in southern invincibility, but diehards cannot be summarized as planters angered by emancipation. Religious Confederates did not have to own slaves to believe that God was on their side. Soldiers need not be manner born to hate and dehumanize Yankees. Slave ownership did not predispose a trooper to have an optimistic view of the battles he fought or heard about through the grapevine. In short, these people and their ethos were peculiar in more ways than one. Their intricate, human motives and perceptions cannot be reduced to a financial and ideological commitment to racial slavery. Confederate defeat was also complex and peculiar for many reasons; its blend of invincibility and capitulation, reunion and rebelliousness was distinctly southern, and white southern at that.[9]

Understanding these people requires suspending hindsight and judgment and seeing them as they viewed themselves. Diehard Rebels were not insane, delusional, or bombastic; they were rational people who saw and fought a war radically different from the one we imagine in retrospect.[10] Moreover, these people were not "representative" southerners; they were often more privileged, more educated, and more attached to slavery than their fellow citizens were.[11] Most scholarship on unconquered Confederates seeks to explain the war's outcome. Some historians dismiss late-war optimism because it undermines their argument that a loss of will doomed the Confederacy. Other scholars define diehard Rebels as typical to demonstrate the strength of Confederate nationalism. Both interpretations belong to old debates about why the rebellion failed. Diehard Rebels can tell us more about southern culture and warfare in general than about Confederate defeat. Finally, this book shows how convictions that repulse us were thinkable and widespread in the nineteenth century. If our knowledge of outcomes tempts us to read the present into the past, our disagreement with the Confederates' cause entices us to criticize rather than explain their values. Throughout the text soldiers express their beliefs in their own words whenever possible. Their ethos seems less astonishing when we immerse ourselves in their language and discern their patterns of thought.[12]

Soldiers' letters and diaries from 1863 to 1865 uncover the wartime perspectives, cultural values, and psychological constructions that convinced Rebels they were invincible. This book's inquiry narrows its source material in two ways. First, to explain a wartime mentality, it ignores evidence available in postwar memoirs and regimental histories. Though these records provide descriptive accounts, their authors rely on memory, and—to an extent far greater than wartime writings—they speak with an audience in mind. According to William Maxwell, "In talking about the past we lie with every breath we draw." Memory "is really a form of storytelling that goes on continually in the mind and often changes with the telling. Too many conflicting emotional interests are involved for life ever to be wholly acceptable, and possibly it is the work of the storyteller to rearrange things so that they conform to this end." For this reason, postwar accounts cannot answer wartime questions. Second, by centering the inquiry on 1863–65, this work studies a period when the volume of testimony was most affected by casualties, war shortages, unreliable mail service, and the acceleration of military campaigns. This problem is most acute for the final operations of 1865. For example, few of General Lee's men had the time or means to record their observations during the critical period from the evacuation of Richmond on April 2, 1865, to the surrender at Appomattox a week later. To compensate for this documentary silence, this book includes accounts soldiers wrote a month or two later, when the chronicles were based on wartime writings and their tone rings true. This was a difficult decision to make, but the available evidence offered few options.[13]

Despite these source restrictions, this book enjoys an embarrassment of riches when compared to the evidence available to scholars of other wars, cultures, and eras. More than 750,000 men fought for the Confederacy, and more than 80 percent of them were literate. By writing to loved ones and keeping copious diaries, Rebels and their Union counterparts left behind more written evidence than exists from soldiers of any previous conflict. Moreover, these records compare favorably to documents from twentieth-century wars because unlike troops from these later struggles, Civil War soldiers encountered no government censors. They could and did reveal their hopes and fears, speculate about coming campaigns and the war's conclusion, express their motives for fighting and enduring, and criticize anyone and anything. Their writing provides historians with an incomparable glimpse of nineteenth-century America. Archives, historical societies, universities, and libraries preserve thousands of these letters and diaries, and books and journals have published hundreds of the better collections to accommodate scholars and a substantial reading public.[14]

By including the accounts of troops and officers from across the Confederacy, *Diehard Rebels* uses rich evidence to compare the experiences and perspectives of diverse soldiers in disparate locations. By relying on written evidence, this book privileges the educated. Nonetheless, in this study, enlisted men and officers expressed common convictions and knowledge. Privates from small farms and colonels from plantations shared similar mentalities of being unconquerable, and neither rank seemed better prepared for defeat. Perhaps the style of command melded the mentalities of troops and leaders. Civil War officers marched, camped, fought, and died beside their men in a manner that was less common in other American wars. The ethos of invincibility also transcended class lines. As this book demonstrates, diverse beliefs and actions contributed to the ethos. Many of these elements drew from war experiences and did not reflect class issues or slavery, thereby making the ethos more attractive to yeomen than was Confederate nationalism, which seldom strayed from masters' aims and ideology.[15]

This work also contrasts Rebels in three groups: the Army of Northern Virginia, which defended Richmond; the Army of Tennessee, which fought General William T. Sherman's force in Tennessee, Georgia, and the Carolinas; and the Army of the Trans-Mississippi, which opposed Federal troops west of the river. The evidence reveals significant variation in opinion as well as striking similarities in the attitudes of Confederates who fought from Virginia to Texas. The text explores these comparisons in depth. This book favors the voices of the infantrymen, cavalrymen, and artillerymen who fought in these main theaters over accounts written by Confederates whose war service was more unique or unfortunate, such as partisan guerrillas, sailors, and prisoners of war. Adding many of these latter viewpoints threatened to turn an already diverse discourse into a cacophony. Finally, the content of diaries and letters showed striking similarities— the confidence soldiers displayed in letters also appeared in their most private chronicles. Significant occasions when correspondence differed from journals, such as after the Battle of Franklin, receive attention in the text. Likewise, the tone of correspondence addressed to men, women, and children is similar if not indistinguishable because troops often meant their letters for the eyes and ears of everyone back home.

Rather than follow the war's final years chronologically, each chapter corresponds to an element that diehard Rebels used to bolster their faith in Confederate invincibility. The first two chapters explore belligerents. At a basic level, every soldier's view of the Civil War depended on how the sides were drawn. The language, images, and abstractions that defined "us" and "them" helped troops grasp enormous struggles and kill with impunity. Specifically, chapter 1 shows how religion shaped Confederate identity. Convictions that God controlled history and favored the rebellion convinced thousands of soldiers that their Maker would providentially deliver independence when the time was right. This chapter reminds us that Christianity permeated nineteenth-century life and shaped most Americans' worldviews. For many Rebels, faith provided the bedrock for notions of invincibility. Chapter 2 examines how abstractions of the enemy influenced soldiers' images of the war and its contingencies. By underestimating or barbarizing the Union, Rebels envisioned a foe that was too inept or too evil to win a war directed by God. Taken together, these chapters demonstrate that

Confederates pictured themselves and their adversaries in Manichaean terms that left no doubt as to which side was right; they drew the sides of the Civil War in a way that made Union victory inconceivable, even impossible, within their worldview.

The next two chapters shift the focus from belligerents to the war itself. Chapter 3 explores how soldiers remained confident within their immediate surroundings. A host of issues, including comradeship, disorienting combat conditions, and the spectacle of Confederate numbers on parade grounds and enemy corpses on battlefields, assured many Rebels that they were holding their own against great but surmountable odds. Chapter 4 examines how troops perceived the distant war, the corners of the conflict that touched far-off theaters, the North, and overseas. Troops used hearsay, irresponsible media coverage, and propaganda to envision a war that was rosier than the truth but just as believable from the soldiers' vantage point. This chapter pays close attention to a force that influenced every soldier's life but seldom receives attention from historians—that is, camp rumors. The gossip of war covered immediate campaigns, distant battles, political events, home front issues, and foreign affairs in a fog of optimism that reflected and affected soldiers' view of things. Taken together, chapters 3 and 4 illustrate how warfare appeared chaotic and ambiguous to those who waged it. The first two chapters show how perceptions of belligerents clarified a messy reality and pointed unequivocally to Confederate victory, and chapters 3 and 4 reveal how warfare near and far obscured the course of the Civil War's final years.

Chapter 5 studies the price and legacy of southern invincibility, covering the final campaigns of 1865 and the surrenders. The influences examined in previous chapters continued to affect soldiers' mentalities up to and even past capitulation. As the Confederacy faded into oblivion, diehards articulated their ethos in a series of resolutions sent to newspapers and the Confederate Congress. Written in early 1865, these documents constituted the diehards' final attempt to rally their countrymen. The resolutions present a litany of southern invincibility and demonstrate the centrality of soldiers' notions of being unconquerable. By the spring of 1865, the cognitive and emotional supports for Rebels' confidence had withstood years of setbacks, but surrendering questioned Confederate faith like no other challenge. Some troops discarded the ethos when events finally impinged on their reality and ended the world they knew. Others overcame the initial shock of defeat and used the culture of invincibility to escape trauma and dishonor. Instead of crippling them after surrender, old notions of southern superiority helped diehards remain defiant. Many of them surrendered and took oaths of allegiance but stayed rebellious to the core. The conclusion studies diehards' final acts as soldiers, considers the long-term impact of Rebel notions of invincibility, and compares the Confederate experience to other cultural reactions to defeat. The central elements of Confederate invincibility—southern righteousness and northern barbarity—evolved into the Lost Cause legend. While other scholarship locates the cult's origins within the socioeconomic and political tensions of postwar life, this book stresses the links between wartime and postwar beliefs.

In the end, the history of diehard Rebels reveals southern culture as a continuum rather than a succession of Old South, Confederacy, and New South. It recovers how a generation of veterans lived through all three eras and strove to maintain their values and identity within the crucible of war, emancipation, and reunion. Many historians follow Faulkner's lead and stress how defeat changed the South.[16] Confederate failure and Reconstruction altered southern politics and the economy but did not reshape white southern culture.[17] If anything, the Union war effort and military occupation hardened white southern resistance to cultural change. Rebels responded to anomie by preserving their innermost convictions. In this important way, white southerners remained unconquered for generations.

Their persistence complicates the legacy of the Civil War. The most popular studies of the conflict depict an inevitable struggle that strengthened the nation and expanded equality as America transformed itself in the fires of fratricide.[18] These works stress common courage and convictions, a rebirth of freedom, and reconciliation after a brothers' war. But this sanitized war can corroborate buff history and southern "heritage" claims that glorify and obfuscate the past. Missing are the broken promises of emancipation, intense hatreds, and persistent southern defiance that darkened the war and unraveled its conclusion. This book retrieves a murkier war: people prayed to a God who slaughtered armies of abolition; soldiers spawned images of enemies that haunted them for the rest of their days; battles were chaos, the distant war a jumble of rumors; myopic perspectives clouded chronology, erased turning points, and defied a collective rise and fall. The war formally ended in 1865, but the bloody conflict spilled into Reconstruction and stained posterity.[19]

The power of religion depends, in the last resort, upon the credibility of the banners it puts in the hands of men as they stand before death.

—Peter L. Berger, *The Sacred Canopy*

The Smile of Providence

Confederate Religion and Invincibility

Moments when people encounter mortality or when societies confront crises reveal the strength of religious beliefs.[1] With death pervasive and anomie on all sides, the crucible of war may be the ultimate test of a people's spirituality. In the American Civil War, Confederates lofted banners of faith for all to see. Their beliefs graced government documents, filled newspaper columns, accented military reports, and enriched thousands of diaries and letters. A host of influences, including the tenor of antebellum southern evangelicalism, the government's uses of Christianity, and the encompassing presence of spirituality in the armies, convinced many Rebel soldiers that God favored their cause and would deliver them victory. Even in the final months of the struggle, soldiers displayed remarkable confidence that the Almighty would save them from ruin if they fulfilled their obligations to him, if they upheld their covenant.

By providing assurance that God blessed the Confederacy, religion fostered a strong expectation of victory—even a mentality of being unconquerable—among many Rebels. This belief that they were on the winning side of Providence colored Confederates' perceptions of the military situation and delayed the most stalwart defenders' realization of the rebellion's fate. While confidence in ultimate triumph was a reason in itself for soldiers to adopt Confederate religion, the men sought Christianity because it bestowed two invaluable gifts: an explanatory system to make sense of the war and a code of behavior to guide them past the temptations of camp and the perils of combat. Secular institutions rivaled but seldom matched these gifts. Thousands of men carried southern evangelicalism with them to war and thus intuitively gained a religious worldview of the conflict. Thousands more found religion after encountering carnage and thereby acquired a belief system that enabled them to overcome terror and maintain reality. From 1863 to 1865, Rebel armies were perhaps the most religious legions ever assembled on American soil.

Through the final years of the struggle, thousands of Confederates continued to have faith in God's favor and Providence. On Christmas Day 1864, Edward Crenshaw sat in his winter quarters hoping for holiday joy or "good news from our armies to cheer me." None came. "But the blessed Thought that God, in his infinite mercy, gave his only begotten son as an atonement for our sins, cheers me and gives me new life." "I will not despair when we have such a God to aid us," Crenshaw reasoned, "for he has said that he will protect the weak and aid those who are deserving and he will hear the prayers of those who call him in an humble and contrite spirit.—He will do what is best for us; his will will be done and not that of our enemies." Crenshaw did not fathom that God's will could correspond to northern war aims. In a letter to his father, Reuben Pierson bluntly expressed his confidence in God's favor: "While we . . . fight in a holy and just cause we need have no fears of being enslaved by so brutal and cruel enemies as those against whom we are fighting." According to Pierson, "God who rules the destiny of all things and is a God of wisdom and of justice will never suffer a determined and Christian people to be overcome by a cruel Tyrant but will be their deliver[er] as in the days of old." Pierson reasoned that a God who led "the children of Israel dry-shod through the Red Sea" could and would find a way to give the Confederacy its independence.[2]

In the end, Confederate religion yielded equivocal results. On the one hand, spirituality offered the men immeasurable benefits. Christianity countered the fear of death, promoted discipline and morality, relieved the stresses of combat and fatigue, encouraged communal bonds, and alleviated boredom. Rituals of faith connected thousands of soldiers to peaceful memories and to loved ones worshiping back home. On the other hand, religion prolonged and intensified the conflict. Ministers and civic leaders quoted Scripture to justify warfare. Many even encouraged increased destruction and carnage as a purge for national sins. Because the religious code of behavior for many white southerners equated fighting for the Confederacy with doing God's work, Christianity encouraged thousands of devout Rebels to stay in the ranks despite increased hardships and mounting death tolls. In the end, thousands of southerners convinced themselves that only God could conquer them, and he was their greatest ally. While praying to their Prince of Peace, Confederates developed a mentality that extended the suffering of millions.[3]

ᏧᎳ ᏧᎳ ᏧᎳ

The conviction that God favored their cause and would providentially deliver them independence continued to hearten many Rebels in the final years of the war, in part because the roots of these thoughts were deeply embedded in southern religion and the American mind. Three developments in antebellum religion particularly influenced this wartime belief: the growth and separation of evangelical Protestant denominations in the South, antebellum clerics' support of slavery, and the millennialism of American civil religion. In all three elements, southern identity gravitated toward God and away from the North. This heavenly focus raised Confederates' perceptions of their country and cause to a sacred level. In other words, many soldiers continued to expect ultimate triumph because their religion conceived the South as divinely chosen for greatness.[4]

Facing failure and desolation, South Carolinian Richard Furman tried to reassure himself that "as the Lord is great in his Mercies, we are thereby encouraged to hope." He braced himself against a grave future with the conviction that "God has promised Strength equal to the Day of Trial," and commensurate to the challenge, "so will the Glory and Joy of Victory be to the faithful soul." In Kentucky, a kindred spirit, James Smith, found similar comfort in God's promise of providential deliverance: "'The Lord hath his way in the wilderness and all things obey his might.' I trust he will yet bring good out of this evil."[5] Furman and Smith were not writing about the ravages of war and the rebellion's need for divine aid; the failure they feared was an irreligious South, and the bleakness they encountered was the ungodly landscape of the region in the 1790s, not the charred fields of the Confederacy in the 1860s. Similarities between the ministers' language and Confederates' words of faith illustrate that wartime spirituality owed much to antebellum evangelical inheritances. Views and practices central to Confederate religion first became popular in the South during the Great Revival of 1800–1805. In the final years of the Civil War, Rebels still saw the conflict through a spiritual framework strikingly similar to the worldview of Furman and other turn-of-the-century southern clerics. These connections confirm that Confederate religion was more than useful propaganda or wartime delusions fabricated by a people unwilling to accept defeat. Confederate religion constituted the society's reflexive use of its traditional beliefs when it needed them most.

The South had missed the Great Awakening that transformed and expanded religion in New Jersey, Pennsylvania, and Massachusetts during the 1730s and 1740s. Victory over Great Britain raised southern evangelicals' hopes that their denominations, unlike the Anglican Church, would profit from their heritage as outlawed, dissenting churches that had rallied to the patriots' cause. Instead, the first decades of the republic brought spiritual decline. Fewer southern men joined the clergy. The region seemed more interested in expanding its physical boundaries than its spiritual awareness. Empty pews attested to the depopulation of the East as families trekked to Kentucky and Tennessee. Coming at a time when churchmen anticipated growth, this depression hit hard.[6]

How southern Christians perceived this secular winter and hoped for a brighter future exhibits important parallels to Confederate religiosity. Living in a time when the populace lacked both scientific explanations for natural calamities and social theories for the rise of secularism, turn-of-the-century Christians accepted sacred answers for the otherwise inexplicable changes in their world. They calmed their apprehensions with the faith that an omnipotent deity controlled all their affairs. Just as no soul could avoid God's judgment, nothing God created was beyond his command. Scripture described the minuteness of divine care: God controlled the falling of sparrows and numbered the hairs on human heads. On a daily basis, God directed the course of nature, people, and civilizations. Using this system of thought, Furman and his fellow Christians reasoned that God not only knew of religion's waning in the South but was using it for some higher purpose.[7]

But why would their Maker sanction religious depression? Churchmen answered that God allowed Christianity's decline to show southerners the shallowness and futility of a society separated from him. In their view, the Almighty would revive spirituality in the South after the populace recognized the dangers of religious estrangement and repented its sins. In other words, if God wanted to teach southerners the worthlessness of life without him, the poor state of southern religion would improve when Christians learned the lesson and sought reconciliation. The process of change for the entire section was envisioned as the path of an individual's conversion magnified. Clergy imagined that God would respond to the South's penitence with an intense and widespread religious revival that would contrast in goodness the evil of the spiritual void. What had been a place of iniquity would become God's chosen land. Where there had for decades been spiritual darkness, there would now be sacred light. The South's turning toward God would provide a blessed example for the world.[8]

The evangelicals' perspective, however, significantly minimized human responsibility for problems and solutions. Congregations could pray for renewed awareness of God and address the sins that might have caused their current dilemma, but the situation was permitted by their Maker and would be rectified by him alone. Christians infused the past, present, and future of the South with a celestial presence that guided human agency. If a heavenly force governed the universe with minute management, individuals—indeed, entire nations— were a part of God's march through time. The belief in Providence (or the idea that God directed history toward a moral finale) assured Christians that their suffering was meaningful and finite, but it also entrusted outcomes to God and marginalized people as witnesses who at best sustained hope, prayed for deliverance, and sought signs of God's work.[9]

Southern churches nevertheless did not idly wait for deliverance. Theirs was not a blind trust in Providence but a mixture of secular and sacred thinking, a blend of human responsibility and divine guidance. They envisioned a covenant with their Maker, and clergymen told their congregations that God would bless them with a religious revival if they fulfilled their duties to him. Right living could accelerate time and encourage Christ's return. To elicit God's mercy and forgiveness, thousands of southerners fasted and prayed. Dating back to Old Testament times, the fasting ritual was a public confession and transformation that symbolized the discarding of sinful living in favor of a higher, holier existence. Church leaders had for centuries called for fast days and on them exhorted people to forsake worldliness if they wished to see God. Prayer represented a direct admittance of one's dependence on the Creator. Throughout the region, churches and their denominational authorities repeated these acts of humiliation to elicit God's help.[10]

By openly addressing the spiritual decline and seeking reconciliation, southern clergy not only informed believers of the seriousness of the declension but also planted the seeds of hope that a great revival would come with divine forgiveness. But expectation alone could not ignite widespread religious awakening. As John Boles notes, "Only in areas where there is a network of churches and a community of believers, where there exists a widely accepted set of beliefs about how God works in history to effect the redemption of humankind, and where there is a strong sense of social and cultural crisis that can easily be interpreted by contemporaries as susceptible solely to a religious resolution— only when these preconditions are met is a notable revival possible." In the first decade of the nineteenth century, these circumstances finally pervaded the South, and a long-awaited awakening shook the region.[11]

The Great Revival of 1800–1805 evangelized the South and "southernized" evangelical Christianity. Southerners gathered at massive outdoor meetings and released pent-up emotions and expectations. Under the heavens, they constructed a "sacred canopy" to enclose their culture and infuse it with spiritual answers. But as more slaveholders and their chattel found religion in biracial churches, southern clergy found themselves forced to either champion the institution or jeopardize their standing in society. Developments within and outside the region made the decision an easy one for most southern ministers. During the ensuing decades, membership in Methodist, Baptist, and Presbyterian churches grew faster than the total population, and evangelical Protestantism in general became orthodox throughout the land. While northern evangelicals faced challenges from Catholicism, the varied beliefs of immigrants, and secular -isms, southern Christians marveled at their prosperity and unity. Unconsciously at first, southern church leaders and their congregations began to regard their spiritual growth (and economic prosperity) as signs of divine favor. They reasoned that God must approve of their religious practices and social institutions— why else had he blessed their region with a miraculous revival, years of rising spirituality, and significant economic prosperity?[12]

Nebulous assumptions about the South's special place in God's heart crystallized in the ensuing sectional debates over slavery. By attacking the morality of slave owners and their society, abolitionists struck a blow not only at the peculiar institution but also at southerners' claims to divine favor. Northern radicals described the South as brutish, sinful, lazy, and aristocratic, terms antithetical to how southern Christians saw themselves and their culture. Throughout the region, evangelicals responded with ironclad scriptural defenses of human bondage that compared southern practices to those of the Israelites and prophets. The particulars of proslavery doctrine are not relevant here: what matters is the way in which evangelicals used the exchange with abolitionists to distance their society from the North and connect it to God's ways as these church members interpreted them. Church leaders' defense of slavery and the South not only created a "gospel of disunion" but also foreshadowed the ethos of invincibility and Lost Cause legends. By contending that southern culture enjoyed divine sanction, evangelicals attempted to place it beyond the reach of mortal criticism and to vilify its enemies as infidels and apostates who challenged God's order. This was their direct intention and the immediate impact of their efforts in the South. Indirectly and over time, their assertion of divine favor encouraged the conviction that God would protect southern society from all perils.[13]

Decades of sectional arguments continued to polarize the country and expand southerners' perceptions about their society and its place in history. This trend accelerated with the denominational schisms of the Presbyterian (1837), Methodist (1844), and Baptist (1845) churches. Splitting ostensibly over slavery, southern evangelicals worked to convince themselves and their congregations that God had ordained the split and favored them over their northern brethren. On one level, clergy were consciously striving for legitimacy after the sectional rending of religion. On another level, the prosperity of southern religion and society in general after the denominational breaks encouraged the conviction that God blessed the South regardless of whether or not clerics sought validation.[14]

Though it is tempting to attribute the South's belief in divine favor to the origins of southern evangelicalism, religious proslavery doctrines, and the denominational schisms, another influence anteceded and helped to foster these developments: the millennialism of American civil religion. Since the revolution, church figures and laypeople north and south had combined the Puritan faith that Pilgrims founded a new Israel with the republican ideology that the young nation represented humanity's greatest experiment in government. The result was a civil millennialism that sanctified the United States' place in the divine plan for history. In 1847, the Reverend William Anderson Scott of New Orleans succinctly outlined America's providential pedigree: "God has a great design for this Continent and for our generation. As the Jews of old—as the Apostles—as the Reformers—as our fathers of 1776—so are we, as a race, and as a nation, a peculiar people and called to a high and glorious destiny." That destiny, according to Frederick A. P. Barnard, president of the University of Mississippi, was "the political regeneration of the whole human race." As sectional tensions increased, many white southerners believed that their region was fulfilling the American mission.[15]

Sacred and secular trends fostered the growth of civil religion throughout the antebellum decades. Typologies between America and biblical Israel were popular in evangelical sermons. Most clergy shared an eschatology that supported millennial visions. Westward expansion, burgeoning nationalism, general prosperity, and widespread optimism encouraged notions of manifest destiny. Citizens and travelers distinguished the young nation from "decaying" Old World monarchies. With the birth of Mormonism, some Americans even contended that God had visited their land in biblical times. These trends coalesced into a national ethos that heralded the United States as the redeemer nation, the bearer of a new age of civilization. From the pulpit, clergymen espoused this ethos by placing the country at the forefront of providential designs.

Such a climate of antebellum southern religion profoundly affected thousands of Confederate soldiers. Born during the Second Great Awakening, Rebel troops matured in a culture of religious intensity and contentiousness. Those who participated in the movement saw the outer world as infused with a divine presence. Southern clerics professed time and again in revivals, denominational schisms, proslavery arguments, and civil millennialism that this presence favored the South. Regional prosperity, harmony in biracial churches, and the growth of southern religion were considered signs of Providence's smile. Strikingly, many of the sacred practices and convictions Rebels carried in the trenches around Petersburg hearkened back to the actions and words of Furman and other turn-of-the-century evangelicals. [When Christian Rebels espoused confidence that God favored them, they voiced a fundamental American belief.]

෧෨෨෧ ෧෨෨෧ ෧෨෨෧

When the war came, religious Confederates agreed that God's hand created and shaped the struggle. Having used Providence to explain disparate events, including poor and abundant crops, births and deaths, and religious declensions and revivals, it was axiomatic that southerners would interpret the national contest as divinely ordained. As a religious pamphlet that circulated through Confederate camps claimed, "The only proper view of this Revolution, is that which regards it as the child of Providence." Similarly, Thomas Dunaway told his Virginia Baptists in 1864, "The calamities and scourges which befall nations, are ordered by and are under the control of an Allwise though mysterious Providence." Elder Dunaway admitted the difficulty of discerning God's intentions for the war but contended that to deny Providence "is to close the book of Revelation and plunge ourselves into inextricable difficulties." Denying a divine presence in the contest "is simply to assume that God has created a world of intelligent beings 'in his image and after his likeness,' and abandoned them and given them up to

their own government and delusions, while he continually takes care of inani-
mate nature and governs the natural world by well-established laws."[16]

By using Providence to explain the conflict, Confederates admitted a host of
related beliefs into their perspective on the war. If the struggle was an act of
God, the Confederacy's fate ultimately lay beyond human agency. As one Rebel
expressed it, "He holds the destiny of our nation, as it were, in the palm of his
hand." The soldier was certain that God "directs the counsel of our leaders, both
civil and military." Likewise, a chaplain told his brigade, "The Great God sits at
the helm of the ship of war, to vindicate the doctrine that the battle is His." In
a position reminiscent of evangelicals' perspectives in the 1790s, devout Rebels
viewed the war as an inevitable event and considered themselves pawns in a
celestial plan. Moreover, a belief in Providence did not permit accidents or fortune. Every effect had a cause, every death served a purpose, and every victory
or defeat meant something. Seeing the Almighty directing the carnage not only
helped Americans fathom the magnitude of the struggle but also averted the
blame for deaths numbering in the hundreds of thousands.[17]

On February 4, 1863, a national day of thanksgiving, William Rees examined
this common conviction for his flock of Methodist Texans: "In the consideration
of this subject, the Providence of God, we must guard, on the one hand, against
the barren and icy rocks of Atheism, that would resolve God to a dead idealism,
or inert abstraction; and, on the other, the wildfire and phosphoric corruscation
of fanatacism, that would father on God all subjective vagaries of the enthusiastic
day-dreamer." Exhibiting the craft of a good sermonizer, Rees employed polar
extremes—icy atheism and fiery fanaticism—to locate his faith in Providence at
the center of southern evangelicalism. Nevertheless, the pastor believed what
he professed, and the starkness of his language illustrates white southerners' unquestioning faith in God's Providence.[18] During its short existence, Confederate
religiosity evaded barren atheism with ease; the challenge came from the flames
of enthusiasm and fanaticism. Within the maelstrom of warfare, soldiers and
civilians—even the South's religious lights—became so caught up in the contest
that they saw signs of God's favor in the most minute or gloomiest circumstances.
Kindled with antebellum assumptions and enflamed by wartime propaganda,
the conviction that God favored the Confederate cause spread like wildfire and
blazed throughout the final years of the war. If Pastor Rees could have distanced
himself from the struggle at hand, he might have seen the phosphorescence of
a volatile faith that "fathered on God all subjective vagaries."

Many church leaders called for a national repentance to acquire divine favor.
They averred that God controlled the war's outcome and would deny the rebellion success until its people fulfilled their obligations to him. "As all sources
of good are at His disposal," the Reverend J. L. Burrows warned in a sermon
published for the troops, "so are all causes of evil." Burrows explained that God
controls "the demon of war" and "overrules the wrath of man so that it shall

effect His purposes." In short, without divine blessing, the Confederacy could expect not only the leveling consequences of Union victory but also the wrath of God. A Virginia Baptist cogently expressed the Confederacy's alternatives: "With the smiles and approbation of God on our cause and country, no army, however numerous or powerful, can conquer us. On the other hand, no matter how weak our enemies, without His blessing we shall be overcome." Only by "humbling ourselves and acknowledging our dependence on him" could Rebels gain divine approval and thus victory.[19]

But during these days of high patriotism, calls for penitence and reform were less popular than nationalistic claims that the rebellion had already secured divine sanction. For many southerners, impulses to legitimize the new government and justify the war merged with antebellum assumptions of regional sacredness to form an ironclad faith in God's support. On a fast day devoted to humiliation, the Reverend Joseph Atkinson told his North Carolinians that "a conflict waged in self-defense for all that man holds dear, and consecrated by the martyr-blood of the best men in these Confederate States—by the solemn voice of all our religious convocations, of all Christian churches and above all by the visible favor of Almighty Power, cannot but terminate happily." Atkinson went further when he interpreted the ebb and flow of victories as signs of God's intervention on behalf of the rebellion. After reverses including the sinking of the *Merrimac*, the surrender of New Orleans, and the capture of Roanoke Island and Nashville, "when brought to the lowest point of public depression and of conscious dependence, our deliverance was at hand." According to Atkinson, during this nadir of Confederate fortunes, when General George McClellan's massive army threatened Richmond, "God poured the spirit of dauntless heroism into the hearts of an whole people—soldiers, legislators, leaders, alike." Such narratives accomplished two ends, downplaying southern misfortunes by highlighting the peoples' resolution and insinuating that God would never abandon his Rebel followers: they would win the war no matter how desperate the military situation.[20]

Widespread Confederate ideology and symbolism encouraged faith that the rebellion followed providential designs. From the war's inception, Confederate institutions described themselves as uniquely sacred. Spiritual idioms permeated the discourse in legislative halls and military headquarters as well as chapels. While Confederate founders met in Montgomery, Alabama, Henry Timrod, the unofficial poet laureate of the Confederacy, penned these lines:

At last we are
A nation among nations; and the world
Shall soon behold in many a distant port
Another Flag unfurled!
Now, come what may, whose favor need we court?

And, under God, whose thunder need we fear?
Thank Him who placed us here
⌊ Beneath so kind a sky.

Unlike the U.S. Constitution, the Confederate document explicitly mentioned God. The legislature placed the epigram "Deo Vindice" on the national seal. During the war, President Jefferson Davis proclaimed nine days of national prayer, thanksgiving, and fasting. Congress and state legislatures called for many more such occasions, and on one of them Davis prayed "that his sustaining grace be given to our people, and his Divine wisdom imparted to our rulers; that the Lord of Hosts will be with our armies, and fight for us against our enemies; and that he will graciously take our cause into his own hand and mercifully establish for us a lasting, just, and honorable peace and independence."[21]

Confederate clergy approved of this approach and wrapped their cause with the mantle of divine favor. As one minister exclaimed, "How fraught with thrilling incidents of Divine interposition, is the short, but eventful history of our government! In reviewing the past, let us thank God, and take courage." Shortly after Gettysburg, a chaplain reminded a brigade of Robert E. Lee's men that "large armies and great powers do not always conquer the smaller and weaker. The Bible and history show that the reverse comes nearer being true." After recounting at length how Macedonians, Athenians, Romans, Englishmen, and Russians had beaten their enemies despite enormous odds, the chaplain addressed the history of his congregation. According to him, from Manassas to Gettysburg, the Confederate army had always vanquished larger forces, often whipping five hundred thousand enemies at a time. As the chaplain put it, "Often they have more than doubled you, and yet they have never beaten you. Under God you have always mastered the field." By this interpretation, the history of Lee's army paralleled biblical accounts of the Israelites' miraculous triumphs. Just as outnumbered forces led by Moses, Joshua, and Gideon slew thousands with the aid of divine power, Lee's men scattered the northern multitudes by God's blessing.[22]

Many prominent clerics drew explicit typologies between the Confederacy and biblical Israel. As one minister claimed, "David broke off from the first Israel under the reign of the house of Saul. . . . Davis broke off from the second kingdom of Israel under the reign of her first King, A. Lincoln, and established the second kingdom of Jerusalem." The first chapter of Jeremiah was a popular scriptural choice: "Then the Lord said unto me, out of the North an evil shall break forth upon the inhabitants of the land and they shall fight against thee, but they shall not prevail against thee; for I am with thee." Such Scripture persuaded innumerable southern evangelicals who interpreted the Bible literally.[23]

As the war continued, members of the clergy saw the Confederacy's survival after successive Federal onslaughts as a sign of God's help. The longer the rebellion withstood the war storm, the more miraculous it seemed. In 1863, Bishop George F. Pierce described his young nation: "With her foot planted on the right and her trust in God, undismayed by numbers and armaments and navies, without the sympathy of the world, shut in, cut off, alone, she has battled through two long, weary years, gallantly, heroically, triumphantly, and today is stronger in men, resources, faith and hope than when Fort Sumter's proud flag was lowered in her maiden arms. It is the Lord's doing, and it is marvelous in our eyes." The following year, the Reverend D. S. Doggett remarked, "It is a fact of no small import, and of no little consolation, that a war-storm of three years' duration, has neither wrecked nor dismantled the goodly ship of our fortunes; but that she stands firmly, with her bow to the blast, gradually making her way to the harbor." Another minister, Stephen Elliott, concurred and echoed Pierce's language: "We have assuredly had everything against us; numbers overwhelming, hate bitter and cruel, resources without stint, the command by our enemies of the ocean and the rivers, the ear of the world shut to us, the cry put upon us of slavery and barbarism. With all these things have we been contending for three weary years, through storm and sunshine, in cold and hunger and nakedness, creating as we fought, weeping while we labored, reaping courage and endurance from the fields sown with the blood of our children, and yet through the mercy of God, we stand this day unconquered and defiant, looking to final success with as full assurance, as upon the day when we threw down the gauntlet under the walls of the ocean girdled Sumter."[24]

Southern clergy supported the war effort with actions as well as words. At recruitment rallies, ministers connected Confederate military service to doing God's work. When men left for war, church leaders collected provisions for them and assisted their families. Religious organizations provided critical supplies and labor to hospitals. Hundreds of ministers joined the ranks as chaplains or fought as officers and common troops. Some churchmen expelled members of their congregation who withheld their sons from the draft or otherwise defied government directives. A Georgia soldier summarized a typical Sunday sermon: the minister "ruined skulkers speculators and all persons who owed money allegiance to their country and were defrauding the Govt or his neighbors out of his dues said such persons were dishonest and did not merit the freedom they enjoyed, exhorted us to obey the Laws of Congress and of the States & the orders of commanders said we were due that to them." Such exhortations illustrate the iron bond between Confederate church and state. As Emory Thomas explains, "Among all the institutions in Southern life, perhaps the church most faithfully served the Confederate army and nation. The press was often fractious on policy and tactics; the schools weakened or closed; but the church usually remained constant and seemed to thrive on the emotional and physical sacrifices of wartime."[25]

Confederate religion reached the troops through chaplains' sermons, military orders, government proclamations, family letters, and, most voluminously, millions of pamphlets printed and circulated by the religious military press. Despite major challenges in financing, producing, and distributing these publications, as late as May 1865 the religious military press poured out a steady stream of sermons, reports, and stories that glorified the Confederate cause and its Christian soldiers. Concerned with saving soldiers' souls, the preachers turned editors of these papers also instilled confidence in the cause. "At first," Kurt Berends explains, the editors "clearly differentiated between the cause for God and the cause for the South. But as time went on, it became increasingly difficult to tell the two apart." Merging the causes "created and explained a framework of beliefs—a worldview—that sustained an unvanquished optimism for southern independence." Editors used Scripture to sanctify the rebellion; compared northern and southern armies, societies, and churches; and fused civil liberty and religious freedom. In the end, millions of pamphlets conflated serving the Confederacy with following Christ, fighting Yankees with killing infidels, and winning independence with fulfilling providential plans.[26]

Confederate soldiers' religious worldview attested to the strength of southern evangelicalism and the effectiveness of denominations' war efforts. Faith in Providence and God's blessing affected soldiers' perspectives on many levels. Within their personal war of camping, marching, and fighting, confidence in God eased stress and explained hardships. Soldiers also used belief in divine favor to explain their army's fortunes and to comprehend prolonged revivals within the ranks. Beyond their immediate realm, soldiers drew on assurances of divine aid to find silver linings in news from distant campaigns and to promote an inextinguishable trust that they could not lose with God on their side.

Religious Confederates believed in a God of Battles who orchestrated everything within the maelstrom of war. Envisioning an Old Testament Jehovah imposing his will helped soldiers make sense of the horror, power, and chaos of battles. Cannons did not indiscriminately smash charging legions—God did, and with purpose. He orchestrated the movement and administered the fates of all combatants. Devout troops would have agreed with the way one minister described the Seven Days' Battles: "If our eyes could have been unsealed during those seven days . . . we should have seen an angel, terrible as that which smote the host of Sennacherib, hurling back the multitudinous cohorts of our self confident invaders, filling their ranks with confusion, dismay, and death." It was a powerful typology. Sennacherib, king of Assyria, ridiculed God, demanded gold and silver from the Israelites, and marched on their capital, Jerusalem. In earthly might, Sennacherib outmatched Hezekiah, king of Judah and defender of Jerusalem. Sennacherib boasted that his chariots had scaled mountains in Lebanon to cut down its tallest cedars; his ranks had reached remote lands, drunk foreign waters, and dried the streams of mighty Egypt. But Hezekiah was a pious leader who prayed and fasted. When Sennacherib's host camped on the outskirts of Jerusalem, the angel of the Lord wiped out 185,000 Assyrian soldiers, and Sennacherib fled in shame. McClellan's ignominious retreat from the Confederates' Jerusalem, despite the superior size of his army and his self-confident air, seemed a telling parallel to the sacred story. Rebels had no trouble catching the moral of the story: the outcomes of battles were beyond mortal reach; God decided everything and favored the pious.[27]

Religious Confederates viewed themselves as pawns moved by this God of Battles. Surviving the struggle was beyond their control and in the hands of the one who oversaw the paths of bullets and the fates of men. Troops used the mystery of Providence to explain how they passed through the surrounding death of battles unscathed. God shielded them for his own purposes. Many Rebels could only thank the Almighty for prolonging their lives. After fighting at Burgess Mill in February 1865, Joseph Manson confided in his diary, "I am not able to express my gratitude to God for having covered our heads in the day of battle. His good providence has spared us." After Spotsylvania Court House, a muddy hand-to-hand struggle that affected the hardest veterans, Robert Stiles wrote home, "Nothing but God's Providence over us has shielded us from greater losses. . . . God has been very near to both of your boys I hope and believe darling Mother." Two weeks later, Thomas Hampton wrote that "since the 7th of May 1864 we have passed through the severest scenes of wreaking war that can be Imagined in which I have been miraculously preserved in many cases with my Co[mpany] for which I see the alwise providence of God demonstrated in evry days conflict."[28]

Devout Rebels were perhaps fatalists for accepting their status as pawns, but they also believed that God protected the lowliest trooper who prayed with true reverence. Like turn-of-the-century evangelicals, Confederate soldiers entwined secular and sacred thinking, seeing a world in which human agency and divine power could work in concert. Simple prayers, such as William Casey's "May God be my shield and protection in the day of a fight," enabled soldiers to entrust their fate to God and thus to ease fears and anxieties concerning death. In October 1864, William Nugent admitted, "It is dreadful to contemplate the many, many dangers which continually surround us, and yet I do not feel alarmed, because my trust is in the Great Ruler of the Universe. In the midst of danger I feel a trust in a higher power that enables me to bear bravely up and I have a hope of getting safely through this pernicious war." After a fight, Stiles wrote, "I trust He enabled me to do my duty on the field & certainly with greater composure than hitherto." John Cotton told his wife, "I dread this fite for I think the cavalry will have a heap to do and I dont no whether I will ever get out of it or not but I only have to trust to him who runs all things for my safety I hope he wil gide me safe threw the storms of battle and then return me safe home to you and our dear little ones."[29]

Some men were so convinced of a connection between personal piety and God's protection that they encouraged family members back home to lead moral lives on their behalf. "Pray for me and tell every colored *Christian* on the land to do the same. But do it in faith," Casey wrote to his mother. "For it is writen in the fifth Chapter of James that, 'The effectual fervent prayer of a righteous man availeth much.'" North Carolinian John Francis Shaffner wrote home, "We should all pray without ceasing to Him to continue to bless our arms with success, until we have achieved a glorious and decisive victory and driven the invaders from our soil." Resolutions sent home by five Georgia brigades summed up soldiers' requests: "We earnestly and sincerely request our friends in Georgia to remember us in all their supplications at a throne of grace: praying that we may be enabled to continue steadfast in the foregoing resolve; that we may secure, through Divine grace, the salvation of our souls; that God may preserve our lives through the coming campaign, nerve our arms in freedom's contest, and crown our labors, privations, and toils, with Southern independence, peace, and prosperity." "Remember," South Carolinian Theodore Honour told his wife, "prayer is a mighty weapon." Honour stressed human responsibility for divine aid; the pious could wield God's favor like a sword. He urged his wife, "Put your trust in Him who alone can help in this our time of need." Honour promised her, "I owe my safety thus far to the prayers of my loved wife, my Pious Parents, and myself." Texas cavalryman Dunbar Affleck must have been comforted by his mother's words: "God *has* mercifuly protected you through many dangers—and—He will again hear the prayers of your mother which daily ascend to His throne of Grace for your continued preservation from danger—moral as well as physical." Mary Downman reassured her husband that his safety was in her prayers: "I do pray so earnestly that your life may be precious in the sight of Our Father—it is so precious to me."[30]

Either for their own safety or for the salvation of loved ones, soldiers evangelized to family members who lacked religion. When Casey found God, he hoped that his act "will be beneficial to the whole family," including his brother in arms. In a letter to his mother, Casey wrote, "Give my best to Pa and tell him that I say that enough of his life has been already devoted to the world. Ask him for my sake to think of it[,] to ponder the question. But he is not yet too old to be good. I would almost as soon hear that Pa had become a Christian, as to hear that war had ended." John L. Sheppard wrote to his mother, "If we are again united I hope & pray that it will be as a Christian family." He asked her to "stir up Pa, talk to the children . . . tell Pa to try hard & be a good deciple & pray to God & I know he will be improved." When Charles Fenton James learned that his sister attended dancing parties, he feared that her conduct would jeopardize God's protection over him in battle. He wrote her a strong rebuke: "Suppose that while you were upon the dancing floors, you were to hear that one or both of your brothers had fallen in some battle, what would be your feelings then? . . .

And do you have any guarantee that such will not be the case when you go to the ball room?" James chastised his sister for neglecting her duty not only to God and her country but also to her brothers in uniform. In a world where God's hand touched everything, a person's conduct could have far-reaching consequences.[31]

These Rebel exhortations suggest that some troops felt a religious separation from the home front. Civil War armies could be intensely spiritual, and warfare often isolates a soldier from his family and his former self. This observation should not be taken too far, however. A shared religion united some Confederates with distant loved ones, and the divorce of soldier from society may be a more modern phenomenon. Some devout Rebels nevertheless felt a sacred disparity between the army and the civilians it protected. After his furlough, an Alabama captain observed "that citizens at home were more demoralized than are the soldiers." He attributed the difference to faith: "We have more religion among soldiers as a mass than now exists among citizens." Mississippian Harry Lewis also commented on "the deplorable state of religion at home." He told his mother, "The opposite is the case in the army," where "crowds flock" to church. Some diehard Confederates blamed civilian sin for the nation's critical condition. Georgian W. R. Redding despaired that "Satan is reaping a great harvest now" and was convinced that the armies of darkness and the war would persist until "our People will get right [with] God." Redding prayed, fasted, and attended church, but, he admitted, "the longer I live the less confidence I have in human beings." He wished that everyone at home could hear the Word of God as it was expressed in sermons for the troops.[32]

Beyond their personal lives, many soldiers saw God empowering entire armies. Prayers for personal safety also contained supplications for their side in the struggle. "I've had an anxious day," Edgeworth Bird understated during the Battle of the Wilderness. He prayed, "God bless our friends and watch over them tomorrow and give us a great and crowning victory." Just as survival in contests like the Wilderness could seem divinely ordained, victories against great odds and within horrific maelstroms also appeared miraculous. Devout soldiers saw the God of Battles fighting for them. At Resaca, Captain Samuel McKittrick noted, "the hand of God appeared to be signally on our side." Having "just returned from another Battlefield that proved to be favourable to us," Hampton explained, "under the divine protection of God we was victorious." In many Confederates' eyes, officers deserved praise for sound leadership and troops garnered respect for their courage, but God alone was the agent of triumph.[33]

Over time, some Rebels came to expect divine favor and the victories it would bring. Praying for God's help before a battle and giving him credit after a triumph was one thing; presuming divine aid and triumph was another. While he stood between William Sherman and Atlanta, Frank Batchelor assessed his army's chances: "Our Army is large, in good spirits, have all confidence in Genl [Joseph E.] Johnston, and looking to the God of battles feel assured of victory."

The same week, Nugent wrote to his wife, "You may look out for rapid movements, startling combinations, heavy fighting and a crushing defeat to the Yankee army by the blessing of a Good Providence." A North Carolina lieutenant noted that Lee's army was "more determined & confident" during the constant fighting of May 1864 because "under the smiles of God when the wild conflict is joined, we will triumph." In December 1864, a Mississippi sergeant thought, "We can yet achieve our nationality with the aid of the All powerful God of battles." These veterans understood the importance of manpower, morale, tactics, and sound leadership, but God's blessing trumped these earthly matters. They saw the Almighty as a constant, invincible ally who would wreck the enemy in coming battles. They could not conceive that God planned anything else.[34]

Rebels traced the will of God and his love in reports from distant theaters. Reviewing engagements in early 1864, Thomas Goree pronounced, "God has certainly blessed our armies this year." He explained, "Whenever we have met the enemy—in S.C., Fla., Miss, Tenn., Ky, Va., and N C., the victory has been ours, with apparently very little effort on our part." The span of these victories and the fact that little Confederate resistance was required proved that God's hand was involved. For Goree, no man—and certainly not Jefferson Davis—could manage simultaneous triumphs across thousands of miles. Only God could. Goree prayed, "May these small victories be the harbingers to greater ones, and then may our Noble Country having won its independence be long blessed with peace." Weeks later, when Confederates won a victory at the Battle of Mansfield, a soldier in the Army of Tennessee added it to the list of triumphs that Goree recited and came to the same conclusion: "God is certainly smiling with favor upon us this year." Across the Mississippi, Edwin Fay saw the 1864 campaigns in the same light: "God in his mercy has favored our Arms this Spring." Troops considered combinations of victories that spanned the nation—regardless of their significance—signs of God's work on the Rebellion's behalf. Those who sought proof of divine favor found it in the news. In May 1864, after reading "a summary of our late successes" in the *Richmond Enquirer*, Alabama private James Pickens wrote in his diary, "From all phases in which it can be viewed our cause is progressing favorably and a glorious future with peace, independence, nationality & happiness . . . is awaiting us." Instead of being concerned about southern arrogance or pride after these victories, the private prayed, "God guard us against a show or spirit of uncertainty." Confidence in God's love was not a sin; doubting divine favor was. With supreme confidence, Pickens wrote, "We may calmly await the operation of His hand in . . . our affairs."[35]

As this evidence suggests, many Rebels based their confidence in ultimate triumph not on bravado but on religion. Soldiers witnessed God's hand at every level of the war effort; his domain spread from the individual soldier to the nation. The Almighty shielded soldiers' bodies in combat, led their armies to victory in campaigns, and oversaw their country's bid for independence. As William

Heartsill concisely remarked, "Kind Providence is with us in this great struggle." This simple, unwavering conviction shaped Rebel perceptions in innumerable ways. On this particular occasion, Heartsill interpreted the rainstorms that helped Confederate crops as signs of divine partisanship. Because Providence explained God's hand in history, the idea influenced how soldiers perceived the war's progress and expected it to end. St. Paul's assurances to the Romans gave troops comfort and courage: "All things work together for good to them that love God, to them who are called according to His promise." The Bible seemed to promise Confederate independence. On the same day that Heartsill construed rain as a sign of God's allegiance, Hampton illustrated that this Scripture affected some Confederates' perspectives on the war: "All things work together for good to them that love God & believeing that we are such I hope we may be profited in our trials." A sermon printed for the troops echoed this faith: "If we, as a State, and confederation of States, officially and privately, nationally and individually, trust obediently in God, He will be our deliverer." Southern evangelicalism proclaimed that a soul who loved and confided in God would be saved; Confederate religiosity promulgated that a nation that cherished and trusted Jehovah would be preserved. South Carolinian James Drayton Nance reflected on the power of this belief: "Whenever I have been inclined to gloominess, on account of our difficulties and dangers . . . I have found relief and hope in the reflection that there is a just and merciful God who reigneth and will not abandon us and suffer our enemies to triumph over us." Faith released him from fear of defeat and responsibility for victory: "We have only to do our duty and leave the consequences to Him."[36]

The potency of this conviction is evident in an ambiguous thought present in many soldiers' writings: as Casey put it, "If God is for us, who can be against us?" This sentence touches a core assumption of Confederate religion and the ethos of invincibility. Interpretations of it hinge on the first word. *If* could represent the conditional and mysterious nature of providential aid. Perhaps Casey and others meant that no one could be certain of God's allegiance in war, but if he were for their side, no one could defeat them. This view stresses that Confederates had to secure God's blessing by fulfilling their covenant with him, by seeking him with true reverence. Nugent expressed this perspective: "We have nothing to fear if we have the approving smiles of Heaven and are true to ourselves." Jehovah directed the fate of nations: only if God were on their side could no one defeat them. The meaning changes dramatically, however, when *if* is interpreted as a synonym for *because*. Perhaps Casey and others meant, "Because God is for us, who can be against us?" Herein the soldiers have assumed divine sanction and thus feel assured of ultimate victory—with God on their side, they cannot lose. This latter interpretation seems closer to many soldiers' meaning, as Hampton unequivocally stated: "I feel assured that God is for us & who can be against us."[37]

Such statements should not be dismissed as figures of speech, because they illuminate people's mentality during the war. The ambiguity of Casey's assertion probably served a purpose. He and others could sound stalwart in their confidence in the cause while actually meaning to stress how much the rebellion's fate lay beyond mortal control. Perhaps the meaning of the phrase changed as the war continued. Were Confederates more likely to emphasize their dependence on divine aid (the first interpretation) in the war's first years or its last? Conversely, were Rebels more likely to stress their confidence in divine favor (the second interpretation) in the war's first years or its last? Common sense and historical hindsight might suggest that southerners often expressed certainty in God's allegiance when things were going well at the war's outset and concern over seeking celestial help when conditions declined in the war's final years. It is equally likely, however, that southerners focused on their covenant with God at the start of the war, when his demands seemed clearer and more attainable, and swore that he favored them in the war's final period, when the stakes and casualties were highest. In other words, perhaps Confederates believed in divine favor more as the war worsened because they needed to trust in God's help as the struggle intensified.

To sustain a trust in God's favor, however, Confederates—like southern evangelicals from earlier times—needed signs of hope and blessing. How and where did Rebels discover reasons for optimism in 1864 and 1865? Inflating the importance of distant victories was one kind of proof, but there were many others. Because they connected their country's military success to its piety, public manifestations of faith were "bloodless victories" toward their final triumph. In particular, national days of thanksgiving, prayer, and fasting brought the Confederacy closer to God and thus closer to independence. As Elliott affirmed in a fast-day sermon, "We have so often seen the gathering fury of our enemies dispersed by God in answer to our humble prayers—scattered and rolled back in blood and confusion—that we come to day boldly to the throne of Grace, firmly believing that our prayers, and supplications, if offered with pure hearts and clean lips, will return to us laden with blessings from the Lord of Hosts, the God of the armies of Israel." James agreed with Elliott and offered a popular opinion among soldiers when he told his sister, "It is a notable fact that we have never yet met with disaster immediately after a fast day. Our arms have always been blessed with success; and not until the people, in the exultation that follows success, have forgotten the giver of all victory and rejoiced in their own strength and given themselves up to pleasure, have our armies met with reverses." Soldiers found other evidence that connected national piety to military outcomes. Virginia artilleryman James Albright claimed that "the attacking party always gets the worst of Sunday engagements." A North Carolina chaplain concurred, arguing that even General Lee's assaults failed on Sundays. For these men, the connection between piety and military success was tangible.[38]

National fast days rededicated people to the cause and raised their expectations of success. This chapter has already explained how late-eighteenth-century evangelicals used fast days to prepare the South for the Great Revival of 1800–1805. By addressing the spiritual declension, pledging to live better lives, and praying for an awakening, many southerners began to expect the revival. Though many conditions were necessary for its growth and pervasiveness, the revival was in some respects a self-fulfilling prophecy. Confederates used fast days in the same manner. Numerous Rebels acknowledged some of their sins, pledged to serve their country better, and prayed for peace and independence. In a society that believed God answered sincere prayers, the thought of millions of prayers ascending on fast days convinced untold thousands that the Almighty would deliver them from northern peril. Praying for victory and independence would hasten their arrival.

Many Confederates recovered from the despair of Gettysburg and Vicksburg by increasing their religious activities and observing the national fast day on August 21, 1863. When the Army of Northern Virginia returned to its native soil in mid-July, a revival swept through its ranks. The exact origins of the awakening are difficult to discern. The Pennsylvania campaign convinced some Rebels that they placed too much confidence in themselves and General Lee when they should have trusted God. Gettysburg was a message from Heaven. Many soldiers were simply grateful to God that they had survived the campaign. Other troops seemed to seek communal activity to overcome the trauma of the hellish battle. Whatever the cause, the revival's effect was clear: it lifted the army out of despair and rekindled its faith in ultimate triumph. Men throughout the army renewed a promise to trust God as their deliverer. A South Carolinian reported that his brigade listened to sermons every morning and held prayer meetings every afternoon. Mississippian Robert Moore's brigade met more than once a day "to worship that Being in whom all trust for our deliverance." God would provide for those who trusted him. As one private expressed, "When we hear of a victory gained, how thankful we ought to be to our Maker, who is able to see us safe through this struggle if we will only put our trust in him."[39]

In August, the national fast day reinforced soldiers' faith in victory through God. Alabamian Sam Pickens was impressed by a sermon he heard at General Richard Ewell's headquarters. The reverend chose 2 Kings 6:16 as his verse: "For they that are with us are more than they that are with them." Pickens recalled in his diary that the minister "exhorted us to have faith & be a better people." The congregation inspired Pickens, too. He estimated that more than one thousand troops, scores of lower officers, and ten generals, including Lee, attended the service. Another preacher used the fast day to steel the resolve of his audience. He told them he was happy that he was not addressing "faint-hearted whiners, who cry peace, peace, when there is no peace, and who would sell his country or desert his country's flag." He considered pleas for peace "the essence of cowardice," which was the enemy's specialty. If "we stand by our arms," he promised his listeners, "ready to strike at all times for our country and our country's honor," the Yankees will whimper for peace.[40]

The revival and fast day accelerated the nation's recovery from the disasters of July, but other events within the army reinforced this transformation of morale. President Davis's amnesty to deserters augmented the ranks, and when the period of mercy expired, executions affirmed every soldier's duty to his comrades and country. It must have been a strange dichotomy, watching condemned men being killed one day and sinners being saved the next. On September 5, 1863, Sam Pickens witnessed ten executions: one fellow was shot sixteen times before he died. On September 6, Pickens saw for the first time baptisms by immersion: sixteen men joined the church that day. Though paradoxical, grim justice and joyful religion worked together to rejuvenate the army. Returning convalescents increased the ranks, and grand reviews of entire corps showcased the army's power. A Louisiana sergeant noted that scores of wounded men had returned to his company, "all of them . . . can whip twice their number of yankees any day," and thousands had recently joined the church. Two months earlier, these soldiers had suffered their worst defeat; now they faced the future confident of victory.[41]

In September, faith in triumph spread to the Army of Tennessee. When General James Longstreet's Corps joined that army, the men brought conviction as well as material strength. The confidence expressed by the Army of Northern Virginia echoed in the Army of Tennessee. A Georgia soldier hoped "that God will bless us soon in answer to the many fervent prayers that have been sent up for our Country." A lieutenant believed "when we do meet the enemy, God will give us the victory." An Alabamian confirmed, "I don't think anybody is afraid of the result." Likewise, a corporal did not fear the next battle: "Trusting in all wise Providence, I feel confident that we will be successful." Their prayers seemed answered, their divine favor confirmed, on September 19 at Chickamauga. Joshua Callaway shared the glorious news with his family: "We have routed them and run them off. They are said to be crossing the river and leaving as hard as they can. 'Thanks be unto God who giveth us the victory through our Lord Jesus Christ.'" For devout Confederates, the cause of victory was transparent: God delivered Chickamauga to the Rebels because they rededicated themselves to him.[42]

This bond between religious faith and military triumph continued through the end of the war. On November 16, 1864, Captain Samuel Foster went to church on a national fast day and estimated that seven hundred men attended the service. In March 1865, Richard Maury noted, "This is the day appointed by Mr. Davis as a time for Fasting, humiliation and prayer—that we may entreat a merciful God to forgive us our sins—to stand on our side and to give us victory." Manson hoped "that the prayers of all our people would be increasing until God pours out His blessing upon us." For Foster, Manson, and many others, the power of prayer could be quantified: God would assure Confederate independence when enough Rebels prayed with true reverence.[43]

Revivals within the ranks remained compelling symbols of Confederate piety and God's presence. North Carolinian Richard Webb was convinced that 1864 was the final year of the war because "God has given us so many tokens of good in converting so many hundred soldiers." Webb wrote home, "I don't believe that God will deliver us over into the hands of our enemies, while we take Him to be our refuge and strength." In October 1864, an artilleryman thought "our prospects are yet bright" because of evangelicalism among the troops. He reported, "The revival is spreading & pouring in our Battn, & among our infantry support. Four out of five officers, in one of our batteries have been hopefully converted & many of the men. I mention the officers first, only because religious awakening is less common among them, & they are likely to exert more influence for good. . . . God be with us." Historians have noted how revivals countered fears of death, provided diversions in camp, promoted discipline, and fostered primary group cohesion among Christian soldiers. Revivals were also significant for the spectacle of piety they produced. Just as grand reviews and sham battles impressed soldiers with their army's material power, great revivals awed the men with their collective moral strength. The sight of thousands of comrades seeking God's forgiveness and protection convinced many Rebels that their army was as holy as Joshua's Israelites. McKittrick, a captain in the Army of Tennessee, admitted, "It is an impressive scene to see a large mass of sinful creatures standing upon the brink of eternity, worshipping perhaps for the last time in this world." When McKittrick's pious soldiers fought nine days later, he believed that "the hand of God appeared to be signally on our side." Stiles was equally impressed with the sound of a reverent army: he wrote to his sister, "It would do you good to hear the hymns ascending all along the line of battle about dusk each evening. It will not do to rely on these religious features of our army in any self-righteous, self gratulatory spirit; yet it is encouraging to be thus assured of God's presence & blessing with us. Do not be too confident, yet you may encourage an almost bouyant hope in these days of constant repeated victory." During the Atlanta campaign, one soldier observed, "There is a better moral tone exhibited here than I have ever seen among soldiers. Thousands have been converted and are happy Christians. Nearly all our first Generals have joined the Church and the army is fast becoming literally a God-fearing soldiery. This I regard as a very favorable omen and as strongly indicative of our success. In fact our men look upon success as certain." Each baptism or conversion of a soldier increased God's favor and brought the Confederacy one step closer to peace and independence. Fast days and revivals produced a spectacle of piety that reinforced the propaganda that consecrated the rebellion. Revivals in the ranks had tremendous importance for white southern evangelicals. Witnessing "the greatest revival I ever saw," as one Rebel put it, convinced Confederates that God was working through them—they were agents of Providence.[44]

⚬⚬⚬   ⚬⚬⚬   ⚬⚬⚬

Antebellum evangelical inheritances, church propaganda, and spectacles of piety sustained many Rebels' faith into the final period of the war, but do these influences explain why so many soldiers still thought God favored their cause after strings of major defeats? Old notions of southern sacredness might survive the conflict's first years, when the rebellion thwarted Union offensives and stymied Washington strategists, but how could these assumptions withstand Gettysburg, Vicksburg, the Overland Campaign, and the March to the Sea? If victories were signs of celestial aid, why were successive defeats not portents of Almighty wrath? Many men in the ranks voiced concerns about southern sinfulness and deemed Confederate reverses signs of national depravity, but few Rebels doubted that God would save them in the end. Rare was the southerner who thought that God had forsaken the cause.

If Providence was the religious conviction that spawned Confederate confidence in divine help, theodicy—a religious accounting for the existence of suffering and evil—preserved this view through the hellfires of 1864–65. Worldviews perish when they fail to explain the hardships their adherents face. In the war's last stage, a host of anomies challenged the Rebel worldview: soldiers wondered why God had permitted foreign hordes to occupy Confederate soil; why God had overseen the deaths of hundreds of thousands; why God had directed slaves to leave their masters and join the enemy ranks; why God had allowed famine and destruction in a land of plenty; and where God's mercy was in the sick pens of Libby Prison, the charred remains of Columbia, the bloodbath at Franklin, Tennessee. In the end, Confederate theodicy did not dispense joy to overcome the war's anguish—that was not its primary purpose. As sociologist Peter L. Berger explains, "In situations of acute suffering, the need for meaning is as strong as or even stronger than the need for happiness." Theodicy had to answer questions about death, evil, and anguish for all Confederates, from the uneducated boy in the trenches to the plantation mistress.[45]

For soldiers, death and defeat offered the toughest challenges to their worldview. Because they envisioned God's work everywhere, religious Confederates held God accountable when grapeshot turned their most devout comrades into pulp or when enemy forces beat Rebel armies that fasted and prayed. How did they reconcile such destruction of the faithful? Evangelical Christianity explained death without equivocation. Death was God's bidding, and the loss of any comrade was a signal for the living to repent and prepare for their end. Moreover, for believers, death delivered triumph, joy, and entrance into God's kingdom. Sheppard lost two brothers in the war, but faith solaced him in the face of their deaths and his own mortality. Sheppard reminded his mother "that we have a friend above to take care of us. I have put my trust in him & prayed that he would let me live to see you all again, but if my prayer is not granted I know it will be for some wise purpose." Sheppard's evangelicalism washed away any notion that death was random or malicious. God had taken his brothers, and if he saw fit, the Almighty would take him, too.[46]

Defeats more directly confronted Confederate assumptions. If the Confederacy enjoyed divine favor, why was it losing the war? Within the Rebel worldview, setbacks were not signs of divine anger, because God loved those who believed in him. Many Rebels thought major reverses resulted from God chastening his people for their sinfulness. After all, if the Confederacy were blessed with divine sanction, no amount of Union victories could lead the enemy to ultimate triumph. God was punishing the rebellion as a father disciplines his child. From this perspective, adversity and hardships tested the young nation's faith and galvanized its national character. Some southerners drew parallels to the American Revolution: the Continentals suffered through Valley Forge before they reached Yorktown.[47] As a Louisiana Rebel told his father, "God will never suffer a determined and united people to be enslaved and though many of us may never live to see the day I feel assured that our separation from and freedom of the yanks is sure. . . . Our fore fathers endured the revolution for 7 years under far more advantages than we have to endure. Why may we not with their examples before us go on & take courage at our past successes?"[48]

Religion softened the impact of major defeats for thousands of Rebels. In July 1863, troops looked to God after Gettysburg and Vicksburg. In Tennessee, Callaway admitted, "We have received a series of staggering blows" that had halted Confederate progress. "Nevertheless, I am not out of heart," he said, because "our trust is in God and our cause is just." Callaway sent verse to his wife to express his view of the war's course:

> Judge not the Lord by feeble sense,
> But trust him for his grace.
> Behind a frowning Providence
> He hides a smiling face.

However dire the present situation, Providence would smile on the Confederacy in the end. Likewise a Louisiana soldier considered Vicksburg "a sad misfortune" but had "little fear of the final result" of the war. He used Scripture, including Ecclesiastes 9:11, to support his faith: "Our hopes must rest on the God of battles who hath assured us that the race is not to the swift nor the battle to the strong." He expected "adverse fortune" to "darken our prospects but in the end we will come out conquerors." South Carolinian Tally Simpson deemed Vicksburg a major blow that foreshadowed the fall of other southern cities, including Savannah, Charleston, and Richmond. "These cities will be a loss to the Confederacy," he reasoned, "but their fall is no reason why we should despair." Simpson wrote to his wife, "If we place implicit confidence in Him and go to work in good earnest, never for a moment losing sight of Heaven's goodness and protection, it is my firm belief that we shall be victorious in the end." The corporal could not fathom the reasons for major setbacks, but he was convinced that "God's hand" caused them, "and He is working for the accomplishment of some grand result."[49]

This steadfast faith accompanied Confederates through the horrors of 1864. After a month of the grinding Overland Campaign, Casey admitted that he was "very nearly broken down from fighting and working." Even worse, he learned that all his family's slaves left with enemy forces that ravaged his home. Casey wrote to his mother, "I know that you are not in good spirits But you must try and put your trust in the Lord, and every thing will turn out for the best." The next day, Sergeant Rawleigh Downman tried to console his wife over the death of a close friend. "Look to Him & call upon Him for strength," Downman advised. "Whom he loveth He chaseneth—and we must bear his rod with resignation though to our mortal eyes it seemeth grevious. In all things let us bless God though at times his hand he laid heavily upon us." Downman was rather awkwardly quoting Hebrews 12:5–7: "My son, despise not thou the chastening of the Lord, nor faint when thou art rebuked of him: For whom the Lord loveth he chaseneth, and scourgeth every son whom he receiveth. If ye endure chastening, God dealeth with you as with sons; for what son is he whom the father chasteneth not?" The message was clear and comforting: God punishes those he loves, so Confederate defeats offered proof that white southerners were God's children. Piety meant accepting the dire course of events without question.[50]

When Confederates speculated about which southern sin had provoked divine wrath, they seldom considered slavery. Clergy occasionally pointed to the southern treatment of slaves as God's provocation, but soldiers preferred other explanations. Nance thought God sent defeats "to chasten that boastful and self-confident spirit with which we entered . . . this contest." Nance considered southern bravado a national sin that God was beating out of the Rebels. In his view, Rebel élan fostered heroism, but God's chastening was a test of southern "fortitude . . . a virtue much rarer than heroism." Shaffner disagreed. For him, the concept of a national sin was a comfortable way for Christians to ignore their individual shortcomings. He thought that "the prevailing idea of 'National Sin' as the cause of our present chastisement" was an "error." For Shaffner, "a nation's Guilt is but the aggregate sum of *Individual* sins," and God would continue to punish Confederates until they personally repented. John William McLure focused on the national sin of extortion, which, he told his wife, was a "crime [that] has submerged our whole land, & until we rid ourselves of this we can not expect Heaven to reward us with blessings." Arrogance, impenitence, and greed: countless Confederates pointed to these sins not to slavery. The peculiar institution was so deeply embedded in southern culture that few diehard Confederates considered the possibility that human bondage was immoral. The correspondence of James Blackman Ligon, a member of Hampton's Legion, illustrates this mentality. Ligon's mother complained that her ungrateful slaves were abandoning her. "Now Mother," Ligon responded, "I hope if every negro and every dollar's worth of property you possess was to be destroyed in an instant, that you would feel like it was caused by a higher power and to greave after any thing is a besetting sin." From Ligon's perspective, owning slaves was not a sin, but grieving over the loss of property was, because God had willed it to be. Ligon tried to convince his mother that her slaves "have been a perfect neusance and distraction." Their absence would be a blessing in disguise; an inscrutable God had planned this event for some greater good.[51]

Confederates considered chastening a temporary situation: God brought setbacks to discipline Rebels, not to bless Yankees as victors. Many soldiers expressed this point, none more clearly than J. Frederick Waring in 1865: "I know that God will bless this land. We have sinned and he is now chastening us, but he will *never, never* deliver us over to our enemies."[52] This belief shielded troops from the consequences of major defeats and braced them for the war's length. Baking under a July sun in the trenches of Petersburg, Henry Calvin Conner surveyed the stalemated front and admitted that the present campaign might not be the last. Conner desperately wanted to win the war and return to his wife, but he tried to console both himself and her: "We must trust the issue to God alone and he will in his own good time bring it about when he thinks we are prepared for it." In December, peace with independence seemed even more remote, but Conner stuck to his beliefs. With Sherman inching toward Savannah, Conner stoically remarked, "It seems as tho we are destined to lose more of our country yet but we have no cause for despondence." God, not General Sherman, was directing these calamities. "Surely it is for our sins as a nation and people that we are suffering this dredful scorge of war and if we will forsake our sins and turn to god he will remove his rod of chastisement from us and give us peace and prosperity when he sees we are prepared for it." For religious Confederates, the surest route to independence was national penitence, not conquering the peace. Within their faith, many Rebels harbored an implicit assumption that it would be easier to earn God's forgiveness than to conquer the North. As one minister exhorted on a fast day, "More effective than disciplined brigades, armed with the deadliest implements that science has invented—more effective than heaviest ordnance most skillfully served—is the favor of the Lord; and that favor can be gained." When Atlanta fell, McLure thought the news was "decidedly discouraging . . . yet I comfort myself with the belief that such a seeming great calamity had not been sent to us without a design by the great Ruler of Nations." Henry Alexander Chambers shared McLure's perspective: the loss of Atlanta "lengthens the duration of this cruel war. . . [God for some good purpose has seen fit to bring this upon us. Let us submit to His will." Devout Rebels such as Conner, McLure, and Chambers did not need to explain major defeats or dwell on their real-world consequences because religion clarified such setbacks: God intended these calamities for a higher purpose, and all would be well in the end. Confederate armies could lose battles and abandon territory without changing the war's outcome, because God loved them.[53]

From 1863 to 1865, many men imagined that God and the Confederacy would overcome the gloom just as sunlight inexplicably pierced ominous storm clouds or ended the darkest night. In July 1863, after Gettysburg and Vicksburg, Simpson thought God "will roll the sun of peace up the skies and cause its rays to shine over our whole land." In August 1864, a chaplain wrote, "I have never seen our boys in such fine spirits, being perfectly elated with their recent success, many of them think that the 'Bow of Peace' will soon brake through the dark clouds." Soldiers with Terry's Texas Rangers used similar language when they thanked civilians for a new battle flag in September 1864. They promised the women who sewed it that "the dark cloud which has so long lowered above you is dispersing, and through its gloomy folds glimpses of the silver lining appear." The flag included the inscription, "God defend the right." In February 1865, Manson prayed, "Oh God be with me & clear up all darkness & dispondency." Manson knew that "tho all seems dark He can bring deliverance." Weeks earlier, James Keith still believed "the end may not be far off & the sun of peace with happiness in every ray may yet shine out to gild the evening of our days. . . . [T]he eye of faith see[s] only the silver lining of the cloud & look[s] to him who has promised never to desert those who put their trust in him." As late as March 1865, Crenshaw also sought brightness amid the gloom. He confided in his diary, "The South is being sorely tried, and if she is not found wanting in the balance, the dark clouds of adversity will soon clear away from her horizon and the bright sun of victory will shine out resplendently." Despite countless setbacks and amid deepest gloom, diehard Confederates still expected the heavens to shine in their favor.[54]

Men who possessed this view focused on the thinnest silver linings and chased rainbows until the war's end. Rebel theodicy explained defeats and encouraged hope. Faith offered soldiers assurances that God watched over them and an escape from their present circumstances. Weeks after Gettysburg, Moore thought, "How very sweet it is to commune with God. What a dear friend is Jesus to those who live in constant prayer with him." For some Confederates, the comforts of religion were so great that a spiritual mode of thought became almost a preoccupation. On October 27, 1864, one such Rebel, Manson, started a diary that could more appropriately be called a prayer book:

I begin today to note down in this little book, the dealings of God with my
soul. . . . My mind is drawn towards my kind heavenly Father in love & praise.
I have enjoyed more of his Favor during the past months than ever before. . . .
My happiness consists in meeting with Him in secret. I love to commune with

my own heart & be still. The world has lost much of its power over me & I feel that I can cheerfully exchange the greatest attractions [of this world] for the smiles of my blessed Saviour. I have solemnly given myself in Covenant to God to be His in time and eternity. His kind hand has been thrown around me & my life has been prolonged. . . . Oh God show me the path of duty & incline my heart to walk therein. Through this day be very near me. May it be a day of sweetness to my poor soul & prepare me for the trials that may be before me & bring me off. . . . Bless the dear ones of my heart. Receive us all to Thyself at last for Jesus sake. Amen!

Manson's concentration on the divine makes his record one of the most remarkable diaries of the Civil War. Manson replaced subjects commonly found in soldiers' accounts with celestial elements. Instead of writing about the torn earth of Petersburg or his home in Brunswick County, Virginia, Manson described Heaven. Instead of focusing on family ties to his wife and children, Manson stressed his covenant with Jesus Christ. Instead of admiring officers such as his able brigadier, William Mahone, or his colorful corps commander, A. P. Hill, Manson praised God. Instead of detailing the daily traffic of men and arms, Manson scribbled down the movements of his soul as it sought God beyond the horrors of war. And if he should perish in battle, instead of hoping that he would die facing the enemy, Manson prayed, "Oh God may I be found with my face towards the Celestial City & my Armor on."[55]

Manson began his diary in the trenches of Petersburg, where thousands of his comrades found religion because spirituality helped soldiers construct and maintain reality. In 1864, the war entered a new phase as Generals U. S. Grant and William T. Sherman ceaselessly pushed toward their objectives, Richmond and Atlanta. Even the most hardened veterans felt the physical and mental effects of the change. They were accustomed to set battles of one to three days followed by months of recovery. Now they fought and marched by day and dug and guarded trenches at night. It was one of the most profound changes in a war on the cusp of modernity. The war's acceleration no doubt affected the frequency of prayer meetings, but the unparalleled destruction of this final chapter compelled more men to religious reflections. After sharing years of terrible carnage, soldiers watched scores of comrades die within months. In the constant fighting from Dalton to Atlanta, Samuel Vann's company lost forty-four men killed and severely wounded. "We have 19 men in the Co. here now," Vann explained. This attrition compelled Vann's comrades to participate in prayer meetings despite "balls flying around the congregation all the time." Vann surmised that a soldier only had "to look around and see how our ranks have been thinned out" to repent and seek God. It is not a coincidence that more chapels were built along the trenches of Petersburg in 1864–65 than had been constructed in camps during the previous winter.[56]

Casualties encouraged reflection for reasons other than personal salvation; men sought religion not only for entrance into the next world but for explanations of this one. The loss of friends and the growing infrequency of letters from home deprived soldiers of contact with the people who helped them make sense of the conflict. As Berger explains, "The subjective reality of the world hangs on the thin thread of conversation." Discourse with comrades and family members reaffirmed what was real in a chaotic and lonely environment. Many Rebels who were divorced from these connections bolstered their tottering perceptions with the reassurances of evangelicalism. At prayer meetings, soldiers bonded with fellow survivors and found answers for the carnage and filth that surrounded them. Sheppard noted, "As a general thing the men *all* attend Service whenever held before or after a Battle." W. L. Curry, chaplain of the Fiftieth Georgia Infantry, cataloged the extent of religious activity among his men in the summer of 1864: "A prayer-meeting at sunrise, an inquiry-meeting at 8, preaching at 11, a prayer-meeting at 4 for the success of our (Confederate) cause, preaching again at night, was the usual programme of the day. . . . We usually had from fifty to seventy-five brethren at these. . . . The religious interest of the brigade seemed more general than I had ever seen it before." A Mississippi infantryman noted, "We have prayer meetings every night when we dont have preaching." He hoped "the good work will go on until we receive a great blessing nationally as well as Spiritually."[57]

꧁ ꧁ ꧁

The constancy and influence of Confederate religion exhibit the power of intangible, subjective elements in warfare. Evangelicalism's aid was more essence than substance. Instead of giving the rebellion legions, provisions, or currency, Christianity bolstered these material needs in transient ways: revivals galvanized troop morale, fast days sanctified hunger and want in the cause of patriotism, and clergy damned extortionists. Most central to this study, Confederate spirituality never whipped a Union army, but it created an ethos that colored every engagement as either a divine triumph or a holy chastening, thus undermining the objective significance of reversals. Moreover, because Rebels' theory of providential deliverance maximized God's role and minimized human responsibility for the ultimate outcome, it underestimated the very factors that caused Confederate defeat: deficient supplies and manpower, crippling inflation, international isolation, a strangling blockade, the disintegration of slavery, northern strength and determination, and disaffection within the ranks and at home. For devout Confederates, all these elements were dwarfed in significance by their faith and the will of God. Spiritual matters trumped material concerns. As one news editor put it, "The example is being afforded on the grandest scale of the superiority of the *morale* over the *physique*." The weaker side would win because God favored it.[58]

As the struggle worsened, some clergy espoused intemperate views that bolstered soldiers' confidence in divine favor. Paul Escott correctly judges southern churchmen "the staunchest propagandists for the Confederate cause." Funeral sermons illustrate the virulent partisanship of some clergy. Elliott, a Protestant Episcopal bishop, was especially guilty of demonizing the enemy and sanctifying the cause. When Confederate fortunes waned, Elliott preached that "reconstruction was an impossibility. Whatever sacrifices and sufferings the Southern people had bourne, or might have to bear, independence would be cheap compared to an association with the Northern fanatics."[59] At the funeral of General Leonidas K. Polk, Elliott's friend and fellow clergyman, the bishop delivered a blistering diatribe. For dramatic effect, Elliott turned northward to address his enemies:

> And now, ye Christians of the North, and especially ye priests and bishops of the church who have lent yourselves to the fanning of the fury of this unjust and cruel war, do I this day, in the presence of the body of my murdered brother, summon you to meet us at the judgment seat of Christ . . . that awful bar where the multitudes whom you have followed to do evil shall not shield you from an angry God; where the vain excuses with which you have varnished your sins shall be scattered before the bright beams of eternal truth and righteousness. I summon you to that bar in the name of sacred Liberty which you have trampled under foot; in the name of the glorious Constitution which you have destroyed; in the name of the temples of God which you have desecrated; in the name of our Christian women whom you have violated; in the name of our slaves whom you have seduced and than consigned to misery; and there I leave justice and vengeance to God. The blood of your brethren crieth unto God from the earth, and it will not cry in vain. It has entered into the ears of the Lord God of Sabaoth, and will return upon you in that day of solemn justice and fearful retribution.

Elliott was too certain of his cause and convictions to fathom that he too bore responsibility for "fanning the flames" of a cruel war.[60] In another funeral sermon, John Paris preached over the bodies of twenty-two North Carolinians executed for desertion. He did not eulogize the dead, who had been "wicked and deluded men," but instead damned their "heinous and ruinous crime" because it was too prevalent in the army. Paris proclaimed, "I am not sufficiently skilled in language to command words to express the deep and unutterable detestation I have of the character of a deserter." He reminded the men that "the true Christian is always a true patriot," and "we never were born to be the slaves of the Yankees."[61]

Other ministers espoused equally fiery rhetoric. Anticipating the destruction of 1864–65, one chaplain appealed to the manhood and patriotism of the members of his brigade and informed them, "You who have offered your lives upon your country's altar, cannot fail to sacrifice your property rather than entail a cruel state of bondage upon your offspring." He beseeched the men, "When the enemy comes in like a flood, to overwhelm your land in desolation and woe, let us put our trust in the God of battles and strike like men determined to be free!" One preacher presumed to know the Union's limits in manpower and promised Confederates that the enemy's "pompous pretensions break down by [its] sheer incapacity to sustain them." He reported that the Federals "are now putting forth all their might for one grand onslaught, with no possibility of re-peating it, on the same scale." What of the manpower shortages in the South? "The case is entirely different with a people like ourselves, acting on the defen-sive," he proclaimed. "The limit of our endurance is comparatively indefinite. Our expenditure of men and means is so far less, that we may render ourselves invincible either by the number of our foes, or the duration of the war; and availing ourselves of auspicious advantages, we may force the enemy to his last experiment." On May 1, 1865, when the rebellion was forced to its "last exper-iment," a chaplain preached to his soldiers in the open woods. With thousands of other Rebels surrendering or deserting across the Confederacy, the chaplain chose Revelation 2:10 for his Scripture lesson: "Be thou faithful unto death, and I will give thee a Crown of life."[62] Another minister chose a fast day as the appropriate time to warn soldiers that failing to "discharge their duty" to the Confederacy meant they "were dishonest before God."[63]

These messages were potent within the war's context. Many factors, includ-ing evangelical inheritance, needs within the army, and theodicy, encouraged soldiers to accept the partisanship of church propaganda. As the war intensi-fied, so did soldiers' convictions. What started as a belief in Providence and an assumption that Confederates were holier than Yankees grew into a sense of invincibility—God favored the rebellion; therefore, it could not fail. Nugent bluntly expressed this faith: "God is on our side." Instead of hoping that their country was on God's side, many Rebels came to share Nugent's belief. How did these convictions differ? The first, more consistent with evangelicalism, en-visioned the Creator as an unknowable arbiter over battlefields whose design was Providence's progress. Hoping the Confederacy was on God's side empha-sized citizens' obligations to him as well as to their country. Some strands of this thought persisted in fast-day sermons until the end of the war. Clergy continued to implore Rebels to repent of their sins so that they would deserve divine aid. But over time, even fast-day sermons came to highlight the Confederacy's spe-cial place in God's heart and to stress that he was directing them to victory. This emphasis signaled the second, more fanatical vision of God as an omnipotent and ever-present ally whose plan called for Confederate independence.[64]

Southern clergy did not bear sole responsibility for this shift, though millions of religious pamphlets written and circulated by members of the clergy greatly affected the change. American millennialism, Rebel spectacles of piety, and ul-timately the soldiers' personal and collective views also fostered this fanatical perspective. The men relied on God for assurances that no other source could provide. This chapter has demonstrated that soldiers relied on divine protection in combat. In the maelstrom of battle, no other source—not comrades, fortifications, weapons, tactics, or heroism—could shield men from death; only God could. From a Christian perspective, no other body—not the president, a general, a trusted friend, or even an entire army—could protect soldiers' families from destitution or invasion the way that Jehovah could. Thousands of Rebels no doubt hoped and prayed for that protection as Federal armies wrecked the home front. Finally, when Confederates suffered one setback after another in 1864 and 1865, no other element—not foreign powers, Copperheads, General Robert E. Lee, or even devotion to the cause—could guarantee victory the way that God's favor could. Because of these comforts and the other benefits of religion, Christianity was a powerful sustaining force for Confederate morale throughout the war and particularly during its final period.[65]

Most Confederates retained their notion of a national covenant with God, but their focus shifted from human obligations to divine rewards. In 1862, the language in a sermon revealed the lure of this shift: "So long as we shall deeply feel our dependence on God alone, and put our trust in Him, He will favor us, and our progress will be irresistible as the march of time." By 1864, the change in perspective was evident. While Lee's troops fought a continuous campaign against Grant's army from the Wilderness to the trenches of Petersburg, Confederates read religious pronouncements: "The progressive proofs of God's good providence, in our behalf, strengthen the conviction that the period of our deliverance is not remote. Step by step, have we been led through the bloody scenes of our national drama, by the most manifest interposition of his hand. . . . Have we been brought so far, only to be abandoned in the last stage of the journey, and to perish in the passage, as a monument of Divine delusion?" Most Confederate soldiers did not think so. Within their worldview, defeat would signify that God had tricked and forsaken them, and that was unthinkable. When Union forces wrecked the Shenandoah Valley in October 1864, a Virginia private remained confident because God "has never yet deceived any who trusted Him. He never will." The private reminded his father, "We are in the *right* & 'thrice armed is he whose cause is just.'" Shifts in the southern covenant seem apparent to us, but thousands of Confederates missed the change because their faith provided constancy in the struggle. From their perspective, their religion from childhood sustained them through the perils of war.[66] One soldier perfectly expressed this conviction in a February 1865 diary entry. He chose verses from Psalm 71, "Thou which hast showed me great and sore troubles, shalt quicken me again, and shalt bring me again from the depths of the earth. . . . For thou art my hope, O Lord God; Thou art my trust from my youth."[67]

The Mask of Cain

Enemy Images in Rebel Minds

The fall of Richmond stirred Herman Melville to explain the war as best he could in verse. One of his poems, "On the Collegians," explored the images and thoughts that compelled students to leave the liberal arts for warfare:

> What troops
> of generous boys in happiness thus bred
> went from the North and came from the South,
> with golden mottoes in the mouth
> to lie down midway on a bloody bed.

To Melville, the mottoes of honor, duty, and "Truth's sacred cause" seemed partial and emotive, like the lives of the young men who had died for them. Whatever their particular motivations, their ardor and cause coalesced to form the "mask of Cain," the abstractions soldiers created to conceal the enemy's humanity. For four years, Americans covered their countrymen's likenesses under a veil of hatred, prejudice, and fear. Both sides came to view the other as Cain, a jealous, scheming character who kills his own brother, and saw themselves as Abel, the innocent victim who enjoys God's favor. For these reasons, Melville alluded to the first fratricide and Americans called their conflict the brothers' war.[1]

The sacred story had striking parallels in the nineteenth-century South. By 1860, somehow the people who were most like them, their northern countrymen, had provoked white southerners' greatest fears and sharpest contempt. Though they had come to America from the same places and had spilled blood together in the revolution, southerners viewed northerners as culturally alien.

Though the majority in each region worked on family farms and belonged to the same economic class, southerners considered northerners socially inferior. Though they worshipped the same God, southerners saw northerners not only as morally deficient but as evil incarnate. By obscuring major commonalities and magnifying minor differences, the mask of Cain—white southerners' perceptions of the North—precipitated secession and war.[2]

Though some elements of the mask were peculiar to the South, the process of dehumanizing the enemy is universal. All belligerents fight at least two enemies. On one hand, they face actual opponents—the individual people, in all their complexities, who fill the ranks and support the other side's war effort. On the other, they fight the imagined foe—the caricatures, devoid of individuality, that animate fear and hatred. Confederates used a spectrum of colorful images to identify the opposition, but they usually crammed Unionists into one of two categories: inept, inferior adversaries or evil, barbaric ones. From the time they enlisted to oppose a menace they had not seen, Rebels used these abstractions to motivate themselves and justify their actions. Their former countrymen to the North did the same thing.[3] As civil war engulfed the nation, the adversaries' identities and causes were formed in opposition, both literally and figuratively. As historian Susan-Mary Grant explains, "Conflict—ideological as well as military—between the Union and the Confederacy helped each side construct and then defend its relative position." Confederate nationalism reinforced this creation and exaggeration of differences. In war—particularly civil war—patriots brand the enemy as an ignoble opposite as a means of affirming the right to be hostile and free. Scholars have correctly observed that many white southerners abandoned the Confederacy as the war worsened. But soldiers' writings and other cultural evidence suggests that hatred for the North and love for the South grew in 1864 and 1865. As the war intensified, Rebels' hatred for the Union deepened not only out of vengeance but also because the quest for nationhood required more justification when sacrifices multiplied.[4]

If the whole Confederacy deprecated the Union to justify secession and war, individual soldiers abstracted the foe to absolve themselves of murder. Abhorrence of killing and guilt spurs soldiers to simplify the enemy. Hiding opponents' humanness—their integrity as individuals and their bonds of affection—behind the mask of Cain enabled troops to kill without considering it a damning sin. Only by denigrating and dehumanizing northerners could Rebels maintain their sanity against the heaps of dead men for which they were personally and corporately responsible. Enemy stereotypes joined a host of elements, including group absolution, instinctual action acquired through drilling and experience, the chain of command, "combat high," and the mechanical and physical distance between a soldier and his target, that diminished individual responsibility. These factors, compounded by the unprecedented destruction of the war, made abstractions of the enemy necessary.[5]

Stereotypes, however, came with a heavy price. Skewed perceptions of the enemy stimulated men to fight and absolved them of guilt, but caricatures also shaped how soldiers interpreted the other side's actions, measured their resolve, and handled defeat. Speaking from experience, scholar and veteran Paul Fussell admits that abstractions of the enemy create "a perceptual and rhetorical scandal from which total recovery is unlikely." Fussell understands how the mask of Cain permanently alters people's worldview. "Looking out upon the wartime world, soldiers and civilians alike reduce it to a simplified sketch featuring a limited series of classifications into which people, in the process dehumanized and deprived of individuality or eccentricity, are fitted." During the Civil War, Rebel abstractions distorted how Confederates fought and thought about the conflict, and each image of the North was insidious in its own way. Viewing the Yankees as inept opponents severely underestimated the Union's power and resolve. Deeming the enemy barbaric conjured visions of defeat too terrible to permit. Both stereotypes pointed to Confederate victory: the weak foe assured Rebels that they would win; the brutal one convinced them that God would never allow Union triumph. Classifications for the enemy included a number of colorful characters, including fanatical Puritans, brutish mercenaries, immigrant trash, and cowardly shopkeepers, but Rebel abstractions could not encompass images that prepared white southerners for reunion. Because the mask of Cain could not portray the foe as God's favorites, conquerors, or fellow countrymen, many Confederates could not conceive of defeat. Reconstruction meant their worst nightmares coming true. For these reasons, the mask of Cain encouraged the culture of invincibility and created a "rhetorical scandal" from which many Confederates never recovered.[6] How could they lose to inferiors? How could they reunite with barbarians?

ᏫᎳᎧ ᏫᎳᎧ ᏫᎳᎧ

Disparate elements within and outside the South composed the mask of Cain. Some of its parts preceded the war. The antebellum southern economy influenced abstractions of the North in at least two ways. First, without exaggeration, slavery made "the South" and by contrast "the North" and the sectional division. From colonization through nationhood and territorial expansion, the South's peculiar labor system—more than climate, ethnic, or political variations—delineated the regions. It was the major disparity between countrymen who, from a global perspective, shared more than they differed. Second, agrarian life produced close but confined worlds of daily existence that imparted a strong localism to many southerners' perspectives. Common whites (those who filled Rebel ranks) seldom ventured beyond their neighborhoods, let alone their counties or states. As one scholar of this class notes, "Counties were too large to provide the intimacy needed for the close bonds of a locality." This condition increased southerners' affections for home and their suspicions of outsiders or anyone who lived a starkly different life. Moreover, settlement patterns compounded this mentality. When thousands of southerners migrated closer to the frontier, they generally moved farther from population centers. The men who accomplished these arduous moves exhibited a level of personal competence that affirmed their familial authority and individualism. This sense of control over one's sphere of possessions and of "rural isolation" fostered an "intensely provincial" worldview in many white, southern men. Having become "masters of small worlds," they resented meddlers who challenged their home rule.[7]

Antebellum southerners who traveled north often had the effects of parochialism amplified by how alien the North seemed. Every year, thousands of southerners headed north to avoid the heat, recuperate at popular springs, sightsee, or attend schools. Some of these tourists reported positive differences in the North as a way of improving southern culture and economy. Others enjoyed the bustle of city life and honored patriotic treasures like Independence Hall in Philadelphia or Faneuil Hall in Boston. But these southerners often perceived themselves as travelers in a foreign land. Moreover, most of the people who had the time and means to visit the North were planters and slaveholders; hence, those who were most dedicated to the "southern way of life" conveyed biased accounts of the North with both the authority of their social position and that of a firsthand witness. John Hope Franklin notes that these travelers persuaded "those who had not been there that northern intentions toward the South were sinister and that when one dealt with the North at any level, he did so at his own peril."[8]

Whether or not southerners visited the North, many of them accepted the Cavalier legend, not slavery, as the explanation for sectional dichotomies. The story claimed that opposing sides of the English Civil War had settled the regions: Roundheads colonized New England, and the royalists, or Cavaliers, inhabited Virginia and the Carolinas. These warring parties were also described as ethnically distinct: the Yankee—Roundhead line was Saxon, and the planter—Cavalier ancestry was Norman. Derived from different blood and settled in disparate climates, each side developed unique principles and traits. Northerners formed a leveling, industrial, enterprising society, while southerners created an aristocratic, agrarian, leisurely world reminiscent of English gentility. In 1855, William Yancey offered his version of the thesis with characteristic partisanship:

> The Creator has beautified the face of this Union with sectional features.
> Absorbing all minor subdivisions, He has made the North and the South;
> the one the region of frost, ribbed with ice and granite; the other baring its
> generous bosom to the sun and ever smiling under its influence. The climate,
> soil and productions of these two grand divisions of the land, have made the
> character of their inhabitants. Those who occupy the one are cool, calculating,
> enterprising, selfish, and grasping; the inhabitants of the other are ardent,

brave and magnanimous, more disposed to give than to accumulate, to enjoy ease rather than labor.

Yancey's language stamped regionalism as inevitable. In his speech, the differences between North and South were not the result of opposing economics or politics but a product of Creation and, therefore, divinely ordained. The national crisis appeared as natural and unstoppable as the glaciers that had shaped northern landscapes and, according to Yancey, the region's future inhabitants. By "absorbing all minor subdivisions" under the aegis of sectionalism, Yancey not only fortified distinctiveness as he saw it but trumped national affiliations.[9]

The Cavalier thesis may be bogus genealogy, but it is not harmless myth. Its ethnic explanation for regional differences was more significant than the particular qualities it assigned to denizens of each section. The legend overshadowed the shared legacy of the revolution with a longer record of belligerency that divided American ancestors not only in the English Civil War but also as Saxons versus Normans at the Battle of Hastings eight hundred years before the U.S. Civil War. How many people knew the full extent of this historic division is an important consideration. To be sure, the legend attracted slave owners more than yeoman farmers. Nevertheless, even southerners who did not believe they descended from near royalty received the message that northerners and southerners were separate folk who had never seen eye to eye.[10]

The legend appealed to southerners because it offered them flattery, self-absorption, and ethnography while obscuring slavery's mark. The theory showed no genuine interest in the North and instead used the section as a foil for southern greatness. The story pitted the perfect Dixie, a land of honor, grace, leisure, abundance, hierarchical harmony, and political brilliance, against the sooty North, a realm of hypocrisy, banality, labor, avarice, social leveling, and political corruption. One side embodied the final citadel of chivalry; the other represented the vanguard of degeneration. And, of course, southerners descended from "better stock" than northerners. Finally, by using ethnography to explain regional variance, the legend not only confirmed sectionalism (while other theories could have discounted it) but also evaded the stain of slavery. Yancey failed to note the reasons that southern Cavaliers "enjoy ease rather than labor."[11]

While these developments fostered abstractions of the North, different elements in the South and the nation promoted the belligerency that turned these images into vehicles of prejudice. Here the clashes over slavery were paramount. As Eric Foner writes, "The political wars of the 1850s, centering on the issue of slavery extension, had done much to erode whatever good feeling existed between the sections." Indictments against southern morality simmered within northern debates over slavery in the territories and the comparative value of northern and southern society. This underlying slur galled a culture predicated on honor. W. J. Cash expresses the potency of southern honor when he considers what motivated a Rebel to fight: "Allow what you will for *esprit de corps*, for this or for that, the thing that sent him swinging up the slope at Gettysburg . . . was before all else nothing more or less than the thing . . . which elsewhere accounted for his violence, . . . the conviction . . . that nothing living could cross him and get away with it." The roughness of southern life bred this militant defense of honor. Despite pretensions of aristocracy, much of the region remained an "agricultural frontier" that demanded grit and resourcefulness. Most southern white men were accustomed to working with their hands and settling differences with them. As more and more of these men identified the abstract North as a threat to their world, their life in a "fighters' fatherland," as John Hope Franklin calls the antebellum South, predisposed many of them to consider aggression an appropriate response.[12]

The venomous rhetoric that spouted in Congress and splashed across southern newspapers during the 1850s illustrated the severity of regional divisions. James Hammond's "mudsill" speech enraged the North and sold more than twenty-five thousand copies in the South. Firebrands on both sides were transforming difference into grotesqueness. In 1856, a Georgia editor summed up the southern abstraction: "Free society! we sicken at the name. What is it but a conglomeration of greasy mechanics, filthy operatives, small-fisted farmers, and moon-struck theorists? All the northern, and especially the New England states, are devoid of society fitted for well-bred gentlemen. The prevailing class one meets with is that of mechanics struggling to be genteel, and small farmers who do their own drudgery, and yet are hardly fit for association with a southern gentleman's body servant." Such statements split the nation as much as did the substantive issues from which they drew their poison. Over time, Americans had come to view each other as strangers, as contrasting Others, and finally as enemies. In December 1860, Georgia Senator Alfred Iverson helped to complete this degeneration: "Sir, disguise the fact as you will, there is an enmity between the northern and southern people that is deep and enduring, and you never can eradicate it—never! You sit upon your side, silent and gloomy; we sit upon ours with knit brows and portentous scowls. . . . We are enemies as much as if we were hostile States. I believe that the northern people hate the South worse than ever the English people hated France; and I can tell my brethren over there that there is no love lost upon the part of the South." Once southerners considered themselves a separate people, fomenters could present nationalism not as the last resort but as the logical solution to sectional tension.[13]

Secession and warfare both hardened sectional polarities and changed antebellum archetypes into more complex perceptions of the foe. Action supplanted rhetoric and seemed to clarify things. Though the South's fate was more uncertain after secession than before it, nationhood appeared to settle issues. Decisions of allegiance brought people into clearer focus: southerners became either Confederates or traitors, and northerners accepted their role as the enemy—

the ultimate Other. President Abraham Lincoln's call for troops recast the paranoid as clairvoyants; the North was indeed conspiring to subjugate the South and revoke American freedoms. Confederate nationhood also transformed expressions of sectional enmity and discord into affirmations of patriotism and southern unity. Finally, resorting to blows heightened the significance of the times—decades of sectional arguments were about to be decided. C. E. Montague (though writing of a different conflict) captures the spirit of 1861: "The great throw, the new age's impending nativity, Fate with her fingers approaching the veil, about to lift—a sense of these things is a drug as strong as strychnine to quicken the failing pulse of the most heart-weary of moribund raptures."[14]

During the war's early stages, images of inept enemies and barbaric foes coexisted. Antebellum stereotypes combined with war enthusiasm and early Confederate victories to portray northerners as weaklings. Rebels inflated their resources, talents, and resolve and underestimated their adversaries' chances. In this climate, a man who did not indulge in bellicose boasts that he could whip ten Yankees risked being branded unpatriotic or, worse, a coward. Fort Sumter and Manassas convinced many Confederates that pasty Union men were no match for southern steel. The Cavalier myth seemed prophetic; northern forefathers had won the English Civil War, but southern gentlemen were righting the old wrong. In the New World, in another civil war, grimy Yankees were crumbling before stalwart knights of the sunny South. Confederate officers from the master class fashioned themselves as romantic Cavaliers guarding order and honor against twisted zealots. Some contemporaries and subsequently historians noted the inconsistency of evangelical Protestants admiring Catholic gentry instead of Cromwell's army, but war enthusiasm often brushed aside such details. Early triumphs compounded Confederate narcissism by fostering an undying faith in certain commanders and a culture of invincibility. After Manassas, for example, many Rebels contracted the "victory disease," a term the Japanese used eighty years later to describe "the fatal hubris of invincibility" that consumed many of them after Pearl Harbor, Singapore, and the Philippines.[15]

The portrait of an inept enemy that Confederates produced from these impressions was so flexible and durable that it survived successive Rebel defeats and in some form even outlasted the Confederacy. The image depicted Federal armies as motley bands of weaklings, city dwellers, bounty hunters, dandies, and cowards. Bluecoats were immigrants who could not speak English, mill-town boys who never owned horses or guns, urban scum who enlisted for pay, and New England snobs who polished their buttons and boots but failed as fighters. A Virginia artilleryman considered the enemy "starving Irish who fight for daily bread" and "Western scoundrels . . . spawned in prairie mud." They were unhealthy specimens shrunken by factory work who could not possibly beat legions of southern men raised in the rustic outdoors.[16] Their motive paled in comparison as well: Yankees fought for money, while Rebels strove for freedom.

For many Confederates, the Army of the Potomac embodied this perception of the foe. Lincoln's prized army was a collection of white-gloved recreants who could march in step and impress Washington socialites but withered before Rebel bullets—they were parade-ground heroes and battleground failures. The slew of commanders who failed to rival Robert E. Lee—braggarts like John Pope and Joseph Hooker, the sadly incompetent Ambrose Burnside, and George McClellan, the blood-shy general who aspired to Napoleonic stature—seemed to prove northern inadequacies. The portrait of an inept enemy fostered a sense that the Confederacy was unconquerable. As a Georgia private expressed, the "degraded set of Northern people" could never suppress "a noble and respectable squad of Southerners."[17]

The most common name used for the Federals, "Yankees," encapsulated the idea of a pathetic foe. The term lumped all northerners into a caricature of New Englanders as hypocritical reformers, cold industrialists, money-grubbers, and self-righteous Puritans. Branding men from Maine to Minnesota, regardless of their accent, vocation, or ethnicity, as Yankees perpetuated the Cavalier myth that northerners were the natural-born adversaries of everything southern. Only race could discount a northern soldier from being a Yankee, for African American troops were seldom called Yankees or even black Yankees. For Rebels, Yankees were white opponents who represented the mirror opposite of southerners, the warped and alien Others who had forsaken the revolution and threatened southern existence. Some Confederates maintained images of inept northerners until the end, underestimating the Union's power and resolve while its massive armies overwhelmed them.[18]

Images and music spread the stereotype of inept Yankees across the Confederacy. Cartoons, a medium that claims to offer truths through simplified, imaginative sketches and commentaries, thrived on perceptions of the enemy. Southern illustrations that stressed northern incompetence depicted Lincoln as inexperienced and quixotic. In February 1863, the *Southern Illustrated News* printed a particularly effective cartoon, "Master Abraham Lincoln Gets a New Toy." Instead of being depicted as a patriarch, Lincoln appears as an ugly, awkward brat who has discarded his old dolls (representing previous commanding generals Winfield Scott, Irwin McDowell, John C. Frémont, Nathaniel Banks, John Pope, Ambrose Burnside, and George McClellan) in favor of a new one, "Fighting Joe" Hooker. Shelves stacked with the discarded dolls and Lincoln's foolish grin as he holds up his new toy general illustrate both the wooden ineffectiveness of Union generals and the boyish immaturity of the president's leadership. A blank "Proclamation" on the wall mocks the significance of the Emancipation Proclamation.[19]

A similar drawing by Adalbert Johann Volck, a talented cartoonist and Confederate sympathizer from Maryland, depicted Lincoln as a jester presenting the Union war effort as a puppet show. The ridiculously garbed Lincoln introduces

"Master Abraham Lincoln Gets a New Toy." Courtesy of the Hargrett Rare Book and Manuscript Library, University of Georgia Libraries.

the war effort in Shakespearean style and admits that it is a comedy: "Your honours[,] players . . . are come to play a pleasant comedy. . . . Is it a Comedy . . . a Christmas Gambol or a turning trick[?] . . . No my Lord it is more pleasing stuff. . . . [I]t is a kind of history." A banner at the base of the stage advertises "great American tragedians, comedians, clowns and rope dancers in their favorite characters." These great performers are Lincoln's cabinet members and generals reduced to puppet stature. Some of their poses are particularly clever: General Benjamin Butler slumps in the background holding a whiskey jug; Secretary of War Simon Cameron (a notorious grafter) hangs from his own string; and a puppet of a common soldier lies dead and alone on stage right. Secretary of the Treasury Salmon P. Chase mans the box-office window, and a skeleton raises the curtain. Such men would be no match for Confederate leaders.[20]

Because the northern press openly criticized Lincoln and the Union war effort, northern artists drew hundreds of cartoons depicting incompetence in Washington. In fact, the range, volume, and regularity of northern magazines

*"Lincoln and His Puppets." Reprinted with the permission of the
Maryland Historical Society.*

outmatched southern periodicals to such a degree that Confederates may have entertained themselves more with northern cartoons than with Rebel ones. In August 1863, *Frank Leslie's Illustrated Newspaper* printed "The Naughty Boy Gotham, Who Would Not Take the Draft," a commentary on the New York City draft riot. The artist personifies the city as a churlish child in a high chair who tosses his food, labeled "draft," at Lincoln, his startled mother in a dress and bonnet. A girl identified as Philadelphia sulks in the background. Confederates interpreted the draft riots and such northern depictions of them as signs of the enemy's internal deterioration and impending collapse.[21]

Confederate poetry and camp songs also spread the image of inept northerners. As a medium, music was particularly effective at glorifying the new nation, demarcating battle lines, and simplifying the issues and stakes involved. Recent histories of the nineteenth century suggest that the sounds of the Civil War profoundly affected how participants understood the conflict. In particular, music pervaded the soldiers' world: songs wooed men to volunteer, entertained them in camp, sustained them on the march, fostered camaraderie, and consoled them before battle. Some men even sang to calm their nerves within the din of combat. The widespread popularity of music reflected both the sentimentalism of the time and soldiers' search for meaning, comfort, and pleasure in a dreary world.[22]

Songs that portrayed weak opponents emboldened southern men with promises that the war would be an adventure, not a nightmare, and the foe would be laughable, not terrifying. "Call All! Call All!" exemplifies the belittling approach with references to the enemy as small animals and "Doodles":

> Whoop! The Doodles have broken loose,
> Roaring round like the very deuce!
> Lice of Egypt, a hungry pack,
> After 'em, boys, and drive 'em back.
> Bull-dog, terrier, cur, and fice,
> Back to the beggarly land of ice;
> Worry 'em, bite 'em, scratch and tear
> Everybody and everywhere.

By so explicitly dehumanizing the enemy, the songwriter implies that killing the foe would be as easy as squashing a bug:

> Want a weapon?
> Gather a brick,
> Club or cudgel, or stone or stick;
> Anything with a blade or butt,
> Anything that can cleave or cut.
> Anything heavy, or hard, or keen!

"The Naughty Boy Gotham, Who Would Not Take the Draft." The cartoon carried below its title a line of dialogue from "Mammy Lincoln": "There now, you bad boy, acting that way, when your little sister Penn takes hers like a lady!" Courtesy of the American Antiquarian Society.

Any sort of slaying machine!
Anything with a willing mind,
And the steady arm of a man behind.
Want a weapon?
Why, capture one! Every Doodle has got a gun,
Belt and bayonet, bright and new;
Kill a Doodle, and capture *two*.[23]

In "The Old Rifleman," Frank Ticknor belittles the foe by evoking the back-woods nonchalance of American folklore. Like Davy Crockett and other legendary heroes, Ticknor's old rifleman brushes aside the northern threat with natural courage and years of experience. The fellow grabs his buckskin suit, powder pouch, flint, and, of course, "Old Bess" to "see if seventy-six can shoot / As sixteen used to do." Ticknor connected the Federals to the stock villains of the American past: speaking to Old Bess, the rifleman exclaims,

We've seen the red-coat Briton bleed!
The red-skin Indian, too!
We never thought to draw a bead on Yankee-doodle doo!

Though shocked and saddened by the fact that northern countrymen have forsaken the common experiences and collective glory the sections had won together, the old soldier has a chilling solution for the "meddling" Federal: "There's only this to do: / Select the black spot in his eye and let the daylight through!"[24]

The message Confederates received from these words and images was clear: Yankees are easy to kill and defeat. Union leaders and soldiers appeared as children, women, dogs, lice, and puppets. None of them could compete with southern men. Diverse events and figures, particularly in the early years of the war, supported Rebels' perceptions of an inept foe. In addition to Lee and Stonewall Jackson, Confederate cavalry leaders often provided the most colorful evidence that southern intelligence, courage, and ability surpassed northern numbers. When Nathan Bedford Forrest, John Morgan, John Mosby, and J. E. B. Stuart humiliated Federal opponents, they produced an entire genre of legends. Raphael Semmes, captain of the *Alabama*, mimicked these men's successes on the high seas. In addition to Fort Sumter and Manassas, Jackson's Valley Campaign and Lee's defense of Richmond during the Seven Days' Battles offered proof of Rebel military superiority.

But as the war intensified, the enemy appeared more frequently (to Rebels and in their writing) as invading hordes. War is terrifying, and even a people as self-confident as the Confederates shivered at the specter of blue columns pouring across the border. Some Rebels imagined this nightmare at the war's inception when Lincoln called for thousands to quell the rebellion. Secession commissioners warned politicians from sister states to join the Confederacy or stand alone against "the same fell spirit, like an unchained demon, [which] has for years swept over the plains of Kansas, leaving death, desolation, and ruin in its track." In other words, the barbaric image of the North did not replace an earlier, inept version of the Federals halfway through the conflict. The stereotypes coexisted during the war and in the minds of southerners. As the conflict worsened, however, a barbaric view of the adversary gained currency and influenced how white southerners viewed the war and faced defeat. The shift had dire consequences. While the caricature of an inept foe promoted ridicule, the figure of a savage enemy evoked hatred. The weak Yankee was fallible, and Confederate victory seemed certain. The barbarian, however, could be demonic or inhuman, and defeat at the hands of such a foe would be nightmarish. The war became a struggle for survival.[25]

By 1863, a barbaric figure pervaded Rebel depictions of the enemy. Numberless, mercenary thugs lusting for southern loot and women composed the minions of this image. If the Army of the Potomac and its carousel of commanders represented the inept foe, William T. Sherman and his grim, unstoppable force embodied the brutal nemesis. Like pestilence, these dusty columns seemed to take everything of value (including slaves), leaving want and destruction in their wake. Their targets seemed to be women, children, and old people—not armed Confederates. After the Vicksburg campaign, Mississippi governor Charles Clark told his citizens, "We are invaded north, south, and west by a vindictive foe, who is desolating our borders, burning our dwellings, insulting our people, and inciting our slaves to insurrection." Clark preferred death over "base submission" to such enemies: "Let the last of our young men die upon our banner, then let our old men, our women, and our children, like the remnant of the heroic Pascagoulas, when their braves were slain, join hands together, march into the sea, and perish beneath its waters." Because their behavior disregarded the rules of chivalrous warfare, enemy soldiers appeared as demons, vandals, heathens, and animals. An Atlanta newspaper editor depicted the Union as "the myrmidons of a tyranny that is as coarse as it is brutal and ferocious." White southerners fought "not only against the hosts marshalled at the North, but the refuse of European prisons and penitentiaries, of men who hire themselves to cut the throats of innocent men, women and children." Worse still was the foreboding that endless reserves just like them waited at home for their chance to despoil Dixie.[26]

To demonize the enemy, Rebels elicited savage and racist monikers, including "barbarian," "vandal," "abolitionist," and "miscegenator." In May 1864, a Confederate mother told her son how proud she was that her boy was fighting "the *vilest foe* the sun ever shown on which makes the sacrifice the greater." One Rebel yearned "to sweep from the face of the earth the base and amorous race of Puritans which has so degraded itself and villified and slandered the Southern ladies." He often called the enemy "miscegiators" because of his conviction that miscegenation was "the new doctrine which has gained such popularity in Yankeedom." Louisiana infantryman Reuben Pierson thought Hell "would refuse such beings admittance." The Confederate religious press also propagated these stereotypes. Historian W. Harrison Daniel finds that "the denominational newspapers referred to Northerners as barbarians—modern-day Vandals, Huns, and Goths—who were seeking to gratify their 'hellish lusts' at the expense of Southern womanhood. On one occasion a religious newspaper printed the letter of a soldier-minister who argued that it was a religious duty to try to cut the throats of the 'monstrous' Northerners."[27] These barbaric images challenged the North's claims to higher civilization and loftier war aims. According to the Rebels, no Union war aim could conceal the baseness of northern aggression or compare with the justness—indeed, the righteousness—of Confederate self-defense. White southerners used Scripture, including Numbers 10:9, to support their case: "Go to battle without any fear, and strike boldly for your homes and your altars without any guilt. The right, in such case of self-defense, will be on your side."[28]

The barbaric image of the North drew strength from its diverse sources. Reid Mitchell argues that Confederates adapted the brutal figure from stock villains of the American past. Sketching a savage enemy mirrored Americans' apprehensions of Indian braves and articulated Rebel fears that Federals, like the Indians, threatened women and children. Framing Union soldiers as mercenaries hearkened back to old republican suspicions of the professional soldier/automaton as "the pliant tool of despotism" and expressed Confederate anxieties that the Bluecoats would do anything for pay. In other words, both pictures conveyed an invaded people's terror that foes would use warfare to commit monstrous crimes. Savages, by definition, did not know the rules of civilized warfare, and automatons would ignore laws when ordered to do so. Mitchell's analysis is appealing because it highlights Confederates' belief that they were continuing rather than forsaking the American experiment. By painting Yankees with the same brush that colonists and patriots used to mark enemies, Rebels legitimized themselves as the true heirs of the spirit of 1776.[29]

The Union's hardening war policy and the Emancipation Proclamation amplified the barbaric image. Rebels believed that Yankee rulers harbored evil plans behind a facade of reunion and abolition. For many Confederates, restoring the Union seemed a northern excuse to pillage and subjugate the South. Likewise, freeing the slaves really meant the elevation of blacks over whites, miscegenation between Yankee troops and slave wenches, and the rape of southern ladies by freedmen and Negroes in blue uniforms. Governor Clark warned Mississippians, "Humbly submit yourselves to our hated foes, and they will offer you a reconstructed Constitution providing for the confiscation of your property, the immediate emancipation of your slaves, and the elevation of the black race to a position of equality—aye, of superiority, that will make them your masters and rulers." Such jarring images illuminate Confederate fears that the enemy challenged the foundations of southern society and manhood. As southern men, Confederate soldiers drew their identity and authority from the submission of white women, the inferiority of blacks, and the ownership of land. As the war worsened, the enemy threatened to topple these pillars of the Old South. Stories of Union troops raping white women twisted the meaning of female submissiveness and challenged the masculine honor of men who swore to protect southern women. Defiant slaves and black troops upended racial hierarchy. Blue columns occupied and confiscated southern property. By 1864, Confederates perceived the North as trying to erase southern civilization and southern manhood. Federal actions substantiated Confederate propaganda.[30]

But the propaganda came first. Confederate poetry and camp songs spread the barbaric image of Unionists before hard war strategies and emancipation coarsened the Rebels' war. Confederate songs that called men to arms used the barbaric image to great effect. In July 1861, the newly recruited Kirk's Ferry Rangers held a barbecue in Catahoula, Louisiana. After ladies presented a flag to the unit, a glee club sang "Confederate Song," an anthem written for the men by their captain, E. Lloyd Wailes. The ballad warned the troops,

Northern Vandals tread our soil,
Forth they come for blood and spoil,
To the homes we've gained with toil,
Shouting "Slavery!"

The slavery of which Wailes wrote was a Yankee vow to enslave white southerners, not an outcry against black bondage.[31] Verses that luridly depicted a Federal onslaught could have sobered Confederates to the odds they faced, but the songs intended and achieved a different result: terror heightened both the urgency of the call and the heroism of those who answered it. By representing the enemy as countless and ghastly, these ballads valorized Confederate regiments as bands of boys willing to oppose a nightmarish force with gallant but mortal hearts.

By darkening Dixie's borders with hordes eager to steal southern land and women, the songs voiced men's gravest fears and presented them with two honorable options: victory or death. "The Southern Cross," sung to the tune of "The Star Spangled Banner," vilified "the Puritan demon" and envisioned Rebels

with our front to the field,
swearing never to yield,
Or return, like the Spartan,
in death on our shield.

The tune "Call, All! Call All!" included all southerners in a sacrificial effort for independence:

Shoulder to shoulder, son and sire!
All, call all! To the feast of fire!
Mother and maiden, and child and slave,
A common triumph or a single grave.

The message was unmistakable: kill or be killed, defend loved ones or watch them perish.[32]

The enemy appeared in Rebel music as "Yankee despots," "foul mudsills," "rowdies, thieves, vagabonds," "bootblacks, tinkers," "*black*-guards," "Northern scum," "Vandals," "Hessians," "hellish gnomes," "wild fanatic men," and "ruffian hordes."[33] All these slurs elevated Rebels through contrasts: the darker the invaders seemed, the more radiant the defenders felt. Some ballads made explicit comparisons: "They're *hired* by their master, 'Abe'—*You* fight for *Liberty*."[34] Such ballads claimed superiority for the Confederacy in three elements that were sacred to white southerners: blood, cause, and valor.

Soldiers' writings show that music inspired the troops and helped them express their beliefs. In March 1864, Samuel Meetze, a North Carolina infantryman, swore, "I reather die then be com a Slave to the North." Suspecting that the war was entering its final phase, Meetze used song lyrics to express his views to his sister: "We will conquer or we will die. Tis, for our honer and our names . . . [w]e rais the battle cry." Only weeks before his surrender, a Virginia artilleryman composed a song, "We Fight until We Die," with a central verse:

The Yankee thieves have pillaged
Many a Southern home,
And our sweethearts, wives & children
Now penniless do roam.
. . . .
Let vengeance be our cry
While for Southern Independence
We'll fight until we die!

Some of these oaths may have been posturing, a romantic nod to Sir Walter Scott in heroic times. But many Confederates convinced themselves that their South stood between war and annihilation. Surveying their options, the diehards preferred the company of dead comrades over that of barbarians and blacks.[35]

Perhaps the strongest war verse was written by a Confederate prisoner of war, S. Teakle Wallis. From prison, Wallis sent "The Guerillas" to the *Richmond Examiner* in the hands of a paroled comrade. The ballad begins with "a friend" reporting atrocities to a group of Confederate irregulars. The passerby first details the enemy's mistreatment of defenseless civilians:

The shrieks and moans of the houseless
Ring out, like a dirge on the gale.

I've seen from the smoking village
Our mothers and daughters fly;
I've seen where the little children
Sank down in the furrows to die.

The narrator then stirred racist fears:

They are turning the slaves upon us,
And with more than the fiend's worst art,
Have uncovered the fire of the savage,
That slept in his untaught heart!
The ties to our hearths that bound him,
They have rent with curses away,
And maddened him, with their madness,
To be almost as brutal as they.

As a response to these atrocities, the traveler and the guerrillas swore an oath:

Let every man swear on his blade,
That he will not sheathe nor stay it,
Till from point to hilt it glow
With the flush of Almighty vengeance,
In the blood of the felon foe.

The threat to women and property, including slaves, pervades Confederate verses and soldiers' writings. The patriarchy of southern manhood rested on female submission, landownership, and racial superiority. The Union war effort challenged all these elements of southern male identity and could revoke a fourth: political rights. Many Confederate soldiers believed that losing these pillars of manhood would doom them to slavery or subjugation.[36]

Soldiers also found the barbaric image in political cartoons. Volck's best work propagated evil stereotypes of the enemy. In an 1863 drawing, Lincoln drafts the Emancipation Proclamation in a room filled with satanic symbols. A tiny demon holds his inkwell, hoofed feet adorn the table legs, and a vulture's head keeps the curtain open. Racism charges the image as well. A portrait of John Brown and a scene of the slave revolt in Santo Domingo decorate the wall. In a second painting, naked blacks impale men, stab babies, and carry off women. The table is carved with horned heads of African Americans. Volck hints at cowardice with a Scottish cap that covers a Union sculpture and a liquor decanter. In the center, a scowling Lincoln scribbles away with one foot on the Constitution.[37]

While Volck's work associated Lincoln and the Union with Satan's forces, other drawings depicted Lincoln himself as the Devil. These cartoons and others that dehumanized the North represented the most extreme pictorial abstractions of the enemy. *Southern Punch* printed an illustration of Lincoln as the

"Proclamation." Reprinted with the permission of the Maryland Historical Society.

"Prince of Darkness" because Satan was "the first to Rebel against constituted authority." The irony of seceded Rebels painting Lincoln black for his constitutional transgressions was lost on the artist and probably on his readers, too. In the scene, a dark Lincoln Devil abducts Lady Liberty and leads her to his "infernal regions." As they fly above a thunderstorm, the goddess pleads, "Monster of Perdition, let me go!" "Never!" Lincoln replies, "You have been preaching about the Constitution too long already." An artless caricature from the *Southern Illustrated News* perhaps best captures perceptions of the enemy. The drawing, "Masks and Faces," shows "King Abraham before and after issuing the Emancipation Proclamation." A towering figure reveals the face of Satan hidden behind a mask of Lincoln. The proclamation rests at the figure's feet, and the scaffolding atop the unfinished Washington Monument resembles gallows. Here is the extreme impact of enemy stereotypes: the imagined foe becomes the true enemy, and the actual enemy is a mere deception. [38]

ᕗᙏᙏᕰ ᕗᙏᙏᕰ ᕗᙏᙏᕰ

A close study of Confederate letters and diaries reveals a pattern: as the war intensified, the enemy appeared more frequently as barbarians. Antebellum stereotypes and early war propaganda contributed to the mask, but soldiers found plenty of evidence in their war experiences to support base images of

"Abduction of the Yankee Goddess of Liberty." The original illustration bore the description: "The Prince of Darkness (Abraham Lincoln) bears her away to his infernal regions." Courtesy of the Museum of the Confederacy, Richmond, Virginia.

MASKS AND FACES.

Yankees. On occasion, troops expressed respect for northern adversaries, but denigrating the opposition was too central to the process of warfare for soldiers to give it up. From 1863 to 1865, many conditions—some unique to the soldiers' lives and others common to the white South—deepened abstractions of the enemy. Union armies validated Rebel caricatures by introducing two features in the final campaigns that were tailor-made for the barbaric image of them: total warfare and black soldiers.[39]

Few actions confirmed Rebels' views of the enemy and deepened their animosity for Federals as much as the Union's total war offensives. Overwhelming legions of Yankees trampling crops, wrecking railroads, burning homes, freeing slaves, stealing valuables, and leveling cities actualized white southerners' greatest fears of the enemy. These images multiplied in 1863 when the United States abandoned its limited war strategy. Pierson witnessed this "hard hand of war" in Virginia after Gettysburg, writing to his sister, "I for one would welcome death a thousand times rather than live to behold a day of reunion with such a hateful . . . band of robers, murderers & inhumane creatures as we are now fighting." He thought that the world "cannot find a parallel for their beastliness." Lee's army heard accounts of terrible atrocities in counties occupied by the enemy. From Loudoun County, Virginia, came a report that "four young ladies . . . were violated in their beds at home." When Virginian Green Samuels heard the story, he prayed, "God grant when we meet the enemy, we may be able to punish them for the horrid barbarities inflicted upon the helpless citizens within their lines." Samuels wanted vengeance "meted out to these devils in human form." When the Federals inaugurated total war offensives, Confederates like Pierson and Samuels expected the worst.[40]

Rebels in the western theater experienced similar circumstances in 1863 and reacted accordingly. Weeks after Vicksburg fell, Sergeant Edwin Fay watched the enemy level Brandon, Mississippi, and then wrote to his wife in Arkansas, "The Yanks remained in Brandon all night burning the principal part of town and left on their way back to Jackson, which together with Canton they have burned up before. Ashes and charred remains of all kinds of buildings mark their course everywhere." Fay vowed, "I shall never cease to hate them" and instructed his wife to kill any Yankee who threatened her: "Keep that pistol loaded . . . and if the Yankees come to Minden . . . wear it on your person, never be without it and the first one that dares insult you blow his brains out." Fay fumed, "I expect to murder every Yankee I ever meet when I can do so with impunity if I live a hundred years. . . . Peace will never be made between me and any Yankee." William Nugent was equally incensed. From Okolona, Mississippi, he vowed, "The day of retribution is coming, and when it does, woe to the worthless invader, who has had no mercy." Like Fay, Nugent prepared for a war of extermination. In his opinion, the enemy "count time & men as nothing, esteeming the length of the war as of no moment. . . . [S]o be it." The Mississippian thought that invaders could never "conquer and possess so widely extended a country" as the South. "They may & doubtless will impoverish the people as they go along," he reasoned, "but this only leaves a thousand foes behind them who will rise upon their stragglers and put an end to their useless lives." Nugent wanted to unleash the Mississippi cavalry on the "vandal hordes who are infesting our borders." He thought it best to "concentrate our forces and wipe one army completely out before we begin an attack elsewhere." In this way, he hoped to clean the Confederacy of all Yankee scum.[41]

The campaigns of 1864 further confirmed the enemy's barbarism. Marching past General Philip H. Sheridan's work in the Shenandoah, a Virginia private exclaimed, "The Yankees left their mark of fire behind them." J. Tracy Power notes that Lee's men referred to the enemy as "vandals" and "miscreants" with greater regularity after Sheridan's campaign. When Sherman ordered the expulsion of all disloyal southerners from Atlanta and refused to exchange prisoners, a

Louisiana soldier spouted that such conduct "shows the true Yankee trickery of those inhuman vandals." Across the Mississippi, another Rebel witnessed "the hand of a more savage foe" in 1864. He noted in his diary, "Our camp is the ruins of a magnificent plantation." He slept "amidst a perfect forest of blackened chimneys." Similar vistas seared Rebels' images of the enemy throughout the South.[42] Scholar Wolfgang Schivelbusch notes how the Union's total war strategy strengthened Confederate stereotypes of the enemy: "The reason found for this behavior was, along with the innate cowardice and lack of sportsmanship of the pinched Yankee soul, the fact that the Union army consisted in large measure of immigrants, the 'trash of Europe.'" When Private Richard Waldrop observed that "the wrecks & ruins of burnt mills & barns meet the eye on every side," he surmised, "surely Providence cannot always favor such a system of warfare—a system that snatches bread from the mouths of helpless women & children." God's vengeance would be "swift and terrible."[43]

Though total war offensives were meant to crush the Confederacy's will, evidence suggests that targeting civilians strengthened Rebel resolve and hatred. Marching through Culpeper County, Virginia, Spencer Welch thought the region was "totally devastated . . . without a fence or a planted field of any kind." Welch could not fathom how the locals survived, "yet they do actually continue to live there." Moreover, the destruction increased the citizens' determination to fight. Welch reported, "They are intensely hostile to the Yankees, and there is certainly no submission in them." When Virginian J. Kelly Bennette passed the broken walls of a plantation, he commented, "These still stand silent witnesses of the ruthlessness of those who would win us back to the bond of brotherly love." He heard that the Yankees had given the women who lived there an hour to collect their valuables but then stole or destroyed everything the women carried. Reunion with such fiends was inconceivable.[44]

The impact of desolation may have been greater on soldiers who did not witness it firsthand. Anxieties about loved ones and ghastly stories dogged the minds of far-off veterans. From Richmond in November 1864, a Georgian had "no doubt the hated swarm of Yankees have passed over" his home like a plague of locusts. A soldier in the Army of Tennessee exclaimed, "Citizens that live between here and Dalton sometimes come to us and say that the Yanks treat our people back there as mean as they can. . . . My God what will become of us?" The validity of some reports could not be denied. In June 1864, a Virginian's comrade received ominous mail from his sister: "She says the enemy has been at his father's and have done them an infinite amount of harm. They took all the negroes, all the meat and chickens and broke open every lock in the house and stole everything they could carry away which would be of any use to them or their families." Alabamian Elias Davis feared that "they have visited our neighborhood." "I have seen so much distruction of property in [Virginia] and so much distress in consequence of it that my heart sickens when I think of Yankee

Raiders visiting [the] section of country where live those near and dear to me."
When reading a New York newspaper, James Izlar learned that Sherman was
in Izlar's hometown, Orangeburg, South Carolina, and found it "impossible to
describe my feeling upon reading the announcement. Wife and child homeless
& houseless wanderers, the hard and honest earnings of years perhaps a total
loss." He asked for God's protection against "the indignities of a cruel foe."[45]

Of all the actions they witnessed, the shelling of cities particularly galled Confederates because they lacked the strength to silence the barrage and suffered
to watch it. In Petersburg, Paul Higginbotham wrote to his brother after a day of
"terrible cannonading" that "the Yankee batteries . . . are plenty close to tear the
town to pieces," he lamented. Within days, tents and pine board shelters dot-
ted the ground around Charles Blackford and the First Corps Headquarters—
citizens were clinging to the army for protection. "Many of these people [are]
of some means and all [are] of great respectability," Blackford observed, meaning they were white southerners and infinitely finer than the attacking soldiers.
"Yesterday, about the time they thought the people were going to church, [the
enemy] commenced a tremendous cannonade, as if with the hope of killing
women and children en route to church." Visiting the city on a twenty-four-hour
pass, John Walters found fires burning in four places. "These were caused by the
incendiary shell that the enemy were throwing," he concluded. "As the smoke
of these fires rose in the air they presented an excellent mark for the enemy,
and they were not slow to avail themselves of it." Fellow artilleryman James Albright considered the enemy who shelled the city "fiends" and "vandals." Seeing
defenseless women and children fleeing the city convinced Albright that God
would rectify the situation.[46]

Federal bombardments convinced Rebels that they faced barbarians. With
Confederate troops standing before them, the Yankees preferred to terrorize
helpless civilians behind the lines. Union strategists hoped these actions would
make war so terrible for the Rebels that they would lose all taste for it and quit.
Instead, the shelling of Petersburg and Atlanta convinced white southerners that
they faced cowards and bullies who shied away from honest combat. Confederate soldiers and civilians shared this conviction. A South Carolina woman considered the Yankees "a hard set of demons in the shape of human beings some of
them look to me as I imagine the imps of Satan would look." During the shelling
of Atlanta, Tennessee infantryman William Sloan visited the city to thank some
women who had cared for his wounded brother. Sloan "found them deep down
in the earth under their house." While he was there, a woman left the shelter
for a few moments, and "a huge shell ploughed through the room she was in."
She survived, but Sloan noted that "a number of casualties have been reported
among women and children in the city." "That is Brute Sherman's mode of warfare," he concluded.[47]

Federal total war policies fed an already flourishing genre of Confederate propaganda: the atrocity story. Retaliation for atrocities, real or imagined, had motivated belligerents on both sides since the war's inception. The northern press accused Rebels of shooting at ambulances, bayoneting the wounded, and poisoning wells. According to Federal reports, the Confederates cut off the heads of Union dead, boiled their meat, and made souvenirs and utensils from their bones. The southern press claimed that Yankees bayoneted and shot Rebel prisoners, slit the throats and cut out the tongues of Confederate wounded, and fired at Rebels while they helped wounded Federals caught between the lines. Some stories suspected the Yankees of using poisoned bullets.[48]

By the war's final phase, Federal actions and Confederate fears expanded the focus of atrocity stories from the battlefront to the home front. The southern religious press printed accounts of Federal soldiers beating civilian men and raping their wives and daughters. While Sherman's army tramped through Georgia, a cavalryman was convinced that "the yankeys are destroying everything before them and ravishing women." Most accounts of sex or rape involved blacks. Historian James Silver notes that a "sure-fire method of creating a feeling of disgust for the Yankees" was to depict them in "captured cities parading up and down the streets with Negro women on their arms." Stories of black soldiers or slaves raping white women produced the greatest loathing. Malinda Taylor wrote to her husband, a soldier in the Army of Tennessee, that "there was a Negro burnt to death in Eutaw the other day for taking a white lady of[f] her horse and doing what he pleased with her." Similar accounts of "miscegenation" emanated from occupied Atlanta. Arkansan Thomas Key reacted to a "gloomy story of . . . the disgusting equalization of the whites and blacks under Sherman." According to rumor, "a big black negro man" propositioned "one of the most respected young ladies in the city." Key fumed, "The thought of such an occurrence arouses every nerve in my body for vengeance, and I feel like crying: 'Raise the black flag and let slip the dogs of war.'" Whether true or false, these stories vitalized Rebel images of invading hordes and muddied delineations between legitimate acts of war and crimes, between myths and reality.[49]

Atrocities were important because they seemed to unmask the enemy's intentions. Accounts of rape exposed the "true" impetus behind freeing the slaves: racial amalgamation. Reports of pillage and dominance uncovered the "actual" design for restoring the Union: subjugation of the white South. These perceptions, whether accurate or not, expressed Rebels' gravest fears and elevated their cause and self-identity. Terrible accounts reified the Confederates' self-image as innocent victims, as an oppressed, besieged, and violated minority deserving of independence and free of guilt. War correspondent Michael Ignatieff observes that "people who believe themselves to be victims of aggression have an understandable incapacity to believe that they too have committed atrocities. Myths of innocence and victimhood are a powerful obstacle in the way of confronting responsibility." Southern editors stressed this theme of Confederate innocence.

Commenting on Sherman's March to the Sea, an Atlanta newspaper described "the muffled and strangled screams of ravished maidens," "the weak and feeble prayers of suffering old men and women," and "the spirits of honest men, who were murdered."[50]

Atrocities demanded justice, and quests for retribution motivated many Rebels through the war's final years. Historian James McPherson argues that revenge "became almost an obsession with some Confederates."[51] Soldiers expected a divine reckoning against the enemy. For many Rebels, the Yankee mode of warfare reinforced the conviction that God favored the Confederates and would deliver them from these northern demons. North Carolinian John Bratton thought that "the war has assumed a feature more horrible and awful than any ever reached." He anticipated "the pillage and robbing of our people and utter destruction of property by these raiders, but our blood is being chilled and flesh made to creep with horror at the recitals of outrage upon our women." Bratton confided that such atrocities had "not stirred blood-thirsty feelings in me" because he was certain that God would be "an avenger." Richard Waldrop was angered by the sight of killed cattle and sheep left in passing fields. The Yankees slaughtered the animals "not because they wanted them, but only to gratify their devilish malignity." Waldrop took comfort in the conviction that "justice will not always slumber & when it does awake & visit upon them the rewards of their evil deeds," he prayed, "may I be alive to see them." Other Rebels volunteered to do God's work for him. When a Virginian heard of enemy atrocities "that would make a devil blush to commit," he vowed, "Vengeance is mine, saith the Lord." As the army recuperated from a previous campaign, he was eager for an opportunity to punish Yankees "for the horrid barbarities." Sam Lockhart told his mother "of the most desperate outrages I ever heard of" committed by Ulysses S. Grant's men. In response, Lockhart wanted to raise the black flag. "Such men ought to be killed they ought not to be treated as Prisoners of war at all. They ought to be hung as soon as caught." After hearing atrocity stories, untold numbers of Rebels agreed.[52]

As these quotations suggest, because Confederates abstracted Federal soldiers as a universal, stereotypical foe, the crimes of individual Unionists reflected not the faults of those persons but the barbarity and cowardice of the undifferentiated enemy. Consequently, Rebels were not overly concerned with bringing to justice the actual perpetrators of an atrocity—any Yankee would do. This mentality made any foe a legitimate target of vengeance, including Unionist citizens of the South, northern civilians, and prisoners of war. When Federal armies increasingly harassed southern civilians, Rebel troops yearned to visit northerners, who had escaped the atrocities of war for years. After seeing an abandoned neighborhood in Petersburg, Walters admitted that "the unchristian hope will rise that, should our armies succeed in capturing any of the Northern cities, a full retribution may be meted out to them, for only by that means can they be taught the horrors through which this glorious old Commonwealth is struggling to her freedom." General Jubal Early fulfilled Walters's wish when his army plundered and burned Chambersburg, Pennsylvania, in August 1864. The news pleased Walters: "I am glad that at last our generals are laying aside a Little of their Christian forbearance, and by inaugurating a stern system of retaliation, are fighting the enemy with weapons with which they have fought us for the last three years. Possibly the blazing roofs of Chambersburg may induce the people of the North to look at this war in an entirely different light from that wherein they have been accustomed to view it. Well done, General Jubal A. Early! Oh! for the power to whisper in your ear that Pittsburgh is also in Pennsylvania." Georgian Edgeworth Bird also applauded the destruction of a town devoid of military value. He considered Chambersburg's fate a just retribution: "Pennsylvania has burning homesteads and desolate wives. The beautiful town of Chambersburg is a black, charred mass. There is retribution at last."[53]

The emancipation and Federal enlistment of thousands of former slaves further enraged Confederates and confirmed their perceptions of Yankees. Total warfare proved white southerners' suspicions that northerners were barbaric oppressors. Emancipation and black Union soldiers verified Confederate fears that Yankees were racial fanatics. Many Rebels believed that blacks were victims not beneficiaries of the Federals' actions. Clinging to the notion of slaves as property, some Confederates stressed that Union armies stole rather than freed blacks. Other Rebels thought that deceitful Yankees freed slaves to provide labor and cannon fodder for the northern war effort. A Georgia soldier told his wife, "A negro who knows what is for his good will never let the Yanks get him." Another Confederate believed that emancipation spelled doom for the blacks and consoled a friend whose slaves had left, claiming, "They will no doubt regret the day they left their comfortable homes, and kind Master and Mrs— but poor deluded things, they know not [what] suffering is before them." White southerners mocked the morality of emancipation rather than facing the facts. Believing that blacks had been deceived by Union soldiers was more agreeable than accepting that slaves were justified and smart to flee their masters. Expecting a terrible future for runaways was more palatable than anticipating racial equality or superiority for blacks. To denigrate the enemy and ease their own fears, Confederates highlighted evidence of the Yankees' disregard for blacks. A Confederate lieutenant wrote home that the enemy abandoned blacks during a hasty retreat. During the pursuit, his men found black children "lying in the woods nearly dead." As a punishment, the lieutenant "made the Yankee prisoners carry the little darkies that were broken down. It was an amusing sight to see the little darkies with a leg on either side of a Yankee's neck marching to Petersburg."[54]

As the lieutenant's punishment implies, Rebels ridiculed Federals' involvement with blacks. One Confederate denigrated the enemy with remarks such as, "The Yankees marched a line of battle, composed of white negroes and black negroes." In his eyes, white northerners had descended to blacks' racial status because of their association in a biracial army. A South Carolina soldier laughed at a dream he had in which Henry Ward Beecher and other abolitionists were "married to the blackest, dirtiest, stinkiest . . . negro wench[es] that can be found." A Virginia officer wished that "all the Yanks and all the negroes were in Africa." Some Rebels even hurled racist insults at enemy pickets. At Vicksburg, a defender asked the Union soldiers, "Have you Yanks all got nigger wives yet?" At Atlanta, a Confederate asked, "What niggers command your brigade?" and "Have the niggers improved the Yankee breed any?" Mocking the enemy's racial policies was another way of belittling the North and its war aims.[55]

Rebels' pity and ridicule ended, however, when African Americans entered the fray. Facing black opponents implied a parity between former slaves and Confederate soldiers that many Rebels could not stomach. When Nugent learned that "Lincoln demands that we treat negro soldiers upon an equality with our *whites*," he predicted that "the war will not be conducted in a civilized way hereafter." Black Federal troops meant race war. Armed blacks roaming the countryside, murdering and raping whites—the nightmare that had terrified white southerners for centuries—seemed to be coming true. Confederates tried to halt the impending terror by convincing blacks that white southerners would stop at nothing to maintain superiority. A soldier manning Lee's trenches confessed that the men in his unit abruptly ended a cease-fire when they realized that black Union troops had replaced white ones. Other Rebels showed no remorse over the murdering of black prisoners at Fort Pillow. A South Carolinian soldier was "glad that Forrest had it in his power to execute such swift & summary vengeance upon the negroes, & I trust it will have a good influence in deterring others from similar acts." By killing black prisoners, Rebels revealed not only racist rage but also a chilling psychological distance from their victims. A Confederate song that celebrated Fort Pillow expressed the dehumanizing effects of war:

> The dabbled clots of brain and gore
>> Across the swirling sabers ran;
> To me each brutal visage bore,
>> The front of one accursed man.[56]

In August 1864, Higginbotham witnessed the horrendous product of these influences at the Crater: "Between 5 & 600 Negroes & white scoundrels now lie buried in the trenches, and in front of them several hundred more are lying there blackening Corpses in solemn warning to the survivors." Viewing the same corpses, Walters morbidly quipped, "But for their hair and differences of features, the whites could not be distinguished from their colored brothers."[57]

For Walters and others, the enemy was a mass of inferior beings who deserved terrible deaths for introducing a race war.

The trench warfare of 1864–65 placed thousands of adversaries within rifle-shot and earshot for months on end. Though this physical proximity seemed to magnify the conditions of skirmish lines (where enemies sometimes fraternized), the closeness of opposing trenches intensified animosities. The constant sniping that Rebels reported confirms the antagonisms of life in the trenches. Samuel Vann vividly expressed the impact of sharpshooting "in the ditches" outside Atlanta:

> Fighting has been going on very rapidly ever since I came in[to the trenches], and I have been here about four hours. While I was sitting on a log conversing with my friend Jim Anderson about five minutes ago a ball was shot into the log about four inches from me, and they are constantly falling among us. . . . I hear a ball pass by me every syllable I make, and since I have been writing there has been two men shot through the body right here in camp. Poor fellows, I think they will die. I am sitting behind a tree to prevent being shot until I get this letter wrote, and the balls are constantly striking the tree that I am behind. . . . I may be writing to you for the last time. . . . [O]ne poor fellow is out there on the ground crying to God for help.

Outside Petersburg, Bird's unit lost men every day: "Sharp shooting on both sides is murderously active and accurate. Yesterday, a Capt. Jones, 17th Georgia, and a private of 2nd Georgia were passing each other in the narrow covered way of the main trenches. Each raised his head a little too high, and a ball passed though the brain of each." Endless sniping in the trenches took on the aura of a shooting gallery in which each desensitized shooter was the other side's dehumanized target. Knowing that the Rebels lacked adequate rations, Grant's marksmen implemented a tactic that epitomized this blunt atmosphere: "The Yankee sharp shooters kill the town milch cows that are grazing as far as 700 yards in rear of our trenches—1100 yards from them. And then they have killed our boys who venture back to them to cutt off the beef." Such behavior gave Confederates a new term for the foe: "assassins."[58]

Sniping combined with monotony and squalor to make life on the front almost unbearable. "Oh! for a long march through the valley or somewhere else where the same objects will not be the alpha and the omega of each day's existence," wrote one defender. Another Rebel wrote that "we all live under ground," and a third admitted that "times is a little squaly down hear" in the ditches outside of Richmond. Being "in the muddiest most disagreeable place you can imagine" increased hatred for the enemy who pinned them there. Philosopher and World War II veteran J. Glenn Gray conveys why a war-weary soldier often hates his foes with greater intensity:

Are they not responsible for the hard, uncomfortable life he is forced to lead? Were it not for them he would be at home with his wife or girl friend, enjoying his favorite food or sport or other amusement. His mood may become one of deep resentment or smoldering anger against the cause of his present misery. He wants to make them pay for this long-continued disruption of his life, "they" being not the enemy in general so much as that group opposite his position at the front. The more cramped, painful, and unbearable his physical and psychological environment becomes, the more he is likely to be filled with a burning vengeance, which demands action for its alleviation.

Constantly dreading an assault, witnessing the snipers' toll, dodging mortars, and suffering in cramped, filthy quarters embittered men on both sides of the line. Moreover, Rebels who persisted in the trenches understood that the enemy could quit and go home without endangering his country and loved ones. Because Confederates lacked such assurances, these disparate circumstances soured Rebels and fed a fierce determination to save Richmond and Atlanta, to outwill the Yankees.[59]

Trench warfare suggests that military life enhanced the mask of Cain in ways that civilian experiences did not. "The binary deadlock, the gross physical polarization of the trench predicament," reinforced dichotomous perceptions of the enemy. Paul Fussell observes this development in the trenches of World War I: "'We' are all here on this side; 'the enemy' is over there. 'We' are individuals with names and personal identities; 'he' is a mere collective entity. We are visible; he is invisible. We are normal; he is grotesque." Physical nearness to the entrenched enemy did not unmask him; earthworks hid his movements and cloaked his intentions. In other words, protracted contact with the foe increased fear of the unknown (What are they doing over there?) and produced the tensions associated with extended contact and high troop concentrations.[60]

Rebels' impressions of individual Union soldiers also exhibit how close proximity to adversaries could increase the psychological distance between friend and foe. The obvious fact that most of the Federals that Rebels observed closely were captured, wounded, or dead hints at how circumstances (and the conditions of the enemy in them) affected soldiers' perceptions of the other side. Besides an occasional expression of pity for such opponents, these encounters reinforced Confederates' low opinions of the other side and confirmed stereotypes. Under the veil of postwar reconciliation, veterans recalled a brothers' war in which enemies fraternized and helped each other. This unusual behavior existed, but most interaction across the lines was anything but cordial. As McPherson puts it, "If soldiers' letters and diaries are an accurate indication, bitterness and hatred were more prevalent than kindness and sociability." The wartime writings stress broken cease-fires, insults, trickery, and retaliation. For example, a Mississippi private admitted that his comrades called Yankees over to trade goods and captured the unsuspecting men.[61]

For many Rebels, enemy corpses represented the folly of Federal invasions. In June 1864, Robert Stiles found himself near Malvern Hill, "the old hill of fire & terror," and Frazier's Farm, "which gave me my first real view of a field after the battle fought & the victory won." Investigating the old ground, Stiles discovered "piles of human bones—sculls bare & ghastly crunching under the horses feet & wagon wheels, & many other memorials of the former invasion & defeat." Surveying the scene, the Virginian remarked, "Grant has ever to the last followed the track of McClellan, only he does not do quite so well." Dead Yankees marked the site of Confederate triumphs because the adversaries left too hastily to care for their own. Over time, Rebels described enemy corpses with indifference. After artillery had repulsed the foe, William Casey "had the pleasure of seeing some of their dead lying in the ditch." A Tennessean surveyed the enemy dead after an unsuccessful charge during the Atlanta campaign, counting forty-seven bullet holes in one of the Yankees and joking, "He was too dead to Skin." Such language bares the hardening of war. Samuel Foster noted, "We cook and eat, talk and laugh with the enemy dead lying all about us as though they were so many logs." The common sight of dead Yankees also dehumanized survivors who wore the same uniform.[62]

Confederates who looted the dead often confirmed their opinions of Yankee depravity. Surgeon Urban Owen searched dead Unionists who died in his care. While rifling through the knapsack of a dead Iowan, Owen found "a certificate belonging to a lady in Georgia, certifying that her husband had died in the Southern army & that there was money due to him for his services in the army." Owen surmised that the barbarian "had robbed some widow's house" and stolen the certificate as a souvenir. The doctor also enjoyed reading the dead men's letters. Many Confederates stressed the immorality and lewdness of enemy correspondence. Fay concluded, "One would certainly form a very exalted opinion of the Yankee nation to judge from the letters captured both from their soldiers, home & from their wives to the army." Fay claimed, "I have never yet seen a decent Yankee letter and I have read many since I have been in the Army."[63]

Prisoners offered Confederates a unique opportunity to interrogate the enemy, and Rebels had no difficulty categorizing real Yankees within narrow stereotypes. The despondency and fear that affected prisoners' demeanor seemed to confirm Yankee inferiority and barbarity. Captives appeared weak, divided, shifty, critical of Federal leadership, and ethnically diverse. In March 1865, Richard Maury declared a group of 476 captives from Sherman's army "the most villainous looking set of scoundrels that I ever saw anywhere." "And these fellows we are assured are a fair specimen of Sherman's forces," he quipped. What word better than *specimen* expresses that Rebels observed captives as representative samples of the enemy? Maury was shocked and pleased to find so many of them "wretchedly clothed," without shoes or hats. He failed to realize that poorly clad Confederates had probably stolen the prisoners' articles. Maury even surmised that the blankets protecting their feet had been snatched from Carolinians. Mississippian Edmund Eggleston noted that "three or four hundred Yankee prisoners with hang dog countenances and ragged dirty clothes passed our camp." The captives looked drained of will, defeated. Likewise, Alabamian Sam Pickens watched "a lot of Yankee prisoners" being transported to Savannah, Georgia. "They were by far the most filthy, miserable, wretched set of human beings I've ever seen," Pickens remarked. When North Carolinian Richard Webb interrogated some captives in November 1864, they confirmed his suspicion that the enemy was deeply divided over the course of the war and the presidential election. They said "they were put into the fight, because they were for McClelland." Webb apparently failed to consider that the northern men would tell him what he wished to hear. Captives told South Carolinian David Crawford that Grant had deceived them with "orders that Richmond had fallen." The news supported Crawford's opinion that "their army is pretty demoralized" and "fighting themselves." Prisoners told Lieutenant Leonidas Polk that Grant's ranks were terribly sick. Polk wrote home, the "prisoners say, whom we capture daily, that they are almost perished, & that his army is very much demoralized. They all look the worst I ever saw & say the rank & file of their army have despaired of taking Richmond." Other captives begged for food and water and swore that they fought to feed their families. When a Georgia captain heard this, he concluded that "men who fight for money are easy whiped [and] we who fight for our wives and children our homes and Property cannot be whiped." He saw no correlation between the enemies' professed motives and his own. Instead, Yankee words were music to Rebel ears, validating Confederate perceptions that the war was going well for the cause.[64]

The spectacle of hundreds of Union soldiers being marched to prison, like the sight of scores of Union dead, also gave Confederates the impression that the war was going better than it was. In August 1864, Albright counted thousands of prisoners, including "a great many foreigners," who were being sent to Richmond. An Alabama infantryman guarding Petersburg told his wife that large numbers of Yankee prisoners "are coming in almost daily" and "four or five hundred were sent off last week." Such sights especially affected men like William Heartsill, who guarded prisons far from the frontlines. Stationed in Tyler, Texas, Heartsill and his unit maintained a stockade that swelled to more than three times its original size in April and May 1864. On April 15, 1864, eleven hundred Yankees arrived from their defeat and capture at the Battle of Mansfield. In autumn 1864, North Carolinian James B. Jones guarded thousands of prisoners in Virginia, remarking in his diary that hundreds of new Yankees were "arriving and leaving all the time." From afar, this congested traffic of enemy captives seemed to confirm reports of recent victories. Neither Heartsill nor Jones expressed the idea that the volume of prisoners could also indicate the Federals' enormous manpower.[65]

Deserters also reinforced Rebel images of the foe. By stressing Confederate desertion as a cause of defeat, historians have (unintentionally) shifted our gaze away from thousands of dissatisfied Federals who deserted the winning side. In many respects, Sherman's and Grant's troops suffered hardships in the final campaigns that rivaled the plight of their opponents: Grant's ranks sustained unprecedented casualties, and Sherman's footsore columns trekked hundreds of miles. Troops who abandoned the Federal cause presented a disaffected demeanor and often shared Confederates' opinions of Federal commanders, emancipation, and the war's progress. In May 1864, Creed Thomas Davis reported, "Now and then some of them may be seen coming into our lines—deserting. A squad of 20 has just come in. The Yankee army is said to be very much demoralized." After the Wilderness and Spotsylvania Court House, Union deserters who met Pierson's unit "report their loss as being the heaviest of any battle of the war—between 50 & 75 thousand in all & over ten Gens. in all." In June 1864, deserters from Sherman's ranks informed John Cotton and his comrades that the Federal army was critically short of rations, so much so that mules and horses were starving to death. After Kennesaw Mountain, Captain George Knox Miller claimed that deserters from Sherman's army "come to us every night." In October 1864, eight deserters surrendered to North Carolinian Abe Jones while he was on picket duty in Virginia. They favored McClellan in the upcoming election and promised that Little Mac "will get a Majority in Yankee Army." Though Unionists probably talked this way to ingratiate themselves with their captors, Rebels deemed Yankee deserters accurate representatives of the enemy. The northerners were jaded, cowardly, unprincipled, and conquered. Some Yankees claimed that thousands of Federals would desert if given the opportunity. Others did more than reinforce Rebel stereotypes; they informed Confederates of Federal plans and aided in the capture of unsuspecting comrades.[66]

Contact with Union prisoners and deserters perpetuated the Rebel myth of Federal cowardice. Bell Wiley observes, "The overwhelming majority of Confederates remained firm to the end in the conviction that the majority of Yankees were lacking in the stuff that it takes to make good soldiers." Rebels often discounted Federal valor by claiming that Yankee prisoners were drunk. George Binford thought that Sherman's officers "make their men drunk to assault our lines[, and] prisoners attest the fact for a great many have been taken intoxicated." In the battle, "their men were drunk and charged up within ten or twenty steps of our lines. One, a Col, came over in our ditches, too drunk to know what he was doing." A cavalry captain in the Army of Tennessee was convinced that the enemy "never make an attack until drugged with whisky." Walters agreed that Union bravery "must not be taken as an evidence of superior courage, as the men were more than half drunk." No evidence substantiates these bizarre and persistent charges of northern drunkenness. Perhaps Federals falsely admitted to drunkenness to appease their captors; perhaps the effects of adrenaline, fear, and fatigue made them appear intoxicated. Whatever caused the phenomenon, its effect was clear: viewing the enemy as drunken cowards helped to sustain a belief in Rebel superiority through the final period of the conflict.[67]

෮ඟ෨ ෮ඟ෨ ෮ඟ෨

Though circumstances of war explained why the enemy destroyed plantations or appeared powerless as captives, Rebels preferred to consider such actions and impressions evidence of the other side's inherent cruelty or weakness. Confederates treated captured, deserting, wounded, and dead Yankees as specimens that confirmed their stereotypes. Nevertheless, even if soldiers had not manipulated such encounters to prove their prejudices, total war, black troops, and trench warfare would have deepened Rebel animosities and solidified caricatures of the other side. It is difficult to discern when northerners most resembled the grim legions of the Confederate imagination: when their shadowy figures encircled Richmond with bristling trenches, when their columns charred the countryside and darkened southern doorways, or when their skin was black.

Still, the blatant partisanship of many Rebels' views of the North seems extravagant—these perspectives ignored mountains of evidence that confirmed Federal determination, courage, competence, and idealism. Perhaps civilians, whether distant from the real foe or victims of enemy destruction, can be pardoned for maintaining simplistic, passionate images of Yankees, but how is it possible to excuse soldiers who still branded northerners as cowards after witnessing thousands of adversaries die bravely? In the end, regardless of all the factors that shaped these abstractions, two forces necessitated soldiers' biased perceptions of opponents: the need for psychological distance from their victims and the nation-building process. The mask of Cain serves an important role that may be universal in warfare: soldiers and nations need to denigrate the enemy to justify death and destruction.

Scholars accept the prevalence of enemy stereotypes, but few historians consider the long-term implications of these images. The same elements that contributed to troops' perceptions of the enemy also influenced how soldiers envisioned the war's possible outcomes, and some Rebels paid a heavy price for so severely underrating their foes. Most Confederates used abstractions of the enemy as lenses through which they estimated Federal resolve and predicted scenarios of victory and defeat. Because these abstractions presented simple, partisan views of the other side, it is no surprise that they failed to represent the war's concluding period accurately. Underestimations of the enemy and rumors of northern internal division fostered Confederate dreams of a looming Federal collapse. Drawing from the stereotype of the weak Yankee, many Rebels expected masses of thin-blooded, greedy northerners to quake at rising casualty lists or falling stock prices and demand peace. This vision of implosion was remarkable for its popularity and consistency throughout the South.[68]

Other Rebels believed that political division or financial ruin would convince the West to secede from the East.[69] Forecasts for a northern collapse appealed to Confederates for various reasons. Like many Confederates' faith that God would deliver them victory, hopes for Federal self-destruction illuminated a path to victory that did not require military triumph. Both possibilities shifted the responsibility for victory away from the Confederacy. Ironically, many of the troubles Rebels foresaw in the North, including financial trouble, political infighting, and division between east and west, described the Confederacy's internal problems. By the final phase of the war, Rebel currency was worthless, governors openly defied the president, and Union control of the Mississippi effectively split the southern nation into eastern and western halves. Perhaps Rebels wished their headaches on the enemy. As Fay remarked, "I want to see the Yankee nation without a Govt. enjoying what they are so fond of, a state of Anarchy and confusion." Perhaps ascribing internal problems to the enemy on a magnified scale minimized the seriousness of predicaments within the rebellion.[70]

Just as images of a weak foe helped to produce dreams of northern collapse, portrayals of a barbaric adversary promoted nightmares of brutal subjugation. Many Confederates considered total war campaigns and the proliferation of black troops evil portents of the South's future should the rebellion fail. Though Federals increased the destructiveness of their 1864–65 campaigns to convince Rebels to surrender, total war had the opposite effect, instead persuading many Confederates that capitulation was worse than death. Some soldiers received letters from parents and spouses who suffered occupation and devastation. Fred Fleet's mother wrote to him that "death is far preferable to subjugation to the vile Yankees—I know something about it now." As the war intensified, even religious propaganda told soldiers to grasp independence or expect colonization, miscegenation, or even extermination at the hands of the brutal North. In the end, visions of northern collapse and southern subjugation induced many Confederates to prolong the war to obtain the former and avoid the latter.[71]

Like Confederate religion, soldiers' perceptions of the foe clarified the struggle and provided meaning for their hardships. The extent to which Confederates relied on images of the Yankees as inept or barbaric shows the importance of these figures to the Rebels' worldview. But all abstractions, no matter how valuable, distort reality—a conundrum endemic to warfare. If Rebels saw their victims and assailants as complete human beings, they risked undermining their ability to perform as soldiers. But viewing the foe in an abstract framework—simplifying the other side (or half) of the war—precluded Confederates from seeing the conflict with greater comprehension. While Rebels twisted theodicy and evangelicalism to convince themselves that God would deliver them victory,

Confederates also warped the enemy into caricatures that appeared too weak or too evil to win a war that God oversaw. Either way, the result was a powerful determination to continue fighting an enemy that had become so alien to most Rebels that they could not bear the thought of reunion. This problem would severely affect surrendering and the postwar South.]

I doubt if any soldiers in the world ever needed
so much cumulative evidence to convince them
that they were beaten.
—Union General John M. Schofield, *Forty-six
Years in the Army*

Without a Murmur

Confederate Endurance and the Immediate War

According to Prussian theorist Carl von Clausewitz, armies with "true military spirit" exhibit a number of traits: cohesion in combat, unshakable faith in the cause, pride, obedience, trust in commanders after defeat, and physical strength. All of these characteristics emanate from "the single powerful idea of the honor of its arms." This spirit, which separates some armies from others, can only be reinforced by two sources: frequent exertions to the limits of human endurance and memories of victory. Clausewitz argues that "nothing else will show a soldier the full extent of his capacities." Like strong trees, armies endowed with this spirit "survive the wildest storms of misfortune and defeat." The Confederacy withstood the "wildest storms" of 1863 and 1864 in part because its two veteran armies, the Army of Northern Virginia and the Army of Tennessee, imbued this military spirit with a conviction that they were unconquerable. The summer of 1863 brought twin disasters, Gettysburg and Vicksburg, to these armies' theaters, yet they persevered and remained hopeful. The 1864 campaigns tested their endurance and faith even more. While an enemy force twice its size pushed and pummeled the first army to the gates of Richmond, its veterans maintained an aura of invincibility around themselves and their general, Robert E. Lee. Likewise, while an enemy host twice its size maneuvered the second army to the outskirts of Atlanta, its troops believed in themselves and their general, Joseph E. Johnston. During these contests, the sources of military spirit continued to replenish Rebel armies: men suffered unprecedented hardships that steeled their resolve, and veterans not only remembered past triumphs but interpreted present engagements in a positive light.[1]

In hindsight, their behavior seems delusional. How did "true military spirit" withstand adversity, deprivation, and attrition? How did the ethos of invincibility survive the turning points of 1863 and 1864, all of which went against the rebellion? Abstractions, such as the belief in providential aid or the barbaric foe, persisted through the toil and turmoil of 1863–65 because hardships from the concrete world strengthened those convictions. How Rebels interpreted their immediate war and persevered through it requires another explanation. Daily suffering, constant setbacks, and unprecedented carnage must have affected these men, so how did they remain hopeful? Clausewitz's formula for a veteran army offers part of the answer. Endurance and past glories inspired thousands of Confederates to continue the war. Historians who stress comradeship and ideology further illuminate Rebel motivation. As a World War II veteran expressed it, "It took me darn near a whole war to figure what I was fighting for. It was the other guys. Your outfit, the guys in your company, but especially your platoon. . . . When there might be 15 left out of 30 or more, you got an awful strong feeling about those 15 guys." Casualties strengthened the bonds among Rebel survivors. A third, murkier factor affecting morale involved how Rebels perceived their surroundings. Throughout the war's final campaigns, many Confederates grossly misjudged the odds they faced and the battles they fought. This chapter recaptures and explains Rebels' clouded but strangely confident view of their immediate war.[2]

For many reasons, scholars have explained the conduct of Confederate soldiers who deserted late in the war better than the behavior of those who fought to the end. Our understanding of the dire conditions that surrounded Rebels— the widespread destruction, overwhelming odds, and harsh living—combines with our knowledge of the war's outcome to render desertion a more rational act. Accounts by Confederates who remained in the ranks illuminate how different the war looked from a combatant's vantage point. Though these Rebels saw bad portents, they also found good omens that colored their immediate war. Poor supplies, anxiety for home, fatigue, attrition, destruction, and war weariness convinced some men to desert but emboldened others to further resistance. In other words, diehards were not oblivious to their surroundings; they understood their conditions and circumstances as well as those who quit. Yet the trials that broke the will of some soldiers strengthened the spirit of others. Fortitude emanated from a number of sources. Being young men, most Confederates sought to convince themselves and others of their masculinity, and enduring severe hardships without complaining or quitting signified manhood. Comradeship enforced these gender norms. Camaraderie provided friendship but also pressured veterans to withstand unending squalor before the eyes of peers, who mattered most.[3]

Diehard Confederates suffered through the same hunger and squalor that disheartened others. The ever-hopeful did not enjoy a privileged position. Deficient supplies told even the most stalwart fighters that the Confederacy was in trouble. Ironically, a land so abundant with agriculture and devoid of industry primarily lacked food and forage, not ammunition and guns. All soldiers felt this penury when the army reduced rations in 1864. From 1861 to 1863, soldiers received three-quarters of a pound of pork or bacon or one and a half pounds of fresh or salt beef per day. New regulations cut their standard to half a pound of pork or bacon for campaigning troops and a third of a pound for stationary units. Men of every rank grumbled. Private Creed Thomas Davis said every soldier knew that such rations were "barely sufficient to sustain life." Captain Charles Blackford concurred, "I merely eat to live, and live on as little as possible." He described his fare as "corn-bread and poor beef,—blue and tough,—no vegetables, no coffee, sugar tea or even molasses." Georgian Edgeworth Bird was sick of "beef so lean that it does not cast a shadow." "That's my diet now," he complained, "a streak of lean and a streak of fat." South Carolinian Thomas John Moore groused that the cornmeal was "black and dirty and even seemed as if the cob had been ground up with the corn." Louisiana Private Lafayette Orr was "nearly starved out on corn bread" and considered conditions "myty gloomy at the present time." Still, Orr "never disspared yet and never doubted our sucksees." Similar statements abound. Grumbling was the soldiers' time-honored right, and many Rebels observed it, but such protests did not always signify despair. Despite their complaining, Davis, Blackford, Bird, Orr, and thousands just like them remained hopeful and stuck it out to the end of the war.[4]

By enduring hunger together, Confederates deepened the "true military spirit" of their veteran armies. The hardships that induced some to desert united other sufferers and raised their pride. Diehards supplemented their diet and sustained their spirits by foraging together and sharing food from home. Foraging, or getting food without paying for it, included everything from hunting and fishing to outright theft. South Carolinian R. E. Elliott griped that the government gave him "one quart of parched corn . . . to march on all day!" But he insisted, "I am not unhappy nor am I discouraged" because "we have enough to eat of course along the roads." By foraging and sharing their loot, the members of Elliott's group proudly sustained themselves with delicacies that "have found their way to our fire." For such men, the message was clear: incompetent government officials could disappoint them, but the veterans would not fail each other. As Davis boasted, "We are independent of the Government for rations." While defending Petersburg during the winter of 1864–65, Davis worked for local civilians in exchange for food. When he received no rations at all, the private "shucked some corn for a farmer in the neighborhood, for which he promises to pay flour." Later that month, Davis cut two cords of wood for a woman in return for a bushel of potatoes and a bushel of turnips. In South Carolina, Percy

Nagel's comrades picked plums and fished to supplement their rations. Food was scarce, but diehards like an Alabama cavalryman swore that they "can live and fight on what we get."[5]

In the final years of the war, comradeship served as both a positive force that inspired selfless behavior and peer pressure that favored superhuman endurance. In the presence of friends, Confederates pushed themselves to extremes to prove their manliness. Frank Adams exemplified this impulse in early 1865 when he claimed, "I can stay in the army as long as any body." Blackford witnessed the effects of this mentality on Hood's Brigade in January 1864. Campaigning barefoot on frozen ground, the men left bloody footprints on the snow and ice. "Shoes are very scarce," Blackford explained, and "the men get pieces of raw hide from the butchers, and, after wrapping their feet up in old rags, sew the hide around them, making a clumsy ball, which they wear . . . until it wears out." Despite their pitiful condition, "there was not a murmur" from the men. Lieutenant Green Berry Samuels observed a similar scene in November 1863 when thousands of Lee's troops slept under the stars on a wintry night "without a murmur." Samuels concluded, "These noble men take pride in their sufferings, their hardships and their dangers." The warrior's code glorified troops who silently weathered combat and wretchedness. Facing the interminable war, Adams concluded, "There is no use crying it cant bee helped." Quiet endurance—or, as the soldiers put it, suffering "without a murmur"—affirmed Confederate soldiers' masculinity and veteran status. The phrase became a mantra for Confederate troops. Army surgeon James Brannock marveled, "The world [has] never produced such soldiers." "Boys, delicately raised & cared for tenderly at home, are marching day & night, though cold & wet, over mountains & rocks, *hungry, fatigued & barefooted* & that too . . . without a single murmur." Sergeant Reuben Pierson swore, "I have never known a heartier or hardier set of men in my experience than the members of Co. 'C'," because "they live on $\frac{1}{4}$ lb. of bacon and one pound of flour and never murmer." Charles Andry wrote to his mother from the defenses of Mobile, "Tell father . . . he may flatter himself of having a son who though raised in the lap of luxury, has passed through the most infernal ordeal of privations . . . & of misery without a murmur." Andry's perseverance even confirmed his ability to take his father's position as the family patriarch: "I shall make it a true pleasure to assist him, in his old age, in any capacity which my limited qualifications will allow me." Soldiering was a maturing process for thousands of southern men, and doing one's part in battle and on the march without complaining was considered a sign of manhood. Class also shaped their peer pressure. Elite young men like Andry persisted to confirm that a luxurious life had not spoiled them, while common southerners endured to show that they were as good as any other man.[6]

One of the severest trials for Confederate soldiers, particularly in the war's final period, was the uncertainty of conditions at home. Many men withstood personal privations better than they abided thoughts of their suffering families. Wild rumors and sensational newspaper reports supported paranoid visions of devastation and starvation. Moreover, conflicting intelligence could mock troops' limited breadth of information and leave them wondering whether the enemy had destroyed or bypassed their homes. After hearing that the enemy had plundered his county, Fred Fleet wrote home, "I hope the reports are exaggerated, but I am almost afraid to hear the true account." Edwin Leet admitted to his wife, "I have been very uneasy since the Yankeys were at Woodville, I heard that they had been through your neighborhood and destroyed everything." Paul Higginbotham told his brother that he had not heard from home for nearly a month, "so you may know how anxious I am to hear from the folks. After hearing the raiders had gotten into Amherst, I was almost crazy to learn what damage was done, and as is always the case, we heard a thousand different reports. Todays paper says that they treated Ladies near McIvers Depot too bad to write here." Seasoned Confederates learned that anxiety and misinformation could combine to shake the firmest morale.[7]

Historians have long noted that such circumstances encouraged men to desert for their family's sake. Throughout the war, good soldiers reached personal limits of endurance and left the army. In February 1864, North Carolinian J. S. Gooch was discouraged by poor rations and the war's length. "Iff any man was worn out with any thing I am with this war," he complained. Gooch watched comrades desert to Union lines every night and did not blame them. Even stalwart Confederates despaired when steady veterans fled the ranks. Lieutenant Thomas Boatwright admitted that the desertions "really [make] me feel despondent relative to our final Independence." Alabama infantryman Elias Davis noted that twenty-five men from another Alabama regiment had deserted the trenches of Petersburg and commented that "some of them had been good soldiers" and were trying to go home.[8]

The deserter's rationale is easy to understand; how others resisted the temptation to leave or lacked it altogether is more difficult to comprehend. While a host of factors, including military authority, ideology, comradeship, and the culture of invincibility, kept men in the ranks, particular elements helped them to cope with threats to loved ones. As Christians, many Rebels endured such anxieties by praying for divine protection for their families. As partisans, Confederates used the Federal menace of the home front to confirm their low opinion of the foe and inspire renewed resistance. As veteran troops, many men considered civilian hardships an unfortunate but unavoidable element of warfare. Instead of deserting to rescue parents, spouses, and children, many soldiers told loved ones how to face northern destroyers. Blackford admitted to his wife, "To think that my whole family, wife, child, mother, sister, are probably this very morning subjected to the insults and indignities of a band of freebooters makes my blood boil." Blackford nevertheless sent his wife dispassionate instructions: "Should the yankees come you must stand your ground"; hide food and valuables in the slave's mattress, "as the yankees will, I suppose, respect her race"; or lend supplies "to the commissary department, returnable in kind." Higginbotham "was glad to learn the Yankees did not get to Fathers. . . . But they will no doubt try another [raid] before long." He told his brother what "to do at home in case the Yankees should come again. . . . Run off the horses, and every thing else that they would be likely to carry off." When Brannock noticed in the papers and "heard though various private sources" that Federal columns had sacked his hometown, he told his wife, "The thought haunts me day & night that my wife & children may be without a home to shelter them." Yet he comforted himself with the thought "that they have true & tried friends who will never permit them to want for food & shelter." Sergeant Marion Fitzpatrick encouraged his wife, "Enjoy yourself whenever you can and look ahead to brighter times." He expected that the Confederacy's fortunes would soon improve but admitted, "Of course it is a dark time with the women who are left almost unprotected at home." "But as true and patriotic Southern ladies," Fitzpatrick reasoned, "I hope you will bravely stem the storm and successfully land on the shore of Liberty." Such was the extent of the sergeant's advice and comfort. Men like Blackford, Higginbotham, Brannock, and Fitzgerald had plenty of reasons to flee to their loved ones. Instead, they faced the trials of war with pragmatic clarity and hardened sensibilities—fulfilling their duty seemed the surer route to ending the struggle, and they expected their families to agree.[9]

In 1864, Rebels had more to fear than conditions on the home front because Union leadership brought the same relentless pressure to the battlefield. The continuous campaigns of 1864 caused unparalleled suffering for troops on both sides. Gone were the years of confined engagements and short battles nestled within long periods of inactivity and recuperation. Now the great armies traveled within each other's shadow and clashed almost daily. As Earl Hess explains, the war's final phase packed "several battles with the intensity of Gettysburg and Chickamauga into a compressed time span, each one linked by only a few hours or days of maneuvering into positions while under the guns of an alert and desperate enemy." General Ulysses S. Grant expressed the grim tenacity of this struggle in a dispatch he sent to Washington after fires had cremated his wounded in the Wilderness: "I propose to fight it out on this line if it takes all summer." It took all summer, fall, and winter and part of the following spring.[10]

The men who served in these campaigns fought, marched, entrenched, and guarded by day and night for months. Fatigue and filth dogged their tracks. Nine miles from Richmond on May 28, 1864, Charles DeNoon told his parents, "I am tolerably well, considering the fatigue I have undergone for the last 24 days hard fighting and marching. Our Regt. fought the Yankees for 11 hours on the 25th. It was one continuous roar of musketry." A few days later, Creed Davis scribbled in his diary that he had slept for just three of the past forty-eight hours.

Writing to his wife from the battle line, Captain Samuel McKittrick explained, "We have been ever since the 7th of May marching around or lying in line of battle all the time. We have marched, I suppose about 150 miles by day and night. . . . My dear; it is a hard struggle for independence." Three weeks into the campaign, South Carolinian Theodore Honour used a moment of quiet to clean his one pair of socks and undershirt. "I tell you," he commented to his wife, "Virginia is the place to bring a fellow down to *dirt*." Six weeks into the campaign, Higginbotham was "nearly broken with fatigue and want of rest." The strain of being "exposed to Shelling and Pickett firing nearly all the time" was taking its toll. He and the men were "dirty as Hogs, and full of *Buggers*" because they had no chance to clean themselves. Though he carried a fresh shirt in his knapsack, the Virginian could not "afford to put it on yet" because the campaign seemed infinite. These conditions produced an irritability that coursed through Higginbotham's letters. He complained about the flies, the heat, rotten apples, bad water, "the sound of cannon and musketry," and the war in general. Such correspondence illustrates that suffering "without a murmur" was sometimes a metaphor for selfless endurance rather than reality. Most soldiers complained of the strain and pined for peace at some point, but they also upheld the ideal of sacrificial service and stayed in the ranks through their darkest hours.[11]

Men of every rank wore the effects of unremitting warfare on their faces and frames. Gaunt and ashen, many Rebels seemed to age years, and some men never regained their youthful health and countenances. Constant toil put Thomas Hampton in the hospital with diarrhea. He wrote to his wife, "You do not know how much exposure & hardships we have gone threw since [the campaign began six weeks ago] & not much prospect of things getting any better soon." From May to August, Hampton's weight dropped from 162 pounds to 137. When Hiram Williams went home on leave, friends did not recognize him until he spoke. Captain George Knox Miller of the Army of Tennessee admitted, "I thought I had seen much of war but the last two weeks experience has been the most trying of any." Miller could "barely speak above a whisper" from lack of sleep and exposure to the elements. He was "fighting all day & marching during the night. I did not know my powers of endurance before." On July 7, General Lawrence "Sull" Ross wrote to his wife, "I am nearly worn out, and was surprised upon looking in a glass at my care worn and haggard Expression. It seems to me I look ten years older than when you saw me last. I have rested only one day since my last letter to you [April 26], been fighting all the time." Generals A. P. Hill and Richard Ewell broke down from exhaustion. Hill suffered from mysterious, possibly psychosomatic, maladies. Ewell, who had lost a leg earlier in the war, never resumed command. Even Lee fell sick during the campaign. In Georgia, General John Bell Hood, with a crippled left arm and without a right leg, fought on though he had to be tied to the saddle. The youngest Confederate to command an army, Hood changed from one of the most striking and vigorous figures of the war to a haunting and sallow specter—a living metaphor for the crippled rebellion.[12]

While hunger and fatigue emaciated individuals, attrition decimated the ranks. Though Lee and Johnston tried to conserve manpower by maintaining strong defensive positions, even headlong, murderous charges by the Federals killed irreplaceable Rebels. From May to September, General Ross's brigade shrank from 1,000 to scarcely more than 200 men as the troops fought eighty-seven engagements in one hundred days. After Atlanta fell, the Ninth Texas Cavalry counted 110 active members out of the original 1,000 who had started the campaign. Its brigade contained only 686 of the roughly 4,000 horse soldiers who had originally composed the outfit. Whether or not Confederates admitted the fact, the Federals' persistent pounding was shrinking Rebel units beyond recognition.[13]

Veterans understood attrition, and some felt it stalked them. In February 1864, Williams returned to his unit after a sixteen-month absence. "What a change from the company in which I first volunteered two years ago," Williams lamented, noting that "three of my old mess are dead, [and] several are wounded or disabled for life." He cataloged the losses: "Aughe has lost a leg and has gone. Springsteed is gone. Bradley is wounded, a dozen or more are prisoners at the North, while many of them are dead. Their graves are scattered from Dog River all through Mississippi, at Columbus, Deer Creek, and Vicksburg, to this place." "Such is war," he concluded. On May 7, 1864, surgeon Spencer Welch walked past the dead and dying of the Wilderness: "As usual on such occasions groans and cries met me from every side. I found Colonel James Nance, my old school-mate, and Colonel Gaillard of Fairfield lying side by side in death. Near them lay Warren Peterson, with a shattered thigh-bone, and still others who were my friends." Honour watched his company shrink from fifty-two to eighteen men during the first weeks of May 1864. In June, Grant Taylor's brother-in-law and messmate, Ide, fell into Federal hands while on picket duty. "I feel very lonely to-day for they never make any better men than Ide. And a brother has he been to me and I feel that I have lost a true friend." Taylor's company numbered only thirteen.[14]

On June 3, 1864, Henry Berkeley's artillery unit lost fourteen men at Cold Harbor. The day started as most others did, with Berkeley and his close friend, Edmund Anderson, sharing breakfast. The sounds of combat separated them when each man ran to his cannon. When one of his messmates, Bob Winston, fell, Berkeley took his place. "While the death storm" claimed men and horses all around him, Berkeley marveled at Colonel William Nelson and Lieutenant George Hobson, who "walked up and down on the top of our breastworks and gave the orders calmly and deliberately." "Tears trickled down Hobson's cheeks as he saw one after another of his brave men go down before this terrible hail." A shell decapitated fifteen-year-old John Christian, who had joined the army just six weeks earlier.[15]

After the battle, Berkeley learned that Anderson was mortally wounded. Praying "that it might be better with him than I hear," Berkeley had guard duty and could not see his friend. At three in the morning, a lieutenant offered to take his place, and Berkeley raced for the field hospital. He did not get far before a comrade stopped him and said that Anderson was dead. Berkeley went to see the body and noted that his friend "looked perfectly natural." By morning, Berkeley discovered that all five of his messmates were casualties. The carnage was so severe that Nelson ordered Berkeley to write to his family and made the mail boy wait for the letter.[16]

Within days, a sharpshooter killed Hobson while he was arranging the burial of two comrades. His loss seemed too much for some men to bear. Robert Stiles wrote home, "My faith is nigh staggered Mother," because Hobson was "the bravest, cheeriest, most generous spirit in the world" and the "saddest of all the losses of this frightful war." "Ah! dearest Father, how dead, *dead, dead* my youth is!" he exclaimed. "Every battle takes some friend," while other comrades succumbed in Union prisons. Recalling the war's cost, Stiles admitted, "I loved George Hobson & them all,—more than I knew before, & every few moments the sight of the crushed & hopeless—perhaps raving or sinking widow rises to bring dimmness over the struggling eye of faith, that 'would see Jesus.'"[17]

The loss of able leaders and veteran troops changed the character of companies and regiments. Samuel Vann remained confident that although "there are not many of us dirty Rebels here[,] . . . what few of us are here are in fine spirits and can whip many a Yank yet." Nevertheless, Vann admitted that his company numbered only nineteen, "so small that it does not require many officers." Survivors often had to fill many roles. DeNoon found himself in charge of his company because the captain was sick, the lieutenant was wounded, and the sergeant was dead. Berkeley acted as gunner, sergeant, and lieutenant, while "Col. Nelson acted as chief of artillery, and our Capt. Kirkpatrick was commanding our battalion. This left us with only one commissioned officer, Bill Harris, recently acting as lieutenant." "This shows our heavy loss since leaving winter quarters," he commented. "We started out with four lieutenants; three of these have been killed and the [fourth] has not been seen or heard of for two months." Such casualties compelled Berkeley to write, "Our line of march is marked by the graves of the fallen." In the end, decimated ranks not only depressed the survivors but raised the possibility that units would be consolidated under new leadership and designations, a prospect that angered veterans, who took pride in their regiments' names and records.[18]

Veterans who lost comrades and saw their companies shrinking became increasingly critical of shirkers and exempts who could alleviate manpower deficiencies. Within Petersburg's trenches, Welch estimated that "we need ten or fifteen thousand more men here, and we could easily get them if the able-bodied exempts would come on here, but they seem to have become hardened to their disgrace." He wished such men had "seen our poor fellows Thursday night coming in wounded and bleeding and shivering with cold." Believing that the soldiers "who suffer and have often suffered in this war are the last ones to say surrender," Welch blamed the Confederacy's dire condition on stay-at-homes and predicted, "If the South is ever overcome, the contemptible shirkers will be responsible for it." On the same day, October 2, 1864, Johnny Jackman railed against the "rats" who exaggerated the severity of their wounds to avoid returning to the field. Jackman was recovering from a June head injury and gleefully watched from his hospital bed in Americus, Georgia, as medical examiners caused "great consternation among the 'rats'" and hospital attendants. The doctors sent "all who were able to pull a trigger to the front." The affair reminded Jackman "of traders examining [live]stock."[19]

In October 1864, troops across the Confederacy regained hope when Richmond issued General Order 77, a measure that sent thousands of exempts and detailed soldiers to the front lines. Though the order sapped manpower from the Confederate economy, transportation networks, and medical centers, veterans hailed the change as an improvement for the besieged nation. Welch described a roundup of able-bodied men in Richmond that sent "about twelve thousand men" to the front. "Many of them . . . were gentlemen of leisure." Policemen captured them "in all parts of the city and [sent] them under guard" to a collection point. "Officers were seized in the same way on the streets" and, despite their objections, assigned command of the new units. When authorities grabbed a medical officer, he "would plead that he was due at his command and that he was a noncombatant, but they would tell him he was the very man they needed to attend to the wounded." Summing up the story, Welch admitted, "It delights soldiers to hear of these things. It does them good all over [and] the miserable skulkers almost die of fright." His account exudes the perspective and pride of a veteran. Because soldiers considered their sacrifices emblems of the highest patriotism and the strongest masculinity, they often disregarded the value of male noncombatants. Many veterans were so focused on the military side of the war that they missed the glaring fact that men were also required to produce food and ammunition, transport supplies, treat the wounded, and support civilians.[20]

Soldiers who required these noncombatant laborers, such as quartermasters, straddled the manpower dilemma. As Thomas Elder watched the government press able-bodied men into the army, "giving the whites muskets and the blacks spades," he was happy that "Genl Lee seems determined to give Grant a lively time." But Elder also complained that "this order takes every man I have, without exception" from the quartermaster's department. Likewise, Bird doubted that the disabled workers he was promised in return for his drivers could perform adequately: "Teamsters should be able-bodied to attend well to the teams and do the heavy, rough work generally before them, but of course it is best to try it. In the present stress of the country, all these men are required, at least that is the verdict of those in command." Other veterans applauded the general order but wished that exceptions could be made for certain friends and family. Lieutenant John McLure knew that circumstances demanded harsh measures, but he feared that a friend with defective eyesight would be sent to the front lines. While campaigning in the Shenandoah Valley, Creed Davis learned that his father was now manning Richmond's trenches. Within weeks, the old man fell and sprained his ankle. Elder, Bird, McLure, and Davis were diehard Rebels who often expressed how much the Confederacy needed more men. When their demands were put into practice, however, the results lacked the simple justice and clear-cut success they had envisioned.[21]

Many other soldiers praised the order without discussing how local military needs might differ from national demands or how their manpower gain signified a loss for the Confederacy elsewhere. In November 1864, Lee's army obtained fifteen thousand men from conscripted noncombatants and recuperated veterans. Moreover, another twelve thousand men from the detached Second Corps came back to Richmond in December. Not only did bolstering the ranks of Lee's army drain labor from essential industries, but the return of the Second Corps signified failure in the Shenandoah and the abandonment of that vital farmland to Sheridan's forces. Veterans seldom mentioned these points, instead stressing that fresh troops negated the losses of 1864. Overestimating the reinforcements at "thirty to forty thousand troops," John Walters believed that these fresh arms would combine with the already "stubborn resistance" exhibited by Rebel defenders to deliver the enemy a crushing defeat. Walters even wished for a massive Federal advance "while we are in as good condition to receive it as we are," because "unless [Grant] can bring at least three men to our one, he will find that though he may say the 'Rebellion is on its last legs,' yet he has not the power sufficient to throw it off of them." Fleet told his parents, "Genl. Lee has been considerably reinforced lately, and you need not be surprised to hear of some move similar to that made in the summer of '62," when Lee had repulsed the Army of the Potomac from the gates of Richmond. Considering the army's growth, Fleet assumed, "We will be much stronger than we have been at any time since the campaign of this year commenced and with the continuing smile of Providence, who can doubt our success?"[22]

The arrival of reinforcements coincided with Lincoln's reelection. For diehards, both events signified a longer war, which was not a pleasant thought. Even stalwart Rebels had to reconcile perseverance with their yearning for peace. The war's monotony bothered Moore. "No change ever comes," he complained, "the hours, days and weeks are as much like each other as two black eyed peas." Staring at his diary, Williams admitted, "There is so much sameness about these days of duty. The same week over and over again that I find it impossible to narrate the events of each day so as to make it at all interesting." Williams asked himself "a score of times a day" when the war would end. On Christmas Day 1864, Walters confessed, "I try to think otherwise, but sometimes I fear that we will never be at peace again." A young artilleryman garrisoned in Charleston Harbor stated things plainly enough: "I am tired being a soldier."[23]

[The war's length and destructiveness also hardened soldiers to the gore that surrounded them. Prevalent sights of shrieking, wounded men, bloated corpses, and disemboweled friends took a heavy toll on many veterans. Soldiers' desensitized language revealed how much these scenes affected them. Blackford told his young daughter that amputated limbs sticking out of a shallow grave made "a very horrid sight, but one we get used to."]When Robert Trieves informed a woman of her friend's death, he failed to restrain his graphic description of the "horribly torn & mangled" body. He told the woman that "the terrible missile struck him in the left side above the hip, crushing the same, & entering his bowels, which were torn & protruded thro' the wound, which was very large." Countless impressions such as this one separated Blackford, Trieves, and other veterans from the innocence and parlor-room politeness of the civilian world. As Fleet put it, the war "deadens the sensibilities and destroys the finer feelings of us all."[24]

Other soldiers' actions, more than their words, showed how hardened they had become. Some troops habitually plundered dead Yankees. David Crawford's comrades left the trenches at night to grab food, canteens, blankets, coats, and tent flies. Honour looked on as a Rebel showed off a handsome silver watch he had snatched from a dead Yankee. "These fellows have been in the war a long time," Honour explained, and the men "talk of all sort of war scenes with the utmost indifference." Standing on an old battlefield, Boatwright was repulsed by the skeletons but more appalled by the behavior of his friends.["Many of the boys picked up the skulls" and tossed them around "as if they were toys." Others were pulling up corpses and searching the pockets.]"One of the men took up a mans arm or the bone of it and commenced breaking it to make a ring." The fellow "said it would make a nice white ring." Boatwright hoped "never to witness such a scene again." When a shell exploded within Berkeley's artillery limber, it decapitated one horse and tore the legs off of two others but left the rider of the headless horse unscathed. He was "covered from his face to his knees with the brains and blood of the horse," and Berkeley "could not help being amused at his appearance, yet it was an awful gruesome place to be amused."[25]

Such experiences convinced some Rebels to quit the war, but most Confederates braved the conditions and fought on. The same elements that motivated deserters united diehards, because, as Clausewitz explains, "A soldier is just as proud of the hardships he has to overcome as of the dangers he has faced." The terror and squalor of 1864 fostered a "true military spirit" within Confederate ranks that marked them as veteran armies. This phenomenon reminds us that Rebel forces changed in ways that do not fit within our grand narrative of the war. As Confederate armies changed over time, negative developments such as increased privation, desertion, and attrition could have positive consequences. Rebels complained occasionally (as all soldiers do), but many of them venerated each other for enduring the war "without a murmur." By doing so, they inadvertently used comradeship to push each other to extremes. Attrition gradually sapped armies of their power, but it also strengthened the bonds among survivors. Desertion further depleted the ranks but also winnowed units of the disheartened, thereby increasing the concentration of diehards in Rebel forces. If Confederate armies seemed more defiant than ever late in the war, these developments help to explain why.[26]

The year 1864 did more than separate the disheartened from the diehards: it widened the gap between soldiers and civilians. The unprecedented suffering and carnage convinced many troops that they alone sustained the nation. Soldiers from across the South believed that the armies remained hopeful and patriotic while the home front sank into despondency and corruption. South Carolinian James Drayton Nance told his wife, "If I entertained any fear for the success of our cause, it would be rather from apprehension of the decay of the spirit of the people, than that of the army. I have always observed that there was more hope, cheerfulness and spirit here, than at home." During William T. Sherman's March to the Sea, Henry Calvin Conner admitted that the Confederacy was losing territory, but he was more concerned about the people losing faith. "I fear that thare are many at home who are destitute of both honour and patriotism," he wrote to his wife. Conner felt that the military situation would improve "in a short time" if shirkers responded to the call for more troops, but "nothing short of a file of men with the bayonet could push them to the front." Veterans like Nance and Conner suspected that they were doing more for the Confederacy than anyone else was. When reports of civilian despair reached the front lines, soldiers felt betrayed by the millions they were fighting and dying to defend. When North Carolinian Henry London heard rumors that the state legislature sought a separate peace with the United States, he flew into a rage. London vented to his father that such citizens deserved "the terrible vengeance of an indignant army, of men who for the last four years have been baring their breasts to hostile bullets and fearful diseases, while the cowardly wretches have been at home aiding & abetting their countrys foes by treasonable measures."[27]

Camaraderie fostered this cliquish notion that soldiers deserved more praise than civilians. Many citizens' wartime writings exhibited steadfast faith in the Confederacy and its independence.[28] But the milieu of army life reinforced the ethos of invincibility in ways that civil society did not. When soldiers observed that the army exuded higher morale than the home front, they may have been self-righteous, but they were also insightful. For civilians, the death of a soldier could lead to two responses—increased devotion to the cause for which the man had died or revulsion toward the war that had stolen a loved one. Soldiers rarely expressed the second sentiment when they lost a good friend or family member. Dead comrades cemented troops' devotion to the cause. Fletcher Brabham admitted that the absence of familiar faces around campfires "puts a gloom over me," but "we have our consolation [that] in a great and glorious cause their fate was sealed." When Mississippian William Nugent and his regiment occupied an old battlefield, "it makes the war-feeling creep instinctively over us. Beneath this soil there sleeps many a martyr to the sacred spirit of liberty. From their graves comes up an all-pervading sense of our ability to accomplish our independence." Moore sent condolences to his overseer after the man's son was killed at the Crater. Moore was "sad to think that such good men should fall by foul hands of a despicable foe!" He prayed, "Heaven grant that we may yet live to inflict punishment upon such wretches as have snatched him from us!"[29]

[Survivors in the thinning ranks could reinforce each other's morale in ways that civilians could not.] Lieutenant Harry Lewis of the Sixteenth Mississippi Infantry understood that the army's atmosphere encouraged higher morale than the home front. He explained to his mother, "You don't know what a relief it was, in one sense . . . to come from Miss. where if the people are not whipped, they delight not to dwell upon and delineate the bright sides of the Confederacy" to return to the armies in the heart of the nation. In March 1864, Lewis returned to Lee's army in Virginia, "where thousands of veteran soldiers, representing every army in the Confederacy, rove to and fro, loud in their expression and firm in their belief that the Southern States eventually will emerge from the smoke of the conflict covered with honor and purified by the terrible ordeal through which she will have passed." Lewis was "so pleased with the temper and mettle of our troops" that he hoped "great things for the present year." In January 1865, Fitzpatrick admitted, "We have some croakers here but not so many as you have there at home." He hated to hear such men talk but figured "it is natural for some" to be gloomy. Regardless of what others said or did, Fitzpatrick had "no distant dream of ever giving up." He promised his wife that "Yankees may kill me but will never subjugate me." He meant it. Fitzpatrick was mortally wounded on April 3, 1865, days before his comrades surrendered at Appomattox.[30]

This separation between soldiers and civilians is fascinating because Confederate troops were not professionals. Civil War armies were composed of farmers, shopkeepers, mechanics, college students, and a handful of men with prior military training. War was a radical departure from Rebels' normal world, and many of them disparaged the cadre of West Pointers in charge. Units of neighbors and family members marched to war together and maintained close ties with those at home. Nonetheless, the experience of war separated veterans from everyone else. As military scholar and veteran Samuel Hynes explains, "War is more than actions; it is a culture. Military traditions, values, and patterns of behavior penetrate every aspect of army life and make the most ordinary acts and feelings different." For some Rebels, the difference was so profound as to create two wars, the one they fought and the one their families and other civilians watched and read about in the papers. Clausewitz understood the phenomenon: "No matter how clearly we see the citizen and the soldier in the same man, how strongly we conceive of war as the business of the entire nation, opposed diametrically to the pattern set by the *condottieri* of former times, the business of war will always remain individual and distinct. Consequently for as long as they practice this activity, soldiers will think of themselves as members of a kind of guild, in whose regulations, laws, and customs the spirit of war is given pride of place." Despite the many ties between battlefront and home front, the soldiers thought and fought a war that was distinctly theirs. Without this insight, we cannot fathom how so many Confederates remained defiant through the hellfires of 1864. As one Rebel described the situation in January 1865, "The people in parts of Georgia, Alabama & the Carolinas are ready to submit; but the real country is the army—it [is] unconquered and unconquerable."[31]

But Clausewitz argued that victories were as important to military spirit as endurance and activity. How did Confederate armies retain their cohesiveness after major defeats at Gettysburg, Vicksburg, Atlanta, Franklin, and Nashville? To be sure, Rebels won battles after these disasters. Mansfield, Kennesaw Mountain, and Cold Harbor were undisputed victories that revived diehards' confidence in themselves and the cause. But these victories alone could not have sustained Confederate armies. A more complete answer lies within soldiers' perceptions rather than military historians' accounts of 1864. Scholars often present a bird's-eye view of battles. Maps that follow campaigns from the crow's vantage point epitomize this perspective. Using historical hindsight, maps summarize the complex designs and actions of armies in a dispassionate and accurate manner. Arrows, lines, and other symbols represent the experiences of thousands of men in a way that connects to a sweeping, coherent narrative. The soldiers who fought these campaigns (as well as their officers) lacked this complete picture and instead saw warfare from a worm's-eye view. Battles and other events seemed too close, too incomplete, and too foggy for participants to discern much beyond their immediate surroundings. This uncertainty gave optimists room to dream—each new battle might be the one that decided the war, and any minor tactical gain could grow to strategic importance. From the bird's-eye view, the Confederacy seems doomed in 1864. From the worm's-eye view, however, the rebellion appeared closer to victory that year than ever before.[32]

Confederates who fought in 1864 preserved their myopic, hopeful, perspectives in letters and diaries. For a number of reasons, soldiers claimed victories in battles that historians consider stalemates or Confederate defeats. Rebels tended to underestimate their losses and to exaggerate enemy casualties, in part because Federal armies often suffered greater casualties and frequently left their dead and wounded in southern hands. Confederates also followed strict definitions of a tactical victory. Whenever they retained control of the field or thwarted the enemy's intentions, Confederates declared themselves winners. But by focusing on the current situation, many Rebels missed the greater implications of a series of engagements. For example, General Johnston's men claimed victories whenever they repulsed Sherman's assaults, but many Rebels failed to admit that their overall retreat toward Atlanta eclipsed such minor successes. Finally, such thoughts did not merely materialize late in the war as a response to major setbacks: some Confederates had been inflating their military success since 1861.

Two beliefs reinforced soldiers' optimism. First, Rebels maintained an unquestioning faith in most of their commanders. Even when they suffered severe hardships or high casualties, the troops seldom challenged Lee or Johnston's decisions. This obedience muted criticism of how the campaigns were directed and freed the troops from explaining how success would be achieved. Even men who admitted that they saw no path to independence trusted their commanders to find a way. Second, most Confederates thought that one great victory—a Confederate Cannae—could decide the war in their favor. Despite three years of oscillating fortunes and inconclusive campaigns—after the mammoth carnage of Shiloh, Antietam, Gettysburg, and Chickamauga buried thousands but failed to destroy either army—many veterans still believed that a brilliant tactical success would decide the struggle. The dramatic, unprecedented scale of the 1864 contests amplified soldiers' conviction that this decisive battle was imminent. As the war worsened, accelerated, and pushed Confederates to the limits of their endurance, the troops anticipated this all-or-nothing showdown both because momentum seemed to be leading toward it and because they wanted peace more than ever. However inaccurate or naive these perceptions seem today, they sustained Rebels' hope through the worst military circumstances and long past the point where victory seems possible in hindsight.[33]

Gettysburg is called the high-water mark of the Confederacy, the northernmost line of Rebel reach from which everything diminishes to Appomattox. The image of Pickett's men repulsed strengthens notions of a sea change: a tide of men returned defeated, never to touch those heights again. Perhaps novelist Michael Shaara tells the tale best in *Killer Angels*. While survivors streamed past him, General James Longstreet "thought to God: if there is any mercy in you at all you will finish it now." According to Shaara, at this terrible moment, Longstreet knew that "the army would not recover from this day. . . . He knew that as a good doctor knows it, bending down for perhaps the last time over a doomed beloved patient." Watching burial parties ascend on the fallen, Longstreet thought, "All that was left now was more dying. It was final defeat."[34]

Confederate diaries and letters from Gettysburg tell another story. Not only did Lee's men persist without a premonition that they had lost the war, but many refused to believe they had lost the battle. Jedediah Hotchkiss, a topographer for Lee's army, met Pickett's Division after the charge. On the night of July 3, he found them "scattered all along the road; no officers and all protesting that they had been completely cut up." The men were angry that other units had not supported them enough to take the heights. Hotchkiss noticed "despondency in the army at our great losses, though the battle is regarded as a drawn one." Mississippian Robert Moore agreed that Pickett's division was "badly demoralized" because they had "captured the enemy's works but were forced to abandon them." Moore conceded that the army was "cut up & disorganized & has failed to carry the enemy's position," but he refused to use the words *defeat* or *retreat* in his diary. When Lee's troops returned to Virginia ten days later, Moore summarized the situation: "We fall back from no fear of the enemy but that our army is in no condition to move forward & we are too far from our base to remain here." Both Hotchkiss and Moore described Lee's army as "cut up." Such phrases undermined the notion that Confederates were merely returning to their base of supplies. Though diehards proclaimed the battle a draw, some of their language suggests that the campaign was costlier than they would admit.[35]

Many Rebels wrote similar assessments as parting shots of the campaign. Bird was so committed to refuting the idea that Gettysburg was a Confederate defeat that he devoted four letters to the subject in less than two weeks. Four days after the battle, he stressed that the enemy was "impregnably posted. . . . They had rock walls built on the mountain side and tops." Gettysburg's terrain rose to great heights in Confederate memory. On July 12, the Georgian remembered "hurling our army against the heights and mountains of Gettysburg"; in Bird's opinion, conquering them was a heroic but impossible assignment. Welch agreed: "We drove the Yankees three miles from the battlefield to a long range of high hills, from which it was impossible to dislodge them." A South Carolinian considered the enemy's position "barren mountains, as formidable as Gibraltar."[36] These men practiced a double standard without hesitation. Confederates claimed victories at battles, like Fredericksburg, where terrain helped them achieve success, but when the enemy used such tactics to its advantage at Gettysburg, Rebels considered the engagement a draw.

Lee's men supported their arguments with inflated casualty figures. Gettysburg was the bloodiest battle of the war. The Union army lost twenty-three thousand men, a quarter of its troops. The Confederates suffered worse. The battle cost Lee twenty-eight thousand killed, wounded, or missing, more than a third of his army. Despite this carnage, Rebels who fought at Gettysburg were convinced that the enemy had lost more men. Bird heard "the Yankee's acknowledge to a loss of thirty thousand." He figured, "Ours could not have been half of that." This false disparity raised troops' spirits and helped them deem the battle a success. As one soldier wrote, the Rebels "inflicted a much heavier loss on the enemy than they received, notwithstanding their terrible disadvantage." South Carolinian David Aiken thought Confederate casualties were slightly higher, "about 18,000 or 20,000 men," but he insisted that "the enemy's loss must be vastly larger, for we captured 11,000 prisoners." Pierson thought Lee captured "over twenty thousand prisners, several pieces of artillery and an immense amount of small arms and ammunition." Though Pierson admitted that Confederate losses were "heavy," he assumed the enemy had suffered "30 to 50 thousand" casualties, while "our loss will fall much short of these figures." The message behind calculating the enemy's greater losses was clear: Lee's army invaded northern soil and inflicted horrific losses on the enemy despite being on the offensive against an impregnable position. This assessment, shared by innumerable Rebels, meant that Gettysburg was not a defeat.[37]

The aftermath of the battle seemed to support this rosy perspective. When the vestiges of Pickett's division returned to their lines, Confederates prepared for a Federal counterattack. None came. Rebels stressed this fact to bolster the widespread opinion that the enemy soldiers would have suffered worse than Pickett's men if they had been courageous enough to cross the same field. Bird pointed out that the Yankees "retreated at the same time our fellows fell back and did not attempt to follow up." He claimed that "captured officers say they would have had to abandon all their positions [before Pickett's charge], if [the Confederate bombardment] had kept on thirty minutes longer." In other words, lack of ammunition caused the outcome to be less than a complete Confederate victory, and the enemy conceded this point. Welch also stressed the enemy's refusal to attack: "On the night of the 3rd General Lee withdrew the army nearly to its original position, hoping, I suppose, that the enemy would attack him; but they didn't dare come out of their strongholds, for well they knew what their fate would be if they met the Confederate Army of Virginia upon equal grounds." Pierson argued, "We whipped the enemy too badly for him to attempt to follow us" and surmised, "The yankees dread to hazard an engagement with the army under Genl. Lee on anything like fair ground; they know we are superior in valor to their men and therefore they always seek some advantages of position." Such rationalizations transformed the defeat at Gettysburg into proof of Union cowardice and inferiority.[38]

In hindsight, Gettysburg was a staggering defeat for Lee and his men. The Pennsylvania campaign ended in failure and devastated the army, especially its officer corps. Popular perception depicts the battle as the turning point of the war, the moment when the tide of Confederate victory subsided. Understanding how Rebels persisted for years after the battle, however, requires considering how the campaign looked from the participants' perspective. Their rationalizations may seem dubious, but they were genuine and consistent with the way Confederate soldiers viewed the war from beginning to end. Similar reasoning—particularly the inflation of casualties and misrepresentations of tactical outcomes—brightened Rebel perceptions of the battles they fought throughout the war. The impact of this pattern of thinking was clear after Gettysburg. Bird was convinced, "We did whip them at Gettysburg, but at awful loss." He considered the battle an "unfortunate victory." Pierson reasoned, "We have lost many noble and gallant men but we should have lost equally as many in a battle of Virginia and besides we would not have procured a single lot of supplies." South Carolinian Tally Simpson thought Lee "attacked the enemy, and tho he gained the advantage and held possession of the battlefield and even destroyed more of the foe than he lost himself," the Army of Northern Virginia "lost heavily" and had to recover before resuming the offensive.[39]

Not every Confederate at Gettysburg considered it a draw, and many diehards tempered their earlier claims to victory as time and distance provided a different perspective. The tremendous amount of space some men devoted to proving that the battle was not a disaster suggests that even the most devoted Confederates could not easily dismiss Gettysburg's terrible results. Some troops resolved their view of the campaign by anticipating future success. For them, Gettysburg would mean less and less with each Confederate victory. In August, the army's rejuvenation began in earnest. Men recovering from wounds and illnesses reinforced the army. A religious awakening and martial reviews revived the ranks as well. When General Benjamin G. Humphreys assumed command of General William Barksdale's brigade, he quoted his fallen predecessor in his first order to the men. According to Humphreys, Barksdale's last words had been, "The Rebels are invincible. Although repulsed to-day [they] will be victorious to-morrow." After Gettysburg, diehards were more eager than ever to fulfill Barksdale's prediction.[40]

While eastern troops convinced themselves that Gettysburg was not a defeat, western soldiers tried to fathom the fall of Vicksburg. On July 4, 1864, General John C. Pemberton surrendered thirty thousand Rebel defenders to Grant. Within a week, Confederates raised the white flag over Port Hudson, and the Mississippi River rejoined the Union. In his memoirs, Grant argued, "The fate of the Confederacy was sealed when Vicksburg fell." Many historians agree. The event certainly spread despair across the South. Confederates grieved over Pemberton's surrender more than they despaired over Lee's failure. The news staggered troops close to the disaster, but within weeks many of them regained composure. Nugent at first reacted to the news with gloom and disgust but ultimately downplayed the significance of Vicksburg. Four days after the surrender, he wrote, "One thing is sure the River must be surrendered to the Yankees and our country now belongs to them by right of conquest." Nugent expected that "the war will soon be terminated one way or another . . . and we will either be defeated absolutely or some compromise made that will restore the old Union." Vicksburg temporarily convinced Nugent that the Confederacy had lost the war.[41]

Twenty days later, Nugent sounded like a new man—or, more accurately, like his old self. He regained his faith in the cause and its ultimate triumph. "After the fall of V.burg," he confessed, "I entertained the most gloomy forbodings." Demoralization throughout the army and "the submissive spirit of the people" had depressed him for a time, but Nugent now predicted an outcome different from defeat and reunion. "If I am not greatly mistaken," he conjectured, "the possession of the River will prove a conquest barren of results." The enemy's great triumph would somehow prove inconsequential. A month after the surrender, Nugent was sickened by civilians who "are almost ready now to *submit absolutely* to old Abe's will and kiss the rod that strikes them." He urged his wife, "Do not be discouraged, but with a firm reliance upon Almighty God, be trustful, hopeful." He admitted, "Since the fall of Vicksburg I have reflected a great deal." After a month of thinking, Nugent was "now satisfied that the calamity will result in ultimate good & force us to the adoption of some more decided plans of action." Vicksburg would invigorate the Confederacy and awaken Rebel leaders to a more successful strategy. "We must get rid of the slothful, gold-laced & thin-strained gentlemen & let young America have a swing at the *cannibals*," he hollered. The new "war-policy . . . must be no dilly-dallying, no tardiness, no timidity in our counsels. We must fight ever, fight bravely, and contend for every inch of ground, falling back only when our warm and patriotic blood shall have watered & dyed the soil of the sunny South." By mid-August, Nugent had convinced himself that civilian gloom after Vicksburg was an "abnormal condition [that] will not continue long." He predicted, "Men's minds will very soon acquire a healthy tone," as his had, "and if they will only exert their influence to keep stragglers in the army we will soon conquer our enemies, achieve our independence & have PEACE." Six weeks earlier, Nugent had expected to be conquered or returned to the old Union; now he argued that Confederate victory was imminent if civilians encouraged stragglers to do their duty. His transformation reveals how resilient the ethos of invincibility could be. Gloom and despair could trouble diehards for a while, but they often restored their faith during the worst circumstances.[42]

Before the 1864 campaigns commenced, Rebels across the Confederacy predicted outcomes as bright and hopeful as the southern springtime. The men envisioned climactic clashes and final showdowns that would secure victory and independence. Welch believed "if we whip the Yankees good again this spring they will quit in disgust. Their cause is not just, like ours, and they are sure to become discouraged more readily." At Dalton, Georgia, George Binford pronounced the Army of Tennessee "as strong as if not stronger" than ever before, "and the soldiers [are] in high spirits and eager for the fray." Binford expected that "we will assume the offensive" and "see Mr. Grant flanked on both sides. Our army is in splendid condition and the only topic is an onward march into Tenn. & Ky." Brannock concurred: "Rest assured that you will hear a good account of Johnston's Army during the next twelve months," he told his wife. "Our prospects seem very cheering. The general impression is that the War will close this year. At any rate, whether it closes in twelve months or twelve years, we have passed the crisis & can never never be a subjugated people." Nugent was so confident the war would close in 1864 that he told his wife, "I can afford to transport a scanty wardrobe until then." "You may tell your friends that I say we are not near whipped; and the Yankees will find it out this spring." Nugent predicted "one more grand fight in Georgia; after that we may expect nothing more than raids" from the enemy.[43]

Similar forecasts came from Virginia. Before the campaign began, South Carolinian Franklin Gaillard traveled with Longstreet's Corps through the Confederate heartland as it returned to the Army of Northern Virginia. He noted high morale "from all quarters." "The Army, Government, and the people seem now to be working together harmoniously to the one great end of independence." Gaillard thought 1864 "is unquestionably a year of promise to our cause." In Virginia, infantryman Elias Davis was so "convinced this war will have virtually closed" before autumn that he predicted the Confederacy would win without much of a fight. Davis wrote to his wife, "We are not expecting to do much fighting here this year." "One general engagement some time this spring" was possible, but there was no doubt of the result: "All are sanguine of our success." Lieutenant Robert Tutwiler speculated with his fellow officers about the coming campaign. Many of them assumed that "Genl. Lee will advance . . . and they predict that the 'big battle' will be fought on the Potomac, very probably on the other side." Wherever the battle was to be fought, Tutwiler and his friends thought "it is evident when the campaign does open it will be 'a short and bloody one.'" Like many others, Tutwiler was "strongly inclined to the opinion that this year will see the end of 'this cruel war.'" When Pierson assessed Lee's troops, he announced, "The general health and spirits of this army are altogether unsurpassed by any band of soldiers that history either modern or ancient give an account of and all are eager for the opening of the spring campaign in the full belief that we will be blessed with some grand and glorious victories."[44] These statements display a striking confidence. Eight months after Gettysburg and Vicksburg, while massive Union armies prepared to annihilate them and torch the Confederate home front, Rebels sensed that their nation was nearer to victory than ever before.

A multitude of influences supported Confederates' high expectations. Brannock and many others hoped for victory because they yearned to go home. He told his wife, "It would make [me] very happy to think that I could be with you before the summer is over to help you in your garden, enjoy your nice flowers,

& eat some of those good old-fashioned vegetable dinners which we used to have." Samuels wrote to his wife, "Should we defeat Grant this spring I hope to *see you* and dear Lucy in a few months." Others underestimated Federal resolve. Welch thought the Confederacy could withstand a disastrous campaign but the enemy could not. In his opinion, another year of high casualties and futile offensives would drown the North. Conner agreed: "The enemy will make one more desperate effort to take Richmond," but the northern home front would not abide another defeat. Conner heard about "a good deal of dissatisfaction springing up in the North in regard to the war and some of thair leading men do not hesitate to say that thair only hope is based on Grants success and should he fail as no doubt he will . . . thay will be no longer able to support the war." Other troops, including Nugent and Elias Davis, exhibited groundless bravado perhaps to convince their families and themselves that the war would end soon and without disaster.[45]

High estimations and genuine hopes for the upcoming campaigns resulted in part from the enormous troop reviews that Generals Lee and Johnston orchestrated. When the weather improved, the generals collected, inspected, and displayed their forces so that the men could witness their armies' size, precision, and pride. With hundreds of unfurled flags, thousands of polished rifles and gleaming bayonets, legions of prancing cavalry, column after column of smart-stepping veterans, rows of cannons, and a cadre of commanders atop beautiful steeds, reviews raised morale like no other events except victories and revivals. As noted in previous chapters, physical spectacles impressed the men on both emotional and cognitive levels. Chapter 1 explained how evangelical meetings displayed an army's holiness with both passionate service and the staggering sight of hundreds of participants. Grand reviews had a similar impact on soldiers' pride in their military prowess. Troops saw that they belonged to a giant force composed of crack units and storied brigades. Moreover, reviews provided the perfect remedy for the dull isolation of winter quarters. Men who had for months seen only their closest comrades now saw Alabamians, Carolinians, Georgians, Floridians, Kentuckians, Mississippians, Tennesseans, Texans, and more. The entire South seemed gathered together for imminent victory.[46]

Spectacles of prowess deeply impressed the veterans. Brannock considered a review of his corps "a fine sight—I never saw a finer looking body of men." He thought that "a new spirit seems to have been infused into the army since Genl Jo. Johnston took command." Seeing "3 lines of men 2 rank deep reaching near 3 miles" convinced Hampton that his was "a beautiful Army in good trim & high spirits." The memory of being routed at Missionary Ridge the previous November seemed irrelevant: as Hampton put it, "It does not look much like we was badly whiped to see the amount of troops at this place." Thomas Key agreed: The "army presented itself in the best condition that I have ever witnessed it." "Thousands of hardy soldiers marching to the notes of the shrill fife and bass drum . . . looked grand and cheering." According to Key, everyone felt "confident that the next battle will result in a great victory for this army."[47]

Massive sham battles provided a similar spectacle and gave the men practice at tactical maneuvers. Using blank cartridges, entire corps advanced and retreated against each other. Key thought that "the dark lines of men made a grand display as they moved in battle array, their guns glittering in the sunlight." The rattle of musketry echoed off the surrounding mountains and "sounded very much like a real battle." Hampton described a sham battle as a "magnificent sight." Four lines of men were drawn up in opposition to each other and reached "over a mile & a Half." "They marched up in some 50 yards of each other & fired with all of the artillery & small arms." In addition to their officers, "thousands [were] there to witness the scene," including many ladies from Atlanta. After participating in several big combat simulations, Orr told his brother, "We have better armies in the field now than we had twelve months ago, and we are better armed and better dissipland; and ower men are in better spirits." The experience emboldened the young man: "Why should we give it up nowwhin so many of ower brave comrads have fell and so much blud have been shed. I ask you as a brother fight it out to the last, never give it up, and bee put on an [equal] footing with the negros. I say no. I will fight them ten years [illegible] independence. I have never dissponded yet. I have passed through several hard fought battles, and I can tell you I have all ways stood to my post." The only news that discouraged young Lafayette was word that the girls back home were marrying shirkers. Men enjoyed sham battles so much that they organized them without approval from headquarters. Nagel explained the protocol to his mother: "One brigade would challenge the other, they would meet at night each man armed with a torch in one hand, & a large pine bush in the other." By torchlight, the brigades "had regular pitched battles, threw out skirmishers, have reserves, & every thing like real war; their bugles would sound the charge, & they would rush upon each other as if in earnest." The only casualty was an old fellow whose "splendid flowing beard" was singed close by an opponent's torch. For some soldiers, the spectacle of sham battles and reviews lasted well into the active campaign. In June 1864, Fleet told his parents, "If you could only *see* the Army, you would never feel any anxiety about Richmond. Lee is stronger than when the fighting commenced & his men, as well as those of the gallant [P. G. T.] Beauregard are in the best possible trim." The sight of their numbers both heartened Confederates and distracted them from the enemy's superior manpower.[48]

No Confederates had more confidence in themselves and their leaders than Lee's Army of Northern Virginia. As J. Tracy Power notes in his study of the army's final campaign, "Many officers and men simply assumed that a Confederate victory was both forthcoming and inevitable," and "predictions for the coming campaign differed more in their degrees of enthusiasm than in questions of whether the Army of Northern Virginia would succeed." As Tutwiler related,

"Every soldier feels as confident of success as if we had already achieved it."[49] Their confidence came from a keen awareness that they had beaten their opponents more often than not during the war. Lewis was unfazed by the news of Grant's arrival in Virginia, believing that no amount of "reorganizing and reviewing" in the Army of the Potomac could erase the central issue: "We have repeatedly routed and vanquished" them. Though many of Lee's best and bravest men were dead, the army took comfort in the knowledge that its surviving veterans sustained the spirit and ability of their fabled units. In early 1864, the Confederate government insured the army's veteran composition by requiring all men whose three-year enlistments were expiring to stay in the ranks. Richmond also bolstered military manpower by expanding the draft age limits to seventeen and fifty, eliminating substitutions, and abolishing most exemptions from service. Regardless of the law, thousands of old volunteers reenlisted "for the war" as a response to massive reenlistments in the Army of Tennessee. In February 1864, Lee told his army that the wave of voluntarism "gives new cause for the gratitude and admiration of their countrymen." He hoped that the movement would "extend from army to army until the Soldiers of the South stand in one embattled host determined never to yield."[50]

The most hardened veterans could not have predicted the devastation of 1864. The eastern campaign began with gruesome battles at the Wilderness and Spotsylvania Court House that decided little. Belligerents pushed each other's lines forward and backward, making it difficult to measure which army held the field. Diehard Rebels nonetheless considered themselves victorious.[51] After the Wilderness, a Virginia lieutenant thought that "our success so far has been as decided as brilliant." He suspected that Lee's next move would "drive [Grant] into the Rappahannock" and secure independence. Foremost in soldiers' claims to triumph were misconceptions that they had driven the enemy for miles when in fact the final lines were almost identical to the adversaries' initial positions.[52] The most certain outcome of these battles was bloodshed. During the first week of active campaigning, Grant's troops suffered thirty-two thousand men killed, wounded, or missing, a total that amounted to half of Lee's army and a loss that exceeded the casualties of "all Union armies *combined* in any previous week of the war." The Rebels had lost about twenty-one thousand men, and their leaders had paid the heaviest toll. Twenty of Lee's fifty-seven commanders of infantry corps, divisions, and brigades were sacrificed, while Grant lost ten of his sixty-nine officers of that rank.[53]

Witnessing so much carnage fostered inflated casualty figures. Through word of mouth, Rebels convinced themselves that Grant had lost 50,000 men at the beginning of the campaign. John Hampden "Ham" Chamberlayne wrote home that "we have punished the Yanks dreadfully. . . . [T]heir loss must touch 50 to 60 000 all told—They still move against us, but feebly." Stiles concurred that Grant "is awfully repulsed—his losses in killed & wounded being at least 3 or 4 to 1; probably the disproportion is even greater. I really presume his loss will sum up 50,000." Like Chamberlayne, Stiles described the enemy's recent attacks as "feeble." Chamberlayne told his sister, "Do not be too confident, yet you may encourage an almost bouyant hope in these days of constant repeated victory." David Crawford agreed that the Union "army is pretty well demoralized" by its excessive losses. He passed on a rumor "that they are fighting themselves, it is said that they are liquored to fight, some of our Corps saw some of them drunk." Blackford thought that "50,000 would not cover the enemy's loss," while DeNoon confirmed that the "Yankee loss [is] supposed to be 55 to 60 thousand. Our loss [is] estimated at 10 to 12 thousand." Army surgeon John Shaffner estimated Confederate losses at 15,000 and Union casualties "from 40,000 to 75,000." Abel Crawford heard similar casualty figures while defending Petersburg: "It is believed by a great many of the leading men that this is the last fight. I understand that Gen. Lee says it is the last."[54]

Tactics help to explain why Rebels overestimated the enemy's casualties. By fighting on the defensive, behind breastworks, Lee's men cut down countless Union advances. Rebels watched Grant's dead and wounded pile up, and despite the intensity of the campaign, Confederates found their work straightforward and the results predictable. South Carolinian James Tinkler told his parents, "We lay behind our works and let them advance on us and when they would come up in forty or fifty yards we would pour our fire into them and just mow them down." Another Confederate noted, "Our troops are in excellent spirit, and say they want only plenty of ammunition, and plenty to eat, and then let the Yankees come." Grant's stubbornness, exhibited in his bullheaded charges and unwillingness to retreat, seemed to play right into Rebel hands. Shaffner marveled that "any other Yankee general would have acknowledged the defeat and gone back across the river, rested two or three months, and then made another attack." The North Carolinian could explain Grant's persistence only as an act of God: "God has placed Grant in command, who will exhaust all the armies of the North and make this the Waterloo of the war and will continue to attack until he is almost annihilated." How else could veterans understand the unrelenting carnage? Each new Federal assault was awash in blood, killing more of the enemy and bringing the Confederacy closer to independence.[55]

Despite the bloodshed, terror, and fatigue, Lee's men remained high-spirited and hopeful. Captain J. J. Young's report that "we have been successful in every fight" and "our men are in the best of spirits" clearly shows that the soldiers' perceptions and their spirits were mutually reinforcing. While the fighting escalated around the crossroads on May 9, Walters claimed, "Our troops are in the best of spirits." After the horror of the Bloody Angle, Elder wrote, "Our men are in excellent spirits and express a willingness and determination to die in the ditch rather than that Grant should get to Richmond." A week later, still fighting at Spotsylvania, Elder announced that his men "are in good condition and ready for another fight. I don't suppose the world ever saw a more determined better contented people under similar circumstances than is presented by Genl Lee's army at this time." Trieves agreed that the army "is in good spirits & confident of victory." Success in mowing down Union assaults convinced Lee's men that the war was ending in their favor.[56]

Though Grant's massive army maneuvered toward Richmond and Petersburg, Confederates continued to repel the enemy's assaults and won lopsided victories at Cold Harbor and the Crater. Such events convinced many Confederates that their army could still outsmart, outmaneuver, and outlast the enemy. Welch wrote to his wife, "It now looks as if our army will have to lie in line of battle all summer to keep the Yankees back. Poor devils! How they do long for Richmond! Our minds are prepared to endure anything rather than submit to them, and the nearer they get to us the more determined we are not to yield." The Federal disaster at the Crater convinced Higginbotham that "Grant, great as he is thought to be by the Northern Fanatics, is no more a match for our Noble Lee." Lieutenant John McLure concurred: Grant no longer worried him and his comrades. They doubted that the Union general could be "more successful in his future enterprises than he has been in the past, & these as we all know, have been miserable failures." Captain Elias Davis also thought that Lee was Grant's "master in the art of war" because the great Virginian had "managed to kill five of Grants men whilst he was killing one of ours." Artilleryman James Albright spread the rumor that Lee had proclaimed the Battle of the Crater "the most brilliant affair of the war."[57]

Though neither side could know it at the time, the Crater exemplified the strategic deadlock that would grip adversaries around Petersburg and Richmond until April 1865. Tactical blows continued to bleed both armies but failed to break either one. While detached units in the Shenandoah Valley and western armies from Georgia to the trans-Mississippi replicated the fluid campaigns of the early war, the trenches in eastern Virginia foreshadowed the frozen stalemates of World War I. As they settled into the trenches, some diehards predicted they could hold out against any odds for any period of time. As Thomas Goree told his brother, "We are quietly settled down here, I suppose for the winter, or until Genl. Grant arrives at the conclusion that it is useless for him to longer expend his energies & resources in a vain endeavor to take Richmond." Goree thought Grant persisted because "he does not know what else to do. He knows that to storm our works would destroy his army. And, whatever way he turns, he can't go far before he encounters Confederate bayonets." Boasted Goree, "You all in the Trans-Miss. Dep't. need have no fears about Richmond unless Grant can get a *much* larger army than he has at present." Welch agreed: "Grant has come to a dead halt before Petersburg and Richmond." Fleet compared the Confederate position to the siege of Sebastopol, which lasted eleven months during the Crimean War. As Fleet argued, "The allied armies of England and

France remained in the trenches before Sebastopol in a climate far colder than our own and certainly men fighting for liberty and right, dearer than life itself, can endure as many hardships as troops contending for political advancement and military honors have shown themselves able to bear." Despite the strain of life in the trenches, thousands of Lee's men vowed to outlast the foe. As Walters wrote, "Having put my hand to the plow I shall finish the row."[58]

⌒〰〇 ⌒〰〇 ⌒〰〇

In early May 1864, while the campaign for Richmond ignited in the Wilderness, the advance for Atlanta began in three mountain passes south of Chattanooga, Tennessee. Each campaign's beginning foreshadowed its character. In Virginia, Grant and Lee traded blows day and night in search of the decisive battle that would win the war. In Georgia, Sherman and Johnston maneuvered around each other in the hopes of securing victory without the bloodshed of a complete offensive assault. Their armies matched the numbers contesting in Virginia: ninety-eight thousand for Sherman and sixty-five thousand for Johnston. If the seemingly interminable combat in Virginia challenged Confederates to find hope in high enemy casualties and minor tactical gains, the seemingly unending retreat in Georgia challenged Rebels to retain hope that the culminating battle, whenever and wherever it was fought, would be a stunning triumph. The faith that thousands of these soldiers kept in their generals and comrades is remarkable not only because of their constant retreating but also because their army lacked the glory garnered by Lee's troops. One reason for their confidence was their veteran status. These men had lost many battles and had changed commanders often since their first day at Shiloh in April 1862, but they knew how to fight and believed they would win under the right general and circumstances. An Alabama soldier expressed this mentality well: "General Johnston has infused new life into the army and we feel that now is the time to retrieve the misfortunes which have befallen us in the past and if we can meet Sherman on anything like an equal footing we have no fears of the result."[59]

On numerous occasions, Confederate success in Georgia appeared and vanished like a mirage. At Dalton, Resaca, and Adairsville, Rebels prepared to pound Sherman's advancing columns, but each time the Union army outflanked the Confederates and blazed a path toward Atlanta. Lacking a complete picture of the campaign, troops wondered why they retreated from positions as sure as a turkey shoot. One soldier thought the rocky terrain at Dalton offered Johnston "the strongest natural position I ever saw."[60] At Cassville, Johnston promised his troops that the time and place for fighting had finally arrived. "By your courage and skill," Johnston claimed, "you have repulsed every assault of the enemy. . . . You will now turn and march to meet his advancing columns." The speech electrified the troops. Jackman described it as "Napoleonic." Cheers erupted through the ranks. According to Brannock, "Our lines of battle were formed immediately, every body in the highest spirits, & the men, although so worn out with fatigue & loss of rest, were eager for the great struggle & confident of victory." But after waiting with anticipation for hours, "we were startled by an order from Gen. [William J.] Hardee to pack up in all haste & to leave *immediately.*" General Hood, usually anything but overcautious, feared that his flank was being passed by a large enemy force and called off his attack. The threat turned out to be a cavalry detachment, but the Rebels lost their chance to strike. That night they retreated again.[61]

Pulling back after Johnston's glorious pronouncement affected morale. When the order to retreat reached Brannock and his men, "we were perfectly astounded," he wrote. "For the first time the men begin to grumble & become dispirited." To further rankle them, the frantic retreat was "sort of a dog trot all the way," with artillerymen and teamsters whipping their horses and officers hollering for the men to close ranks. John Cotton told his wife, "There is a heap of our men thinks we are whiped because we have fell back." He hated "very much haveing to give up so much of our own cuntry to the enemy to bee destroyed." Everything they passed would soon be at the mercy of the enemy. Sergeant John Hagan commented on the beautiful wheat fields. They were "the finest I ever saw," and it sickened him to know that "it all will be destroyed." Other Rebels were distressed at the sight of fleeing civilians. Cavalryman Stephen Jordan suffered to watch panicked women and children: "It is an ugly sight to see," he wrote. Miller saw "thousands of families fleeing from happy homes. . . . Mothers frantic with fear flying with their little ones in their arms." Looking back, Miller could chart the enemy's progress by the columns of smoke rising from refugees' homes, "a sight I never wish to behold again." Miller confided to his wife, "I thought I had seen much of war but the last two weeks experience has been the most trying of any." The captain and his comrades faced a new kind of war.[62]

The soldiers' distress is understandable, but it is difficult to comprehend why so many troops still trusted Johnston and remained hopeful. Brannock admitted, "We still believe that he knows what he is doing." The Tennessean assumed that Johnston's backpedaling had an underlying strategic purpose. J. P. Cannon concurred: "Usually an army becomes demoralized when it has to fall back continually," he argued, "but we have enough confidence in our commander to believe that when the opportunity comes he will strike the enemy a blow which will stop his aggressive movements." According to Mississippi Sergeant Edmund Eggleston, "The day and night marches are very trying on the men but as yet no evidences of demoralization are exhibited." Chaplain Robert Franklin Bunting reported, "Every confidence is felt in General Johnston." "Although [the troops] do not relish so much falling back . . . they believe it will bring the more crushing defeat upon the foe at last." Atlanta newspapers agreed that Johnston was luring the enemy into a trap. A rumor even circulated through camp that Johnston was retreating "in obedience to a positive order from Richmond, ordering him not to bring on an engagement for four days," presumably because reinforcements were on the way.[63]

Fighting on the defensive gave Rebels the impression that they were severely punishing the enemy. This conviction is curious, however, because the two sides' casualties for the Georgia campaign were about equal—Johnston's men were not inflicting the two-to-one losses on the enemy that Lee's troops were achieving in Virginia. In fact, up to the final week in May, Sherman's losses were less than Johnston's. Nevertheless, Samuel Foster pronounced the fight at Adairsville "all one sided, that is we kill them and they can't hurt us." Hampton estimated Union casualties at seven thousand and Confederate losses at three thousand, when both forces had lost about four thousand men to that point. "I do not think that either [figure] is fair wrong," he told his wife. James Hall concluded that "so far we have everything to encourage us. Our loss has been slight while that of the enemy must have been very heavy since General Johnston has compelled them to attack our breastworks in almost every instance." Cannon believed that the Rebels "have inflicted a loss of at least three to one, but Sherman, having such a large force, can flank and compel us to fall back when it suits him." He figured that the coming battles, even if they were not large, would "reduce his strength before reaching Atlanta, so we can give him battle with something near an equal force. If we can do this we feel sure of a great victory."[64]

Assuming that they were beating the enemy in each engagement may have provided diehards with a way of compensating for the ignominy of retreat. This could explain Binford's curious assessment: "In every charge we slayed them with but little loss on the whole retreat." Similarly, Brannock admitted that throughout the retreat, "we have the consolation of knowing that, all this time, the enemy are suffering worse than we are." More than any physical evidence, the Rebels' psychological need to sustain morale encouraged the opinion that Sherman's army was in terrible condition. Confederates looked for any sign that the Yankees were suffering. One cavalryman thought that the enemy was "living as severely as ourselves" because there were no sutlers in Sherman's camp.[65]

Some troops even disparaged the enemy for flanking instead of fighting. As Cotton put it, "We will whip them yet as soon as we can get them to fite us." Grant Taylor agreed: "The Yanks have flanked us and caused us to fall back. We invariably repulse them when they attack us. But they wo'nt come up and give us a general battle. If they would I believe we could whip them. The army is in fine spirits and have full confidence in themselves if we could have a fair fight." Nugent also wrote home that "our men look upon success as certain whenever we get old Sherman to fight us squarely and quit his everlasting flanking." According to Nugent, "Whole corps have charged Divisions of our army and have always been repulsed with great loss." Frank Batchelor concurred that Sherman "gets worsted every time he assaults our breastworks, and seems afraid to open the big fight." Instead of admitting Sherman's success at penetrating into enemy territory without fighting a major battle, Rebels such as Cotton, Taylor, Nugent, and Batchelor deemed the Bluecoats' maneuvering a sign of Yankee cowardice or trickery. To ease their frustrations, Confederates convinced themselves that Sherman's movements only postponed his destruction.[66]

Diehards' hopes for the campaign seemed fulfilled at Kennesaw Mountain. Chafing for an opportunity to smash the Confederates and seize Atlanta, Sherman ordered the type of assault Johnston had been goading him to do since the days at Dalton. On June 27, Union divisions funneled into a devastating field of fire on Kennesaw Mountain. Using the terrain for defense, as they had since Dalton, the Confederate veterans unleashed enfilading volleys and close-range artillery fire on their exposed assailants. When Sherman realized his mistake and called off the fight that afternoon, he had lost three thousand men, while the Confederates had suffered fewer than six hundred casualties.[67]

Rebels considered Kennesaw Mountain proof that they could and would crush the Federals whenever the two sides engaged in a direct fight. Once again, possessing the battlefield encouraged Confederates to magnify their estimates of Federal casualties. Where the fighting was most intense, J. Litton Bostick said, "The ground was strewn with the Yankee dead and wounded." He heard that General Patrick Cleburn's division had killed one thousand Federals while losing only eight men. Other Confederates stressed that the enemy "were repulsed at every point with terrible slaughter" or "repeled . . . with dreadful slaughter." On June 29, Private Thomas Jefferson Newberry watched Sherman's troops bury their comrades under a flag of truce. He told his father, "They have bin busy a burying their dead all day." Watching the enemy collect corpses smashed beyond comprehension or charred by fire convinced many Rebels, like McKittrick, that Kennesaw Mountain was "a great victory." The battle persuaded Miller that "Gen. Johnston's army . . . still presents a defiant front to the hosts of Sherman." According to Miller, the Union general "saw proper to hurl his drunken mercenaries against our lines and in every instance only left a gory field and filled his hospitals with the mangled and dying." Many Confederates found no evidence of victory more conclusive than the spectacle of enemy dead.[68]

Kennesaw Mountain colored Rebel perceptions of the entire campaign. The day before the contest, Rebels read newspapers that assessed Sherman's casualties for the campaign at thirty thousand men. The actual number was closer to seventeen thousand. After Kennesaw Mountain, Cotton claimed that "from there own accounts we have killed and wounded betwixt 50 and 75 thousand of there men" since Dalton. General Johnston shared this appraisal, guessing that Confederate casualties (excluding the cavalry) numbered almost ten thousand and presuming enemy losses "six times as great." Brannock figured that "Sherman has lost at least 30 or 40,000 men while we have not lost one fourth that number." In their assessments, many Confederates reiterated their positive impressions of the battle's one-sided results. Cannon surmised, "A few more engagements like that will reduce Sherman's force so he will not have so many to send around our flanks." A staff officer figured that if the enemy "keep up the work as they did yesterday [at Kennesaw Mountain,] their army will be used up before the summer is over and we will have a clear road to Nashville."[69]

Kennesaw Mountain also confirmed many Rebels' faith in Johnston and his strategy. Batchelor summed up the army's situation three days after the battle: "Our Army is large, in good spirits, have all confidence in Genl Johnston, and looking to the God of battles feel assured of victory." Brannock predicted, "Johnston is drawing [Sherman] farther & farther, & when the proper time arrives will no doubt *crush his army completely*." For Brannock and others, including General Johnston, strict military concerns trumped all other considerations. As long as the army avoided destruction and frustrated the enemy's advance, the amount of territory the Rebels surrendered hardly mattered. In the end, these diehards would sooner give up Atlanta and preserve the army than wreck themselves against Sherman's enormous force in an attempt to save the city. They hoped that their conserved legions would somehow catch the enemy forces making a mistake and ruin them. This Fabian perspective transformed the meaning of otherwise apparent sights of Rebel defeat. Charred crops were not portents of failure but necessary losses that robbed the enemy of supplies. Ruined railroads and burned bridges were not Confederate misfortunes but impediments to the enemy's progress. Retreating was not an admission of defeat but rather a cagey elusiveness that permitted the army to fight another day.[70]

As Sherman inched closer to Atlanta in July, some diehards tried to convince their families that the city was expendable. On July 12, Miller admitted that he was "reconciled to the loss" of the city. "I would regret very much to leave it to the foe but am satisfied that it would not be done unless it is for the best." According to Miller, "the moral effect" of Atlanta's fall "would probably be greater than the material" loss of the railroad hub and supply center. Miller accepted "almost anything that does not cause our army to disband," because "while we can keep that in the field I have no fears of the result." In fact, Miller stated, "I dont remember a time within the last year that I felt more confident of our final success than of present." While working in an Atlanta hospital in July, army surgeon Urban Owen stoically watched Johnston's men move essential items to Augusta. The move panicked civilians but not Owen. Despite seeing "people . . . fleeing the wrath to come," Owen thought that "our prospects of final success were never more flattering than at present." Sergeant John Hagan warned his wife, "You must not be suprised if you hear of our being in Atlanta or even of our giving up Atlanta. Gen Johnston well Knows he has but few men & no whear to get more . . . so he will make his fight a successful fight." Despite their long retreat to Atlanta and signs that they would surrender the city without a fight,

Miller, Owen, Hagan, and their Confederate brethren still trusted Johnston and expected to win.[71]

But not all Johnston's men shared this rosy outlook. Benjamin Seaton was tired of retreating. Within two miles of Atlanta, Seaton wrote, "It seams as we have gone as far as we ought to go unless we intend to give up all of our country and not fight anymore and that is not the idey—it is victory or death." Williams agreed and asked, "Will this falling back never come to an end?" While some of his comrades disregarded Atlanta's fate, James Bates wrote home, "I am very much afraid Atlanta will fall into the hands of the enemy, & it will be a most serious loss to the Confederacy—both on account of the rail road & the extensive manufactories here." Many men registered their disgust and despair by deserting. Hampton was shocked to discover that some of his brigade's deserters hailed from his home county. Other troops stayed in the ranks but grumbled. Hagan, for one, was unimpressed by their talk: "Some of our troops grow despondent but it is only those who are all ways despondent all good Soldiers will fight harder the harder he is prest but a coward is allways ready to want an excuse to run or to Say they or we are whiped." Hagan espoused a strict warrior's code, enduring hardships and setbacks without complaint or despair. In his view, those who failed to follow the code were cowards.[72]

Johnston's strategy won over many of his soldiers but did not please Confederate president Jefferson Davis. When a message from Johnston implied that the Army of Tennessee would abandon Atlanta without a fight, Davis removed the general on July 17 and appointed Hood to the command. The news sent shock waves through the army. Like Federal troops' affection for George McClellan, Confederates loved Johnston because he put their comfort and safety first. Foster concluded that Johnston "has so endeared himself to his soldiers, that no man can take his place." According to Foster, "We have never made a fight under him that we did not get the best of it." Nugent also thought that the army had succeeded under Johnston's leadership—had whipped the enemy in every engagement, had been well fed and clothed, had never been led to slaughter, and had always inflicted heavy casualties on the enemy at little cost to the Rebel ranks.[73]

Whether or not they supported Johnston, many troops expected results from Hood's appointment because the young general was a fighter. After months of weary marching and digging, Rebels anticipated the decisive battle for Atlanta. Sergeant Robert Banks, a Mississippian, said that Johnston's "removal fell upon us so unexpectedly that it made all feel sad—but we do not lack confidence in our present commander." The men sensed that Hood's aggressive leadership would press the issue and reveal the fate of the Confederacy. For weeks, Bates had been impatient for a showdown. He predicted, "If we win this fight here and Lee in Va. is successful I believe we will have peace in six months but if we fail in this summer campaign the war in my opinion *will be protracted indefinitely.*" "Remember this & see if I am not a prophet for once," Bates told his sister. Hampton agreed that "there will be Stiring times in this department soon" because of Hood's appointment. He expected that "a general engagement will come off in a few." Brannock forecast that "the next ten or twelve days will decide the contest for Atlanta" and claimed that "most military men think that Sherman's campaign will end in disaster."[74]

Within two days of taking command, Hood fulfilled expectations by assaulting Sherman's troops that encircled Atlanta. In eight days, the young commander cost his army fifteen thousand casualties while inflicting only six thousand on Sherman's troops.[75] Despite conclusive and ruinous results, the troops' perceptions of these battles varied from disgust to elation. Some men understood that Hood's aggressive tactics would bleed the army to death. Williams observed, "Hood will soon ruin his army at this rate. It will not do for the weaker army to charge the stronger." Recounting Hood's first assault on July 20, Banks claimed, "We whipped them." Banks stressed that his regiment had planted its colors on the Union breastworks and captured 152 prisoners but failed to mention that the Rebels had also ultimately retreated to their own lines, leaving their dead and wounded behind them. Banks even discounted the fact that his regiment suffered a ghastly 22 percent casualty rate, stating that "out of 210 men we lost only 48 so rapid was the charge." As had happened in countless previous battles, Rebel combatants found ways to claim victory. Nugent thought that his new general "has so far done very well and gives evidence of some ability—but at what fearful cost." The Mississippian estimated that Hood lost eight thousand men and "inflicted more than a corresponding and relative damage on the enemy." Though Banks and Nugent knew that Hood was losing men at an alarming rate, they still considered these battles Confederate victories.[76]

Many Rebels praised Hood's leadership. Brannock considered Hood's assaults "successful" and inspiring. "We have captured, according to the latest estimates, about 4700 prisoners & upwards of 30 pieces of artillery." He claimed that Hardee's corps had "attacked the enemy . . . completely routing them & driving them from their entrenchments with great slaughter." Though Brannock admitted that a few more such offensives would wipe out his division, he announced that the battles had "almost entirely done away with the dissatisfaction of the army at the removal of Genl Johnston." Hampton also applauded Hood's leadership throughout the punishing engagements, concluding that the enemy "have been badly cut up on both wings since Hood has had command." Hampton expected Sherman to "be turned back at this place as we are receiving additions evry day & our men are quite buoyant although there are a great many of our men droping into the hands of the Enemy & running away." Within weeks, Hampton assumed that "Gen Hood has checked the forward movements of the Enemy & if the Enemy does not look sharp [Hood] will give him a complete

Flogging as the Troops are confident & determined." Seaton even believed that "the enemy loss is vary heavy and ours is quite small to thers."[77]

After the Confederate offensives, both sides settled down for a siege in which neither army gained an advantage for a month. Union probes failed to break the defenses, and Rebel cavalry failed to sever the enemy's supply line. Nevertheless, rumors circulated through the gray ranks that their horse soldiers were loosening Sherman's grip on Atlanta.[78] When most of the Union army left the trenches on August 25–26, however, Hood and his men supposed that the Bluecoats were finally retreating. Rebels and Atlantans rejoiced and claimed victory for four days. Eggleston visited the enemy's "abandoned line" the day after they "evacuated." Predictably, he thought that "their works are greatly inferior to ours." While Confederates celebrated, Sherman's columns slid south to cut Hood's last supply line. On August 30, the Rebel commander discovered his adversary's intentions and sent two corps to intercept the Federals. It was too late. The Union army crushed these corps and launched a powerful counterattack. Facing annihilation or surrender if they remained in town, the Confederates evacuated the city to save the remains of their army. Atlanta, a symbol of Confederate tenacity second only to Richmond, now belonged to the enemy.[79]

Soldiers who had praised Hood days earlier now blamed him for the disaster. Nugent voiced a popular verdict: "Sherman completely out-generaled Hood." Foster bitterly remarked that Hood "has virtually murdered near 10,000 men around Atlanta trying to do what Joe Johnston said could not be done." General Ross noted, "The troops are much dejected and abuse Genl Hood. . . . They all call loudly for the Old hero Genl Johnston." After defeat, Johnston's leadership seemed more valuable. Troops seldom mentioned that the fall of Atlanta would have been the logical outcome of Johnston's chronic retreating. Instead, men focused on Hood's high casualties, even though many Rebels had downplayed those losses before Atlanta fell. "When Johnston left this Army," Ross commented, "it was the finest and best army I Ever heard of to the number, but now it is hacked and the men will not charge Breastworks, and is 20,000 men weaker now than when he left." Hiram Smith Williams's diary entry for the day Atlanta was lost exudes depression: "The great struggle is over. Atlanta is being incinerated. Our Corps was put in motion early this morning. . . . The troops are already demoralized and such straggling I never saw before."[80]

Many Rebels found ways to downplay the implications of their failure. In their letters and diaries, soldiers used false reports, dubious reasoning, and blind faith to boost their morale. Even though they had been abandoning territory from the start of the campaign, Foster somehow considered Atlanta "the first piece of public property" the enemy had captured all summer, and he believed that Sherman had paid too dearly for it. Many soldiers assumed the defeat prolonged the war but did not alter its eventual outcome, Confederate victory. Brannock admitted that the loss of the city was "a severe blow to us, but it is by no means fatal to our cause & should not make us despond for a moment." "If we could have held Atlanta," Brannock reasoned, "we would in all human probability have had peace by Spring—as it is we can form no idea when we shall be able to achieve that glorious result, but come it must & will, sooner or later & our independence with it." The Tennessee surgeon suspected that victory was between two and four years away, and renewed devotion to the cause and "a firm reliance upon Providence" were the only ingredients necessary for success. After repeating this reasoning for pages to convince his wife (and himself) that all would be well, Brannock interjected a telling remark: "It is useless to talk about this any more. I wish I could not even think about it any more." Brannock and his comrades were "beginning to 'cheer up' again," but denying the disastrous news was not easy. Bates evaded the cost of losing Atlanta by underrating the city's importance: "The only serious inconvenience resulting from its fall is the loss of the principal Rail road leading to Richmond." Moreover, Bates did "not think Sherman will be able to hold Atlanta," because his supply line, "which is nearly 400 miles in length," should be easily cut. Exiles from Atlanta spread word "that Sherman's army is rapidly being depleted by men whose terms of service has expired." An Atlanta newspaper estimated that more than three hundred thousand Union soldiers would finish their terms of service between August and December 1864. The authors of the report suspected that Sherman had lost ten thousand men during his first two weeks of occupying the city. If enough Yankees refused to reenlist, Sherman would have to evacuate his prize.[81]

President Davis encouraged this agile optimism during a visit to the army after Atlanta fell. Fearing that Sherman's success would wither rebel resolve, the president swooped through the Carolinas and Georgia on a speaking tour. Certain that "nothing has changed in the purpose of [the Confederate] Government, in the indomitable valor of its troops, or in the unquenchable spirit of its people," Davis envisioned victorious scenarios that outdid those created by his troops. Though Sherman commanded a massive army flushed with success, Davis predicted "no chance for Sherman to escape from a defeat or a disgraceful retreat." "The fate that befell the army of the French Empire in its retreat from Moscow will be re-enacted. Our cavalry and our people will harass and destroy his army, as did the Cossacks that of Napoleon, and the Yankee general, like him, will escape with only a bodyguard." Furthermore, Davis charged, "we must march into Tennessee," where "we will draw from twenty thousand to thirty thousand to our standard, and . . . push the enemy back to the banks of the Ohio and thus give the peace party of the North an accretion no puny editorial can give."[82]

General Hood's plans after the loss of Atlanta matched Davis's visions of glory. The army's operations in the fall and winter of 1864 were so outlandish that James McPherson describes them as "scripted in never-never land." The extreme optimism of Hood's strategy proved that even Confederate commanders could be seduced by notions of invincibility. When the Army of Tennessee, still forty thousand strong, failed to sever Sherman's supply line, the troops turned their backs on the superior Federal force and headed for Alabama and Tennessee. Leaving all of Georgia to Sherman's columns, Hood marched toward General George Thomas's sixty thousand Bluecoats with the intention of crushing them and liberating Tennessee. Hood hoped eventually to reach Kentucky, acquire twenty thousand recruits there, and turn east to join Lee's army. Then he expected that the combined Confederate legions would finish off Grant and Sherman.[83]

Returning to their beloved Tennessee brightened troops' perceptions of the campaign. They vowed to reclaim the state from Yankee rule and never abandon it again. Some soldiers' accounts of their operations exhibit so much misinformation and optimism that the march seemed to be an escape from reality as well as a flight from Sherman. Men in the Army of Tennessee seldom mentioned Sherman's impressive March to the Sea. After all, they had left Georgia and did not witness, let alone oppose, the Federals' momentum. Cotton wrote home that the Rebels "whiped the yankeys where ever we come in contact with them[, and] we have torn up a great deal of railroad on our rout." Bates considered Hood's march "one of the boldest movements of the war." Hood used misinformation and rhetoric to encourage this optimism. On October 2 he had his officers report to the men "that we were going to flank Sherman out of Atlanta, and in maneuvering we might be short of rations occasionally, but he would do his best on that point." Furthermore, Hood "expected to have some fighting and some hard marching, and wanted an expression of the men upon it." As Foster reported, "Every man said go." Days later, while on the march, Hood reported to a passing column that "the Yanks were leaving Atlanta in a great hurry." Foster rejoiced, "This army has done wonders! Flanked the Yanks out of Atlanta without firing a gun."[84]

A number of other elements bolstered Rebel morale during the campaign. Marching north without resistance was a welcome change after months of retreating south under constant enemy pressure. As Orr put it, "Marchen is pretty hard, but I had reather march than fight." The troops also felt successful by "capturing" towns they had abandoned to the foe months ago. When the Rebels reacquired Dalton, Brannock counted eleven hundred prisoners, piles of commissary, quartermasters, and medical stores, and miles of wrecked railroad. Foster also claimed Calhoun, Resaca, and Tunnel Hill as towns that the Confederates had seized. Brannock and Foster did not bother to calculate how many towns, supplies, and rail lines were being snatched by Sherman's men. For their part, Hood's men enjoyed tearing up Georgia's railroads. Foster said the troops "are just making a frolic of it." Though skeptical of the campaign at its start, Foster was beginning "to think that Jeff Davis and Hood made a ten strike, when they plan[n]ed this thing. It beats fighting." He was convinced that they had torn enough railroad to sever Sherman's supplies. "Their only chance now to live," he conjectured about the Union army, "is to disband and scatter over the country, and make their way back north as best they can."[85]

In November, when the Rebel army met and repelled advance components of Thomas's force, Confederates misperceived that they were overpowering their foes. Nugent told his wife, "Hood is pushing Thomas who is calling vainly for reinforcements. The prospects are we will soon have Nashville and that the Yankees will be driven into Kentucky, and possibly beyond." As the Rebels headed toward Nashville, Hood made a promise he would soon break. Regimental commanders called their men out and told them that Hood would not *"risk a chance for a defeat in Tenn. That he will not fight in Tenn. unless he has an equal number of men and choice of the ground."* Foster thought, "This was very nice talk, for we all felt confident that we could always whip an equal number of men with the choice of the ground."[86]

Thomas was pulling back, but his army was winding up for a knockout punch, not retreating. On November 30, the Confederates found General John Schofield's troops at Franklin, Tennessee. These Federals had evaded Hood's army at Spring Hill on the previous day and would have been across the Harpeth River and on their way to Nashville, but the bridge needed repairs. While wagons creaked across makeshift spans, thirty-four thousand Bluecoats and more than sixty artillery pieces rimmed the town. Schofield thought the sight of so many defenders entrenched before a two-mile level plain would halt the Rebels and buy time to complete the crossing. He was wrong. Despite having only twenty-two thousand troops within reach of the Union position and only eight cannon, Hood ordered a frontal assault.[87] What followed was carnage worse than Grant's debacle at Cold Harbor. One scholar describes the Battle of Franklin as "the grisliest features of Pickett's Charge and Spotsylvania's Bloody Angle" combined. More than twenty thousand men marched across an unobstructed field of fire; seven thousand of them fell as casualties, including twelve generals. The Confederates also lost fifty-four regimental commanders, half of their total. Schofield lost only a third of the casualties he inflicted on the Rebels and departed during the night for Nashville. The Army of Tennessee had smashed itself beyond recognition.[88]

Even after a defeat as devastating as this one, some diehards claimed victory. Because Schofield's army had left its position during the night, Hood's men controlled the field of battle and thus technically gained a tactical win. Moreover, as on so many previous battlegrounds, the Rebels miscalculated casualty figures and discounted their significance when the toll ran against the Confederates. Vann's account of the battle was typical: "They were well fortified and we had to charge their works, so we put out through shot and shell, driving them from three lines of breastworks, though many of our gallant men fell on the field. . . . They were lying heaped up all over the battleground. Such a slaughter never was seen before on either side. I counted 30 dead Yanks in a space of ground not larger than a common dwelling house. We lost as many killed as the Yanks but we gained a complete victory, driving them to Nashville." Orr offered a similar account of Franklin: "We have had another big battle in which we whiped the enemy, tho with a grate slaughter on our side. Our loss in killed and wounded was much grater than that of the enemy. Our brigade lossed 400 killed and wounded. . . . We completely surprised them and drove them to Nashville. . . . Our brigade only numbers twenty five men." Orr's description of the battle was filled with inconsistent information: they had whipped the enemy but were slaughtered; they had driven the Federals from the field despite the fact that the Confederate brigade numbered only twenty-five.[89]

Did Rebels like Vann and Orr really consider Franklin a "complete victory"? Comparing Confederate letters and diary entries written after Franklin suggests they did not. Throughout the war, diehards' correspondence and journals bore striking similarities, a fact that implies they believed what they wrote and did not embellish accounts for people back home. Franklin was an exception. Vann and Orr sent letters that protected their army's honor and reassured loved ones that all was well. Perhaps they were trying to counterbalance the grizzly reports of Franklin that were sure to spread through the press and informal grapevines. Another letter about the battle demonstrates that soldiers' correspondence could be public expressions of patriotism meant to motivate rather than inform. Bunting and his cavalry unit missed Franklin, but he did not hesitate to call the battle "our great victory" in an open letter he sent to the editor of the *Houston (Texas) Tri-Weekly Telegraph*. Bunting's description of an engagement he did not witness exudes rhetoric: "Stimulated by the charm of the talismanic words that rang in clarion tones from their well tried leaders and with the prayer on their lips, that the God of battles would nerve their strong right arms to cleave the foe to death, those patriots rushed triumphing to the conflict." Pages of similar material "reported" how Texans were fairing in a distant campaign. The chaplain even told his readers that "our next news will doubtless be that Nashville is in our possession." The newspaper printed Bunting's entire letter.[90]

Unlike correspondence, diary entries from Franklin described the battle's true devastation. These more candid reports were written when Hood's army stopped to bury its dead. Counting only one hundred Union wounded, surgeon Henry McCall Holmes assumed that Schofield had "carried off" most of his casualties. But the doctor confessed in his diary that "our loss [was] very heavy." Local citizens passed on disheartening news from the Federals: the enemy "had no idea we would attack, they intended leaving midnight anyhow." Such reports undermined Confederate boasts that they had controlled the field of battle. Holmes began to realize the futility of Franklin. In his diary, Foster called the battle a catastrophe. As burial parties did their grim work, he observed, "some officers have no men, and some companies no officers. . . . Gen.

Hood has betrayed us." Foster considered Hood's order to assault "cold blooded Murder." While others misrepresented the battle in letters, sobered and angry troops like Holmes and Foster knew that the army's frolic through the country-side was over.[91]

Other Confederates, including Hood, still dreamed of a triumphant finale to the campaign. The Army of Tennessee marched toward Nashville. After be-ing pummeled by Schofield's thirty-four thousand troops, the Confederates fol-lowed their opponents to the city, where Thomas had another thirty thousand men behind defenses as formidable as those at Richmond and Washington, D.C. Upon reaching the outskirts of the Tennessee capital, even Hood knew that his twenty-five thousand soldiers could not take such a position guarded by a force more than twice the size of the Confederates. Instead of pulling away to recu-perate or crossing the Cumberland River in an attempt to outflank the superior Union army, Hood entrenched his men within sight of the Federal works and waited for an attack. The Confederate line covered only four of the eight roads that radiated south of the city.[92] On December 15, as a curtain of fog lifted over the scene, fifty thousand Union men rushed down the four unguarded turnpikes and into Hood's right and left flanks. The Rebels withstood massive assaults until darkness halted the fight and then retreated to a stronger, more compact position that covered only two of the eight routes heading south. The next day, Hood's depleted ranks repulsed powerful blows for hours but finally crumpled and fled in chaos. "Such a stampede you never heard of," Orr wrote to his brother. "Men threw away there guns and evry fellow for his self. The officers tried to rally ther men several different times but could not do any thing with them." According to Eggleston, "The infantry ran like cowards and the miserable wretches who were to have supported us refused to fight and ran like a herd of stampeded cattle." The sight was too much for the veteran: "I blush for my countrymen and despair of the independence of the Confederacy" if it relies on "the army of Tennessee to accomplish it."[93]

In two days outside Nashville, the Federals completed the annihilation they had started at Franklin. Thomas inflicted six thousand casualties on the Rebels, including the capture of more than four thousand prisoners, while suffering three thousand losses. He also netted fifty-three artillery pieces, the highest number claimed in a contest by either side during the war. Contemporary Con-federate accounts of the rout at Nashville are rare because the men spent two weeks running for their lives. The rearguard action of Nathan Bedford Forrest's cavalry and luck saved thousands of Rebels from being captured during Christ-mas of 1864. When the remains of Hood's army regrouped at Tupelo, Missis-sippi, at the beginning of 1865, they numbered only half of the forty thousand who had entered Tennessee seven weeks earlier. Hood resigned on January 13.[94]

꧁꧂ ꧁꧂ ꧁꧂

In victory and defeat, skewed perceptions and misjudgments of their immediate circumstances influenced how soldiers comprehended their ordeal. Campaigns had a way of keeping men focused on the present. Troops seldom gazed back to reevaluate the preceding week's engagements because current dangers seemed more pressing. If they looked at all beyond the immediate conflict, soldiers preferred to look forward to prospects for peace and victory rather than backward. With a mixture of bewilderment and respect for Rebel tenacity, Schofield related an experience that exhibited Confederates' distorted perspectives. As waves of Union troops overwhelmed Hood's ranks at Nashville on December 16, Schofield talked to a captured Rebel field officer. Their conversation still perplexed and fascinated the general thirty-two years later. Schofield asked the officer when his men had realized they were beaten and received the answer, "Not till you routed us just now." Schofield at first doubted the response. The Confederates had surely known weeks earlier, at Franklin, that they were finished. But when he reflected on the prisoner's answer, Schofield thought that "he probably told me the exact truth. I doubt if any soldiers in the world ever needed so much cumulative evidence to convince them that they were beaten."[95] By trusting their comrades and generals, miscalculating casualties, claiming victory in defeat, and otherwise magnifying their chances for success, thousands of Confederates convinced themselves in 1864 that the war remained winnable.

In those days Rumor took an evil joy
at filling countrysides with whispers, whispers
gossip of what was done, and never done.
—Virgil, *The Aeneid*

Four

Gray Grapevines

Rumors and the Distant War

Virgil depicted rumor as a "monstrous deformed, titanic" beast. At night the menace never slept but flew over restless populations, shrieking its news. By day rumor perched itself on rooftops and towers, collecting gossip, "bringing great cities fear, harping on lies / and slander evenhandedly with truth." Virgil stressed that rumors altered perceptions of reality. Like a malicious trickster, rumors obscured and spoiled people's search for critical facts. Rumors told stories "of what was done, and never done," and the most potent stories not only inhabited but also changed a milieu.[1] A Confederate soldier offered a different metaphor for rumors. In his view, gossip was a "'grape vine telegraph,' a machine that can be worked by any one" with great effect. According to the soldier, rumors were not external demons that plagued people; rather, men used hearsay to transmit their hopes and fears. Moreover, gossip could "be worked by any one," from the lowest private to General Robert E. Lee. For common soldiers, the grapevine offered an empowering channel of expression wherein "the most ridiculous rumor will be operated as a fact after going a few yards." Unlike Virgil, the Rebel emphasized that gossip reflected perceptions of reality. Rumors promised to unveil circumstances clouded by distance, military secrecy, and general uncertainty. Soldiers used gossip to fill a void. Taken together, these descriptions illustrate the complicated nature of rumors: they are uncontrollable monsters and the products of men; they both affect and reflect reality.[2]

Though rumors peppered Civil War diaries, correspondence, telegrams, newspapers, and even military orders, few historians have closely examined wartime gossip. This neglect is understandable because rumors challenge historians in unique ways. By reflex scholars consign false rumors to the detritus of time and read true ones as news. This separation of fact from fiction lies at the heart of history's search for a verifiable past and a narrative that explains it. But rumors mock our hunt for a fixed historical context and a coherent, complete story. As Ann Stoler explains, they point to a "fractured social reality" in which distinctions between fact and fiction are problematic and knowledge is fragmented and contested. This "epistemic murk," as Michael Taussig calls it, thwarts our attempts to spin a tidy chronological tale out of a tangled past. Another problem also arises. Rumors, by their nature, complicate (and often elude) historians' search for causation. Tracing the roots and effects of current rumors is difficult enough; uncovering the origins and impact of 140-year-old rumors is far more complex. Without a clear line of causation, gossip blurs agents and subjects, actions and reactions. Some Civil War scholars mention rumors, but perhaps for these reasons, no author focuses on the slippery subject. What did Civil War rumors mean to the soldiers who spread them? What can rumormongering tell us about these men and about the universe of war where pieces of gossip flashed and faded like shooting stars?[3]

Most rumors, even those spread in the final months of the war, bolstered Rebel hopes for ultimate victory. Given the poor conditions inside the Confederacy at that time, troops might be expected to have spread dreadful rumors about class divisions, military defeats, financial woes, and the disintegration of slavery. Instead, during the nadir of Confederate morale, diehards intoxicated each other with gossip of improbable victories, northern disasters, and foreign intervention. The distant war—that vast, diffuse conflict that touched remote campaigns, northern politics, Atlantic commerce, and European embassies— encouraged brighter assessments of Confederate odds. Some soldiers even persuaded themselves that independence could be won elsewhere if they persisted on their front and avoided major disaster. In short, soldiers who sought good news to validate death and suffering often found it in the press and in camp gossip that put a positive spin on unsubstantiated reports.

This chapter is divided into two parts. The first section explores how hearsay shaped perceptions of the distant war, searching for patterns in Rebel gossip about military theaters, the North, and overseas. The embellished battlefield reports from chapter 3 reappear here in abbreviated form because they served a second purpose. In addition to heartening the troops who fought those campaigns, these local exaggerations sparked widespread rumors that affected how remote Rebels perceived the military situation. This section stresses that Confederates did not fight in a vacuum; reports from everywhere, whether true or false, informed their war. The second part of this chapter explains why rumors were prevalent and positive. Civil War rumors were stories that reflected and subtly changed a military and cultural milieu. Here the thrill of the hunt is not finding the first Rebel to whisper a rumor but rather collecting and studying the diverse groups and factors that encouraged the phenomenon. Finally, this second part considers why Confederate rumors avoided despair and hysteria when the rebellion lost successive battles and waned.[4]

ᏀᎭᎭᏅ ᏀᎭᎭᏅ ᏀᎭᎭᏅ

Some historians are quick to couple Gettysburg and Vicksburg as twin disasters, but contemporaries treated the events quite differently. Troops across the South expected glorious results from Lee's Pennsylvania campaign, and early rumors seemed to confirm these hopes. One telegraph correspondent followed Lee's army during the campaign, and his first reports declared Gettysburg a victory. As the Confederate wire services buzzed with optimism, southern newspapers used these inaccuracies to build stories. For weeks after Gettysburg, Confederate newspapers heralded the battle as a stunning Rebel victory. On July 13, the *Richmond Dispatch* called Gettysburg "an overwhelming victory." For weeks, estimates of enemy casualties soared, and Confederates speculated that Lee might take Washington or Baltimore. Some of this misinformation can be attributed to wishful thinking. For many Rebels, triumph in Pennsylvania was a self-fulfilling prophecy. Partisans failed to question the validity of reports that supported their expectations. They could not conceive that Lee's "invincibles" could be defeated in a major battle. As noted in the previous chapter, soldiers who fought at Gettysburg spun the battle as anything but a defeat. Their accounts spread to distant corners of the Confederacy, substantiating the telegrams and newspapers.[5]

Assessments of Gettysburg may have been positive in part because Rebels needed good news after the fall of Vicksburg. Confederates seldom viewed campaigns in isolation. Instead, they imagined how events in one piece of the war influenced other theaters, the home front, and abroad. Because diehard Rebels had convinced themselves that they would win the war, they sought positive reports to counter the significance of negative news. Maintaining this reality required victories, and, not surprisingly, waves of wish rumors washed across the Confederacy after major defeats. In July 1863, rosy reports from the eastern theater countered gloomy news from the West. Sergeant Edwin Fay of Arkansas illustrated this tendency in a letter to his wife. "As an offset" to Vicksburg, Fay shared reports of "the total discomfiture of the Yankee Army in Maryland." According to rumors, an engagement just outside Baltimore had killed four Union generals and severely wounded General George Meade, "the successor of [Joseph] Hooker in command of the largest army on the Planet." Fay predicted, "Washington will doubtless be captured," and "a compromise of some kind will be effected which may result in Peace." He admitted this was a "faint hope" after Vicksburg, "but drowning men will catch at straws you know." Viewing the war from Arkansas, Fay knew that Vicksburg's fall was a critical blow, but he dreamed that a brilliant triumph in the East—for example, the capture of Washington—might spin the wheel of fortune in the Confederates' favor. This cycle of good-bad-good news, some of it real and some imagined, clouded the final years of the war. Whenever a major defeat crippled the rebellion, wish rumors raced across the region, confounding people with "gossip of what was done and never done."[6]

Word of the fall of Vicksburg radiated from the city. Troops nearest the Rebel Gibraltar first learned its fate. Days after the surrender, soldiers in Mississippi and Tennessee tried to make sense of the news. The surrender clashed with months of positive reports from the city. Throughout the siege, telegraph operators and newspaper editors had spread stories of stubborn defenders and enormous enemy casualties. Now the wires were silent. Troops at Chattanooga heard a rumor of Vicksburg's fall three nights after the event. An Alabama lieutenant hoped it was not true because "if it is we are badly crippled." Across the Mississippi in Arkansas, Fay weighed the impact of Vicksburg on July 10. He heard that the number surrendered was 17,500; in reality, more than 29,000 officers and men had capitulated. Though Fay thought "it is almost impossible to tell the consequences" of the news, he assumed the worst. Like dominos, "Mobile, Selma, Montgomery, Atlanta, Augusta, Charleston" would fall. In the aftershock of the event, Fay had "little hope of the future." Far off in Maryland, Lee's army heard rumors of Vicksburg's fate on the evening of July 12. Recent newspapers were scarce; some troops lacked papers newer than July 2. Skirmish lines were quiet that night, but Lee's camp buzzed with rumors and counterrumors. A Georgian noted, "First we have a rumor that [Joseph E.] Johnston has driven [Ulysses S.] Grant off. Then, that the place has fallen." He did not trust either report. After receiving "various reports & contradictions," troops in the Army of Northern Virginia conceded the fall of Vicksburg after they crossed the Potomac on July 13.[7]

When the facts could no longer be denied, distant soldiers mourned the loss of the stronghold. Morale plummeted across the South. Men who had maintained confidence in the cause through years of trouble now doubted their nation's survival. Desertion reached epidemic proportions. In August, Corporal A. P. Adamson counted sixty-six men in his company absent without leave.[8] Confederate President Jefferson Davis offered amnesty to deserters who returned to duty within twenty days. In a proclamation to the soldiers, Davis claimed, "Your enemies continue a struggle in which our final triumph must be inevitable." But Confederate spirits were shaken after Vicksburg, and Davis confirmed this fact by devoting much of his speech to dire warnings of defeat. He alerted the soldiers that their enemy "aims at nothing less than the extermination of yourselves, your wives, and children." While Davis warned soldiers that their only alternatives were "victory or subjugation," he promised that "victory is in your reach. You need but stretch forth your hands to grasp it."[9]

Davis's speech boosted morale, but many troops had already begun to recover. This swift upturn seems odd until we examine how soldiers interpreted the bad news. Much of the Confederate grief in the summer of 1863 did not derive from a fear that the war was lost. Instead, many men lamented that set-backs prolonged the conflict. During the preceding winter and spring, soldiers had hoped to win independence with the coming campaigns. As in previous winter quarters, troops yearned to meet the enemy, finish the job, and go home. Vicksburg crushed their dreams of an early peace. As one Rebel explained, "Be-fore receiving news of the sad misfortune I began to imagine that the dawn of peace had already commenced . . . but now a dark pall is thrown over the scene." Joshua Callaway agreed: "We were all cheerful and in good spirits till its fall. Now we are sad and depressed." He grumbled, "The War will last for the next 50 years," making Callaway "almost sick at the thought of the blood, treasure and long war it is going to take before we establish our independence." After Vicks-burg, Fay assumed that the war would continue "till [Abraham] Lincoln & Co. are dispossessed of their office." But Fay remained certain that "we will come out in the end victorious." Within weeks of the disaster, these Rebels shared a more positive mind-set. In their view, losing the Mississippi River merely postponed Confederate independence.[10] As Davis had noted in his speech, setbacks were "temporary reverses." Diehards still believed that their nation was unconquer-able. Georgian Edgeworth Bird insisted, "They *can never* conquer us." Reuben Pierson agreed: "Adverse fortune may for awhile darken our prospects but in the end we will come out conquerors." Army surgeon Spencer Welch reasoned, "Countries have been overrun, and then not conquered."[11]

Confederates also overcame the turning points of 1863 by spreading rumors. For the rest of the summer, streams of optimistic gossip countered the defeats of July, thereby softening their significance and obscuring the course of the war. Word of the New York City draft riots spread throughout the South. The image of Yankees killing each other in the streets elated the Rebels. For Marion Fitz-patrick, the riots were a "bright ray in these dark times." Rumors claimed that the mayhem had spread to Connecticut and New Jersey. Fitzpatrick confessed, "If the Yankees will fight among themselves and let us alone it will please me the best in the world." Other hearsay came from the trans-Mississippi. Lee's army in Virginia received erroneous press reports that General Sterling Price had whipped the enemy in Arkansas, capturing four regiments. The Memphis press convinced Mississippian William Nugent that the Confederacy "will have an ironclad Navy afloat very soon." According to the paper, "The Yankees are ter-ribly alarmed on the subject." Nugent imagined that such a fleet could turn the tables on the enemy and nullify the capture of Vicksburg. Dreaming of "a block-ade of Northern ports and the bombardment of New York & Boston," Nugent hoped "to hear of it" in the press. Others countered Vicksburg's loss with gossip that Confederates had recaptured New Orleans. People from surrendered cities often compensated for their failures by spreading word of the enemy's defeat at other critical points on the river. Citizens from Vicksburg swore that enemy forces admitted "the surrender of New Orleans to a Confederate Fleet and land forces under Gen'l [Richard] Taylor." Fay heard similar reports "from scouts in the vicinity of Port Hudson." [12]

These bogus reports filled the air with good news until more valid reasons for optimism arrived in late September. General Braxton Bragg's victory at Chicka-mauga confirmed Rebel hopes that all was well after Gettysburg and Vicksburg. The earliest news from the battle inflated the enemy's losses to spectacular pro-portions. In Virginia, Sam Pickens heard that Confederates had grabbed seventy cannons and threatened to capture the entire Union army. Fay heard similar ru-mors in Mississippi. Word spread that Bragg had pushed the enemy for eleven miles, taking fifty pieces of artillery on one day and twenty-five the next. Waiting for final word from the battle, Fay and his comrades expected the enemy to be "driven into the Tenn. River." Days later, more accurate reports corrected exag-gerations, but the facts still pointed to an important Rebel victory. "Making all due allowances," Nugent declared, "We have gained a signal victory and have convinced the Yankees that there is life in the 'Old hulk' yet." Chickamauga meant that Rebel armies remained equal to the task. Peace with independence might not be far off after all. [13] Confederates speculated that Chickamauga would improve the war's course. Nugent admitted, "Conjecture leads the way to a thou-sand distant prospects, and I find myself indulging again the hopes . . . that we will have peace on the reassembling of the Lincoln Congress." He knew that "it was no use . . . to conjecture as to the future," but the Mississippian could not help doing so. Fitzpatrick hoped that Bragg's achievements would keep the enemy out of Georgia, Fitzpatrick's home state. Fay shared Nugent's hope that "Bragg's victory will carry the elections in the N.W. states and that I think will be one of the preliminaries of peace." Pickens heard the best rumor of all. Gossip from Richmond claimed that Chickamauga had convinced Europe to recognize the Confederacy. In Virginia, ecstatic troops spread hearsay that plans were in place for recognition in thirty days and peace in ninety. [14]

During the following spring, when the armies resumed active campaigning, rumors of military success multiplied. "As the landscape changed from brown to green," Stephen Crane explained, "the army awakened, and began to trem-ble with eagerness at the noise of rumors." In 1864 Confederates looked to General Lee for hope and victory. Gary Gallagher claims that Rebels' trust in Lee and his ranks was "the single greatest factor engendering Confederate hope after the midpoint of the war." [15] Troops near and far claimed victories whenever the Army of Northern Virginia fought. Not surprisingly, inflated re-ports from the Wilderness, Spotsylvania Court House, and Cold Harbor coursed through the Confederate grapevine. Other, more bizarre rumors demonstrate the depths of Rebel hopes for the Virginia theater. Though Grant's enormous army was pinning Lee's defenders within earshot of the capital, South Car-olinian David Crawford spread rumors that Grant was losing control of his men. Crawford told his mother that the enemy "is pretty well demoralized, it was reported that they were fighting themselves." Rumor had it that Union soldiers were "liquored to fight" and issued bogus reports to boost their flagging confidence. Crawford heard from Yankee prisoners that Grant had falsely reported the capture of Richmond and Petersburg. Other rumors spread that Grant had promised to dine in Richmond on particular dates. When the appointed dates passed, Lee's soldiers relished such stories as proof that the enemy would never take the capital. In one account, the general sent word to Lee that "he expected to dine in the city" on June 18. Lee replied that Grant "would sup in h——ll." Weeks later, the story was that Grant "intended to take his 4th of July dinner in Richmond." Cavalryman James Blackman Ligon declared, "If he gets even a *lunch* in Petersburg it will surprise me." These stories spread across the South to other armies and the home front, colorfully confirming Richmond's safety.[16]

In July an even better rumor captivated Confederates: Grant was dead. A Texas cavalryman serving in Louisiana shared the report with his father. The soldier had heard the rumor from a friend who claimed that a captain saw an official dispatch from General Lee reporting that "Grant made desperate assaults upon Richmond and was defeated and tis said led the last one himself and was killed." The Texan thought the story had merit because it "accords with the report of a woman from Vicksburg that the flag was at half mast on account of the death of Grant." Even better, the story was "corroborated" by a lieutenant colonel who left Richmond shortly before the attacks. According to the Texan, the colonel reported that "Grant's army was completely routed and that ours was in pursuit." The cavalryman thought this "glorious news" but admitted, "it seems too good to believe."[17] Grant's death was reported again later that month. This time, he was watching Union shells explode over Petersburg when a shot from a Rebel cannon tore off his arm, causing him to bleed to death on the surgeon's table later that day, July 17, 1864. Virginia artilleryman James Albright joked, "Grant is *still* dead; but, comes to life occasionally." Despite the wisecrack, Albright was unsure of the truth. For days he could neither confirm nor deny the report, and its elusiveness and optimism teased him. He started to view other information as clues about Grant's fate: Albright thought that the slackening of the Federal bombardment might mean that the enemy had a new commander.[18]

Rumors of Grant's death reveal the tone and transmission of Confederate gossip. At first glance, such rumors aspired to nothing higher than news—they acquired significance by promising timely, critical information during uncertain moments. "Yet on second look," according to a classic study of wartime rumors, "the type of discourse represented in . . . rumors often has a hidden mode of signification" that judges rather than informs. In short, rumors of Grant's death were more than bogus news, they were stories. As Walter Benjamin explains, "The value of information does not survive the moment in which it was new. . . . A story is different. It does not expend itself. It preserves and concentrates its strength and is capable of releasing it even after a long time."[19] The rumor was more than bogus news: it was a story forecasting the end of the campaign. If the eastern front was an elaborate game between Grant and Lee and the former was dead, the Confederates would win the struggle for Richmond. Diehards speculated that Grant's replacement would retreat to Washington and regroup, as so many of Lee's opponents had done in the past. In July 1864, such gossip promised a beautiful release from a tense stalemate of trench warfare under the summer sun. No wonder the rumor spread like wildfire through Lee's trenches.

Confederates also transmitted the rumor of Grant's death because it offered them vengeance. Quests for retribution motivated many Rebels through the war's final period. James McPherson argues that revenge "became almost an obsession with some Confederates."[20] As noted in chapter 2, the shelling of Petersburg galled Lee's men because they lacked the strength to silence the barrage and suffered to watch it. Seeing Union shells fly over their lines and pummel the town, Rebels cursed the enemy for preferring to fire on civilians.[21] Confederates who blamed Grant for this atrocious mode of fighting delighted in spreading the rumor that he died precisely because of his barbarity: a Rebel shell had supposedly struck Grant while he was entertaining himself watching the effect of Federal artillery on the helpless city. A Confederate sergeant admitted, "It is a good story & looks like retribution—hope it is true." Good stories, like this one, stand alone and often contain morals. The rumor was a parable for chivalrous warfare, reinforcing Rebel notions that such despicable enemies could never defeat gentlemen of the South led by Robert E. Lee. Fate would not allow such an unjust outcome.[22]

Word of Confederate victories in Virginia seemed to confirm these cultural assumptions. In Louisiana, Henry Orr relayed to his father the news that "success was still crowning our arms on every hand" and that Lee's troops were "jubilant." According to Orr, there was "no fear for the safety of Richmond." In Georgia, Henry Orr's brother, James, reported to their mother similar "cheering news from Virginia." A Texas cavalryman concurred: "Grant has been repulsed with terrible loss." Troops across the South received glowing reports from every battle Lee fought against Grant: the Wilderness, Spotsylvania, Cold Harbor, the Crater, and other assaults on Petersburg and Richmond. Whether accurate or not, news of heavy Federal casualties and confirmations of Richmond's safety buoyed Rebels' faith in Lee and his ultimate triumph.[23] From a distance, the Confederacy appeared to be winning the war in the East.

The aura that surrounded General Johnston could not match Lee's mystique, but Confederates expressed confidence that the little Virginian would beat General William T. Sherman. After Johnston's victory at Kennesaw Mountain, distant Rebels anticipated a swift and glorious end to the Atlanta campaign. Ligon predicted that Sherman would be forced back to Kentucky "if he does not surrender his whole army" first. In Petersburg, artillerymen were "looking daily for news that Johnston has defeated Sherman."[24] Johnston's constant retreating, however, frustrated Rebels who anticipated a stunning triumph outside Atlanta. Soldiers wanted front-page news from Georgia; they hungered for Sherman's annihilation and grew tired of Johnston's miniscule results and cautious tactics.

For these reasons, distant Rebels expected momentous news when General John Bell Hood replaced Johnston and fought major battles in late July. Remote Confederates celebrated Hood's battles as great victories. Southern newspapers printed extras to cover the event. One Richmond paper claimed, "Atlanta is now felt to be safe, and Georgia will soon be free from the foe. . . . Everything seems to have changed in that State from the deepest despondency." A War Department clerk exalted, "Sherman's army is *doomed*." John Trevillian told his sister how the news appeared at headquarters in Hanover County, Virginia: "Hood in Georgy captured 22 pieces of artillery 2 lines of brest works Killed a General & captured 4 more." He figured that Grant was silent on his front because "we gave old Sherman such a whipping." Henry Calvin Conner spoke for many comrades when he expressed a hope that "Hood will be able to exterminate Sherman before he quits him and recover the whole of northern Georgia from his poluting tred." A Virginia artilleryman hoped that the "glorious news from Atlanta" foreshadowed Confederate occupation of Tennessee and Kentucky.[25]

Inflated reports from Georgia, like exaggerations from Virginia, encouraged wildly optimistic and bogus rumors. Though no major engagement was fought in August, word spread across the South that Hood had thrashed Sherman. In Virginia, Captain W. R. Redding passed on the rumor that "Sherman has been routed from Atlanta." He was "proud to hear of Sherman's defeat" and hoped that Hood's army would "press him into Ohio before they stop." The same rumor reached Fay in Arkansas: "Hood has defeated Sherman & is at present driving him back towards Chattanooga." Rumors of victory when no battle had been fought further misled already misinformed troops. In the end, the Atlanta campaign was too shrouded in hearsay for distant Rebels to acquire an objective assessment of the theater—whether or not they sought an accurate picture.[26]

When Atlanta fell on September 1, 1864, diehard Rebels received the news slowly and doubted its validity. After expecting military triumph all summer, many Confederates could not believe the bad news. In Winchester, Virginia, on September 6, artilleryman Creed Thomas Davis read a Richmond paper that announced "big fights in the neighborhood of Atlanta Ga on the 1st & 3rd" but did not report Hood's evacuation. When Davis and his unit learned the news days later, it became the "topic of conversation" throughout the camp. Davis admitted, "The boys do not reconcile themselves to it so readily." After months of positive rumors, Rebels found it difficult, emotionally and cognitively, to accept that Atlanta was gone. Word reached the Trans-Mississippi Department much later. Separated from the rest of the nation by Union control of the Mississippi, troops in the western Confederacy were often most susceptible to false reports. On September 12, William Heartsill noted in his diary, "We have rumors this evening that Atlanta has fallen, don't believe a word of it." From his camp in Texas, Heartsill did not concede the loss of Atlanta until mid-October.[27]

After reports confirmed Sherman's victory, something remarkable happened: rumors spread that Hood had recaptured the city. A North Carolinian in Lee's trenches first heard of Atlanta's fall on September 3. Two days later, "a rumor was afloat that Atlanta had been retaken with thirty thousand prisoners and with a loss to us of ten thousand men." John Cotton's cavalry unit was in East Tennessee when he heard that Hood had recaptured the city in late September. In Virginia, Albright heard that Hood had acquired Atlanta in early October. Albright considered the news proof that "there is nothing to be discouraged at—all goes well as could be expected."[28] Rather than accept the consequences of losing the city, Confederates spread misinformation that upheld their views of the military situation for weeks.

When rumors of Hood retaking the city proved false, some Rebels sought any sign that Atlanta would be redeemed. John Walters thought General P. G. T. Beauregard's appointment as commander of the Department of the Southwest and General Nathan Bedford Forrest's recent successes meant the Union would have trouble holding the town. Welch was "anxious to hear something from General Hood, for if he can whip Sherman at Atlanta the situation may be entirely changed." He still believed "if Sherman is forced away from Atlanta and we can hold Richmond this winter . . . we shall have peace" with independence. Rebels stubbornly refused to accept the significance of Hood's defeat. In the Petersburg trenches, Major Thomas Elder conceded that Atlanta's fall "cast a shade of gloom over all" and reported that "the Yankees are greatly rejoicing over the event and predict a speedy end of the rebellion in Georgia." But Elder thought that the event was "mere stuff" that "will have its effect in putting off the day of peace" but would not change the war's outcome—Confederate victory. The idea that Atlanta's fate prolonged the war but did not doom the Confederacy echoed Rebels' response to the loss of Vicksburg: both events merely postponed inevitable glory.[29]

Rebel reactions to Atlanta's fall illustrate how positive rumors that preceded and followed bad news could soften the blow of a major defeat. Word from Atlanta followed the pattern of reporting that slanted news about Vicksburg. The first word from other battlefields and campaigns was often optimistic and exaggerated: Johnston had broken Grant's siege of Vicksburg; Hood had battered Sherman outside Atlanta. Soldiers who anticipated good news sometimes accepted these reports as facts. Then troops received a more accurate account that tempered or refuted early declarations of triumph. Finally, a second round of wish rumors followed the bad news. Hearsay claimed that New Orleans had been redeemed after the loss of Vicksburg. Likewise, gossip that Hood had retaken Atlanta and that Forrest had seized Nashville offset gloomy facts and sustained Rebel hopes. When combined, these waves of positive rumors and bad news obscured the war's course and clouded the finality and significance of dire events.

Rumors about Hood's march into Tennessee after the fall of Atlanta exemplify this cycle of good-bad-good news. The army's movement at first elicited optimistic reports. While on a steamboat on the Alabama River, Thomas Hampton heard in early December that "Hood is said to have whiped the enemy at Murphreysborough." Within weeks he received "cheering news from East Tenn I hope it is true it is reported that Breckenridge has taken Knoxville & Chata nuga[.] If so we will soon be all right in that quarter." From afar, Confederates initially celebrated the Battle of Franklin as a decisive Rebel victory. In Virginia, Conner waited for news that Sherman's army had been destroyed or captured in full. Instead, he read in a northern newspaper that Hood had suffered defeat at Franklin. The report did not faze Conner because "any one can see from thair dispatches that thay have gotten the worst of it and I hope Hood may be able to drive [General George] Thomas back and liberate all of our western states." Pickens shared Conner's view of "Yankee accounts." "Altho, they claim a victory they admit that they at dark retreated all night, not halting till within fortifications of Nashville." Given the facts, Pickens concluded that "the boot was on the other leg—the victory was ours."[30]

Such reasoning worked until the Army of Tennessee fled in panic from the battle of Nashville in mid-December. After receiving and accepting many positive accounts of Hood's campaign, Thomas Hampton at first did not believe news that the army was retreating. "I do not put any confidence in such a report," he scoffed. But cold facts accumulated over the next four days, and Hampton started to worry about the safety of comrades who had fought at Nashville. Even after the fall of Atlanta, Rebels expected triumphs from Hood and disasters for Sherman.[31] When the opposite became true, Confederates were cognitively and emotionally slow to accept the news. As with the fall of Atlanta, wish rumors countered the bad news from Nashville. In Louisiana within two weeks of the defeat, Hugh Montgomery spread a rumor that Hood had captured Nashville. On New Year's Day, while the remainder of Hood's force straggled out of Tennessee, Edward Crenshaw recorded hearsay that "Gen. Hood had turned on Gen. Thomas and defeated him. I hope it is true." As in the case of Atlanta, troops spread positive rumors shortly after the disaster in Tennessee in an attempt to ignore terrible implications. This cycle of good-bad-good news continued until the end of the war.[32]

The bewildering interplay between fact and fiction, distant events and innermost hopes, illustrates the deep contingency that marked a soldier's life. On one hand, events big and small, real and unreal, shaped the way that participants viewed the contest. On the other, people's hopes and beliefs gave magnitude and meaning to the plethora of war news. Together, events and individuals spun dense webs of experience more complex than any narrative can portray. A soldier's place and behavior within this muddle affected his perceptions and motives. This insight enhances current scholarship on Civil War soldiers. Since the mid-1990s, historians have explained Confederate troop determination late in the war by pointing to ideology, camaraderie, masculinity, vengeance, faith in General Lee, and the generational values of the last slave owners. All of these elements contributed to Rebel persistence, but none of these factors offered what rumors appeared to provide—tangible evidence that made continued resistance seem reasonable. Without concrete signs for hope, diehards seem fanatical, delusional, or stupid. For this reason, many scholars agree with Reid Mitchell's dismissal of diehard behavior as "insane Confederate optimism." Diehards may have been more devoted to the cause than other southerners, but they were also rational beings who with the help of rumors and other evidence perceived a war that was going better than the Yankees (and historians) claimed.[33]

In addition to the interplay of fact and fiction, a counterpoint between major and minor theaters further complicated soldiers' views of the war. Many Confederates inflated their nation's military condition by emphasizing victories in secondary campaigns. Throughout 1864, smaller Rebel armies, blockade-runners, and independent cavalry commands bested Union adversaries across the mammoth, distant war. Rumors of Forrest's victories spread stories about his exploits, increased his mystique, and seemed to confirm that Confederates were superior. Troops were slow to realize—or at least to admit—that these events, though dramatic, had little to no impact on the central contests in Virginia and Georgia. Instead, many soldiers assumed that a string of minor triumphs and heroic deeds acquired a strategic importance that outweighed their individual value. In Tennessee, Conner reasoned that triumphs in "other places will have a tendency to encourage our troops and also to discourage our enemies."[34] Rebels also surmised that Union setbacks in other parts of the Confederacy could compel Grant and Sherman to weaken their ranks by sending reinforcements. The trans-Mississippi in particular encouraged exaggerations and speculations. Rumors of minor success in that remote theater grew in stature the farther they traveled. At Mansfield, the Confederates inflicted about twenty-two hundred casualties, but word reached the Army of Tennessee that the enemy had lost fourteen thousand men at the engagement. Diehards had convinced themselves that they would win the war, and they treated minor victories as evidence to support that belief.[35]

Generals encouraged their troops' fascination with battles like Mansfield by drafting official statements that informed their men of distant victories. While his soldiers fought through the mud and horror of Spotsylvania Court House, Lee twice alerted his troops of recent success in the trans-Mississippi and the Shenandoah Valley. Walters noted the events in his diary: "Today a congratulatory order from General Lee was read to the troops regarding the successes of Kirby, Smith, and Price in the Trans-Mississippi Department, and Imboden,

James, and Morgan in the Valley." According to an Alabama soldier who heard Lee's congratulatory order, the general claimed to have "official information" of Frederick Steele's surrender to Price. Whether or not he intended to do so, Lee greatly increased the bogus rumor's credibility. The following day, "another order . . . from General Lee was read to the army regarding the victory of Breckenridge over Sigel in the Valley." Lee also officially congratulated Beauregard for his role in saving Richmond and Petersburg that May.[36]

Of all the secondary campaigns of 1864, General Jubal Early's invasion of Maryland captivated Rebels the most. In July 1864, while the main armies fought for Richmond, Petersburg, and Atlanta, Early led a detached corps of fifteen thousand men across the Potomac and marched toward Washington and Baltimore. On July 9, the veteran columns scattered a hastily assembled Union force outside Frederick, Maryland, and raced for the Federal capital. In two days they were five miles from the White House. Northern newspapers and Washington officials screamed for reinforcements because Grant had recently taken the city's garrison to replace his losses in Virginia. Only hospital patients, bureaucrats, and militiamen stood between Early's men and a dramatic reversal of fortunes. Across the sea, the *Times* of London concluded, "The Confederacy is more formidable than ever."[37]

Reading the panic in northern papers and hoping that this third invasion of the North would be the charm, Confederates enjoyed weeks of good rumors and fantastic predictions. Confederates spread a rumor that prophecy surrounded Early's invasion of the North. From a hospital near Petersburg, Theodore Honour told the popular story of a soothsayer, "the Dreamer who said that the 3rd invasion would not only be successful but that it would end the war." According to the prophet, "Lee would dictate terms of Peace on the soil of the enemy." Honour dreamed of the surrender ceremony, the moment when the Confederacy would become "an acknowledged nation by our hated enemies." Infantryman Paul Higginbotham read about Early's advance in copies of northern papers he received from enemy pickets. The news seemed too good to be true, but Higginbotham believed the Yankees' reports of their own misfortunes. The Virginian shared reports that "Grant has certainly sent a Corps to Washington." He suspected that Early had forty thousand men, because the general "would certainly not go into enemy country so far unless he had a pretty strong force." Newspapers claimed that the governors of Maryland and Pennsylvania had called out the militia but men had refused to come. Confederate leadership had exposed the North's soft underbelly. Excited by the prospect of another invasion, Higginbotham told his brother that "a Rumor is flying around this evening, that we will leave here soon[.]I shall not be at all surprised if our entire Army is not on the road to Maryland ere long." The private seemed to think that no one would stay behind to guard Richmond; Lee would once again take the war to the enemy's homeland.[38]

Troops debated whether Baltimore or Washington would fall first. Creed Thomas Davis read that Early was "in the vicinity of Baltimore." Three days later, South Carolinian Thomas Moore spread the rumor that Early had captured Baltimore. "We are highly elated at the news," he said, admitting that the report remained unconfirmed. Giles Buckner Cooke heard from an officer "the glorious news" that Early was within three miles of Washington. On July 17 James Brannock wrote home that "at last accounts our forces had surrounded Washington & were shelling the city. Every body here seems impressed with the idea that we will soon have peace." James Orr believed a Confederate newspaper that placed the invaders both three miles from Baltimore *and* five miles from Washington. The paper also claimed that a Rebel detachment had liberated all the prisoners at Point Lookout, Maryland. Rumors about the men at Point Lookout had been swirling since the beginning of Early's campaign. When Albright heard the rumor, he speculated that if the freed prisoners "can join Early, what a *stew* Washington will be in." He figured that the escapees numbered "at least 12,000" and that "this will be a powerful reinforcement" for Early. Surveying the situation from Atlanta, Urban Owen thought "our prospects of final success were never more flattering than at present."[39] Unfortunately for the Rebels, Early's campaign ended in ignominy rather than victory. Grant sent the battle-hardened Sixth Corps in time to rescue Washington, and when other Federal troops closed on Early's army, the general prudently headed south.[40]

Though many Rebels applauded Early's raid out of vengeance, they also hoped that the terrors of war would convince northerners to advocate peace at any cost. Popular perceptions of the enemy as corrupt, moneygrubbing, ethnically inferior, and politically divided encouraged Rebels to expect ultimate victory through a northern collapse.[41] Confederates thought the war could be won in countless ways: a decisive victory, a series of stalemates, foreign intervention, a collapse on Wall Street, secession of the West, and a northern peace movement were all popular means to independence. The most likely possibility in 1864 centered on the presidential election. If Union armies failed in the spring and summer, war-weary northerners might elect a peace candidate and let the Confederacy go. With this in mind, Rebels eager for peace and independence scanned northern newspapers for war weariness, interrogated Union deserters and prisoners, and collected rumors that substantiated imminent triumph. Confederate gossip about northern disaffection and foreign aid illustrates the breadth of the Rebel conception of the war: southerners grasped the size of the contest and sought signs of hope in countless contingencies.

Confederates used Union information when it substantiated their faith in a burgeoning northern peace movement. Throughout the 1864 campaign, northern editors who opposed Lincoln and his party bolstered Confederate morale as much as or even more than the southern press did. As early as January 1864, Fay conjectured, "We may be able to hold out Twelve months longer but I don't think the Yanks can with the pressure on them. The Presidential Campaign is already beginning to open in their papers." A comment from the *New York Sunday Mercury* concerning the election exemplifies what Rebels highlighted in the enemy press: "It is not to be disguised that the wisest men at Washington, as well as throughout the country, look with fear and dread upon the issues of the coming Presidential canvass. The temper of the people is so excited, the issues so vital, the disturbances—civil, social, and political—created by the war are so profound, that it is feared an excited Presidential canvass will plunge the nation into chaos." Both the *Richmond Sentinel* and the *Augusta Constitutionalist* reprinted this excerpt in April 1864. Confederates accepted such reports as facts, not as the editorial comments they were. In July, James Orr told his mother, "Tis thought by a great many that the war wont last longer as the people of the north and the Northern Congress is getting badly split up. We get Northern papers from the Yankey pickets tolerable regular. . . . Their papers also state that the Northern people are getting tired of the war and all want peace." South Carolinian John McLure agreed: "The northern press carries some cheering symptoms of a returning sense of reason." He told his wife that "everybody here . . . seems to think that a cessation of hostility is really close at hand." When McLure interrogated some Federal prisoners, they told him that "it was too near the end of the war to be killed now." It encouraged the South Carolinian that "so many gave up with so little resistance." Perhaps the enemy's war effort would unravel before the November election.[42]

Hopes that a peace movement would cripple their foes encouraged many Confederates to exaggerate northern internal strife and spread bizarre rumors on the subject. Northern despondency was real in 1864, but Confederates anticipated northern disintegration, secession, and treason. Army surgeon Junius Bragg passed on the story that "Wisconsin Troops will return home as soon as the spring opens, for the purpose of carrying on a partisan war in their own state." The report bolstered Bragg's "abiding faith in our ultimate success." Higginbotham centered his expectations on Ohio, writing to his brother that "some fellow from Ohio is in favor of a Western Confederacy, & a breaking off from the New England States." Higginbotham then related the fact that "the 63rd Ohio Regt., was on picket yesterday, and said that if their officers made them charge our works they intended to surrender, and asked us not to fire on them." He affirmed, "I think now as I always have done, that we will yet gain our Independence, and I firmly believe the time is near at hand." A Virginia artilleryman spread the rumor that the governor of New York had called out the militia to resist Federal conscription. Confederates expected a bloodier revolt than New York City's draft riot of the previous summer, which had claimed a thousand dead and wounded. From Mobile, a Rebel spread the rumor that "a good many of the Yankee prisoners whose term of service is out are taking the oath and joining our side because Lincoln will not exchange for them."[43] These rumors of Union morale depicted more than despondency: they portrayed treason and mutiny at the heart of the enemy's war effort.

As the election approached, talk of financial disasters, peace movements, and Federal divisiveness intensified throughout the Confederacy. Rebels such as Nugent understood that "our main hope now is the disagreement existing among the political parties North." Troops across the South sought and swapped political rumors with an enthusiasm that matched their interest in distant battles. They read northern papers for shifts in public opinion, debated which candidate would best serve Confederate interests, and asked enemy pickets whom they favored. Some Rebels even saw the event as the Almighty's way of ending the war in the Confederates' favor. Fay explained, "God will work it all out for the best in some way I believe. I want to see the Yankee nation without a Govt. enjoying what they are so fond of, a state of Anarchy and confusion."[44]

After months of increasing hope, soldiers anticipated the results of the Democratic convention as if the nomination itself could settle the war. The final days of August were charged with the hopes of thousands. From Virginia, McLure observed, "All are looking with great anxiety to the action of the Chicago Convention, thinking it may foreshadow our future fate." He tried to guard against false hope because "we have been so frequently disappointed" but could not help praying that the Democrats and the North as a whole "may be for peace." A private in South Carolina wrote that "yesterday and today is big with interest to our country. Oh how earnestly do I pray that peace measures may prevail at the Chicago Convention." Elder thought that "there is some hope of peace now" because "the Yankee people seem greatly exercised about peace." Walters noted the "anxious speculation . . . among our troops as to the probable candidate." The next day, Creed Thomas Davis recorded, "The learned Howitzers are already discussing [the convention's] probable results on the war." Though Rebels' expectations were too high, men stuck in trenches nourished each other's dreams that something as faraway and bloodless as the presidential campaign could win the war for them and send them home.[45]

Then the fall of Atlanta boosted Lincoln's campaign and extinguished Confederate visions of a speedy peace. As discussed earlier in the chapter, diehards first denied the facts, then spread rumors of the city being retaken, and finally downplayed Atlanta's strategic importance. Rebels also performed somersaults of reasoning about the presidential campaign. They first favored a Democrat, but after Atlanta fell (and Democratic candidate George McClellan announced his war policy), Rebels convinced themselves that Lincoln's reelection would be better for them. In the wake of Atlanta, McLure trusted "that everything will work out right for us yet." "It may be," he reasoned, that the loss of Atlanta, "now regarded as such an unmitigated evil," might be a blessing in disguise. "It may prevent the election of McClellan whom we might [find a] much harder foe to deal with than Lincoln." Crawford concurred that both candidates would "prosecute the war and McClellan might do so with better judgement." A Mississippi officer suspected that McClellan would offer a reconstructed Constitution that would draw every Confederate state back into the Union except Virginia and South Carolina. He elaborated, "We were all very much depressed when we read McClellan's letter of acceptance. He comes out so decidedly for War that the question is gravely discussed whether Lincoln would not be preferable." The officer did not mention, let alone consider, the strength of Lincoln's war platform, even though a month earlier the same man had written that Lincoln's reelection would mean the war will "be continued to the bitter end regardless of loss or expense."[46]

When reasonable hopes for a Democratic victory and a negotiated peace disappeared, many Confederates predicted far-fetched scenarios that sustained their optimism. Some Rebels reasoned that Lincoln's reelection would induce more states to secede. Brannock favored Lincoln because "if Lincoln be elected it will probably be the cause of revolution in the North Western states & will end in securing our independence." The South Carolinian's prediction gained credibility weeks later when the U.S. judge advocate general, Joseph Holt, accused Copperheads of designing a "Northwest Confederacy" in the heartland. Holt's scandalous report claimed that peace Democrats sought midwestern secession and an alliance with the Rebels. Walters concurred that Lincoln's reelection might cause tidal waves of disunion: "There is a possibility of the Pacific States leaving the Old Union to form a Confederacy of their own, and in this case the Northwestern States will most probably cut loose from the Eastern States and this of itself would end the war." As these soldiers' writings illustrate, Confederates found hope throughout the presidential campaign. When the outcome went against their early hopes, they modified their predictions to sustain their faith.[47]

Foreign intervention comprised another scenario by which the Confederacy could gain independence without conquering its foe. In 1864, a Richmond minister claimed that negotiation with Europe "has become, with us, an exploded idea. *It may be employed*, but its repeated delusions have ceased to tempt the national expectation." He was wrong. Many Confederates still cherished the pipe dream. Rebels pointed out that the United States had won independence from Great Britain with French assistance: foreign armies and armadas (or at least the threat of them) might similarly compel the Union to accept Confederate independence.[48] Whenever Lord Palmerston, Napoleon III, or Confederate emissaries squeaked about European involvement, rumors of elaborate alliances electrified the South.

In March 1864, a wave of rumors flooded the Confederacy. General Lawrence Ross wrote home that a fellow officer had telegraphed him "to the effect that France has recognized the Confederacy." The next day, a captain wrote from Mississippi, "Startling rumors have reached us recently enlivening our hopes and brightening our prospects. It is said that France has recognized us, and Spain and Mexico & Austria." Tennessee artillerist Thomas Key even drafted an article that expounded "the expediency of making a commercial treaty with France and Spain, proposing to give them the exclusive transportation of cotton from the South if they would furnish the navy to open and keep unobstructed the Confederate ports." Key argued that "the colonies made similar concessions to France in 1776" and that the Confederacy was most wanting in naval power "to retake and possess the Mississippi River, and to open her harbors." In Tennessee, Conner considered the rumors so pervasive that he did not bother to include their details in a letter to his wife in South Carolina. An Atlanta newspaper claimed to have heard from another press that learned "from reliable parties, direct through the line from Chattanooga," that Federal commanders "consider war between France and the United States inevitable." According to the paper, a Union general from Ohio "was heard to say that unless the 'rebellion' could be crushed before the close of the ensuing spring campaign, the final success of the United States was extremely doubtful." With France's base of operation in Mexico, the Confederacy would win independence. The paper even announced that New Orleans was the French emperor's first target. In Virginia, Elias Davis heard the rumor from his colonel's brother, who was visiting camp. The man had been in the Trans-Mississippi Department and "he gave us a few items of news from Texas that have never found their way into papers." In particular, he thought that "nothing [was] more certain than a difficulty between France and United States." The visitor entertained the troops for thirty minutes with predictions about the course of the war and its eventual outcome, Confederate independence.[49]

Though persistent hope lay at the heart of most rumors, Confederate gossip from 1863 to 1865 also reveals a rising desperation. At first glance, rumors of military events, the Union home front, and European intervention spread concurrently. All three topics were popular among rumormongers from the summer of 1863 through the spring of 1865. But a close inspection of Confederate gossip reveals a broad pattern. Over time, Confederates looked for victory from sources that were farther from their reach. Before the fall of Atlanta, false reports of military victories seemed credible and thus spread from Virginia to Texas. Military gossip crescendoed in the summer of 1864, when Rebels inflicted ghastly casualties on Federal armies and threatened Washington. After Atlanta fell, rumors of battlefield triumphs dwindled. Confederates who remained committed to independence looked to other sources for optimism. During the summer and fall of 1864, the presidential campaign captivated many Rebel gossips. This period witnessed a profusion of news about northern secession, treason, and mutiny. If military victory seemed less likely over time, Confederates still clung to northern unrest as a way to independence. A soldier in Lee's trenches illustrated this shift. Like many others, James Bivings had thought the 1864 campaigns would win the war for the rebellion. But by June he admitted to his father, "Few seem now of the opinion that the two battles now pending East & West will end the war." Instead, the troops looked to see if the campaigns would "create a powerful peace party & candidate for the Presidency in the North." After Lincoln won his second term, Rebels increasingly talked about foreign intervention. By 1865, when military triumph and Union internal revolt seemed improbable if not impossible, Confederates focused on Europe, the last remaining source of victory. When the final embers of rebellion died out, faint and pitiful talk of world wars and international aid sparked and faded.[50]

All these rumors, whether true, exaggerated, or false, colored Rebel perceptions of the war. Positive news convinced thousands of soldiers that the war was winnable and that the next report from Lee, Johnston, Hood, Early, or the Yankee press could decide the struggle in the Confederacy's favor. As one Rebel explained, troops spread rumors of distant triumphs because they sought "not only immediate results, but the great all absorbing question of a speedy peace." The amount of attention troops gave to other campaigns, the North, and overseas may suggest, however, that the men doubted the chances for success in their own theaters. Men stuck in the trenches of Petersburg or routed out of Georgia imagined that distant armies, northern politics, and foreign affairs could decide the war in their favor. Such thoughts of the distant war charmed troops who sought an end to hardships, bolstered their morale, and thus extended a conflict that seemed far from lost.[51]

⁐⁐⁐ ⁐⁐⁐ ⁐⁐⁐

Understanding diehard Confederates requires considering why hearsay seemed credible to them. A rumor cannot travel far unless it seems possible to those who spread it. Before Atlanta fell, Rebel optimism was reasonable, and wish rumors of Confederate military triumph appeared plausible. Even by Civil War standards, Grant's Overland Campaign was a bloody mess. In seven weeks, the Army of the Potomac lost sixty-five thousand men, the equivalent of Lee's entire army. The carnival of death left Union men hesitant to charge Confederate defenses and more eager than ever for peace.[52] Before September, the presidential election was a wedge that threatened to divide the United States as severely as the 1860 contest had. In addition to heated differences between Democrats and Republicans, both parties split internally. Republicans argued over the war's prosecution and plans for reconstruction, while Democrats differed over continuing the war or pursuing compromise and peace. For months, Republican leaders sought another candidate. Lincoln's nomination in June did not resolve party discord, and during the trying summer months, Lincoln expected to lose the contest. No president had served a second term since Andrew Jackson, and many Americans opposed the principle of reelection, especially during wartime.[53]

Confederates substantiated their opinion of northern morale by following

U.S. finances. As Federal casualty lists lengthened during the spring and summer, Rebels watched the price of gold skyrocket. A price of one hundred meant that a hundred U.S. dollars purchased a hundred gold dollars. Rebels understood that the price rose when northern confidence fell, so they used this number to assess the impact of setbacks. After three weeks of carnage in Virginia and Georgia, Montgomery noted that gold was 210 in New York. When Daniel Scully heard the same, he wrote in his diary, "We now begin to see the end I think. Their money will tumble down fast under accumulated disasters. As Louis the 14th said of his war with the Prince of Orange—'The last guinea will win.'" Scully expected peace within a year. Though the 210 figure was exaggerated, the price of gold rose from 171 to 191 during the last weeks of May. But Rebel rumors and speculations from these facts could be wildly optimistic. Montgomery read in various New Orleans papers that "the State of New York has already commenced repudeating it[s] foreign debt by paying the interest in Greenbacks. The banks of New York City are compelled to pay off the amount that is wanting fifty thousand dollars in gold much to their regret I presume." Many Rebels expected the Federal war effort to self-destruct if the Confederacy withstood what appeared to be the enemy's final, desperate campaigns for Richmond and Atlanta.[54]

But credibility alone cannot explain why gossip coursed through the ranks: the anxieties of soldiering also encouraged widespread rumors. Unable to control where or when the next battle would be fought, troops sought military information that affected their lives. But grand strategy was too important to trust to the discretion of thousands who wrote uncensored letters to every corner of the South. Rumors compensated for scant knowledge and relieved troops' anxiety about the future. Rebel diarists noted that rumors increased before, during, and after combat. North Carolinian William Alexander observed that when "a hard battle was fought . . . the rumors [were] very hot during the day." Walters recorded that the atmosphere of insecurity affected his unit while it waited to fight at the Wilderness. After spending months in winter camp anticipating combat, the men were called to the front before daylight and waited, huddled together, within earshot of the raging struggle. Empty ambulances passed them and soon returned loaded with the wounded. To distract himself, Walters collected rumors that swirled through the ranks and commented on their validity.[55]

Walter's account illustrates how men tried to grasp battles that enveloped them. The rumors promised good news and help from many sides. One report alleged that General Richard Ewell's men had repulsed seven enemy assaults. "He captured some say two, some three, and others four thousand prisoners, together with several guns." Shortly thereafter, rumors circulated that General George Pickett was bringing reinforcements from Fredericksburg and Beauregard was on his way from North Carolina with twenty thousand men. Then Walters heard that General Wade Hampton and his cavalry were "making the circuit of the Yankee army to destroy a portion of the Orange and Alexandria Railroad in their rear." According to Walters, "All these reports admitted of and received much discussion, and it is a great pity that General Lee could not hear and thus profit by the admirable plans of battle which some of our military types drew up under the inspiration of the moment." It is telling that Walters's comrades drew up "admirable plans" for the engagement—they compensated for their lack of control over events by discussing how they would command the scene. Rumor-mongering offered empowerment within a terrifying environment. Psychologist Ralph Rosnow asserts that "the more threatening and dramatic the experience, the more likely it was to be a wellspring of rumor." In the summer months, suspenseful waiting became an everyday activity as adversaries settled into prolonged trench warfare. For the rest of the war in Virginia, the enemy's movements were often heard but seldom seen. Any moment could erupt with fire.[56]

Soldiering's ambiguities and uncertainties also fostered rumors. If troops faced an insecure future, the present often seemed incomprehensible. Whether in combat, on the march, or at camp, soldiers lived in a confined environment—few secrets existed within the company, but ambiguities pervaded the outer world. Confederates pined for the knowledge that mattered most, particularly news from home and other theaters, and they complained when loved ones corresponded at a slower pace. From Petersburg, Higginbotham pleaded to his brother, "Write soon and a long newsy letter." Higginbotham was trying to make sense of the presidential election, Grant's plans, and reports that Federal cavalry threatened his family. Because comrades often came from the same county, they collected and circulated letters in an attempt to piece together the situation at home. Using newspapers, speeches, and military orders, troops similarly constructed a picture of the Confederacy's fortunes in other campaigns. But the distances that veiled far-off places and events also obscured facts from fictions. Sociologist Tamotsu Shibutani appreciates this issue when he defines rumor as "a recurrent form of communication through which men caught together in an ambiguous situation attempt to construct a meaningful interpretation of it by pooling their intellectual resources." In short, because physical boundaries and unreliable channels often denied Rebels accurate intelligence about the subjects that most interested them, soldiers who gathered and shared information were spreading rumors.[57]

These obstacles plagued troops in the Trans-Mississippi Department. Hundreds of miles from the decisive battles in Georgia and Virginia, soldiers in the West collected and traded rumors as if they were currency. This practice encouraged exaggeration. In particular, enemy casualty figures ballooned to incredible proportions. After Spotsylvania Court House, a Louisiana cavalryman heard that Lee and Beauregard inflicted "a loss of 45,000 killed, wounded & prisoners—15,000 prisoners." When the 1864 campaigns began, Heartsill was stuck guarding a temporary prison camp in Tyler, Texas. One day, perhaps out of sheer boredom, he critiqued some rumors that had infiltrated the stockade: Lee had thrashed Grant; Johnston had captured Lookout Mountain; the enemy had evacuated Chattanooga; Kentucky had sent eight thousand cavalrymen to the Confederacy and refused to contribute soldiers to the United States; Forrest had taken Memphis; the soldiers in the black Federal garrison at Vicksburg had offered to surrender the city if they could return to their masters; a resolution to recognize the Confederacy had failed in the U.S. Congress by only seven votes; and Lee's army numbered 287,000 men fit for duty. Heartsill mocked such news, but others accepted it as fact. In October 1864, Montgomery, an officer stationed in Shreveport, Louisiana, told a friend that "the news to day is *without exaggeration magnificent* we have *slaughtered* the enemy before our ranks around Petersburg & Richmond." As he understood the report, the Confederates allowed the enemy to seize the first trench and "then opened on them with small arms, light artillery & from our gunboats in the James." Distance magnified the scale and significance of a skirmish to the point that Montgomery proclaimed, "Such destruction of human life has never been witnessed during our struggle."[58]

The effect of distance on the trans-Mississippi raises an important issue—that is, the dimensions of the Confederacy and its war. Histories are often incomplete without some measurement of the size of a particular time and place. In his masterpiece on the sixteenth-century Mediterranean, Fernand Braudel describes distance as "ennemie numero 1." During the age of Philip II, the size of the sea and its surrounding area presented a constant problem for merchants, generals, diplomats, and kings. As Braudel explains, "However man tackled the obstacle of distance, splintering the oars of close-manned galleys, driving the post-horses to death, or apparently flying over the waves under a fair wind, he always met with passive resistance and distance took a daily revenge for his most strenuous exploits." Weather, war, and physical obstacles could slow travel and correspondence to a languid crawl, thereby creating the unique dimensions of sixteenth-century economics and politics. Despite the invention of telegraphy, steam-powered printing presses, railroads, and other emblems of modernity, for Confederates, distance remained "ennemie numero 1." The telegraph threatened to obliterate distance by liberating information from its human carriers, but distance prevailed for numerous reasons. Politicians, newsmen, soldiers, and civilians were at the mercy of the speed of Civil War news, which seldom traveled as fast as electricity. Without an appreciation of the Confederacy's discursive apparatus—the limits and possibilities of communication within the rebellion—we cannot fully appreciate the world that soldiers constructed from information.[59]

But can the size of the Confederacy and its war be measured? What, for example, was the distance between Vicksburg, Mississippi, and Hagerstown, Maryland in 1863? As the crow flies, Vicksburg was—and is—about nine hundred miles from Hagerstown. For Mississippi soldier Robert Moore, however, the distance was eight days. Moore himself did not travel that length in just over a week, but news of Vicksburg's fall reached him eight days after the fact. The Mississippian was passing through Hagerstown during the retreat from Gettysburg when word from Vicksburg arrived and changed his war. Not only was Moore eight days removed from the disaster that struck his home state, but people had handled that news for more than a week, shifting its color and meaning before it reached him. For this reason, the speed of news—eight days from Vicksburg to Hagerstown—can help us appreciate the size of the Confederacy and its war in ways that crows and miles do not. Of course, the time it takes for one event to reach a single soldier is more suggestive than accurate. A myriad of variables quickened or reduced the rate of information throughout the war for people across the South.[60]

Understanding rumors' impact on soldiers requires a consideration of the speed at which news from distant campaigns traveled to other armies. In his diary, North Carolina infantryman James Jones meticulously documented when intelligence arrived from far-off places. Jones's records confirm that telegraphy did not guarantee timely news for men in the ranks. When telegrams about General John Morgan's cavalry in Kentucky reached Jones's camp in North Carolina, the news was nine days old. Word of Early's victory at Monacacy arrived eight days later. Telegrams detailing Hood's battles for Atlanta were three days old, and news of Lee's army took six days to reach Jones. The North Carolinian was detached from one of the main armies during this period, a situation that probably increased delays. Nonetheless, during the critical May–December 1864 campaigns for Richmond and Atlanta, news spent four to seven days in transit between troops in the Army of Northern Virginia and the Army of Tennessee. Intelligence took three to four days to travel between Rebel forces in the Shenandoah Valley and Lee's troops outside Petersburg. Correspondence with western forces could be much slower. Word of the capture of Fort Pillow reached the Army of Tennessee after six days. News of Forrest's victories took between eight and eleven days to reach the Army of Northern Virginia. As expected, communication with armies in the trans-Mississippi was most sluggish. While fighting the Red River Campaign, a Louisiana artilleryman did not hear of Lee's "victories" at Spotsylvania Court House for seventeen to nineteen days.[61]

These numbers suggest how distance shaped the soldiers' war. Some men received news earlier than others. Getting timely letters from loved ones, being the first to read a recent newspaper, or knowing someone at headquarters could increase the speed of information. Such variables were compounded by innumerable others—the dispatch with which a general made his report, the amount of traffic over the wires, the priority each transmitter gave to a particular piece of news—that thwart attempts to quantify Confederate distances. In short, speed was not constant. Some news raced from army to army, while other reports crept along at a maddening rate. The variability of timetables could be extreme. A

Rebel at Wilmington, North Carolina, an important Confederate port, received news from Lee's army in one day. But a soldier at McClellansville, South Carolina, down the coast between Wilmington and Charleston, did not hear from Lee's army for nine days.[62] An accounting of when troops in different locations first heard about events nonetheless helps to sketch the dimensions of their time and space. Most important for this study, every delay in transmission gave rumors more time to alter or replace news. When Braudel measured distance in the sixteenth century, he assumed that the only obstacle to knowledge was the time required to transmit it. But biased and inaccurate reporting further separated contemporaries from events, and distances could vary according to rank. Braudel was primarily interested in the size of the Mediterranean for its kings. The sea and its surrounding world were surely much smaller for King Philip of Spain than they were for a cobbler in Genoa. The same holds true for men in the service of the Confederacy. Distances were smaller for military and political leaders than for corporals of artillery. Common soldiers were at the mercy of distance, misinformation, and rumor far more than were their generals and governors.

Distance encouraged soldiers across the South to indulge in rumormongering, but the media and Confederate leadership did so as well. The reach of Confederate gossip was so widespread in part because these "official" sources of information contributed to the grapevine. Soldiers often found supporting evidence for rumors in newspaper columns. As the Civil War intensified and lengthened, its titanic proportions challenged the newspaper men who covered it. The difficulties of presenting an accurate picture of war plagued reporters and editors. Journalism, like the war itself, straddled modernity and an older era. Just as the war's weaponry often outran knowledge that could lessen the bloodshed (military strategy and medicine, for example), so too did advances in communication—the telegraph, railroads, and steam-powered presses—outpace ideas like journalistic objectivity that could responsibly handle the impact of nationwide reporting. As a result, thousands of eager readers digested highly partisan and often bogus news in their daily papers. Editors often identified rumors as such in their columns, but patriotism (and catering to their readership) convinced them to prefer positive gossip to negative hearsay. This subtle slant affected the war's image for countless readers. In the end, a host of issues, including inaccurate information channels, speedy circulation, and media competition turned the nation's largest newspapers into enormous rumor mills.[63]

The path of a typical battlefield report reveals how defeats first appeared in the press as victories. Officers fighting a battle often provided the first accounts of it. During the fury, couriers, staff members, and combat leaders encountered a new participant in modern warfare—the professional war correspondent. Though some correspondents had worked in the Mexican War and the Crimean War, the 150 southerners (and 350 northerners) who followed Civil

War armies in search of news were pioneers of their trade with few standards to guide them. Eager for a story, the reporters interviewed any officer they could grab for news from the front lines. With the day's results still inconclusive, having seen but a part of the chaotic action, officers most likely told reporters that they could not speak for the entire army but their own men were performing gallantly. Southern correspondents fashioned these disparate but positive accounts into a coherent story and flashed it to Richmond or Atlanta via telegraph lines while the cannons still boomed.[64]

When editors received these reports, they faced two temptations. First, if they printed the story without waiting for confirmation, they could get the scoop before competing papers reached the streets. Because the steam-powered rotary press enabled large papers to print thousands of copies an hour, editors could put an extra edition of the daily paper in readers' hands while the battle still raged. Second, because editors wished to be the first not only to announce the battle but also to declare it a victory, they were tempted to embellish the war correspondent's already suspect account of the fight. Psychologists Gordon Allport and Leo Postman note this tendency: "The 'news' has already become hearsay, and what the reporter writes and copywriter revises may slip further down the precarious road of leveling, sharpening, and assimilation." Shibutani concurs: "Too much material is made available by the wire services, and each editor must choose which items to include. There is often no time to verify suspicious items, and the temptation to present a 'good story' is difficult to resist." This process explains how battles as devastating as Gettysburg first appeared in southern newspapers as Confederate triumphs.[65]

Wartime shortages of paper compounded the problem. Hundreds of Confederate presses printed fewer pages, published fewer issues, or closed altogether. But paper shortages liberated editors as well, because newsmen could report the stories they preferred and omit the rest for lack of space. With so many positive rumors in the air, the Confederate media could fill papers with good news. Shibutani discovered similar circumstances in Paris at the end of World War II: in 1945, every city newspaper was restricted to two pages, and many of them falsely and repeatedly reported German capitulation. Shibutani explains, "This is not fabrication; an effort is made to create the desired impression through the omission of inconvenient items, the selection of details, and the preferential placement—'featuring' some items and 'burying' others." Of course, Rebel papers still detailed setbacks and catastrophes, but editors also found space for positive rumors that supported their Confederate hopes. Barraged with information and scraping to stay in print, southern editors sometimes slanted the news to please themselves and their readers.[66]

Some press difficulties can be traced to the Confederacy's telegraph offices. According to journalism scholar Ford Risley, "Wild rumors regularly found their way into news reports" because telegraph services were slow, biased, and inaccurate. Subjective reporting affected Rebel understandings of many Confederate disasters, including Gettysburg, Vicksburg, and Atlanta. While Vicksburg's citizens and soldiers desperately needed provisions, news reports reassured the rest of the Confederacy that the Gibraltar of the South was stocked with supplies. Dispatches transmitted false rumors that Grant had lost ten thousand killed and forty thousand captured in attempts to take the city when in reality the costliest Federal assault during the Vicksburg campaign lost just over three thousand men. Many of these bogus reports were spread by the Press Association reporter in Jackson, Mississippi, whose only contact with Vicksburg was with people who had left the town. As for Gettysburg, only one telegraph service reporter joined Lee's invasion of Pennsylvania. The first telegraph reports reached the Confederacy on July 5. On July 6, the telegrams claimed that Lee's men had captured forty thousand enemy troops. Not until July 9 did wire reports, quoting northern newspapers, admit that the Confederates had suffered defeat. Still, even those sober reports promised that "the citizens are hopeful and confident." Accurate pictures of Vicksburg and Gettysburg took weeks to develop.[67]

Inaccurate reporting was worse during the Atlanta campaign. If telegrams about Vicksburg and Gettysburg were marred by incompetence, "a clear sense of morale building was evident" in the reporting of Atlanta. General Johnston ordered that all news from the Army of Tennessee be strictly censored by the inspector general. When Hood took command and bloodied his ranks for no gain, the wires celebrated his assaults: "Atlanta is safe. All are hopeful and in the best spirits." Telegraphs did not report Atlanta's fall until September 4. On the following day, they asserted that "while the fall of Atlanta is regretted, the army and people are not at all discouraged."[68]

Weeks after the disaster, the wires circulated false rumors that Confederates had cut Sherman's supply line and separated him from the body of his army. Throughout October, the Army of Tennessee harassed Sherman's supply line in hopes of forcing the Federals out of Atlanta. These efforts failed. Union soldiers pushed Hood's men into Alabama, repaired the railroad, and embarked on the March to the Sea. Nevertheless, in mid-October, Richmond newsmen desperately sought good news and thought they found some. A preliminary (and false) report claimed that Hood's army had achieved a victory against Sherman in one of these brief engagements along the supply line. The news was too lean and ambiguous for even the editors to embellish, so Richmond papers informed their readers that the news from Georgia was too good to print. They insinuated that Sherman's army had been completely cut off from the North and claimed that reporting the invaders' fate in Confederate papers would give Lincoln and Grant information they could not otherwise gather.[69]

Confederates defending Richmond and Petersburg accepted this nonsense and sent word to their loved ones. Welch wrote to his wife that "there is encouraging news from Georgia, but they will not tell us what it is, because they say they do not want Grant to find out about it." He conjectured that "Hood may have Sherman in a tight place." On the same day, McLure exclaimed, "There are rumors afloat about Richmond that matters are going on most prosperously in Georgia, the news is too good they say to be published to the Yankees just yet." Alexander thought that the Confederate press "deserve mutch credit" for not disclosing the details of Sherman's fate. Crawford remained hopeful more than a week later. "From newspaper accounts," he reported that "Hood seems to have Sherman in a pretty tight fix. I hope he may be able to put an end to that 'great General of the day,' & his army with him." Rebels speculated for weeks about the long-term implications of a victory that had never happened.[70]

Rumors and biased reporting also marked the Confederacy's religious presses. Throughout the war, Christian organizations dispatched millions of newsletters and pamphlets to Rebel armies. According to historian Kurt Berends, the editors of these papers "created a framework of beliefs—a worldview—that sustained an unvanquished optimism for southern independence." Nothing seems to have shaken their confidence in ultimate victory. After the fall of Atlanta, one editor argued that "there was no disaster" because General Hood's "great object was to hold it as long as he could, and to make the possession of it by the enemy cost him as much as possible. This object has been fully attained." In February 1865, another editor reasoned that "the loss of our great cities is probable. This occurred in the Revolutionary war, and occurs in most wars; but if the heart of the people is right, never determines the result." When Richmond fell, southern columnists again compared their circumstances to those of Americans during the revolution: "The taking of Richmond will have no more effect upon the final result of the war than the taking of Philadelphia, (the Capital of the Colonies) in 1777." William Norris, editor of the *Mississippi Messenger*, penned perhaps the most astounding report in March 1865, less than a month before Lee's surrender: "The Confederacy controls the whole situation." According to Norris, Union generals Grant and Thomas "have been whipped so often that we need not take them into the calculation. In South Carolina, Sherman is confronted by an equal force with all the natural advantage on our side. Let Sherman be destroyed, and the supremacy of the Confederacy is established."[71]

When southern leaders insisted that the Confederacy was unconquerable, they reinforced wish rumors and enhanced their credibility. No politician encouraged Rebels' conviction that they were invincible as strongly as did Jefferson Davis. When the Confederate Congress assembled in May 1864, days before the spring campaigns began, Davis promised the statesmen, "If our arms are crowned with the success which we have so much reason to hope, we may well expect that this war cannot be prolonged beyond the current year." After Atlanta fell, Davis traveled by train across the nation, promising victory. A soldier in Greensboro jotted the gist of Davis's speech down in his diary: "President Davis arrives on the train, makes a speech, glorious news from Hood Army, flanks

Sherman &c President speaks in much hope of our future success." The diarist did not record his opinion of the speech, but such optimism reached some of the president's audience. On the eve of Lincoln's reelection, Davis argued that nothing could deny the Rebels ultimate victory and independence—"not the fall of Richmond, nor Wilmington, nor Charleston, nor Savannah, nor Mobile, nor of all combined." Davis discussed foreign intervention, finances, and the unlikelihood of a negotiated peace with the Union until "the delusion of their ability to conquer us is dispelled." The only course to victory he identified was through persistent fighting: "Let us, then, resolutely continue to devote our united and unimpaired energies to the defense of our homes, our lives, and our liberties. This is the true path to peace. Let us tread it with confidence in the assured result."[72]

Clergymen also supported continued resistance and hopes for a northern collapse. Church leaders decried Lincoln's despotism, predicted financial catastrophe on Wall Street, hinted that masses of wretched northerners faced starvation, and labeled the Yankee press a gigantic propaganda machine that controlled a docile public. In April 1864, Episcopal bishop Stephen Elliott argued that Federal armies were not permanently occupying any vital Confederate territory and mocked the enemy's annual advance and retreat in Virginia and Tennessee. He asked his congregation, "Will the people of the United States consent to be maimed and slaughtered through an infinite series of years for the annual honor of marching from Washington to the Rappahannock, and from Nashville to Chattanooga? Impossible!" Considering the reverence thousands of Rebels accorded to sacred leaders, these pronouncements bolstered faith in victory and independence in profound ways.[73]

All these sources—newspapers, telegraph services, religious presses, politicians, clergymen, and the soldiers themselves—spread wish rumors, but why did they do so? Why was Confederate gossip so positive, even after Atlanta? Fear and hatred can spark the imagination and produce rumors as easily as hopes can. Why didn't chatter about catastrophic defeats, enemy espionage, slave revolts, or starvation on the home front swirl through Confederate camps as the war worsened? Why did so few rumors arise that foreshadowed the nightmares of defeat, Federal domination, and racial disorder? Some negative gossip did exist. Atrocity stories followed Sherman's tracks, and news occasionally announced the death of Lee or some other cherished leader, but wish rumors far outweighed despondent ones.

The phenomenon can be explained in part by soldiers' efforts to construct reality. When receiving news that threatened the Confederacy's existence, such as the fall of Atlanta, many Rebels first denied the reports and then spread positive rumors to counterbalance the disaster's impact. According to psychologist Leon Festinger, when social groups face undeniable evidence that challenges how they view themselves or foresee their future, they often band together to discuss the news and through this discourse produce rumors that support their cherished beliefs. In this manner, "a large group of people is able to maintain an opinion or belief even in the face of continual definite evidence to the contrary." Thousands of Rebels committed to independence and living in uncertain times managed to deflect the significance of successive defeats and worsening conditions by unconsciously inventing good news. Thomas Kuhn's concept of paradigm shifts involves the same dynamic. Kuhn argues that scientists sometimes retain theories when increasing evidence discredits those premises because the older beliefs explain the universe. Instead of jettisoning how they perceive the world, scientists label contradictory facts as anomalies until those findings grow to dimensions that cannot be ignored. When Confederates deflected bad news as temporary setbacks, they acted in similar ways.[74]

But cognitive dissonance is only part of Confederates' behavior; emotions also promoted the spread of wish rumors. Some soldiers questioned the validity of rumors but still circulated them because hopeful messages were too appealing to discard. Though Grant Taylor complained, "We hear so many lies we never know what to believe," he spread a report that northern prisoners were taking the Confederate oath and joining Rebel armies. Higginbotham remarked that newspapers "are now, as they always do, making out our prospects bright, but I believe as much of their talk as I please." Higginbotham nevertheless frequently shared reports that bolstered his morale. Soldiers often concluded the telling of a rumor by doubting its accuracy. Statements such as "It seems too good to believe," "If true this is glorious," "If that be so," and "I hope it is true" reveal the tug-of-war between soldiers' intellects and passions. As veterans, they knew that some of these rumors sounded ridiculous. But as partisans, they could not deny the emotions that good news summoned: pride, hope, anticipation, and revenge. Charles Blackford exemplified this internal debate. In the same letter in which he told his wife that "bad rumors are always true while good ones are often false," he could not resist sharing the rumor that Grant had been killed. After Chickamauga, Floridian Henry Holmes jotted in his diary, "Rumors plentiful, nothing reliable." Still, Holmes enjoyed southern newspapers that quoted the New York press's dire assessments of the campaign. When Nugent heard positive news from Bragg's army outside Chattanooga, he admitted that "the result is very vague," but Nugent accepted the way that hope pulled veterans and shaped their view of the war. For him it was axiomatic that Confederates "will have to look a long ways ahead for the 'Silver lining' to the cloud of war," and he did not question the enterprise. "We can," he assumed, "feed ourselves on hope, while events, big with the hopes of millions, are daily transpiring around us." Like countless others, Nugent failed to see the consequences of relying so heavily on hope.[75]

Patriotism, ideology, and group cohesion also fostered wish rumors. By transmitting news of distant victories, northern discord, and foreign aid, troops expressed their abiding faith in the Confederacy. The most active rumormongers were diehard Rebels like Montgomery, who hoped that positive reports in October 1864 "will rouse the dispondent of our land and be hailed with joy and gladness by those of us whose hope, and confidence of victory & independence has not been lost by the temporary gloom." Montgomery spread wish rumors as a way to boost the patriotism of others and serve the cause. As Taussig argues, "It is in the coils of rumor, gossip, story, and chit-chat where ideology and ideas become emotionally powerful and enter into active social circulation and meaningful existence." The Confederacy lacked a central propaganda agency, but diehard Rebels filled that role. However preposterous their claims, wish rumors were difficult to kill because any soldier who publicly denied their veracity ran the risk of appearing unpatriotic or disheartened. This dynamic intensified as desertions increased. When solid veterans silently headed home, they undermined the notion that soldiering "without a murmur" signified patriotism. In such an environment, spreading wish rumors through camp offered diehards a vocal display of loyalty that was less ambiguous than silent endurance. Moreover, when thousands of forlorn Confederates deserted the ranks, they left behind a more homogeneous troop of unconquered southerners. By winnowing ranks of the disheartened, desertion created a better conduit for wish rumors. This self-selection helps to explain why bizarre rumors of northern secession and European intervention swirled through the ranks late in the war. By the end of the conflict, fanatics who sought any means to refute the likelihood of defeat composed a larger percentage of Confederate armies.[76]

Still, it is unclear whether rumors were a cause or effect of homogeneity. Did positive gossip foster group cohesion, or did group cohesion foster positive gossip? The dynamic probably worked both ways. According to Rosnow, "As rumors are retold, strong common interests begin to crystallize, and the loosely bound collectivity becomes more cohesive."[77] Wish rumors promoted a communal perspective on the war; they connected men who spread them, decreased disparate perceptions of events, and sparked hopeful predictions. Even rumors of Grant's death bound together those who heard them. For a week or two, thousands of Rebels from Virginia to Texas wondered if a single Confederate shell had killed the tenacious general and changed the course of the war. Not all individuals had the same reaction to gossip, and particular rumors were not received the same by all men. Widespread rumors nonetheless contributed to the chaotic experience that united soldiers.

The transience of rumors offers historians a glimpse of the past as present. By showing us how the flux of war must have felt to thousands, rumors illuminate the deep contingency of history that Edward Ayers has recently championed. Dense connections between Civil War events and participants linked social, cultural, political, and military issues, creating a world that was far more complicated than any epic tale. Rumors contributed to this environment; they mirrored the times and affected the war experiences of countless Americans. When soldiers recorded gossip in diaries and letters, the information became a part of their war narrative, their attempt to organize and understand the conflict. The Civil War, like all experiences, acquired form and meaning in the stories that participants told of it. Information, true or false, contributed to these individual chronicles and to a larger story of Confederate persistence. As the rebellion faded, a stream of gossip promoted the beliefs that diehard veterans had always wanted to believe: their armies and people were unconquerable, and everything would turn out right in the end. Whether true or false, rumors traveled far and fast because thousands corresponded with loved ones, Confederate authorities lacked censors, and a highly partisan media whirled at top speed. This profusion helped unvanquished Rebels maintain faith through the darkest months of the war.

The Face of Surrender

Diehard Rebels in 1865

Days after evacuating Richmond, army surgeon Blair Burwell stopped by the side of the road and wrote a letter to his wife, Virginia. His writings maintained a doctor's calm amid the chaos. It helped that Burwell knew exactly where he was. This was a familiar spot in Buckingham County, one county west of Powhatan, where his family had lived for generations. Like the Confederate capital, Powhatan now belonged to the enemy. Nonetheless, Burwell told Virginia he was "satisfied to know that you are surrounded by my two dear Aunts and Uncles who will always render you any assistance in their power." The Burwells were important people in Powhatan; perhaps they could weather the storm better than others. He also reassured her that "we are all well & getting on tolerably especially my self who as always looks things in the face hopingly & firmly believing that all will end well." On the next day, Burwell surrendered at Appomattox Court House.[1]

Burwell's note demonstrates the challenges of studying diehard Rebels in 1865. Did the doctor "firmly" believe that "all will end well," or did he write those lines to soothe his worried wife? As an army surgeon, Burwell had looked into countless faces and recognized the telltale signs of death. Yet if his words are to be believed, the doctor looked into the face of his army and did not see its impending demise. As a slave owner, Burwell had much to lose in 1865. Perhaps he reassured his family because the alternative—emancipated slaves and a ruined plantation—was too terrible to fathom, especially while Grant's army swarmed through Powhatan. Nonetheless, Burwell and many of his comrades had believed for years that they were unconquerable. Perhaps, as German scholar Wolfgang Schivelbusch argues, nations and their most loyal patriots fail to forecast their own defeat. Many Rebel diarists were as positive as Burwell to the bitter end, and they did not write such sentiments for the benefit of family. Moreover, if Confederate faith in 1865 represented self-deception, that does not diminish the strength of the belief. As writer Robertson Davies explains, "It doesn't matter if the belief was wrong, or seems wrong to us today; it is the fact of the belief that concerns me." People "may believe what is untrue, but they have a *need* to believe the untruth—it fills a gap in the fabric of what they want to know." Davies warns that "we often throw such beliefs aside without having truly understood them." However we interpret the diehards' documents, they remind us that wrong beliefs shape actions and perceptions as thoroughly as correct ones.[2]

Beyond these issues of interpretation, studying diehard Rebels in 1865 offers historians a valuable glimpse into an unraveling world. The remnants of the Confederacy, like Burwell's note, help scholars observe the believers of an ethos while its supports crumbled around them. In the spring of 1865, another reality and its followers impinged on the diehards' world and ended it. All the beliefs, stereotypes, misperceptions, rumors, and predictions that had carried Confederates to this point in the war (and this book) faced harsh, indisputable facts in April 1865. How did fanatics react to the death of their nation? How did men convinced of their superiority surrender to barbarians? How did Christians certain of God's favor explain Union triumph? In short, what price did these men pay for feeling invincible? Surrender was a defining moment in the lives of thousands of Confederates. Burwell's letter shows that he faced the crisis as a diehard Rebel. If he saw signs of imminent defeat around him, he chose to remain defiant and hopeful. Burwell may have sensed the end and knew that his letter would never be mailed. If so, he wrote those lines not for family but for himself. Burwell may have known that he was not merely on the side of the road in Buckingham County; he was also standing at a crossroads in his life and in southern history. If so, he upheld his ethos at that critical moment. When his world collapsed, Burwell guarded his convictions. Diehards from across the South reacted to surrender in similar ways. Their decision to remain defiant would affect them for the rest of their days and profoundly shape the postwar South.

ᕮᕮᕮ ᕮᕮᕮ ᕮᕮᕮ

As 1865 dawned, news of General John Bell Hood's disaster in Tennessee and the fall of Savannah to William T. Sherman's columns left a pall over the Confederacy. In Alexandria, Louisiana, David Pierson called the news "the worst of the war" and noted that citizens seemed to exude gloom and despair. "Men of sense and position were freely talking on the streets of our being whipped. Such has never been the case before, and it clearly shows the ominous state of affairs." From Petersburg, John Hampden "Ham" Chamberlayne wrote that the "publick mind [is] in a gloomy state here—We must pas thro' a great crisis before Spring. Much to be done & suffered." Edgeworth Bird described "a general tone of depression" and admitted that "the affairs of our country are in a rather gloomy condition." He observed that the people "have lost confidence in the ability of the chief magistrate, and all sorts of opinions are afloat as to what is best to be done." Seeking explanations and a release from their frustrations, citizens were branding Jefferson Davis the scapegoat. Though "every thing looks gloomy, and every one seems to be low-spirited," Edward Crenshaw thought the criticism of Davis was severe and unjust. J. M. Bonner of Louisiana disagreed. If "the Confederacy should fail what would be the verdict of posterity on the subject?" he asked. "Simply this 'Died from the effects of the prejudices of Jefferson Davis.'" Remarking that "this is no time for experiments," Bonner blamed Davis for replacing General Joseph E. Johnston with "an untried man like Hood."[3]

Many soldiers not only observed the prevailing gloom but took part in it. Pierson wrote home that "we are in a bad fix and everybody knows and feels it. If something is not done, and that speedily, all must be lost." In South Carolina, John Cotton admitted that "it looks like the yankeys has got the upperhand of us I would like to here some terms of peace before they run clear over us." He expected that Sherman would take Charleston "without a fite," because "our soldiers are very much dishartened and the most of them say we are all whiped." He even heard "that georgia is holding conventions to no whether to go back in the union or not if she goes back it will look like rest will have to go two I hate the thoughts of going back but if we have to do it the sooner the better I have suffered two much in this war to ever go back to the union willingly." Virginian Henry Berkeley concurred that the "men's spirits [are] dull, gloomy and all are evidently hopeless, waiting for we know not what end." When a female relative called wavering Confederate troops "white-livered men, cowards," Berkeley imagined "how she would face a Yankee battery and a Yankee brigade." "I don't think our people realize how near the end is on us, or what that end will most probably be." "Our cause is hopeless," Berkeley declared, wondering "if I shall ever see home and the loved ones there again." Creed Thomas Davis confided in his diary that he had "spent a dismal day, Closeted with, and fostering dark thoughts." "I am unhappy and scarcely know what to do," Davis cried. "The war continues and misery is on the increase." He wrote that Hell awaited "the Southern people" and then crossed out the line. Some thoughts were too dark to put down on a page.[4]

As these writings suggest, by 1865 even the most confident diehards expected a bleak future. A year earlier, these men had hoped to secure independence by winning the campaigns for Richmond and Atlanta. In 1865, for the first time during the conflict, widespread predictions of victory and peace by Christmas did not spread through winter quarters. This shift in attitude is significant because no single event crushed Confederate morale. There is no particular date when despondency overwhelmed the new nation. In hindsight, Rebel fortunes plummeted after Atlanta fell and Abraham Lincoln won reelection. For participants, however, these setbacks seemed to postpone, not eliminate, Confederate independence. Nonetheless, by January 1865 a more grim reality imposed itself, and diehard Rebels faced this stark change in diverse ways.

Gloom and war weariness compelled thousands of Confederates to desert in 1865. Some of these troops headed home in January and February with the intention of returning to the ranks in the spring. Grant Taylor shared such plans with his wife: "I will write you a secret which I want you to keep. . . . If I live God being my helper I intend to come home next April if I do not get a furlough before then and they do not pay me off. . . . Unless you think I had better stay and bide my time for a furlough. But I do not think I can start into another summer's campaign without seeing you and the children." Taylor planned to go home not because he had lost all hope of winning the war or because his family needed him but because he thought that the war was far from over and could not face another long campaign without first seeing his loved ones. After his unit transferred from Mobile to South Carolina, Taylor was too far from home to execute his plans unless he deserted, and he could not do that: "Now all hope is snatched away only in deserting and I cannot bear the idea of that yet although we are treated like dogs."[5]

Other Confederates deserted in early 1865 and never looked back. Thousands who tired of the war crossed over to Union lines, and thousands more returned home to help destitute loved ones. In Virginia, Creed Thomas Davis noted that "our men . . . are deserting to the enemy by the wholesale." Peter Guerrant reported that "twelve of our Battalion have deserted & gone to the Yankees within the last ten days." From Tupelo, Mississippi, James Orr wrote to his younger brother, Sammie, "The boys is very much dissatisfied. I think a good many of them will desert between now and spring; some are leaving every knight." He told Sammie, "If you should ever have to go into the service, let me advise you to go into the cavelry service; they are what we call life-insured companys." Orr wearied of hard service and high casualties in the infantry: "About the time I become skilled in ditching [trenches], the Yankeys shot and disabled me. . . . This thing what they call chargin brest works is not the thing it is cracked up to be. It is very unhealthy." All wars test human endurance, and many Rebels reached their limits during the winter of 1865.[6]

In addition to war weariness, some men quit the contest because they lost hope of winning independence. Charles Blackford figured that "our men are deserting quite freely" because "it looks very blue to them." Some veterans despaired not because the fall of Atlanta or Lincoln's reelection prolonged the war but because Sherman's stunning March to the Sea exposed the hollowness of the Confederacy. Blackford admitted, "The fact that Sherman marched from Atlanta to Savannah without seeing an armed Confederate soldier is well calculated to make them despondent." William James Griggs, a common soldier from Virginia, expressed his despair with rare candor: "Billy you may see some grounds upon which to build your hopes of final success," Griggs told his cousin, "but as for me I see none." The Virginian despaired because General James Longstreet's stalwart veterans were deserting in droves. Griggs counted twenty-two hundred deserters from the famous First Corps in the fall of 1864 and believed that most of them had gone to the enemy. "If the troops of the victorious 1st Corps are this demoralized what do you expect of men who have known nothing but defeat for the last seven months?" More depressing were General Robert E. Lee's feeble efforts to handle the epidemic. According to Griggs, "Genl Lee no longer uses threats of punishment to prevent this but he simply begs the men to wait until Spring & try once more to retrieve our fortunes but his appeal is vain." Throughout winter quarters "the men swear they do not intend to fight another battle. In my opinion every man killed or wounded after this it wil be cold blooded murder. All know that it is useless for the war to be further persisted." Griggs concluded, "I would be as glad to see the independence of the South established as any one in the State of Virginia but if there is any truth in men we need not longer contend." Facing squalor and long odds, many troops shared Griggs's perceptions in the early months of 1865.[7]

Others despaired because the populace seemed to have abandoned the struggle. "A great many have wondered why there was so much desertion in the army during the last three or four months," Charles Fenton James wrote, "and they have very naturally attributed it to the reverses which we have met with." "But this is not the prime cause," he asserted. Rather, "desertion takes place because desertion is encouraged" by civilians. He told his sister of a comrade who stayed beyond his allotted leave because "the ladies begged him to remain and attend a grand ball which they were going to have." "Such is the story of nearly every man who returns from furlough. They all agree that . . . the people in the country are enjoying themselves more, living higher and dressing finer than before the war. Dancing parties are heard of every where, and the people seem to have lost sight of the fact that a war was going on." James quoted Edmund Burke's argument that "nations are never murdered but they sometimes commit suicide" and prayed, "God forbid that we should be guilty of such folly. Nero fiddled while Rome was burning. Shall it be said of our people that they exceeded Nero and fiddled and danced while the land was draped in mourning?" Other soldiers lamented that the populace seemed not only apathetic but also opposed to the Confederate cause. William Heartsill spent the final months of the war chasing deserters and their civilian protectors. On the same day that Lee surrendered his army in Virginia, Heartsill wrote from Texas that "it is the STANDING duty of all soldiers, and in fact all citizens, to arrest all skulkers and bring them to justice." Weeks later, he caught a deserter who had been absent for two years. Thomas

Hampton volunteered to hunt deserters in the Trans-Mississippi Department and spent the final months of the war scouring the countryside.[8]

Diehard Rebels such as Heartsill and Hampton could not fathom why men deserted their country in its moment of greatest need. George Marion Coiner worked in General Richard Anderson's corps headquarters, where he read reports that tallied the number of deserters. When he learned one February morning that twenty-five men had vanished from General R. R. Johnson's division during the night, Coiner wrote, "If there ever was a time for every man to do his duty it is now—We have no other alternative left us now, but to fight on with a determination and will, unprecedented in the history of any war." When Reuben Pierson received word that some childhood friends had been imprisoned and sentenced to death for desertion by the Confederate Army, he marveled how any man "could not protect an aged parent or a loving sister from the abuses of the rabble" by remaining a dutiful soldier. For Pierson and thousands more, sustaining the Confederate ranks was the only way to protect people at home. Without the armies, there was no country and hence no defense against northern aggression. John Walters, a native of Amsterdam, was equally appalled: "I who am a foreigner with no ties . . . cannot but think it strange and view with the utmost disgust, the picture of men, whose every tie and association is in and of the South, so far forgetting themselves and so reckless of their honor as to desert, and that at a period when more than at any other time their country needs them and their services most. Nor can I see that desertion is any remedy for the evils of hard and scant fare, insufficient clothing, and no pay." Walters pointed out that deserters not only abandoned the cause but further endangered the lives of their comrades who remained in the trenches. Every quitter deprived Lee or Johnston of precious firepower against increasing enemy numbers. Walters worried that the rising desertion rate "bids fair to leave but few of us to contend with Grant when the spring weather shall admit active campaigning." This double abandonment of cause and comrades partly explains why Rebel units executed deserters during the final weeks of the war. On March 2, 1865, the garrison at Galveston, Texas, executed Antone Ricker, age seventeen. Weeks later, James M. Williams, commander of Spanish Fort in Mobile, Alabama, told his wife without a trace of emotion that "last Tuesday we had a military execution— I had charge of it and commanded the brigade which was ordered out to witness it. . . . Two more will be shot here during the next week or ten days—they are deserters from my regiment." The men were Privates Thomas Elam and Elijah Wynn, friends who had deserted together in September 1863. When three men interrupted General Nathan Bedford Forrest's breakfast one morning in March 1865 to inform him they were sick of the war and going home, he had them shot on the spot.[9]

Military defeats raised the rate of desertion. Word of a severe setback reached the ranks in mid-January: the last open Confederate port, Wilmington, North

Carolina, was closed when Fort Fisher fell. The garrison had withstood a barrage weighing 1,275,000 pounds in December, but January's assault with 1,652,638 pounds buried the defenders under a spray of sand and iron. A survivor described the scene as "terrible, appalling, yet sublime." Wilmington's blockade-runners had been a lifeline for Lee's army. The news shocked the Army of Northern Virginia. A North Carolina private confessed, "I was as much surprised as grieved at the fall of Fisher, as I had confidently expected that it would never fall." Many troops tried to sustain hope. Though one Rebel admitted, "Things are now in such a precarious and unsettled state that we cannot tell one hour what is to happen the next," he hoped "every day for something to turn up favourable to us." North Carolinian John Shaffner wrote that "the fall of Fort Fisher below Wilmington is a serious misfortune, but is not a fatal disaster." He claimed that the only consequence was "we will all be compelled to dispense with luxuries for a season." Virginian Fred Fleet even considered the disaster a blessing in disguise: "Gold has already gone down 10 per cent," he claimed, "for the blockade running at Wilmington was the leech which drew the richest blood from our treasury." Fleet saw "no reason that we should despond, but rather that relying on the Lord of Hosts, we should strive with renewed vigor to resist slavery & subjugation."[10]

According to their letters and diaries, many diehard Rebels chose persistence and expressed confidence, while others succumbed to gloom and despair. Indeed, some Confederates' faith seemed limitless in 1865. Though he ranted about civilian apathy, James believed that "the conduct of the southern people in the future will be different" and hoped that "a revolution which is now taking place in the public mind will bring a change" for the better. Bird agreed: "Our affairs look rather gloomy, but I hope yet for a favorable turn in our fortunes. There is a wonderful power and recuperative energy in the South yet." Though he chased deserters across Texas, Heartsill dreamed that "the day is not far off when we will again be permitted to see loved ones at home, and to meet our comrades in arms, and chat over our many dangers and difficulties; and all this I pray, under the FREE and independent FLAG of the SOUTHERN CONFEDERACY." Many troops expressed a stronger commitment to their nation in 1865 than ever before. Georgia sergeant Marion Fitzpatrick told his wife, "I have no distant dream of ever giving up. Yankees may kill me but will never subjugate me." Likewise, Shaffner started 1865 convinced that it would be "better [if] all fill one common grave, than yield willingly to the yoke of the despicable Northman." He expected the next six months to yield "war, cruel, unrelenting war, & not Peace; that is certain as the rising of the sun." Though these veterans knew failure and saw desertion eroding the ranks, they chose to remain defiant and upheld their ethos of invincibility.[11]

Confederate persistence remained possible in 1865 because the elements that bolstered Rebel morale in 1864 still sustained the hopes of thousands during the war's final months. Religion supported them in their hour of need. Chaplains reported widespread revivals in the ranks in the spring of 1865. Soldiers like Lieutenant J. W. Hardie still believed that "God [is] with us. Who shall harm us?"[12] Thoughts of barbarous enemies also steeled Rebels' resolve. Just weeks before his surrender, a Virginia colonel steamed about "the Yankees vilanous treatment of the people of North and South Carolina—outrages of the most scandalous character are openly perpetrated by officers and men upon the harmless ladies and beautiful females who may fall into their hands."[13] Wish rumors proliferated because the chaos, anxiety, and ambiguities that fostered hearsay in 1864 remained pervasive in 1865. Reliable communication channels such as the media and letters from home disintegrated as the postal service failed. Military intelligence also collapsed because the Confederate cavalry—the eyes of the army—was outmatched by greater numbers and superior mounts. The situation was so critical at times that the whereabouts and intentions of entire armies, like Sherman's, were foggy at best. In this climate of uncertainty, Rebels spread positive rumors to offset bad news and to justify their continued resistance. In February, the mystery shrouding Sherman's army encouraged a rumor that his men "had been badly defeated, his wagon train & 8000 prisoners captured." Confederates used rumors in an attempt to convince themselves and others that all was not lost and that the situation was actually better than it seemed. When Hugh Montgomery argued that "though we have met reverses & a gloom has come over the land, the sky is still bright, cheering, and there is every thing in the future to make [us] hopeful & true & cheerful," his straining attempt at optimism suggests that some Confederates wrote of hope as a means of keeping it alive in their own minds.[14]

In January and early February 1865, a wave of positive rumors countered the depressing news. According to an Alabama soldier, as soon as one rumor was refuted, "Phoenix-like another takes its place." Hopeful gossip and rosy speculations bombarded Confederate camps faster than they could be disproved. From Louisiana, Jared Sanders wrote that General Braxton Bragg had not only thwarted General Benjamin Butler's attempt to take Wilmington, North Carolina, but captured seven thousand of his men. Sanders also circulated the rumor that Hood had turned on General George Thomas and captured an entire brigade. Moreover, according to Sanders, Forrest's cavalry had whipped its opponents, marched into Kentucky, and united with General John C. Breckinridge's force. Sanders assured his family that "this news comes from headquarters & is official." Montgomery wrote to a friend that "a Gentleman just from Memphis states that the Yankees there say that they were *damn* badly used up by Hood and really suffered twice as much as we did." Montgomery claimed that the enemy "do not look upon Hoods retreat as a defeat by any means," so Confederates should not do so.[15]

The most positive rumors that swept across the South in 1865 promised imminent peace with independence. When word spread that Confederate Vice President Alexander Stephens, Virginia Senator Robert M. T. Hunter, and Assistant Secretary of War John A. Campbell, a former U.S. Supreme Court justice, were meeting U.S. Secretary of State William Seward to discuss peace terms, many Confederates assumed that the Union was seeking an armistice and a compromise. In late January, William Nugent wrote to his wife that "the Yankee nation is in a great flurry about peace & has already sent three Commissioners to Richmond to feel our Government. They are satisfied we can never be whipped." Alabamian Sam Pickens concurred that the enemy displayed a "nervous desire . . . to have the war ended." A rumored three-month armistice was confirmed by a man from Richmond who "saw it on the bulletin boards." Cotton was less sanguine about the Confederacy's ability to dictate terms, but the news cheered him enough to consider buying a slave. Cotton would have done so except that he had no safe way of transporting the bondsman home. Montgomery figured that the Confederacy "will be obliged to make some concessions" but thought that independence could be achieved by agreeing to abolish slavery. Still, he hoped the Rebels could retain "the priviledge of using our negroes as slaves for fifty or seventy years." These distortions of both enemy resolve and Confederate strength—written within three months of capitulation—exhibit the durability of Rebel faith.[16]

On February 3, the Confederate representatives arrived aboard a Union steamer in Hampton Roads for their meeting with Seward. Onboard, however, they found President Lincoln, who had decided to deliver the Federal terms in person: unconditional surrender, reconstruction, and the abolition of slavery. He refused to consider any armistice short of an end to the war and would not compromise. When a stunned Hunter replied that even Charles I had negotiated with Rebels during the English Civil War, Lincoln rebutted, "All I distinctly recollect about the case of Charles I, is, that he lost his head." The much-anticipated Hampton Roads peace conference was finished before it started.[17]

When weeks of high hopes for peace with independence vanished, diehard Confederates responded with resolve instead of despondency. James thought that "Lincoln and Seward pursued the very course which was best for our safety and independence. Surely their hearts have been hardened, as was Pharoah's, and they are rushing blindly to their own destruction." James expected that "before this campaign of '65 is over they and all their crew will wish they had acted differently." "As sure as a just God rules on Earth," James declared, "a terrible defeat awaits them." Thomas Key wrote that "the terms that Lincoln laid down . . . are so dishonorable that it has had the happy result of uniting our people for a more energetic prosecution of the war." Chamberlayne also observed benefits from "the bursting of the peace bubble": "The whole country here is again in a war fever—We hope great things from it," he wrote from the trenches outside Richmond. Within the capital, throngs met "to express their feelings at the insult offered to the Confederate States by President Lincoln, in his ultimatum . . . 'Submission or Subjugation.'" Creed Thomas Davis thought that the people "have made up their minds for a long war." South Carolinian John McLure expected "a renewed zeal . . . throughout the country." He thought, "A victory or two on our part would change the [face] of things very much, and perhaps open the eyes of the Yankees a little."[18]

Because diehards considered themselves superior to the enemy, the fact that Lincoln would not negotiate with "rebels" infuriated them. The anger stemming from this insult to southern honor infused Confederate writing. "No peace short of subjugation or unconditional surrender," wrote James Albright. " 'Can't treat with Rebels in arms,' they say. Glad of it, for the very effort to make terms has depressed our boys." Edwin Fay responded to the enemy's effrontery by arguing that "they should make the first overtures and propose recognition before I would allow any one of their envoys in my lines." Lincoln's conditions incited some Rebels to vow eternal defiance. "Rather than submit to a dishonorable settlement," Hampton told his wife, "I would prefer a continued war for years." "I say peace never, if slavery is to perish with it," exclaimed Heartsill, "let's fight it out and GAIN all, or fight it out and LOSE all." Richard Launcelot Maury hoped that the enemy's terms would "quiet those miserable criers for peace— and convincing them that there can be no peace, unite them with us in war to the knife, and the knife to the hilt." A North Carolinian in Lee's army thought that "the uncompromising spirit of Lincoln & co. has had a fine effect on the army." Except for independence, "nothing more favorable to our cause could have occurred." The events at Hampton Roads had touched a nerve.[19]

Some Confederate defiance, however, betrayed more than a trace of fatalism. Creed Thomas Davis noted that "our people seem more determined than ever to fight to the bitter end," but he expected that the end would be terrible. "They must see that we will suffer subjugation in the end," he admitted. "Already we walk hand and hand with famine." Davis shuddered when he thought "of the desperate campaign that awaits us in the spring. But I will try and do my duty." A North Carolinian advised his wife, "It is more than probable that we will be crushed this year, but even if we know this to a certainty, we ought not therefore relax our efforts. . . . [I]f we are doomed to irretrievable disaster, let us feel assured at least that we have well discharged our part." A South Carolinian told his wife to "be brave and resolute" and to leave the rest to God. Coiner seemed hesitant when he wrote, "It looks as though we care to fight on for the last ray of hope." He suspected that the enemy had fabricated the peace rumors "as a scheme to dishearten and demoralize the army." "If so, they have been partly successful," Coiner confessed, for "our troops were very much elated at the idea of a negotiation for peace but since it has turned out as it has, the disappointment is truly great." Others seemed to thirst for a sacrificial culmination to the struggle. Crenshaw hoped "that we will fight until the last man, woman, and child in the South is slain. Better death than dishonor." South Carolinian John Sheppard agreed. As he watched authorities line the streets of Augusta, Georgia, with fifty thousand bales of cotton, "getting ready to burn it in case the Yankees come," Sheppard told his mother, "an Honorable & Glorious Death is far preferable to abject Submission to our inferiors—the Yankees." It was quite a statement: two of Sheppard's brothers had already died for the Confederacy. Whether they feared a bloody finale to the war, accepted it stoically, or sought it as a way to sanctify the cause, many Rebels started to foresee a horrid conclusion. [20]

As the full implications of the Hampton Roads impasse sunk in, Confederates responded in several ways. Many soldiers deserted. Others entertained pipe dreams, just as they had after the fall of Atlanta, Lincoln's reelection, Hood's disaster in Tennessee, and other catastrophes. Rumor mills still offered a stream of delusions for those who sought them. Some troops despaired that the end of negotiations guaranteed another season of bloody campaigns and an interminable war. Thousands of Rebels remained in the ranks because comradeship bound them to fellow survivors. Most of these men desired an honorable peace above all else but felt powerless to do anything that might foster a resolution. Others rallied together to convince themselves and the world that all was well. As united voices, regiments and brigades throughout the Confederacy resolved to continue the struggle and swore their constant devotion to the cause. Their tenacity was echoed by their president. Three days after Hampton Roads, Jefferson Davis vowed that the Confederacy would never humiliate itself by surrendering to its despicable foes. He promised the southern nation that its soldiers would "compel the Yankees, in less than twelve months, to petition us for peace on our own terms." Richmond papers described the president's stance as "unconquerable defiance." [21]

Perhaps the strangest reaction to Hampton Roads was arming slaves for the Confederate war effort. Gloom and fatalism were sensible responses; defiance and rage were consistent reactions. But freeing slaves and making them soldiers contradicted the cause as nothing else could. This central paradox of Confederate history—giving freedom to blacks to insure independence for whites—can be interpreted many ways. First, it was a sign of desperation. White southerners refused to consider it until the eleventh hour. Second, it was a symbol of Confederate nationalism. Masters in a slave republic preferred political independence over their peculiar institution. Third, it was evidence of the culture of invincibility. Rebels actually thought that this measure could prolong the war and ensure Confederate victory. [22]

Diehard Confederates argued both sides of the debate. In some respects, the unvanquished reacted to Hampton Roads and the black Confederate question in ways that resembled their reactions to Lincoln's reelection. In both cases, diehards assumed that peace was imminent and would bring victory and independence. When that bubble burst, they presumed the war's outcome was postponed, not changed. Prolonging the contest in 1865 meant recruiting more men, and many Rebels were prepared to accept blacks toward this end. In Louisiana, Montgomery tried to convince a friend of this logic: "You don't seem to like the negro question much," he proclaimed, but, he pointed out, the "press on the East side of the Miss River . . . favor putting them into the army." Montgomery would support "any means by which we can whip the enemy & gain our Independence."[23]

Those who opposed black brothers in arms clung to the ethos of invincibility with even more determination. For them, the war could be maintained and eventually won if white shirkers and deserters returned to duty. Maury took this position in his diary. He considered arming slaves "a *'bitter pill'* . . . to swallow" and hated "the idea of having to lug Cuffee and Sambo into the ring." When he passed black recruits on the streets of Richmond, the colonel noted their military appearance, "their uniforms belts, and side-arms . . . their grey jackets and caps and their blue pantaloons," and found the whole affair preposterous. Maury thought the fiasco would be unnecessary "if the miserable men at home would only do their duty as the soldiers in the field perform theirs." "If they would only stop grumbling, sent back the absentees without leave, leave off extorting, and raise plenty of provisions," Maury figured, "we would undoubtedly prosper much better" than with black Confederates. James McPherson describes such arguments as a "flight into an aura of unreality." Nearly 150 years later, Maury's position may seem bizarre, but his views were consistent with his perspective and beliefs. In the end, both sides of this unusual debate urged their countrymen to rededicate themselves to the Confederacy; they only differed over how best to make that commitment.[24]

Before the spring campaigns commenced, Rebels sought help from other unlikely sources. Rumors of foreign intervention, however improbable they seem in hindsight, captivated thousands of troops in 1865. In January, reports promised an imminent alliance with France or Great Britain if the Confederacy would abolish slavery. Montgomery understood that "the whole world is against Slavery," but he figured if the Confederacy called its labor system "anything else but Slavery . . . recognition & intervention is bound to come." On January 18, Key announced that "France has recognized the Confederacy on condition that these States emancipate the slaves." Days later, he read in the press that an "alliance between England, France, and Spain" was poised to dictate terms to the United States that would recognize Confederate independence. Conversely, Nugent learned from northern papers that the United States proposed a coalition of Union and Confederate armies "to whip England and preserve the Monroe doctrine." Fleet told his father that a Rebel emissary had "borrowed 43 millions in gold from Germany, giving cotton & tobacco as security, & that he proposes to throw 10 millions on the market and thus redeem a great proportion of the currency." An officer stationed in the Trans-Mississippi Department wrote that a friend of his "has Maximilian on the brain, and wants to get to some point in Txs where we will be in striking distance of Mexico." In 1863, Louis Napoleon proclaimed Hapsburg Archduke Ferdinand Maximilian the emperor of Mexico after thirty-five thousand French troops sacked Mexico City and ousted Benito Juarez's republican government. Many Confederates envisioned a North American alliance between southern plantation owners and hacienda landlords.[25]

Talk of foreign intervention flourished after the peace conference fizzled. On February 16, Heartsill suspected that "the situation . . . in North America at this time is such, that foreign powers may force terms unpleasant to both the North and South." Many rumors claimed that European powers would not recognize Lincoln's second term of office, which started March 4, because the southern states had not participated in the election. Montgomery was certain that "after the 4th of March this country will be [a] separate and distinct nation from the U.S. and so recognized by one or more of the European powers." Nugent agreed that "England & France will not recognize Lincoln as President of anything but the Northern States after the 4th of March, and a war seems almost inevitable." When March 4 came and went without an eruption of world war, Blackford nonetheless told his wife, "I think there is some comfort to be derived from the hope of war between France and the United States." Scenarios of peace through foreign aid continued to fill the newspapers through the end of the month. Captain E. D. Cheatham was "inclined to think that something will grow out of the peace rumors." In late March, Crenshaw spread the rumor that a member of the British Parliament promised recognition from Britain and France if the Confederacy "gained a decided success within the next few months." On March 26, a week before the fall of Richmond, David Pierson imagined that a Federal campaign in the Trans-Mississippi Department (perhaps because it bordered Maximilian's domain) might spark foreign intercession.[26]

While rumors of international aid attracted some Confederates, others admonished their countrymen to unite and secure their independence. Enraged by civilian melancholy or by Lincoln's stark demands, many regiments gathered to reprove naysayers, denounce peace negotiations, and rededicate their lives to the cause. As the Staunton Artillery declared on February 1, 1865, "the despondency talked of does not exist in the army." The Virginians were "determined never to acquiesce in any accommodation short of independence." "We believe this to be the spirit of the whole army," the unit's members proclaimed, "and we appeal to the people of our loved homes to respond to it." Because the soldiers sent these resolutions to newspapers and the Confederate Congress, these records illustrate how the veterans directly addressed the country during its darkest hour. To inspire the populace, soldiers evoked the same elements that had bolstered their morale throughout the war's final phase: faith in providential deliverance, perceptions of a barbaric enemy, and warped views of the military situation. Their resolutions provided litanies of Confederate invincibility.[27]

Many public resolutions broadcast a constant faith that God favored the Confederacy and intended to rescue it from defeat. A brigade of South Carolinians promised, "With the aid of Heaven, we will continue the struggle until our independence be achieved or we perish in the attempt." In late January, Virginia infantrymen resolved "under Divine protection, never to submit to the Government of the United States." Other Virginians confessed their "unbounded confidence in our ability, under the guidance of an overruling Providence, to achieve a glorious triumph in the present struggle, directed by that great, good and gallant spirit that has often led us to victory." A Mississippi brigade looked to the Almighty, "the giver of every good and perfect gift," to bring ultimate triumph. "Relying on a just God," the Ninth Virginia Infantry vowed to "reconsecrate our best energies" toward the goal of independence. Heartsill's unit pledged to "fight the incarnate fiend, so long as we have an organized force, and a kind Providence will give us strength and power to wield a sword or aim a rifle." All of these resolutions sought to remind Confederates that with God as their ally, the rebellion could not fail; pessimists were thus not only cowards but also unbelievers.[28]

The troops also enumerated (and exaggerated) the enemy's atrocities to underscore the Confederacy's goodness and to convince the nation that defeat would be worse than Hell. McGowan's Brigade of South Carolinians reasoned that if the Rebels had correctly judged four years earlier "that the enemy intended to impoverish and oppress us, we *now know* that they propose to subjugate, enslave, disgrace and destroy us." Mississippians swore that the enemy was not only "a cruel foe" but "cold-blooded murderers." Virginian infantrymen pleaded with the populace not to be unnerved by "the cruel vindictiveness and angry boasts of our enemy" but to resist "to the last extremity, a foe, subjection to who would make life itself a burden." Another infantry regiment claimed that the enemy had "spared no species of insult nor injury that malice could devise" and planned for the Rebels "worse than Egyptian bondage." "It is better to die freemen than to live slaves," they resolved. The officers and men of the Fifty-seventh Virginia regiment could not fathom how the people could consider "recanting their declaration of independence from the accursed Yankee despotism which once enthralled us," reminding citizens that the enemy had committed "the most fiendish outrages and cruelties; has desolated and destroyed our country and committed every barbarity recorded in the past annals of rapacity, wrong and rapine." Here the soldier who penned the resolutions warmed to his subject: "Now is no time to dream of submission and reconstruction, when the enemy is at our very door; . . . while the shrieks of our insulted women ring ever in our ear; while the smoke of a whole country, consumed and desolated, yet hangs over the lovely Valley of the Shenandoah, and when the flames which destroyed the whole of Central Georgia have scarce died out." Submission would "consign us and our children to a bondage and slavery which would be insupportably base and degrading, and hand us and our posterity down to the latest time, coupled with an infamy to which any thing—even annihilation itself—were far preferable." Bratton's Brigade declared that "the outrages upon us by a base and unprincipled foe, in violation of all the usages of civilized warfare, have created an impassable gulf between the two sections, which must forever prevent all union or affiliation between them." Like most other resolutions, Bratton's document considered subjugation "worse than death." By evoking images of disgraced loved ones, smoldering homesteads, and roving enemy bands, the Rebels hoped to convince their populace that defeat was too terrible to permit. Reconciliation was farthest from their minds.[29]

The soldiers also asserted that the war was not going as badly as civilians thought. The members of a South Carolina brigade told their countrymen, "At every stage of the unequal conflict, the valor endurance and patriotic devotion of our people have secured a succession of victories of which any nation might well be proud." The South Carolinians argued that "the contest is still undecided" and that "timid counsels" and "causeless despondency" within the nation, rather than the enemy's "temporary success," threatened to ruin the Confederacy. The brigade focused on its past triumphs to the point that it seemed unaffected by its recent setbacks. "In the late reverses which have attended our arms" the soldiers saw "nothing which should obscure the light of our former glorious victories, [or] which should create a feeling of despondency or doubt of the ultimate success of our cause." They believed that "one more determined effort is alone necessary to achieve our independence." The resolutions adopted by three Virginia companies exhibited the same preference for past victories over present circumstances. "In the present aspect of affairs," the men confessed, "we see nothing to occasion gloom or despondency, but, on the contrary, we believe that the past four years of war have proved, beyond all doubt, the abilities of the slave-holding States to maintain and protect, against all enemies, the Government which they have established." Other troops reasoned that "we have had our share of victories, and we must expect some defeats." They compared the Confederacy's condition to the despair pervasive in revolutionary America before the victory at Yorktown. "In the language of General [Nathanael] Greene, during the darkest hours of the Revolution, when he was struggling to recover South Carolina, then entirely overrun and suffering under the scourge of Tarlton," the Rebels quoted, "'Independence is certain, if the people have the fortitude to bear and the courage to persevere.'" The Fifty-seventh Virginia Regiment urged the populace not "to hesitate, to falter in the brave, proud course which has hitherto been marked out for them," because General Lee needed only support from the people and government to "lead us again to victory and success, and crown our efforts with an honorable independence and lasting peace."[30]

To culminate their appeal for renewed defiance, many Confederates recalled dead comrades and vowed to defend the cause for which they had died against the enemy that had killed them. A brigade of Mississippians vowed, "The melancholy but sweet recollections of comrades who now sleep in bloody graves, preclude forever for us the sacrilege of a Re-construction." The Ninth Virginia argued, "We owe it to ourselves, to the cause or liberty, and to the memory of those who have fallen in our sacred cause, to resist, to the last extremity." Another Virginia unit proclaimed, "The blood of our brothers, our sons and our fathers call upon us for vengeance." "Their bones lie bleaching on every hill-top and valley, from the blood-stained heights of Gettysburg to the placid waters of the Rio Grande." A South Carolina brigade also claimed that the best blood of the country had been shed and that patriot bones were scattered across the land. The men vowed never to abandon "a cause which has been consecrated by so many costly sacrifices, and crowned by so many illustrious victories." The soldiers admonished citizens that quitting the cause for which thousands had perished amounted to cowardice. The Fourteenth Virginia Infantry declared that anyone who abandoned the Confederacy was "unworthy to breathe the air of freedom, and should, with his posterity, be the serfs of serfs, to the remotest generation." According to the diehards, a nation that quit its struggle for independence deserved infamy for all of history—biblical bondage would plague such a country for centuries. But "the unabated fervor of the veterans of our armies," as the Virginians put it, still stood between the Confederacy and the basest subjugation.[31]

Though soldiers submitted these resolutions to inspire the populace, the act of drafting such vows profoundly affected the troops. In fact, these documents probably inspired their creators more than they influenced their audience. The soldiers' movement to congregate and swear their lives in defense of the rebellion bore a striking resemblance to the religious revivals that swept through Confederate camps. Whether they were animated by concerns for civilian despondency or by inner forebodings about the coming campaigns, troops found strength and comfort by banding together and voicing a faith in ultimate triumph. Soldiers who met and expressed a rhetoric of patriotic sacrifice were also reliving the emotional days of 1861 when they first volunteered to oppose the Union. Memories of fallen comrades and the sight of fellow survivors vowing to fight to the end overwhelmed some soldiers. James wrote to his sister two long letters detailing the ceremony during which his unit composed resolutions: "I now feel as I felt in June '61 when I first enlisted. . . . The same spirit which actuated me then, actuates me now; and I feel as buoyant and hopeful and as confident of the result of this war as I ever felt in the midst of the most brilliant successes." "After four years of bloody war—of hardships and privations," James proclaimed, "the veteran soldiers of the invincible army of Northern Virginia, are speaking to the country." Earlier that day, James's regiment had drafted resolutions to protract the war. A band played martial music while a committee wrote a preamble and resolutions. After the vows passed unanimously, officers and civilian dignitaries spoke at length about the Confederacy's imminent success.

A judge from Kentucky spoke for more than two hours, promising the regiment that "when the Spring campaign opened we would have five hundred thousand men under arms." Another man refused to give a speech but predicted "that the Yankee armies would be defeated in the next campaign and that the war would be over by Christmas." When Lincoln began his second term in early March, Fay presided over a meeting in which the members of his unit reenlisted for four more years. He crowed that for four years, Lincoln had already tried to rule the Confederacy, "but our brave soldiers have been invincible."[32]

How much significance should be given to resolutions meant for public consumption? These statements could be interpreted as face-saving gestures. Brigades may have clamored to affirm their devotion to the cause when desertion was most rampant. When Fleet's brigade vowed "as a body for war to the bitter end instead of any reconstruction," he hoped that the resolutions "will raise us in the estimation of our comrades beyond the clouds of malice and reproach." Fleet's comment suggests that some units penned resolutions to solidify their reputations as diehards. At a time when widespread desertion undermined the integrity of Confederate armies, public expressions of patriotism were an obvious way for troops to separate their cherished regiment or brigade from shame. Moreover, Rebels uniformly identified their units in the resolution titles, thereby leaving no doubt as to which men promised Congress and the people unending service. The resolutions also raise questions because of their formulaic language. After the first statements were publicized, other units may have mimicked the expressions they read in newspapers as a way of drawing attention to their own patriotism.[33]

Other aspects of the resolutions suggest that Rebels meant and believed what they declared. First, the troops supported their statements with the same elements that had bolstered their faith throughout the war. They made their case for persistence with signs of providential favor, images of barbaric enemies, and skewed perceptions of the war's progress. In short, their language and reasoning were the same in 1865 as in 1863. Judging one year's expressions as genuine and another's as false seems dubious. Second, the troops were profoundly affected by the act of passing resolutions. If it had been a disingenuous act, their statements are unlikely to have moved them as much. For these reasons, the resolutions merit more scholarly attention than they have received. More historians examine the debate over arming slaves because it represents a paradox in Confederate history—a slave-holding nation asking its bondsmen to fight for their masters' independence. The 1865 resolutions, however, can illustrate more about the motives and mentalities of the Rebel army, the embodiment of Confederate nationalism.

While wish rumors continued to impress the men and resolutions bolstered their solidarity, faith in God's favor provided the bedrock for Confederate confidence in 1865. People are often attracted to religion in times of great uncertainty and pain, and the nature of Confederate religion connected Rebel adversity to God. Soldiers who viewed themselves as chosen people destined for greatness expected providential deliverance from defeat even as their nation crumbled around them. Thus, Christian Confederates viewed setbacks as evidence of God chastening them rather than as signs of their imminent doom. As a Louisiana lieutenant noted in January 1865, "All that happens to us, is for the good. God will sometimes send us disasters to bring us to our senses." In late February, Hampton wrote to his wife, "I really think that this war will in a short time assume a different character I.E. for our good." "Although things to some may look gloomy," Hampton did not despair because "in God we may look for redemption." Believers considered even the darkest circumstances to be lessons from a loving God. James Izlar, captured during the fall of Fort Fisher, admitted, "Our cause looks gloomy, but I am still hopeful, [because] God is just, God is power." Only the Almighty decided battles and wars. Izlar prayed, "In to thy hands O Lord I commit, all who are near & dear and the justice of our cause." While he prayed, the prisoner heard the church bells of New York City ringing in celebration of another Union victory but believed that Confederate triumph would still come when Jehovah wished it.[34]

The Confederacy observed its final day of national fasting and prayer on March 10, 1865, a month before Appomattox. Across the Mississippi, Lieutenant James Wallace thought this religious day received more pious attention from citizens than any other: "Every countenance bore deep humility and evry church was occupied during the day by the people of God." On the occasion, Key believed "that the Supreme Ruler will soon reward the Sons of Liberty for their prayers with a great victory," because "almost every national day of humiliation and fasting has been followed with some marked triumph on some bloody battlefield." Word of a victory at Kinston, North Carolina, seemed to confirm Key's belief. Troops under General Braxton Bragg inflicted more than 1,200 casualties, most of them prisoners, at a loss of 134 men. In the process, the Rebels halted General John Schofield's merger with Sherman's army. Rawleigh Downman prayed that "God in his great mercy may look with favor on our cause and deliver us from our enemies." Maury's description of the fast day illustrates how Confederates conceived of their relationship with God: he saw the event as an opportunity to "entreat a merciful God to forgive us our sins—to stand on our side and to give us victory." For Maury and thousands of others, divine forgiveness and Confederate triumph were one and the same. Moreover, Wallace, Key, and Maury jotted these lines in diaries, not letters. They did not assume God's favor for the benefit of dispirited loved ones.[35]

The persistence of religious fervor in the Confederacy was evident in the high level of religious activity that continued until the war's final days. As their ranks thinned and their future grew darker, many soldiers needed to believe that God was an ever-present and unswerving ally. James Keith admitted that he derived comfort from looking "to him who has promised never to desert those who put their trust in him." Keith's use of the word *desert* is poignant—shirkers and comrades were disappearing from the trenches, but God was not. A minister who served Lee's troops during the final months of the war noted that "revivals . . . during the winter of 1864–65 were as general and as powerful as any we had at all and only ceased when the army disbanded." Chaplain Richard Webb wrote home, "We are now enjoying a refreshing shower of grace from the presence of the Lord." Scores of men had joined the church since the fast day. Historian James Silver notes that "as late as March ministers of all denominations in Virginia were in the field, addressing the people in an effort to encourage moral firmness and support of the war." In March, chaplain John Paris preached to the men behind their breastworks while bullets whizzed overhead. Less than a week before Richmond fell, Maury still attended prayer meetings daily. Creed Thomas Davis noted in his diary that a local reverend preached to the troops regularly in the last months of the struggle and always brought religious tracts "which he scatters profusely through the camp." Robert Augustus Stiles collected Christian pamphlets and gave them to troops whose units lacked chaplains. Many of these publications were wildly optimistic about Confederate success. "It is pleasant, in the midst of this torrent & rush of earthly burdens & confusion," wrote Stiles, "to turn to the green pastures & the still waters of God's love." "Just to turn away to that blessed great part of our soul's life" offered Stiles and fellow believers a beautiful release from their darkest days.[36]

Rumors and religious convictions affected how Confederates interpreted the news they received in 1865. Somehow, many diehards still managed to claim victories and depict the military situation with optimism. They yearned for good news and interpreted ambiguous reports in positive ways. Maury's 1865 diary exudes his notions of Confederate invincibility. Again, these lines were not public expressions of patriotism. Perhaps Maury remained defiant in his diary because he wished to impress future readers of the journal. In some ways, every diarist writes to the future reader or discoverer of the book, even if that person is the writer. But even if such were the case, Maury chose to identify himself as a diehard Rebel until the bitter end. Thousands of men throughout the Confederacy made the same choice in 1865. This collective decision to remain defiant had profound implications for reunion, reconstruction, and the memory of the war.

Throughout the final months of the war, Maury, an infantry colonel, was in Richmond recuperating from a serious wound. Doctors told him he would never be well enough to return to his regiment, but Maury scoffed at their diagnosis, just as he laughed at "croakers" who predicted doom for the Rebels. "I cannot be conquered, no! Not by the whole Yankee nation," he hollered. When President Davis gave General Lee command of all Confederate forces, Maury thought the news foreshadowed great victories. He knew that the Confederacy "must succeed" in the coming campaign and figured that its chances were "better now, since that great and good man has taken the helm." Maury guessed that Lee planned to take the offensive "and deal Grant a pretty heavy lick." When Lee reinstated Johnston as commander of the Army of Tennessee, Maury trusted that the general would bring Sherman "to grief." "Hurra for Old Joe," he exclaimed, "I bet on Joe." As had so many other Rebels, Maury trusted that his favorite generals could perform miracles against their adversaries.[37]

But February brought news of the fall of Columbia, Charleston, and Wilmington. Maury noted that "some of the weak kneed poor wretches" in Richmond "are terribly frightened" by the bad news. "How glad I am that I possess such a hopeful disposition, and such 'Maury obstinacy,'" he noted—such events did not dampen his spirits or alter his never-say-die attitude. When Richmond citizens voiced anxiety for the capital's safety in March, Maury branded them "cravenhearted." "It is a disgrace to the South and to the very Earth that such men should live," he announced. "They cry out that we are whipped already and must make peace on any terms—confound the scoundrels (alas that we have to fight for them) we are not near conquered yet." Maury viewed the evacuation of Charleston and Wilmington as good news because troops stationed there could now "concentrate against Sherman and no doubt whip him." As Johnston gave up more territory, including Goldsboro and Fayetteville, North Carolina, to Sherman's columns, Maury still hoped that Johnston was saving his smaller force for a dramatic blow that would cripple Sherman. As for Lee, Maury wished that the general would "move upon Washington which must be almost entirely uncovered." Knowing that such a move exposed Richmond and seemed unlikely to work because of low manpower, Maury still wanted Lee to try.[38]

Maury's high expectations for Johnston and Lee seemed to bear fruit in late March when both generals appeared to score triumphs. Outside Bentonville, North Carolina, Johnston's army attacked a detached wing of Sherman's force. "Good news from Johnston as I was sure there would be soon," Maury wrote on March 20. "He has met Sherman and whipped him. . . . Drove him a mile when meeting reinforcements he rallied, and assumed the offensive, but was easily repulsed." Maury claimed that Johnston had captured 1,500 prisoners and three pieces of artillery. In fact, the Confederates had lost 1,500 men while inflicting only 933 casualties. The affair could have been worse, but Sherman let Johnston's men escape because the Federal general saw the end of the war approaching and wanted to spare both sides further bloodshed. Days later, Maury learned that Lee's men had "attacked the enemy near Petersburg, drove them from their works capturing 9 cannon and 500 or 600 prisoners." When Grant counterattacked on March 30, Maury noted that the Union ranks were repulsed until Grant quit, "leaving many dead and wounded Yanks in our hands." Maury either could not or would not recognize that these Confederate attacks were desperate attempts by Rebel forces to avoid being enclosed by larger Federal armies. Three days later, the Rebel defenses around Petersburg crumbled and Grant's thousands headed for the capital.[39]

Though Richmond's evacuation on April 2 marked the beginning of the end, many Confederates who participated in the chaos could not grasp its complete significance. Colonel George Alexander Martin was sick in bed when an officer of his command rushed in to report that Lee's army was in full retreat and that the government had already left the capital. Martin galloped into town to find his men "and if necessary die with them." Instead, he discovered panic and mayhem: "Commissary Stores were being removed or destroyed, wagons drays and other vehicles were loading, or being driven swiftly through the streets, creating a rumbling and confused noise, and their drivers were cursing and shouting, men were hallooing, women screaming, children crying, horses neighing and engines whistling." People, beasts, and loot blocked the streets, and government stores of liquor flooded the gutters. Fires started by Confederates consumed parts of the city and "lent a horrid glow to the surroundings." Gunboats and magazines exploded, spraying pyrotechnics into the sky. Martin could not find his men but gathered that all of Lee's troops were heading west for Lynchburg or Danville while Grant's forces closed around them and claimed the capital. He feared that the fires would burn down the city's bridges before he could escape across one.[40]

After the collapse at Richmond, the city's defenders fought and fled west during a week of disorganized activity. Contemporary accounts of their scramble from Richmond to Appomattox Court House are rare, because few troops found time to eat and sleep, let alone express their thoughts in writing. In particular, the chaos restricted correspondence with family. Those who recorded the events conveyed confusion, fatigue, and disbelief in diary entries. Many chroniclers strove to comprehend the "rather startling intelligence," as Walters put it, that Richmond was gone. Henry Chambers expressed the situation in ways that foreshadowed the Lost Cause. In his diary, Chambers explained that the enemy, "by overwhelming numbers broke over our Petersburg lines." He stressed that "our men fought gallantly, repulsing assaults again and again and that too when the enemy was eight and nine columns deep." The enemy did not merit laurels for its triumph: size rather than skill or courage had decided the contest. "It is a sad thing," Chambers reflected, "for this hitherto never defeated army, to be by sheer force of numbers driven from our lines." Like many of his comrades, the North Carolinian saw the collapse at Richmond as Lee's first defeat. Gettysburg and Grant's successes in the East somehow did not fit the definition of Confederate failure. Many troops echoed Chambers's effort to end the struggle with their honor intact.[41]

As Walters marched west, he tried to prepare himself for the future. "What fate may have in store for us, I cannot imagine, but I fear that the last days of the Army of Northern Virginia is near at hand," he scribbled on April 4. The next day, Walters noted that "many of the men [are] in apparently as good spirits as ever," but the "usual jest" seemed to be "constrained, while the laughter was evidently forced." He doubted that the army could escape the enemy's grasp "as both men and horses are broken down and the rations which were served out today were two ears of corn per man." Walters admitted that he was "almost used up" and worried about falling behind. But instead of dreading the thought of becoming a prisoner, Walters feared that he would miss the army's momentous finale: "Ere many days General Lee will need the service of every man, and though one man can do but little, yet when the death struggle takes place, I should like to be there." Walters sensed that history was being made and wanted to play his part as a diehard Rebel, even if the role made him one of the war's final fatalities. [42]

Downman, a cavalry sergeant, was too busy fending off the enemy to write as regularly as Walters did. As one of General Fitzhugh Lee's horse soldiers, Downman served as the rear guard for the army after it abandoned the trenches. Riding west over hills, across fields, and down country roads, Downman and his comrades stopped to fight at Scott's Corner, Namozine Church, Deep Creek, Tabernacle Church, and near Amelia Court House in just three days. On April 5 they received word that the enemy had seized a line of Confederate wagons and raced to protect the panicked teamsters and precious supplies. When Downman heard on April 6 that a slave was heading toward Downman's home, he stopped and penned a long missive to his wife. "Every thing has been so stirred up since our evacuation of Richmond that I cannot write you a very connected letter," he confessed. Downman's primary concern was reassuring his family, and he used the prevailing chaos to piece together a wishful narrative. The cavalryman promised, "You must not be depressed on account of our defeat at Petersburg" because "the affair was not as bad as you may have heard." Downman went on to inform his wife that the Confederates had succeeded against the raid on the wagon train: "We whipt them handsomely and took about 80 prisoners." Moreover, his unit had "attacked a brigade of Yankee infantry—killed their general a large number of men & captured about 700." What is most striking about Downman's account is his belief that the evacuation of Richmond and the ensuing retreat were not the end of the war but rather the resumption of active campaigning. "I cannot tell you all my adventures since the active campaign commenced," he explained. Still, Downman figured that "this is to be the last regular campaign. If we can stem the torrent we are safe. If not then organized resistance ends and we enter upon the period of irregular warfare & no one can tell how many years it may last." Even though Downman had been in the saddle for days, fighting against great numbers, he still highlighted minor tactical gains and hoped for the best. [43]

While Downman sought silver linings, another cavalryman, Cornelius Hart Carlton, watched as his unit melted away via desertions. Ten or twelve men left during the night of April 3 and went home. On the following night, eight or ten more quit as they crossed the railroad bridge over the Appomattox River. When he fed his horse on the morning of April 5, Carlton realized that more men had disappeared in the dark. Of the forty-nine thousand troops who left the trenches on April 2, only twenty-eight thousand surrendered a week later, the rest having either deserted or been captured during the long scurry. On April 6, Giles Buckner Cooke noted that only a few divisions of the First and Third Corps "had any organization." "The rest of the troops were straggling terribly and rapidly disintegrating." That same day, three Union corps surrounded a quarter of Lee's army at Sayler's Creek and captured six thousand men. When Lee received the news, he asked with astonishment, "My God! Has the army been dissolved?" No, but it was almost gone.[44]

The following day, Grant and Lee started to negotiate surrender via messages passed by flags of truce. But even Lee seemed unable to accept the end, and the correspondence stalled the following day. That night the fires from Union camps surrounded what was left of the Army of Northern Virginia. "What will become of us all tomorrow?" Cooke asked himself. The thought of never seeing his family again was "maddening," and he expected "to be captured or killed" in the morning. "Great God make me strong," he prayed, "prepare me for whatever fate." On the morning of April 9, the Confederates charged the Federal cavalry in an attempt to break out of Grant's tightening grip. The Union horsemen fled, and Rebels seized two cannons. But two corps of Yankee infantry filled the gap and outnumbered the Confederates five or six to one. Lee finally agreed to surrender, though he told an officer, "I would rather die a thousand deaths."[45]

When Lee returned to his lines after completing the proceedings with Grant, Confederates yelled and surrounded him. For years, the men had cheered their general, so the outcry might have been no more than custom. But many of these Rebels were not yet prepared to surrender. As one scholar notes, "Despite their grinding week-long retreat and its heavy losses, more from straggling than combat—despite last night's red western glow of enemy campfires and this morning's breakout failure; despite the coming and going of couriers, blue and gray, and [Lee's] own outward passage through their line of battle . . . many of them were still not ready to believe the end had come." Postwar accounts and legends claim that troops crowded Lee and swore that they "would fight 'em yet" if the general would say the word. Instead, he asked them to go home.[46]

The realization that they had surrendered was too much for some soldiers to accept. "While I knew that things were going badly," David Gregg McIntosh admitted, "I was not prepared for such intelligence, and a thunderbolt from heaven could hardly have shocked me more." Weighing his options, McIntosh decided, "my first and only duty was to my country, and that as long as I could be of service to her I should avoid surrender." He and some comrades who "could not brook the thought of witnessing the spectacle of surrender" tore off their military insignia and escaped through the Appomattox swamp. Chamberlayne fled with McIntosh and wrote to his sister days later that "we refused to take part in the funeral at Appomattox C.H." "I am by no means conquered yet," he exclaimed. Chamberlayne expected to join Johnston's army, and if that force surrendered, he would head for Texas and maybe Mexico. "If the struggle is over I will go abroad & hope to provide a refuge for us all," he wrote on April 21 from Charlotte, North Carolina. Chamberlayne preferred living in exile over accepting a reality imposed by the enemy. Such diehards hurried toward the sunset of the Confederacy, leaving the darkness of the future behind them as long as possible. In May, Chamberlayne rode all the way to Mississippi, swapping horses four times in a furious race against reality. At the end of his remarkable journey, the Virginian said that he had been "guided by what I thought duty," but "in truth, the age of the sword is gone by." No amount of running could recover the past.[47]

Most troops used a series of activities less dramatic than McIntosh and Chamberlayne's flight to help accept the surrender. After hearing the "sad news," Albright "felt like an old horse . . . turned out to die." He cried with his comrades, said good-bye, and "started south" for home. Others mingled with the enemy, especially after Federal troops delivered three days' rations to the famished Rebels. The size and condition of the Union army stunned Walters: "I have seen more of the Yankee army by passing of endless lines of troops, artillery, and wagon trains than I ever saw before, and in view of the immense numbers, unlimited resources, and perfect and complete appointments in all that belongs to an army, my astonishment is not that we were all compelled to surrender . . . but that we were able to stand as we have for four years with our comparatively small numbers, lean cattle, and imperfect equipment." Walters realized that misperceptions of the enemy and notions of Confederate invincibility had sustained the rebellion for months if not years.[48]

Other Confederates were less willing or able to discard the ethos of invincibility. Chambers could not surrender to barbarians. He vented rage and humiliation at "the fact that these worthless fellows whom we have so often whipped . . . can pass with the air of conquerors through our camps and hereafter throughout our whole country." When he considered that enemy legions "swelled by contributions from almost every race and color on the globe . . . can now lord it over us and ours," Chambers cried, "Oh! God how can we bear this!" He was so convinced of the superiority of white southern men that defeat seemed a nightmare, a "mad intoxication" that must be imaginary. He prayed that God would send "some terrible retribution yet . . . upon this motley crew who have waged upon us so unjust so barbarous a warfare!" The diehard's list of enemy atrocities was long and predictable: northern "hell-hounds" had "burned our houses desecrated our altars, plundered our wealth, waged unrelenting warfare upon the aged, the weak, and helpless," and "insulted and dishonored our lovely women!" The barbarians won "by every chicanery, by fraud, by passion, by superstition,—by fanatical religion, by the hope of immense rewards, and by the blandishments of beauty even." No amount of reconciliation could appease men like Chambers.[49]

Perceptions that steeled Rebel resolve during the war soured the experience of defeat. Alabamian Sam Pickens was captured on April 2 during the frantic retreat from Richmond and Petersburg. When his captors fired two hundred guns to celebrate Lee's surrender, Pickens could not believe it: "We can't realize the truth of the astounding events that are transpiring so rapidly." For Pickens and other stalwarts, signs of defeat seemed to be "crowding up on us" because the enemy was imposing its reality. No more could diehard Rebels interpret local engagements and distant news in a positive light: the enemy's world was "crowding" Confederate perceptions, leaving no room to dream. When this happened, the bitter implications of defeat replaced any tangible supports for the ethos of invincibility. Pickens and countless others struggled to escape the full consequences of this change. "Oh! can it be possible that after all sacrifices made— immolation of so many noble heroes it is not to end in our favor—that we are to lose our independence & be in subjection to the Yankees!" Like Chambers, Pickens prayed that God would yet "deliver us out of the hands of our too powerful enemies & bless us with Independence & Peace!" Providence surely had not designed this end. Virginian Kena King Chapman also refused to accept the facts. "The opinion seems to prevail that the war is ended," he admitted, "but I cannot think so—there is life in the old land yet." For many diehards, disputing the facts was easier than discarding an ethos.[50]

News of Lee's surrender sent shock waves across the Confederacy. As reports radiated from Virginia, they had less impact on soldiers who were farther from the event. Three days before the capitulation, Joseph Bryan was riding with Colonel John Mosby's partisans in northern Virginia when he heard of Richmond's fall. "What the ultimate result will be remains concealed from mortals," he wrote. "We can but fight and pray our best." Among the soldiers, Bryan heard no cry for peace but instead "an unusual desire to meet the enemy that we may at least give a few Yanks a satisfactory evidence that all the Rebs are neither dead nor captured yet." Though Bryan claimed that the war's outcome remained uncertain, his language betrayed the facts of defeat—"all the Rebs are neither dead nor captured *yet*." Realizing defeat created an "unusual desire" to show the enemy that Confederates were superior even if conquered. Appomattox, however, decided the course of action for Mosby's men. Instead of proving their supremacy in a final battle, they disbanded and went home on April 21. On that day, Mosby told his horsemen that "the vision we have cherished of a free and independent country has vanished." In Virginia, Mosby clearly understood that the Confederacy "is now the spoil of the conqueror."[51]

Farther away, in North Carolina, news of Lee's surrender swirled through the Army of Tennessee for days before the men accepted it. Unconfirmed reports of Richmond's fall filtered into the army on April 6, 7, and 8. A Confederate congressman from Tennessee addressed some of Johnston's men on April 8. According to William Sloan, "He told us of the evacuation of Richmond by the Confederates, but assures us that the loss of the city would be no disadvantage to our cause, and that Lee's army was in as good spirits and fighting trim as ever." The speech must have had its desired effect, because Sloan reported that "all are in fine spirits."[52] Captain Samuel Foster recorded the army's reactions as the consequences of Appomattox seeped into soldiers' mentalities. He and others were demoralized but still hoped and believed "that we will whip this fight yet." Johnston's troops hoped to bolster their ranks with men who had refused to quit at Appomattox Court House. For weeks, Lee's veterans, refugees, cabinet members, and even Jefferson Davis passed through the western army's camp. These men who had been losing battles since 1862 were still fighting while the remains of their government and its most revered army swept by like debris in a flood. But as men from Lee's army continued homeward, Foster and his comrades started to consider the likelihood that they too would be surrendered. "Of course there is great excitement about it," he remarked, "and there are various suggestions which, if Gen Johnson could act upon would of course save the army" from capitulation. When the men learned on April 17 that Johnston was meeting with Sherman, many veterans discussed their plans for going home, although others did not yet warm to capitulation. Foster noted that "some say the [war] is settled and some say that the difficulty has hardly begun."[53]

As in the past, when troops faced great uncertainty, rumors circulated that offered false hopes and obscured the truth. Talk of foreign intervention rose from the ashes of improbability and charmed the veterans once more. On April 19, Foster reported that "the United States has recognized the Confederacy, and agrees to give us all our rights (and slavery) if we will help them to fight all their enemies." Rather than face their current condition, some troops preferred to imagine an imminent world war: "Some think that the big war is about to commence, a war of some Magnitude. France Austria Mexico and the Confederacy on one side, against England Russia and the U S on the other, and the great battle ground will be in the Confederacy. One plan is for the Confederacy to go back into the Union, then France will declare war with the U S and land her troops on the C S Coast where they will have no opposition, and as the French Army advances through the C S the people will take the oath of Allegiance to France, and our soldiers will enlist under French colors." For days, veterans of the Army of Tennessee sought any scenario but defeat. When Foster realized that Johnston had received no terms short of "submission reunion free negroes &c," he exclaimed, "We have been fighting too long for that." The magnitude of Confederate sacrifices made it harder to accept unconditional surrender. Rebels cherished their endurance and triumphs. Unconditional surrender meant accepting that none of those actions had gained a single concession from the enemy. In the end, the Confederacy's honored dead, its heroism, its tenacity, and its brilliant leadership generated nothing. Foster and many others could not accept these deeper implications of surrender. While negotiations for his capitulation passed between the armies, Foster wrote, "I have not seen a man today but says fight on rather than submit." Diehards wanted something tangible for their accomplishments and pride.[54]

When Johnston's men surrendered on April 26, the Confederacy still had thousands of troops in the Deep South and across the Mississippi, but the nation's two veteran armies were gone. "What a mine of startling events has been sprung upon us in the last fortnight," Bird wrote from his home in Georgia. Bird's ethos could not easily process the facts of defeat. A different reality seemed to explode within his world like a mine, scattering his perceptions to bits. Stunned by the blast, Bird stumbled to gain his bearings. He gathered that "the impression seems to be gaining ground that the war is over" but postponed judgment because "a short time will develop all." Fellow Georgian George Mercer admitted that "we are now passing through a period of deep depression." He listed his country's woes: "Our money depreciated so rapidly that it threatens soon to become worthless. The enemy are penetrating every part of our land with their raiding parties, burning and destroying. One colomn has taken Selma and Montgomery and is moving on Columbus, another from East Tennessee has reached Salisbury, North Carolina, while rumor says another is moving on Augusta, another from Charleston, Winnsboro, South Carolina. Our railroad connections are all being severed and many think we can no longer feed large armies in the field and that we must resort to the guerilla system." Mercer then compared these conditions to those of the enemy, who "does not appear to feel the war at all." The United States was enjoying "wealth and comfort," and "immigration far more than repairs the loss in battle." Moreover, the enemy "boasted that the recent discoveries of petroleum alone will create wealth enough to pay off [the Federal] war debt." These signs that "God appears to smile on their cause" disturbed Mercer, and he tried to brush them aside. "While there is life, there is hope," he proclaimed. "We must continue the good fight and leave the rest to Heaven."[55]

Week by week, veterans across the South repeated the same process of disbelief, anger, and humiliation that tormented Lee's men in early April. South Carolinian D. E. Huger Smith marveled that the Army of Tennessee could accept the "disgraceful terms" offered by the enemy. Like many others, Smith wanted a compromise—an "honorable peace" that affirmed Confederate sacrifices and heroism. Without such terms, the Confederacy seemed a colossal mistake. "Four yrs, hard fighting & the best blood of our country all wasted— worse than wasted!" he fumed. "I cannot think, much less can I write about it." The diehard told his grandmother, "There are few of us who would not prefer a prison to going home upon such disgraceful terms." Smith thought that being one of the last diehards would preserve his personal honor even if southern honor had been lost. When Sloan surrendered in Charlotte, North Carolina, he treasured his final Confederate dollar: "I shall endeavor to keep my dollar the remainder of my life, as a memento of our glorious little Government, and its sad and untimely ending." Prefiguring the Lost Cause, Sloan eulogized, "Never was a government so deserving of success, and never before did men fight against such cruel odds, both in numbers and resources, or meet a more barbarous foe." Similar language would echo throughout the South for generations.[56]

When defeat reached Alabama in late April, it elicited the same pattern of denial and confusion. On April 25, officers in Brewersville spread false rumors to their men during a dress parade. Edwin Leet relayed misinformation to his wife the next day: "We received glorious news . . . stating that General R. E. Lee had had a great battle with Genl Grant, and had killed a great number of Yankeys, and that Grant asked for an armistice, to which Lee had agreed." Leet went on to report that "one hundred thousand of Grants army deserted" when they heard of Lincoln's April 14 assassination and that Johnston "had whipped Sherman badly" in a recent contest. Though he doubted the hearsay, Leet hoped that it was true. In Mobile, Charles Andry knew that the war was over but was "entirely at loss as to what course to pursue." Though he wanted to honor his pledge to the Confederacy as long as it existed, Andry could not earn a living until he swore allegiance to the United States. He asked his father for advice: "Why should I . . . cling to a cause or party which has so little vitality? I think my duty now in considering the present aspect of affairs, (which is so plain,) is to do the best I can to provide for the wants of my wife and child." Because many Confederates lacked formal surrender ceremonies, they sought personal ways to end the war and honorably resume civilian life.[57]

Soldiers across the Mississippi River were the last to receive news from the east and accept its implications. On April 23, Colonel Louis Bringier told his wife to hire out their slaves if she could because their labor was worth gold specie. Pleased by the "cheering news" that John Wilkes Booth had murdered Lincoln, Bringier named his child after the assassin. In Shreveport, Louisiana, David Pierson also drew confidence from the president's death. Moreover, Pierson heard that only part of Lee's army had capitulated, and the latest news from the Army of Tennessee reported that its men were "in good condition and still hopeful." But Johnston's army had already surrendered. When authorities in Shreveport planned a mass meeting "to give confidence to the doubting and despondent," Pierson scoffed at this attempt "to bind up the wounds of the mangled Confederacy with plausible reasonings and sweet words." He preferred that every man simply shoulder a gun and fight.[58]

Weeks after Foster struggled with the finality of defeat in his diary, Heartsill faced the same challenge in his writing. In Texas, Heartsill did not hear of the fall of Richmond until April 16—two weeks after the event and a week after Lee's surrender. Though "Charleston, Savanah, Wilmington, Atlanta, Petersburg, and perhaps Mobile and Richmond have fallen" and though "Sherman has marched triumphantly through Georgia and South Carolina, and is now burning his way through the 'Old North State,'" Heartsill still believed that God would deliver Confederate victory. "It is indeed a bitter ordeal through which He is leading us to independence; but Oh how sweet that liberty [will feel], when obtained by bleeding hearts, and tears of anguish." "Through His Omnipotent power we will yet triumph," he exclaimed. "Through all this dark and gloomy present," Heartsill still saw "a bright and glorious future." He predicted that "the enemy will . . . meet with tremendous, and overwhelming reverses, and that too at a moment when least expected." "May a kind providence protect and shield the right," he prayed. [59]

When news of Lee's surrender reached Heartsill and his comrades, they denied the report and spread hopeful rumors. Some men claimed that England and France had recognized the Confederacy. Others announced that "Emporer Napoleon had landed a large Army on the Texas coast." Sanders also heard that French ships were en route to the Gulf of Mexico and that Parisian men were enrolling in the army at a rate not seen since the Crimean War. Heartsill thought, "We should make one mighty, determined effort. For if foreign powers ever do intend to extend any aid, this is 'The auspicious moment.'" He scorned people who called for peace: "We are NOT whiped, we CAN and we MUST fight; subjugation never." On May 9, the members of Heartsill's regiment met and resolved that they "have perfect confidence in, and will render willing obedience to our Commanding officers; and will not lay down our arms, so long as there is a Confederate soldier to vindicate the cause of Southern freedom." Their colonel urged them to "stand by their country, and if the worst comes to the worst, to stand man to man." [60]

When western troops learned that all their allies east of the river had capitulated, some diehards hoped they could save the Confederacy themselves. Heartsill imagined that "the Trans Mississippi could defy the combined powers of all Yankeedom." Junius Bragg figured, "There is an Army here sufficient to worry the Yankees for a long time." Bragg saw himself and other remaining Rebels on the threshold of glory or subjugation—the choice was theirs. "When thoughts of submission come into our minds," Bragg wrote, "we think of Yankee Masters, a ruined country, Negro equality and the mortification of defeat, and fight on a little longer." Like diehards across the river, Bragg persisted to avoid an unconditional surrender and its attendant horrors. Fay dreamed that western soldiers "could hold out for ten years and worry the Yankees into a recognition of the Confederacy." Fay even envied General Kirby Smith, the commander of the Trans-Mississippi Department, because he had a chance to become the father of the Confederacy and place his name next to George Washington's in the pantheon of national military greatness. Only soldiers who had not encountered Grant's or Sherman's one-hundred-thousand-man armies could entertain fantasies of defying the Union for years with Smith's thirty-five thousand.[61]

By mid-May, Smith's army was that formidable only on paper. Desertion and trans-Mississippians' belief in fighting where and when they pleased left Smith with few men and fewer options. On May 12–13, some of these free-spirited troops fought three Union regiments at Palmito Ranch, Texas. The Federals enjoyed early success, but the Rebels rallied and pushed the enemy down the banks of the Rio Grande. The final Civil War engagement of significant size was a Confederate victory. Smith met with the exiled governors of Louisiana, Arkansas, and Missouri. The civilians wanted to surrender, but their general favored resistance until President Davis arrived to take command. When Smith learned that Davis had been captured in southern Georgia days earlier, the general finally quit on May 26. Smith signed documents that surrendered the last Confederates on June 2. With a stroke of the pen, all diehards who refused to accept defeat were no longer loyal soldiers but fugitives from the law.[62]

෴ ෴ ෴

As the war closed in defeat and ruin, a number of factors sustained Confederates' belief that they and their nation remained unconquerable. First, confidence in victory withstood so much counterevidence because the elements that supported a diehard mentality were often irrefutable, ambiguous, or central to Confederates' worldview. Faith that God favored the Confederacy grounded many Rebels' reality. Bad news did not discredit this fundamental belief; instead, the belief shaped how soldiers interpreted catastrophic events. Likewise, Confederate perceptions of the enemy gave meaning and motivation to thousands who fought and killed the foe. Union successes did not change Confederate notions that the enemy was evil, inept, and unworthy of triumph. Instead, views of the adversary influenced how Rebels grasped the possibility of defeat and compelled many of them to fight harder and to blame southerners for Confederate setbacks. Moreover, the fog of war obscured the full power of Federal armies. Rebels knew they were outnumbered, but they had faced and beaten larger armies throughout the war. Even Lee and Johnston, with all the intelligence they gathered during the final campaigns, underestimated the size of their adversaries' forces. Finally, rumors of Rebel victories, foreign intervention, and northern disasters were too ambiguous, distant, and tempting to refute. By war's end, communication channels were so unreliable that soldiers seldom discerned the difference between hearsay and fact. Soldiers who doubted the accuracy of wishful reports were also skeptical of bad news because it often took weeks to determine an event's validity.

All of these elements persisted because soldiers encouraged each other's adherence to them. With revivals and prayer meetings in the trenches, troops sustained their faith that God would deliver independence. Rebels sang music and told atrocity stories that reinforced their perceptions of the enemy. Troops circulated battle reports and rumors that proclaimed Confederate victories. In the final weeks of the war, Confederate regiments and brigades publicly swore their confidence and devotion to the cause. Men who participated in these resolutions confessed that the activity bolstered their spirits. During the surrenders, comrades looked to each other for advice and solidarity. Some of them, like Chamberlayne and McIntosh, even escaped capitulation together to defy the enemy a little longer. Whether they fled reality literally or figuratively, many diehard Rebels upheld their faith in southern superiority in spite of defeat. Their reaction forecast a troubled peace and contested war memory.

When Johnny comes marching home again,
	Hurrah, hurrah!
We'll give him a hearty welcome then,
	Hurrah, hurrah!
The men will cheer, the boys will shout,
The ladies they will all turn out,
And we'll all feel gay when Johnny comes
	marching home.
		—Patrick Gilmore, "When Johnny Comes
		Marching Home"

Conclusion

The Aftermath of Invincibility

Patrick Gilmore's song, "When Johnny Comes Marching Home," encapsulated how Confederates hoped the war would end.[1] As the song relates, a spontaneous procession welcomed Johnny at the outskirts of town. With joy and fanfare, people who had known him since childhood whisked Johnny through the village. Church bells pealed. A laurel wreath crowned his brow. Throngs of women vied for his attention. The whole town honored and thanked him for his sacrifices. It was the happiest and proudest moment of Johnny's life.

Reality mocked the Confederate dream. While veterans walked or rode home as bands of survivors, the scenes of their fantasy were played out in northern towns. A colossal review of smart-stepping victors marched through Washington, D.C. Uncertainty rather than resolution marked Rebels' final journey as soldiers.

Civil War history often ends at Appomattox Court House or Durham Station, where solemn ceremony suggests finality and reconciliation. Confederate diaries offer a different ending. Rebel soldiers continued their war journals to include swearing allegiance to the United States and traveling home. These actions, not furling flags and stacking rifles, closed Confederates' military careers. Adding extra weeks to the narrative may seem trivial, but these final acts of soldiering change the tone and meaning of the war's outcome. After capitulation, Rebels expected the worst from their enemies, and being forced to swear an oath to the Union seemed to unmask the enemy's intentions. For diehards, the false goodwill at surrender ceremonies became a pompous charade when oath swearing proved Yankees' abusive, arbitrary use of power. Soldiers were also soured by their encounters with southern civilians and the ravaged country. The home front reminded Rebels of citizens' ingratitude and Yankee barbarity. This conclusion to diehards' military career (and this book) illustrates how Johnny really came marching home. He did not come home victorious; he did not come home humbled. Johnny came marching home with a loaded pistol. He came home an unconquered loser, armed with wartime convictions that shaped his postwar identity, ideology, and actions.[2]

Though the military surrenders had been quiet and even respectful, Confederates feared retribution from the government they had defied and the millions they had enslaved. After surrendering, a Virginia officer considered himself "a citizen-slave" of the North. Many soldiers summed up scenarios of confiscation, disfranchisement, imprisonment, and miscegenation in one word: subjugation. One Confederate admitted that the "unknown horrors of *subjugation*" caused him so much anxiety that his hair was turning gray. The abstractions of a barbaric enemy that had steeled Rebel resolve during the war now spawned terrible images for the future. Rumors spread that the terms of surrender included "all Confederate soldiers disfranchised; all property whatever confiscated & turned over to the Yankees; and all commissioned officers exiled." The Yankees were implementing their plan to dismantle the South and southern manhood with it. As one cavalryman explained, diehard Rebels vowed to fight against being "ground to death by being robed of all our negroes, and lands and other property—not allowed to Vote nor hold office any more." He and his comrades suspected the Yankees would parcel Confederate farms to freed people or sell the land to pay northern war debts. Many diehard Rebels expected a future darker than their worst wartime experiences. On the horizon loomed everything they had fought to prevent, all the nightmarish speculations they had read in editorials and political addresses, every enemy atrocity they had heard, every fiendish Yankee trick they had scorned. How these stalwart veterans responded to defeat and its uncertainties would affect the South and the nation for generations.[3]

Many soldiers countered defeat by holding onto military customs and comrades. Amid anxiety, they coveted order, unity, and normalcy. This collective behavior, born in the camaraderie of war, marked their final acts as soldiers. In late May, Junius Bragg watched his division disband as units rather than dissolve as individuals and mobs. One day, 186 troops "formed in an old field" near their camp in Marshall, Texas, "and marched away in order with loaded guns." The next night, "about eight hundred men from the Division left. . . . They went in a body and well armed." Marching off together with loaded rifles served many purposes. It separated these men from deserters, who sneaked away singly and in smaller groups, and it provided safety in numbers against Confederate authorities willing to stop them and lawless bands waiting to pounce on them throughout the journey home. At the end, Bragg counted 132 men and officers left in his regiment: he remarked, "They will, of course, go in small squads," as if there were no alternative to military order. William Ellis and some of his comrades in the Washington Artillery missed Appomattox because they were returning from furlough. When word of the disaster reached them, they held numerous "councils of war" to decide what to do as a group. They could have dissolved all affiliations and headed home, but military conventions mattered within the chaos. Kentuckian Johnny Jackman's regiment met in Augusta, Georgia, and selected as a group the best route home. After considering going home by water from Savannah, they took free passage on railroad cars provided by Federal authorities. Whitelaw Reid rode the cars at this time and observed that the destruction that scarred the passing countryside also marked veterans' faces: "Aimless young men in gray, ragged and filthy, seemed, with the downfall of the rebellion they had fought for, to have lost their object in life." Reid, a northerner, wanted to find a crushed foe. The soldiers, though shocked by defeat, used the rituals of military life to see them through the ordeal. Thousands of them perpetuated this culture of campfire, rank, and bugle call in veterans' organizations until the end of their days.[4]

Whether they traveled home by boat, train, horse, or foot, diehard Rebels encountered signs of defeat along the way. Many of them saw war's culminating acts of destruction: Philip H. Sheridan's work in the Shenandoah, William T. Sherman's path through the Carolinas, and Richmond's burned district. For three days along their trek, Kena King Chapman and his group were "refreshed by the sight and smell of dead horses." They were following "the track taken by Genl Sheridan during the last month when he completely demolished Genl [Jubal] Early." David McIntosh's flight from Appomattox eventually led him past Sherman's destruction outside Cheraw, South Carolina. "The desolate track [was] paved all the way with fence rails, houses burned occasionally, and the country swept bare of provisions, horses and mules." When Henry Berkeley reached Richmond, he walked to Main Street "to take a look at the burnt district." Though a four-year veteran of the artillery, Berkeley was shocked by the spectacle. "One could hardly tell where Main Street had been. It was one big pile of ruins from the Custom House to the wharf." At the dockside, "the Yanks had collected all kinds of debris of war: cannon, muskets, bayonets, cartridge boxes, swords, broken gun-carriages, broken wagons." Standing before the wreckage of the Confederacy, Berkeley thought of "our noble dead" and asked himself, "Is it better with them or with us?" He decided that the dead were better off: "We almost know it is well with them," he reflected, "but who knows what the future holds for us; only God." When Chapman saw Richmond, his reaction was less philosophical: "Old Richmond is sadly changed—all the business portion of the city being a heap of ruins—thanks to the Dutch Irish, and the everlasting 'nigger.'" Fleeing Confederates had torched Richmond, but the bitter veteran blamed immigrant hordes from the North and slaves. Chapman used the mask of Cain and racism to shift the blame for the South's destruction. His diary entry represents one of the first examples of Lost Cause revisionism. In coming decades, hundreds of diehards like Chapman rewrote history to uphold wartime convictions and honor.[5]

During their travels, some troops vented rage and a sense of entitlement. Defeat and the absence of law encouraged base behavior. A chaplain in Robert E. Lee's army witnessed "more stealing in camp" the day after Appomattox "than I ever knew." The problem increased. Thousands of veterans who had suffered for their country stole whatever they needed from Confederate and state storehouses. "I lived for four years on goobers, parched corn and rotten meat," one soldier explained, "and I saw nothing wrong with taking blankets & such from the commissary as they would have been confiscated anyhow by the Yankees." But some "confiscation" was disorderly and indiscriminate. Scores of armed veterans sacked Thomasville, Georgia, in early May. They stole horses, carried off between 75,000 and 125,000 pounds of corn, destroyed books and furniture, and threatened to burn the town. A New Orleans reporter noted, "Ex-confederate soldiers have fought four years without pay, and now they propose to pay themselves." In most cases, troops looted government property first, but they also deprived and terrorized civilians throughout the South. With hundreds of miles before them and empty haversacks, many veterans had no choice but to seek sustenance and shelter from people along the way. But some men took more than their hosts could afford to give. Eliza Andrews, a young Georgia woman, watched as soldiers seized her neighbors' horses in broad daylight. One veteran led a mule away from its pleading owner without a trace of compunction. As he passed Andrews, the soldier asked, "A man that's going to Texas must have a mule to ride, don't you think so lady?" A wartime gulf between the experiences of soldiers and civilians enhanced such callousness. During the chaos and lawlessness of the spring of 1865, veterans who had given everything to protect citizens expected those people to give them everything in return.[6]

Some Confederates fled rather than face the impact of defeat, emancipation, and reunion. The rugged expanse across the Rockies attracted many Rebels. Enough Confederates headed to Texas after the war to make it the most populous state in the South by 1880. Still others preferred to leave the country altogether. On July 4, 1865, General Jo Shelby drowned his battle flag in the Rio Grande and led several hundred cavalrymen into Mexico. One historian estimates that as many as eight to ten thousand Confederates settled in Latin America after the war. Expatriates became filibusters, mining operators, and coffee planters south of the equator. Some veterans even joined the Egyptian army. These Rebels preferred exile in the most alien cultures over coexistence with enemies and freed slaves.[7]

Millions of Confederates stayed in the South and used the war to forge a regional identity as distinctive and defiant as their antebellum slave culture. The seeds of postwar opposition and the Lost Cause germinated in Rebels' experiences as hardened soldiers who had convinced themselves that they could not be conquered by Yankees and blacks. Beliefs that served soldiers during the conflict did not evaporate at Appomattox. Faith in the invincibility of their arms, valor, and cause—convictions seared into the mentalities of thousands of southern men during their formative years—shaped their peculiar postwar identity as unconquered losers. Some evidence suggests that Confederate veterans were more accepting of defeat than were southern civilians because the troops knew that they had been conquered in battle. To be sure, some citizens expressed opinions that betrayed a lack of military experience. More important, Rebels who admitted that they were "whipped" rarely denounced their cause and ethos. Instead of abandoning faith in their superiority, diehards used this deep belief to overcome the humiliation of surrender. Acts of continued defiance—wearing the gray, shunning carpetbaggers, electing Confederate leaders, passing black codes—maintained honor by resisting subjugation. Undaunted by capitulation, white southern men continued their military struggle in the social and political theaters of Reconstruction and beyond.

The central elements of the culture of invincibility—southern righteousness and northern barbarity—evolved into the Lost Cause cult. Instead of doubting that God was on their side, white southerners saw defeat as providential; they viewed their trials in biblical terms and looked forward to resurrection and redemption. Confederate exiles fashioned themselves as the surviving vestiges of God's plan, the stalwart few who would build a shining civilization elsewhere and return to the South at the appointed hour. Religious leaders, including William Bennett and J. William Jones, depicted Rebel legions as God's army on earth. Reflecting on the final months of the war, Bennett recalled, "The anchor of hope held more securely as the storm increased. The serene courage and perfect trust of the Christian soldiers were the richest legacies of those gloomy days." Jones argued that those legacies continued to bless the South after defeat because he "always found our returned soldiers the most tender and impressible part of the congregations."[8] Like defeats at Vicksburg, Atlanta, and Nashville, the death of the Confederacy somehow confirmed God's love of the South and fit within his higher plan for the region. Reconstruction also provided more evidence of northern barbarism. Corrupt carpetbaggers, black armies of occupation, and meddlesome federal agents seemed to confirm northern immorality and justify southern defiance. The destruction of slavery and elevation of black southerners incensed the diehards. Whether or not they had owned slaves, unconquered Rebels thought the enemy misused its power to embarrass and humiliate a prostrate people. Such enemies did not deserve victory and respect. Reviewing white southern behavior after the war, historian David Goldfield argues that former Confederates performed a "mental alchemy . . . on the war itself. They spun the straw of defeat into a golden mantle of victory."[9] To us, white southerners' treatment of defeat seems magical and transformative. To them, it was a continuation of old ways, a response deeply rooted in their ethos. Stubborn conduct after defeat mirrored the diehards' handling of major setbacks throughout the conflict.

Unwavering devotion to the South and their stature as veterans made diehards the natural leaders of the Lost Cause cult and staunch defenders of southern orthodoxy. Unreconstructed Confederates wrote the first histories of the conflict. David Blight describes their efforts as "one of the most highly orchestrated grassroots partisan histories ever conceived." General Early, an icon of diehard sentiment, published his take on the war's final years in 1866. In a recent introduction to Early's work, historian Gary Gallagher notes, "Anyone susceptible to the deeply flawed, though admittedly comforting, notion that national scars healed rapidly after Grant and Lee set a conciliatory public example at Appomattox should read Early's book as an example of widely held opinions in the postwar white South." Throughout his account, Early injected the base stereotype of barbaric Yankees. Addressing his former enemies, Early wrote, "There is a wide and impassable gulf between us, in which I see the blood of slaughtered friends, comrades, and countrymen." Early filled footnotes with atrocity stories and other evidence that the enemy did not deserve victory. He described "delicate ladies, who had been plundered, insulted, and rendered desolate by the acts of our most atrocious enemies." Like so many diehards during and after the war, Early attributed defeat to overwhelming numbers, "an immense horde of foreign mercenaries, incited by high bounties and the hope of plunder . . . flocked to the Federal army," and "southern negroes were forced into its service." Diehards like Early continued hostilities in lectures, articles, and books. Their culminating effort came from their irreconcilable leader, Jefferson Davis, whose two-volume, 1,279-page memoir never admitted a wrong or surrendered an inch to the Yankees. This movement in speech and print elevated Confederates to epic stature and degraded Yankees as artless hordes. As authors, diehards maintained the ideas that had sustained them as soldiers: they minimized slavery's role in the contest and linked their cause with Christian virtues and the legacy of the American Revolution. The Lost Cause cult depicted an immaculate Confederacy that was crucified by an evil government. Advocates cried, "The South will rise again" and intended the analogy to Christ's resurrection. The Daughters of the Confederacy sustained the veterans' worldview and culture deep into the twentieth century. As William Faulkner explained, southern mistresses like Rosa Coldfield lionized diehard Rebels and their fallen comrades with "poems, ode, eulogy, and epitaph, out of some bitter and implacable reserve of undefeat."[10]

Diehards' postwar diaries and letters reveal a deep "reserve of undefeat." Many veterans stressed the superficial, forced nature of reunion. In their view, Federal troops and black henchmen bullied Rebels into swearing an oath to the Union. As Berkeley put it, they "thrust their vile oath of allegiance down our throats with bayonets." George Mercer thought that "the arbitrary power of the United States Government seems to increase daily." He noted instances when former Confederates were harassed, imprisoned, and fined for speaking against the federal government or challenging a Union officer. "The whole country groans under a military despotism," Mercer lamented. In August 1865, Henry Calvin Conner thought that "the United States Government is and has been tottering on its base for many years and the last four years it has been more corrupt than ever and now they have got the South just where they wished it and I look for nothing else but trouble." Wartime stereotypes continued to influence Conner's opinions. He had "seen so much of them and know the nature of a yankee so well that I expect nothing good from them." Another diehard recounted that "some shortsighted creature . . . supposed . . . that I was enjoying the rest from war and toil." The veteran responded, "War would be a delightful furlough to this sort of life." He foresaw "no prospect of improvement" for the nation and sectional reconciliation. In addition to doubting the prospects of reunion, he questioned the fate of freed slaves. "They are free according to Yankee say so but they are the greatest sufferers in the end," he proclaimed.[11]

Such passions seem likely in 1865 or 1866, but diehard assertions of southern superiority persisted long after Appomattox. Stalwart veterans became politicians, professors, editors, ministers, lawyers, and above all icons of southern defiance. As civic leaders and living relics, diehards eulogized and set the record straight. Some added a contemporary veneer to their rhetoric, but their central points remained constant. To the end of the century and beyond, diehards insisted that their cause was righteous, their soldiers incomparable, their leaders demigods. Edmund Jones, a veteran of the Confederate cavalry, became an attorney and served in the North Carolina legislature. This career brought him in frequent contact with the state constitution, a document written during Radical Reconstruction that infuriated Jones. He particularly hated the preamble, which expressed North Carolinians' gratitude to God for preserving the Union. That section "was placed in the constitution by a horde of foreign carpet baggers, assisted by an army of emancipated slaves and a few native scalawags, while the real citizenship of the State were shackled and helpless," Jones explained. The "real citizenship of the State" consisted of diehards like himself. Jones ranted that the preamble "was intended at the time as an insult to the helpless people, and was so accepted." He complained that one of the "woes of the followers of a lost cause" was "the distortion that History makes of their motives and aims," and he vowed to do his part to confront slander. Speaking to a memorial association in 1896, Jones sought to educate the coming generations: "Child of a hero sire! little do you know of the pure flame of patriotism that burnt in the bosom of him whose offspring you are and I fear you know but little more of the matchless courage that for four long, terrible, bloody years, maintained the rights of his State, and the integrity of her laws against a world of arms." He urged his listeners to pass on the heroic legacy of the diehards: "Let the living do justice to the dead. It is a poor boon to ask. You can do no less without being an unfilial ingrate." Thirty years after the war, Jones's words still betrayed passion for the cause and hatred for Yankees.[12]

Diehards delivered the same messages in the early twentieth century. Virginian Charles Fenton James became a minister and president of Roanoke Female College. In 1901, James insisted that the origin of the war was not slavery or even states' rights, which he claimed merely constituted "pretext." The real cause was "the irreconcilable antagonism between . . . the two representative classes of English people who settled these United States." Faithful to the Cavalier myth that had justified secession and fostered enemy stereotypes, James delineated the way that ancient ethnic differences between the "Cavalier" and "Puritan" erupted in civil war forty years earlier. John Shaffner had served as a Confederate surgeon. In 1902 he recalled the profound suffering of diehard Rebels. Weeks earlier, Dr. Shaffner had listened to Booker T. Washington speak and was struck by one of Washington's comments about slavery days. Washington had remarked how much he looked forward to Sunday's breakfast because it included a touch of molasses to sweeten the simple meal. "It occurred to me then," Shaffner recalled, "that very probably at the time this negro boy was happy in absorbing the small allowance of black sweetening; his young master, possibly in camp, marching, or fighting, would have been more happy to have shared in this, at that time, impossible luxury." The point of comparison was clear: blacks complained that they had suffered during slavery, but white southerners endured worse during the war "without a murmur." Speaking to veterans at a Memorial Day service, Shaffner stressed "the propriety of teaching to your children and drumming it into their heads, the many heroic deeds, you and your comrades accomplished during the four years of civil strife!" The soldiers' accomplishments mattered, not the outcome of the war. Echoing wartime exaggerations of the odds, Shaffner insisted, "It should be indelibly impressed on your descendents, that, with blockaded ports;—shut off from communication with the world at large, it required more than 3,000,000 men to overcome, by starvation and exhaustion, less than 600,000 Southerners, and that four long, bitter years were required to accomplish the result." Shaffner concluded, "The heritage left coming generations is one of the grandest in history."[13]

Many scholars stress how the Lost Cause responded to defeat or to postwar socioeconomic changes, but as these statements suggest, the cult also sustained wartime mentalities. Jones, James, and Shaffner used the Lost Cause as a medium through which they could safely express their Confederate ethos. Politically and economically, diehards had to change to some extent after defeat; culturally, they did not. The enemy transformed laws, elections, and labor relations but could not touch white southern culture, which remained unchanged and unconquered. Belief in an unconquerable Confederacy survived as faith in southern superiority. With astonishing ease, diehards shrugged off defeat and celebrated their wartime achievements. Lost Cause organizations censored textbooks to ensure that generations of southerners learned about the superiority of Confederate soldiers and their generals. Veterans taught the same lessons at home. South Carolinian James Eleazar was so accustomed to hearing "Grandpa tell of whipping the lard out of the Yankees on a dozen battlefields" that he assumed that the Rebels had won the war. At age twelve, when he learned about Confederate defeat, Eleazar suffered "one of the saddest awakenings I ever had." Incredibly, Eleazar's story shows that the biased, myopic perceptions of battles that soldiers maintained during the war survived Appomattox, reached the twentieth century, and touched the descendants of the unconquered.[14]

The shared elements of the ethos of invincibility and the Lost Cause raise an important question: How would the diehards' memory of the war have differed if they had won? The Lost Cause commemoration of sacrifice, heroism, and history would surely have occurred if southern society were honoring victors. The memorial rituals, hagiography of generals and Johnny Reb, and base stereotypes of the foe that we view as signs of coping with defeat would have flourished after Confederate independence. Moreover, reconciliation after a victorious rebellion would likely have sacrificed African Americans, as was the case after Reconstruction. Such speculations are not meant to provoke what-if histories; rather, they shift our gaze away from defeat to see the continuity of a white southern ethos. Though southern novelists and historians wish to find irony and trauma in 1865, white southern culture did not hinge on defeat. Robert Penn Warren thought, "In the moment of death the Confederacy entered upon its immortality." This is an elegant idea, but surrendering was not a prerequisite for Confederate perpetuity. White southerners claimed eternal glory through years of wartime trials, not as the consequence of a sudden event like capitulation. Armed with God's love and an undying hatred of the North, the stalwart defenders of the Confederacy immortalized themselves and their nation before defeat. The soul of rebellion lived in the culture of invincibility, a spirit that honored the Confederacy regardless of national sovereignty.[15]

The South today remains the country's most self-conscious region, and historians continue to explore the Confederacy and its end for clues to the source of southern distinctiveness. The memory of defeat, devastation, and occupation differentiates white southerners from other Americans even after Vietnam. But while this experience separates the region from the rest of the United States, it connects white southerners to people throughout the world who have suffered similar calamities. From a global perspective, other Americans are distinctive because they have not experienced such a loss. For this reason, the Confederate culture of invincibility offers historians a phenomenon with deep southern roots and international relevance. How are conditions that veil defeat from the vanquished universal and local? How are diehards from diverse cultures alike and different when they face surrender? Comparisons between Confederates and the German ranks of World War I or Japanese troops of World War II might reveal how people of diverse religions, societies, and political philosophies feel unconquerable. Perhaps the answer lies in certain elements that all soldiers share: the immaturity of youth, the chaos of warfare, the burden of defeat. Perhaps each ethos of invincibility stems from its own culture and the peculiar mode of warfare it engenders.[16]

Three factors shaped Confederate notions of invincibility: the environment of war, the qualities of white southern culture, and the mechanics of group psychology. First, the fog of war obscured reality. Combatants seldom grasped the battles they fought, let alone comprehended the developments of entire campaigns. Wish rumors further distorted the facts and influenced the way soldiers envisioned the conflict and its outcome. Moreover, the war tested troops' endurance before the eyes of hundreds of men from home and thousands of anonymous peers. Camaraderie, often considered a positive bond in soldiers' lives, provided social compulsions that pushed Rebels to greater sacrifices in the presence of friends. Immersed in a culture that prized honor and masculinity, Confederates outdid each other in showing their devotion to the cause, their faith in victory. Remaining optimistic while marching barefoot, eating parched corn, and sustaining wounds were the marks of a veteran, and thousands of young Confederates strove to acquire that status. By stressing how the war's context encouraged Rebel faith, we grasp how the soldiers' convictions were thinkable and widespread. After surrender, factors born in war continued to shape Rebels' views of themselves and their service. The fog of battle and the fog of memory sparked endless debates over the particulars of campaigns. Veterans retraced the chaos, searching for the critical order, the errant division, or the exact location that decided a fight. Some learned that the fog of memory could be as useful as the fog of war when claiming victory in defeat. Comrades also recalled and commemorated their fortitude and suffering. More than any particular victory, the veterans chose resilience as their greatest military achievement.

Second, white southern culture nurtured Confederate notions of invincibility. The South and its culture were never monolithic, but certain beliefs shared by thousands of Rebels reflected their attachment to antebellum life in the region. Drawing from religious inheritances, soldiers believed that God favored white southerners and would deliver Confederate independence when the time was right. Christianity provided a partisan interpretation for Rebel victories and setbacks: triumphs proved God's favor and presence among Confederate legions; defeats confirmed God's love by chastening Rebels for their sins. Using this perspective, many soldiers convinced themselves that they could not lose. White southerners also borrowed sectional stereotypes to depict the enemy as inept and barbaric. Because these abstractions helped soldiers distance themselves from their victims, the caricatures withstood evidence of northern strength, valor, and humanity. Slavery also imbued Confederates—especially officers of the master class—with supreme confidence in their supremacy. In short, Rebels' religious convictions, views of the enemy, and attachment to slavery fostered white southerners' confidence in their cultural superiority. To the end of the war and beyond, this faith confirmed Confederates' right to nationhood. By focusing on how culture encouraged Rebels' sense of invincibility, we see how the war they thought and fought emanated from deep southern reservoirs of meaning. These beliefs persisted in postwar words and deeds. Former Rebels continued to disparage northerners and blacks as inferiors. Within decades, defiant white southerners snatched political control of the South from the unworthy winners. The unconquered and unreconstructed South used its deepest values to justify Jim Crow and terrors that lasted for generations.

Finally, because the soldiers' world was emotional as well as cognitive, psychology can clarify how thousands of Rebels convinced themselves that they were unconquerable. As historian Peter Gay explains, "Psychoanalysis, like history, concentrates on understanding the past, works to make illegible clues legible, and digs beneath surfaces to hidden layers obscured and distorted by the passage of time, or by the writers'—or the public's—need to deny unpleasant truths." Confederates' self-absorption with their culture, cause, and imminent triumph prolonged the war and obscured the likelihood of defeat. In many ways, Confederate nationalism—indeed, all nationalisms—can be seen as a collective form of narcissism: the Rebels favored themselves so much that they separated from and fought fellow Americans to preserve their identity and its most cherished features. As war correspondent Michael Ignatieff puts it, "Nationalism is a distorting mirror in which believers see their simple ethnic, religious, or territorial attributes transformed into glorious . . . qualities." In the end, the narcissism that inspired the Confederacy contributed to its downfall. Just as Narcissus gazed at his reflection while he wasted away, Confederates admired their supreme nation while it faded into oblivion. Thousands of diehards claimed divine favor, praised their armies, discounted the enemy, and resolved to win instead of facing the portents of defeat: deficient supplies and manpower, worthless currency, international isolation, the disintegration of slavery, Union strength and determination, and Rebel disaffection within the ranks and at home. By revealing the psychological underpinnings of Confederate hope, we avoid the impulse to dismiss their faith as irrational, and we comprehend how passions informed reality.[17]

ᎶᏢᎤ ᎶᏢᎤ ᎶᏢᎤ

The myth of Narcissus offers a fitting coda. Ovid wrote,

> In time,
>   the nymph brought forth a son, an amazingly pretty boy,

whom she named Narcissus. For this, her baby, she came to inquire
of the blind seer how he would live, and what fullness of years
he might expect. The prophet replied: "He will live long,
if he does not know himself." Absurd? Or a mystery? No one
could understand or explain what his answer meant. But the truth
came out in its own good time, in his life and peculiar death. [18]

Likewise, diehards' thoughts and actions may seem absurd or a mystery, but the meaning and significance of Rebel culture can be found in the rise and peculiar defeat of the Confederacy. No explanation of the rebellion's fate and legacy is complete without considering how diehards knew themselves and their enemies. By linking the soldiers' context, culture, and dreams, we discern why a people on the brink of surrender expected victory and how the calamitous end shaped their future.

Notes

Abbreviations

Albright Diary   James W. Albright Diary, James W. Albright Books, Southern Historical Collection, University of North Carolina at Chapel Hill

Berkeley Diary   Henry Robinson Berkeley Diary, in Henry Robinson Berkeley, *Four Years in the Confederate Artillery: The Diary of Private Henry Robinson Berkeley*, ed. William H. Runge (Chapel Hill: University of North Carolina Press, 1961)

Brannock Papers   James Madison Brannock Papers, Virginia Historical Society, Richmond

Brothers   Thomas W. Cutrer and T. Michael Parrish, eds., *Brothers in Gray: The Civil War Letters of the Pierson Family* (Baton Rouge: Louisiana State University Press, 1997)

Campaigning   John Q. Anderson, comp., *Campaigning with Parsons' Texas Cavalry Brigade, CSA: The War Journals and Letters of the Four Orr Brothers, Twelfth Texas Cavalry Regiment* (Hillsboro, Tex.: Hill Junior College Press, 1967)

Conner Papers   Henry Calvin Conner Papers, South Caroliniana Library, University of South Carolina, Columbia

Cruel War   Grant Taylor, *This Cruel War: The Civil War Letters of Grant and Malinda Taylor, 1862–1865*, ed. Ann K. Blomquist and Robert A. Taylor (Macon, Ga.: Mercer University Press, 2000)

CWC   Civil War Collections, Confederate and Federal, Tennessee State Library and Archives, Nashville

Davis Diary   Creed Thomas Davis Diary, Virginia Historical Society, Richmond

Foster Diary   Samuel T. Foster Diary, in Samuel T. Foster, *One of Cleburne's Command: The Civil War Reminiscences and Diary of Capt. Samuel T. Foster, Granbury's Texas Brigade, CSA*, ed. Norman D. Brown (Austin: University of Texas Press, 1980)

Granite Farm	Edgeworth Bird, *The Granite Farm Letters: The Civil War Correspondence of Edgeworth and Sallie Bird*, ed. John Rozier (Athens: University of Georgia Press, 1988)
Green Mount	Benjamin Robert Fleet, *Green Mount: A Virginia Plantation Family during the Civil War: Being the Journal of Benjamin Robert Fleet and Letters of His Family*, ed. Betsy Fleet and John D. P. Fuller (Lexington: University of Kentucky Press, 1962)
Hampton Letters	Thomas B. Hampton Letters, Center for American History, University of Texas at Austin
Heartsill Diary	William W. Heartsill Diary, in William Williston Heartsill, *Fourteen Hundred and 91 Days in the Confederate Army*, ed. Bell I. Wiley (Jackson, Tenn.: McCowat-Mercer, 1954)
Higginbotham Papers	Paul M. Higginbotham Papers, 1862–82, Virginia Historical Society, Richmond
Hyatt Papers	Arthur W. Hyatt Papers, Hill Memorial Library, Louisiana State University, Baton Rouge
Infernal War	Edwin Hedge Fay, *This Infernal War: The Confederate Letters of Edwin H. Fay*, ed. Bell I. Wiley (Austin: University of Texas Press, 1958)
Lee's Army	Susan Leigh Blackford, comp., *Letters from Lee's Army; or, Memoirs of Life in and out of the Army in Virginia during the War between the States* (Lincoln: University of Nebraska Press, 1998)
LSU	Hill Memorial Library, Louisiana State University, Baton Rouge
McLure Papers	McLure Family Papers, 1845–1922, South Caroliniana Library, University of South Carolina, Columbia
Nellie	William Lewis Nugent, *My Dear Nellie: The Civil War Letters of William L. Nugent to Eleanor Smith Nugent*, ed. William M. Cash and Lucy Somerville Howorth (Jackson: University Press of Mississippi, 1977)
OR	U.S. War Department. *The War of the Rebellion: The Official Records of the Union and Confederate Armies*. 70 vols. (Washington, D.C.: U.S. Government Printing Office, 1880–1901)
SHC	Southern Historical Collection, University of North Carolina at Chapel Hill
Surgeon's Letters	Spencer Glasgow Welch, *A Confederate Surgeon's Letters to His Wife* (Marietta, Ga.: Continental, 1954)
TSLA	Tennessee State Library and Archives, Nashville
USC	South Caroliniana Library, University of South Carolina, Columbia
VHS	Virginia Historical Society, Richmond

Voices	G. Ward Hubbs, ed., *Voices from Company D: Diaries by the Greensboro Guards, Fifth Alabama Infantry Regiment, Army of Northern Virginia* (Athens: University of Georgia Press, 2003)
Walters Diary	John Walters Diary, in John Walters, *Norfolk Blues: The Civil War Diary of the Norfolk Light Artillery Blues*, ed. and intro. Kenneth Wiley (Shippensburg, Pa.: Burd Street, 1997)
Williams Diary	Hiram Smith Williams Diary, in Hiram Smith Williams, *This War So Horrible: The Civil War Diary of Hiram Smith Williams*, ed. Lewis N. Wynne and Robert A. Taylor (Tuscaloosa: University of Alabama Press, 1993)
Yours till Death	John Weaver Cotton, *Yours till Death: Civil War Letters of John W. Cotton*, ed. Lucille Griffith (Birmingham: University of Alabama Press, 1951)

Introduction. Southern Invincibility and Confederate Defeat

1. Faulkner, *Intruder in the Dust*, 194–95.

2. Rawleigh Downman to wife, January 16, 1864, Downman Family Papers, VHS; Reuben Pierson to Mary Catherine Pierson, March 28, 1864, in *Brothers*, 230–31; Frederick Waring Diary, September 9 (eighth quotation), September 10, 1864 (ninth quotation), J. Joseph Frederick Waring Papers, Georgia Historical Society, Savannah; William Nugent to wife, January 8 (tenth quotation), January 26, 1865 (eleventh quotation), in *Nellie*, 231, 235; John William McLure to wife, February 6, 1865, McLure Papers.

3. Clausewitz, *On War*, 189.

4. This distinction between ethos and nationalism is one of the principal differences between my work and Rubin, *Shattered Nation*. Rubin's book appeared while I was revising this volume. We study the same phenomenon in southern history, but our approach and conclusions vary in many respects.

5. McPherson, *For Cause and Comrades*; Gallagher, *Confederate War*; Berry, *All That Makes a Man*; Carmichael, *Last Generation*.

6. Gallagher, *Confederate War*.

7. McPherson, *What They Fought For*; Reid Mitchell, *Civil War Soldiers*, 168.

8. Ayers, *In the Presence*, xvii. This book enhances Ayers's idea of "deep contingency." While other scholars—most notably, McPherson—have used contingency to illuminate chance and the bonds among political, social, economic, and military events, Ayers sees "deep contingency" as the "intricate connections in which lives and events are embedded" (xix). In other words, Civil War history should portray more than a deterministic web of factors that span the battlefront and home front. History is a humanistic endeavor that seeks to reconstruct how people's individual, emotional wars touched the distant conflict, and vice versa. See McPherson, *Crossroads of Freedom*.

9. Luraghi, *Rise and Fall*, 5; Stampp, *Peculiar Institution*. In this respect, *Diehard Rebels* reinforces Carmichael's *Last Generation*, which studies a group of stalwart Confederates from Virginia before, during, and after the war.

10. Reid Mitchell, *Civil War Soldiers*, 191; Beringer et al., *Why the South Lost*, 87. For more on the perils of such hindsight arguments, see Shy, *People Numerous and Armed*, xiii.

11. Gallagher, *Confederate War*, 72, made the claim that diehard Rebels were representative southerners. He also calls dissident southern communities "atypical" (23). Gallagher identifies the lacunae of my study, but his work is an extended essay that raises questions and challenges scholars rather than a detailed monograph that offers complex analysis and copious evidence.

12. O'Brien, *All Clever Men*, 11; Faust, "The Peculiar South Revisited," in *Interpreting Southern History*, ed. Boles and Nolen, 99; Brugger, "Mind of the Old South," 227. For an excellent example of writing that presents a distasteful mentality without judgment, see Fuller's treatment of her family life in Zimbabwe during the Chimurenga War (1966–80) in *Don't Let's Go to the Dogs Tonight*.

13. Maxwell, *So Long, See You Tomorrow*, 27. Another questionable source I included was William Heartsill's diary, published in *Fourteen Hundred and 91 Days in the Confederate Army*. Heartsill printed his diary after the war and gave copies to friends and relatives. Wiley examined both Heartsill's manuscript and the published work, and I trust Wiley's assertion that the two sources do not differ significantly.

14. Gallagher, *Confederate War*, 28; McPherson, *For Cause and Comrades*, 11.

15. The pervasiveness of the ethos is entirely understandable in light of the cohesion of white southern society for centuries. See Morgan, *American Slavery, American Freedom*; McCurry, *Masters*; Hale, *Making Whiteness*.

16. Woodward, *American Counterpoint*, 276.

17. Cash, *Mind*, 103.

18. Foote, *Civil War*; Shaara, *Killer Angels*; McPherson, *Battle Cry of Freedom*; Ken Burns, *The Civil War* (nine-part documentary, 1990).

19. Since the 1990s, Charles Royster, Edward Ayers, David Blight, and others have reintroduced the dark legacy of the Civil War. This book reinforces their efforts to present a more complicated war. Ayers first called for a "new revisionism" in "Worrying about the Civil War" in *Moral Problems in American Life*, ed. Halttunen and Perry, 145–65.

Chapter One. The Smile of Providence: Confederate Religion and Invincibility

1. Berger, *Sacred Canopy*, 51.

2. Edward Crenshaw Diary, December 25, 1864, in Crenshaw, "Diary," 367; Reuben Pierson to father, January 15, 1864, in *Brothers*, 224; Reid Mitchell, *Civil War Soldiers*, 187–88.

3. Woodworth, *While God Is Marching On*; Genovese, *Consuming Fire*. For different views of Confederate religion, see Beringer et al., *Why the South Lost*; Shattuck, *Shield and Hiding Place*; Logue, *To Appomattox and Beyond*.

4. In *Gospel of Disunion* (3–5), Snay stresses how these same three developments aided the growth of southern separatism and secession. My work shows how these antebellum influences also helped construct an ethos of invincibility that colored Confederates' perceptions of the war in 1864–65. Antebellum religion thus not only contributed to

disunion and the war's beginnings but also affected the last phase of the Rebel war effort and Confederate reactions to defeat.

5. Furman and Smith quoted in Boles, *Great Revival*, 26–27.

6. Boles, *Irony of Southern Religion*, 5.

7. Boles, *Great Revival*, 25–26.

8. Ibid., 28–30.

9. Ibid., 27.

10. Ibid., 31–32.

11. Boles, *Irony of Southern Religion*, 5–6.

12. Ibid., 75–76; Heyrman, *Southern Cross*; Hatch, *Democratization of American Religion*, 220–26; Berger, *Sacred Canopy*.

13. Snay, *Gospel of Disunion*, 53–109.

14. Ibid., 113–50; Schweiger, *Gospel Working Up*.

15. Quoted in Snay, *Gospel of Disunion*, 187.

16. Atkinson, *God, the Giver of Victory and Peace*, 11; Dunaway, *Sermon*, 3–4.

17. Tally Simpson to cousin, July 18, 1863, in Simpson, *Far, Far from Home*, 258; Renfroe, *"Battle Is God's,"* 7. The language Boles used to explain evangelicals' mentality in the 1790s is equally enlightening for the Rebel worldview: "Given their way of looking at God working in history, any event or situation necessarily and irrevocably was destined to bear the imprint of Providence" (*Great Revival*, 25).

18. Rees, *Sermon*, 3.

19. Burrows, *Nationality Insured!* 4; Dunaway, *Sermon*, 11. Faust, *Creation*, and Genovese, *Consuming Fire*, overemphasize the critical tone of the wartime jeremiads. For every critical remark they quote, there exists a laudatory comment that connected Confederate independence to God's plan. The message scholars stress of course corresponds to the thesis they present, but the soldiers themselves highlighted the positive connections between God's law and Confederate values.

20. Atkinson, *God, the Giver of Victory and Peace*, 13, 5–7. Boles and others have noted that early Confederate successes convinced Rebels that they had divine help: "In the heady days following the First Battle of Bull Run, when southern armies won a string of victories in the eastern campaigns and Lincoln suffered through one disappointing general after another, it was easy for Confederate partisans to see the hand of God behind southern success" (*Irony of Southern Religion*, 93).

21. Henry Timrod, "Ethnogenesis," in Negri, *Civil War Poetry*, 3. Davis quoted in Bennett, *Narrative*, 416. On the religious dimensions of Confederate nationalism, see Silver, *Confederate Morale*; Faust, *Creation*, 22–40. Faust describes religion as "the fundamental idiom of national and personal identity" within the newborn nation ("Christian Soldiers," 64) and frames Confederate uses of religion as a self-conscious strategy for legitimacy, "a posture designed to win support both at home and abroad" (*Creation*, 22). According to Faust, this strategy backfired when the internal logic of evangelicalism made religion critical of the nation and its efforts. I have two caveats: first, by framing southern evangelicalism as a strategy appropriate to the exigencies of nation building and warfare, Faust highlights its role in ideology and propaganda to a degree that colors southern evangelicalism as a tool consciously chosen by leaders for its usefulness. I

stress that religion powerfully influenced the worldview of southerners both elite and common. In other words, Confederates did not select religion as a fundamental element of their society; rather, evangelicalism was already woven into the fabric of their culture and worldview. Second, though focusing on elite rhetoric, Faust gives the impression that evangelicalism's criticism of the Confederacy was a national discourse shared by all classes. Many common citizens used religion to criticize actions in Richmond or the conduct of other social classes, but some elements of the evangelical critique were conspicuously absent from the soldiers' discourse. Most notably, Rebel soldiers said little or nothing about how the practices of southern slavery constituted sins against God worthy of divine punishment.

22. Rees, *Sermon*, 11; Renfroe, *"Battle Is God's,"* 7.

23. Quoted in Faust, *Creation*, 28, 29.

24. Pierce quoted in Silver, *Confederate Morale*, 35–36; Doggett, *War and Its Close*, 16; Stephen Elliott, *Gideon's Water-Lappers*, 6.

25. W. R. Redding to wife, April 8, 1864, W. R. Redding Papers, SHC; Thomas, *Confederate Nation*, 246; Silver, *Confederate Morale*; Shattuck, *Shield and Hiding Place*, 51–72; W. Harrison Daniel, *Southern Protestantism*; Boles, *Irony of Southern Religion*; Woodworth, *While God Is Marching On*, 145–59.

26. Berends, "'Wholesome Reading,'" 142, 131–32.

27. Atkinson, *God, the Giver of Victory and Peace*, 5–7; 2 Kings 18–19.

28. Joseph Richard Manson Diary, February, 8, 1865, VHS; Robert Augustus Stiles to Caroline Clifford Stiles, [May 15, 1864?], Robert Augustus Stiles Papers, VHS; Thomas Hampton to wife, May 29, 1864, Hampton Letters. See also Thomas Hampton to wife, May 23, 1864, Hampton Letters; Grant Taylor to wife, February 28, 1864, in *Cruel War*, 227, McPherson, *For Cause and Comrades*, 63; Woodworth, *While God Is Marching On*, 27–39.

29. William Casey to mother, June 28, 1864, William Thomas Casey Papers, VHS; William Nugent to wife, October 12, 1864, in *Nellie*, 216; Robert Stiles to Rosa Stiles, June 15, 1864, Robert Augustus Stiles Papers, VHS; John Cotton to wife, May 26, 1864, in *Yours till Death*, 108. See also Grant Taylor to wife, June 5, 1864, in *Cruel War*, 256. Some soldiers reasoned that God could protect them in battle as easily elsewhere. Frederick Bowen wrote to his cousin, "I was not alarmed in the fight, felt that my Maker could preserve me there as elsewhere, & should I fall it would be all well" (Frederick Bowen to Charlie, October 15, 1864, Frederick Fillison Bowen Papers, VHS). Similarly, Hampton assured his wife, "I want you to cheer up & recollect that the same hand that protected me while quietly following the peaceful avocation of Farming is no less visible here in the Rough & dangerous looking Depth of a life & Death strugle with an Imbittered foe" (Thomas Hampton to wife, July 19, 1864, Hampton Letters).

30. William Casey to mother, April 3, 1864, William Thomas Casey Papers, VHS; John Francis Shaffner to wife, May 25, 1864, Fries and Shaffner Papers, SHC; resolutions from Benning's, Bryan's, Wofford's, Anderson's, and Evans's brigades quoted in Bennett, *Narrative*, 420–21; Theodore Honour to wife, May 7, 1864 (fifth through seventh quotations), May 28, 1864 (eighth quotation), Theodore A. Honour Papers, 1859–65, USC; mother to Dunbar Affleck, May 21, 1864, Thomas Affleck Correspondence and Writings, LSU;

Mary Alice (Macgruder) Downman to Rawleigh Downman, April 10, 1865, Downman Family Papers, VHS; Silver, *Confederate Morale*, 14.

31. William Casey to mother, April 3, 1864, William Thomas Casey Papers, VHS; John L. Sheppard to mother, May 20, 1864, Sheppard Family Papers, USC; Charles Fenton James to Emma James, February 13, 1865, Charles Fenton James Letters, VHS. Casey also disparaged parties in a letter to his sister; see William Casey to [Bell?] Ann Casey, January 31, 1864, William Thomas Casey Papers, VHS. See also McPherson, *For Cause and Comrades*, 64–67; Berends, " 'Wholesome Reading,' " 139.

32. Elias Davis to wife, March 9, 1864, Elias Davis Papers, SHC; Harry Lewis to mother, April 6, 1864, Harry Lewis Papers, SHC; W. R. Redding to wife, April 8, 1864, W. R. Redding Papers, SHC.

33. Edgeworth Bird to wife, May 6, 1864, in *Granite Farm*, 164–65; Samuel McKittrick to Mary Stennis McKittrick, May 17, 1864, in Lewis, "Confederate Officer's Letters," 493; Thomas B. Hampton to wife, February 29, 1864, Hampton Letters. In the same letter, Bird told his wife, "God be with us, and I believe he is. We have done well tho' we are greatly outnumbered." Thomas "Stonewall" Jackson best exemplified this mentality. "For Stonewall Jackson," Royster explains, "the course of combat was divinely ordered. Every incident came from the will of God. Apparent mistakes and confusion only seemed chaotic or disastrous; they were God's way of working out His beneficent intentions for those who loved Him." Jackson "took every opportunity to emphasize God's direction of events. Even some of his shortest, most urgent battlefield notes, let alone official reports, acknowledged his dependence on divine rule" (*Destructive War*, 267–68).

34. Frank Batchelor to wife, June 30, 1864, in Batchelor, *Batchelor-Turner Letters*, 81; William Nugent to wife, June 25, 1864, in *Nellie*, 184; Leonidas Lafayette Polk to wife, May 25, 1864, Leonidas Lafayette Polk Papers, SHC; Edmund T. Eggleston Diary, December 31, 1864, in Noyes, "Excerpts," 358.

35. Thomas J. Goree to Sarah Williams Kittrell Goree, April 26, 1864, in Goree, *Longstreet's Aide*, 123; W. A. Taylor to Mrs. L. M. Nutt, May 6, 1864, Leroy Moncure Nutt Papers, SHC; Edwin Fay to Sarah Shields Fay, May 22, 1864, in *Infernal War*, 397; James Pickens Diary, May 17, 1864, in *Voices*, 271. For more on soldiers' interpretations of news from distant theaters, see chapter 4.

36. Heartsill Diary, June 7, 1864, 207; Romans 8:28; Thomas Hampton to wife, June 7, 1864, Hampton Letters; Rees, *Sermon*, 11; James Drayton Nance to wife, January 1, 1864, James Drayton Nance Letters, USC.

37. William Casey to mother, June 28, 1864, William Thomas Casey Papers, VHS; William Nugent to wife, June 25, 1864, in *Nellie*, 185; Thomas Hampton to wife, April 29, 1864, Hampton Letters.

38. Stephen Elliott, *Gideon's Water-Lappers*, 5; Charles Fenton James to Emma A. James, February 13, 1865, Charles Fenton James Letters, VHS; Albright Diary, August 21, 1864; Richard Stanford Webb to cousin, August 31, 1864, Webb Family Papers, SHC. W. Harrison Daniel, *Southern Protestantism*, 29. Propaganda in the religious military press used the term *bloodless victory*: "Every revival of religion in your midst . . . is a bloodless victory over the enemy of our country" (quoted in Berends, " 'Wholesome Reading,' " 146). On February 23, 1865, Chaplain R. F. Bunting reassured his listeners,

"the Lord has as much to do *now* with the affairs of men, as when the glory of His presence filled the tabernacle . . . or when He conversed with Abraham." Reviewing the three-year contest, Bunting contended that public piety had secured Confederate victories (quoted in Berends, " 'Wholesome Reading,' " 152–53). On June 9, 1864, the *Christian Observer* "proved" that certain fast days promoted Confederate victories: June 13, 1861 (Manassas), May 15, 1862 (Seven Days'), March 27, 1863 (Chancellorsville), and August 21, 1863 (Chickamauga). President Davis called for national fasts on June 13, 1861; November 15, 1861; May 16, 1862; September 18, 1862; March 27, 1863; August 21, 1863; April 8, 1864; November 16, 1864; and March 3, 1865. The actual fast days were observed within a week or so of Davis's announcements; see Silver, *Confederate Morale*, 64–65.

39. Tally Simpson to sister, August 9, 1863, in Simpson, *Far, Far from Home*, 270; Robert Moore Diary, August 16, 1863, in Robert Moore, *Life*, 161; James Barr to wife, July 21, 1863, in Barr, *Let Us Meet in Heaven*, 122–23.

40. Samuel Pickens Diary, August 21, 1863, in *Voices*, 195; Renfroe, *"Battle Is God's,"* 6–7.

41. Samuel Pickens Diary, September 5–6, 1863, in *Voices*, 197–98; Green Berry Samuels to wife, September 12, 1863, in Spencer, Samuels, and Samuels, *Civil War Marriage*, 193; Reuben Pierson to father, August 22, 1863, in *Brothers*, 209. For Davis's August 1, 1863, proclamation of amnesty for deserters, see OR, ser. 4, 2:687–88. A profusion of religious tracts circulated through the army at this time, further enhancing religious fervor and raising morale; see Robert Moore Diary, September 4, 1863, in Robert Moore, *Life*, 164.

42. Marion Fitzpatrick to wife, August 28, 1863, in Fitzpatrick, *Letters to Amanda*, 84; Green Berry Samuels to wife, August 30, 1863, in Spencer, Samuels, and Samuels, *Civil War Marriage*, 192; Joshua Callaway to wife, September 22, 1863, in Callaway, *Civil War Letters*, 134.

43. Foster Diary, November 16, 1864, 145; Richard Launcelot Maury Diary, March 10, 1865, VHS; Joseph Richard Manson Diary, November 16, 1864, VHS; James Alexander Turrentine Diary, March 10, 1865, VHS. W. Harrison Daniel stresses that "fast-day sermons . . . were characterized by their patriotic fervor. . . . Mrs. Mary B. Chestnut once attended a fast-day sermon and confessed that the sermon, 'stirred my blood, my flesh crept and tingled. A red hot glow of patriotism passed over me. There was . . . exhortation to fight and die' " (*Southern Protestantism*, 29). See also Freemantle, *Three Months*, 157.

44. Richard Stanford Webb to cousin, April 25, 1864, Webb Family Papers, SHC; Robert Stiles to mother, October 2, 1864, Robert Stiles to sister, May 20, 1864, both in Robert Augustus Stiles Papers, VHS; Samuel McKittrick to Mary Stennis McKittrick, May 8, May 17, 1864, in Lewis, "Confederate Officer's Letters," 492; William Nugent to wife, June 9, 1864, in *Nellie*, 179; James T. Wallace Diary, May 30, 1864 (final quotation), SHC; Berends, " 'Wholesome Reading,' " 135, 140–41, 146; Robertson, *Soldiers Blue and Gray*, 186–88. Reverend D. S. Doggett avowed, "Our army, to-day, may be called, a church in the wilderness; a church in whose center abides the Shekinah, and on whose front towers the pillar of fire; a church, we hope, fulfilling its destiny, and accomplishing its journey to the Canaan of a permanent national repose" (*War and Its Close*, 15). For

another soldier who noted the piety of Confederate generals, see George Marion Coiner to sister, March 20, 1864, Coiner Family Papers, VHS.

45. As Berger explains, "The individual suffering from a tormenting illness, say, or from oppression and exploitation at the hands of fellowmen, desires relief from these misfortunes. But he equally desires to know *why* these misfortunes have come to him in the first place. If a theodicy answers, in whatever manner, this question of meaning, it serves a most important purpose for the suffering individual, even if it does not involve a promise that the eventual outcome of his suffering is happiness in this world or the next. It would, for this reason, be misleading to consider theodicies only in terms of their 'redemptive' potential. Indeed, some theodicies carry no promise of 'redemption' at all— except for the redeeming assurance of meaning itself" (*Sacred Canopy*, 58).

46. John L. Sheppard to mother, May 20, 1864, Sheppard Family Papers, USC.

47. Boles's insights on earlier evangelicalism again hold true for Confederate religiosity. Like their predecessors, devout Rebels preached that "out of disappointment and pain came patience and strength—lessons long taught by Christianity" (*Great Revival*, 30). Royster explains that Americans on both sides expected—even demanded—the war's destructive nature because they thought a great effusion of blood would purge America of its sins (*Destructive War*). In the war's final period, death challenged Rebels' convictions in multiple ways: theodicy not only had to calm their fears of mortality but also had to convince them that dying for their country remained a sacred act. This challenge was critical after Spotsylvania Court House and Franklin. As the war worsened, Rebel theodicy had to consecrate increasingly futile sacrifices. But they may not have seemed more futile or tragic from the soldiers' perspective if they were still confident of victory and redemption.

48. Reuben Pierson to father, August 22, 1863, in *Brothers*, 210.

49. Joshua Callaway to wife, July 19, 1863, in Callaway, *Civil War Letters*, 114; Reuben Pierson to father, July 19, 1863, in *Brothers*, 204; Tally Simpson to cousin, July 18, 1863, in Simpson, *Far, Far from Home*, 257–58.

50. William Casey to mother, June 19, 1864, William Thomas Casey Papers, VHS; Rawleigh Downman to wife, June 20, 1864, Downman Family Papers, VHS.

51. James Drayton Nance to wife, January 1, 1865 (first and second quotations), James Drayton Nance to Mr. Brantly, January 12, 1864 (third quotation), both in James Drayton Nance Letters, USC; John Francis Shaffner to wife, November 21, 1864, Fries and Shaffner Papers, SHC; John William McLure to wife, September 20, 1864, McLure Papers; James Blackman Ligon to mother, August 25, 1864, James Blackman Ligon Letters, USC.

52. Joseph Frederick Waring Diary, January 1, 1865, Joseph Frederick Waring Papers, Georgia Historical Society, Savannah.

53. Henry Calvin Conner to wife, July 28, 1864, December 14, 1864, both in Conner Papers; Burrows, *Nationality Insured!* 6; John William McLure to wife, September 5, 1864, McLure Papers; Henry Alexander Chambers to wife, September 6, 1864, Henry Alexander Chambers Papers, 1832–1925, SHC.

54. Tally Simpson to cousin, July 18, 1864, in Simpson, *Far, Far from Home*, 258; Richard Stanford Webb to cousin, August 31, 1864, Webb Family Papers, SHC; Joseph

Richard Manson Diary, February 11, January 23, 1865, VHS; James Keith to Sarah Agnes (Blackwell) Keith, January 15, 1865, Keith Family Papers, 1831–1916, VHS; Edward Crenshaw Diary, March 13, 1865, in Crenshaw, "Diary," 382. See also Henry Calvin Conner to wife, October 18, 1864, Conner Papers. The flag ceremony is described by the Rangers' chaplain, Robert Franklin Bunting, in his letter to the editor of the *Houston Tri-Weekly Telegraph*, September 21, 1864, Robert Franklin Bunting Papers, TSLA. For a minister's use of the meteorological metaphor, see Atkinson, *God, the Giver of Victory and Peace*, 5.

55. Robert Moore Diary, July 19, 1863, in Robert Moore, *Life*, 157; Joseph Richard Manson Diary, October 27, December 17, 1864, VHS.

56. Samuel King Vann to Nancy Elizabeth Neel, August 25, 1864, September 27, 1864, in Vann, *"Most Lovely Lizzie,"* 47–48, 53. Lost Cause chroniclers Jones and Bennett recognized that soldiers' religious fervor increased as the war intensified; see J. William Jones, *Christ in the Camp*, 260–61, 353–54; Bennett, *Narrative*, 412, 416. Woodworth, *While God Is Marching On*, supports the claim that the religious fervor in the ranks remained steady and perhaps increased during the final period of the war.

57. Berger, *Sacred Canopy*, 17; John L. Sheppard to parents, June 9, 1864, Sheppard Family Papers, USC; Curry quoted in J. William Jones, *Christ in the Camp*, 504; Mathew Andrew Dunn to wife, August 22, 1864, in Jordan, "Mathew Andrew Dunn Letters," 125; Berends, " 'Wholesome Reading,' " 140–41. Though Curry wrote these reflections in 1867, it is doubtful that he embellished his daily schedule.

58. "The Ball Is Rolling," *Southern Confederacy*, February 2, 1864, p. 2. Explaining how intangible elements such as ideology, religion, and mentality affect the material prosecution of warfare is a promising inquiry for new military history. In the past, the subjective and objective sides of war have often been separated in scholarship.

59. Elliott quoted in *Southern Confederacy*, March 10, 1864, p. 1.

60. Elliott quoted in W. Harrison Daniel, *Southern Protestantism*, 40–41. See also Elliott's April 8, 1864, fast-day sermon, *Gideon's Water-Lappers*.

61. John Paris, *Funeral Discourse*, February 28, 1864, in Chesebrough, "*God Ordained This War,*" 264, 269, 271, 274.

62. Renfroe, "*Battle Is God's,*" 11; Doggett, *War and Its Close*, 18; Foster Diary, May 1, 1865, 172. Berends notes that the religious military press often distorted news from the front to favor the Confederacy (" 'Wholesome Reading,' " 147–48).

63. W. R. Redding to wife, April 8, 1864, W. R. Redding Papers, SHC.

64. William L. Nugent to wife, June 9, 1864, in *Nellie*, 180.

65. These comforts can be traced in the writings of soldiers who varied greatly in their concentration on spirituality. Joseph Manson's manuscripts elucidate these assurances; see Joseph Richard Manson Diary, VHS.

66. Atkinson, *God, the Giver of Victory and Peace*, 10; Doggett, *War and Its Close*, 19; Richard W. Waldrop to father, October 3, 1864, Richard Woolfolk Waldrop Papers, SHC. Confederate religion cracked under the strain of successive defeats and unprecedented destruction, but it withstood the war storm in the sense that it sustained its tenets until military defeat ended the war. Faithful soldiers who aired despondency in 1865 did not question that the Confederacy had a special covenant with God but rather wondered if the people or God had broken the covenant. See Nugent to Eleanor Smith Nugent,

January 16, 1865, in *Nellie*, 233; Thomas Hampton to wife, June 26, 1864, Hampton Letters.

67. Samuel Horace Hawes Diary, February 12, 1865, VHS.

Chapter Two. The Mask of Cain: Enemy Images in Rebel Minds

1. Herman Melville, "On the Slain Collegians," in Melville, *Poems*, 109–11. For more on the Cain myth, violence, and civil strife, see Ignatieff, *Warrior's Honor*, 46–48. The sacred story varies in fascinating ways from faith to faith. It appears in Christian, Muslim, and Jewish texts. Melville blames women for inciting men to make the mask of Cain. Some versions of the story base the murder on a dispute over a woman. Others focus on greed and fortune. For the story as nineteenth-century Americans most likely knew it, see Genesis 4:1–17.

2. Two caveats are important here. First, slavery was a major difference between North and South, and I do not intend to discount the significant divisions it created between the sections. Instead, I mean to address the process by which Americans came to view each other as irreconcilably opposed despite the many common interests and traits that bound them together as a nation and people. Second, by focusing on how southerners came to view the North as alien and hostile, I am not blaming southerners for the conflict. Northerners were just as responsible for creating the mask of Cain, and they used it on southerners; however, they are not the topic of this work. For northern abstractions of the South, see Foner, *Free Soil*; Susan-Mary Grant, *North over South*.

3. Numerous studies beyond Civil War scholarship have informed my work on perceptions of the enemy. In particular, see Dower, *War without Mercy*; Fussell, *Wartime*; Lepore, *Name of War*.

4. Susan-Mary Grant, *North over South*, 161.

5. For soldiers' psychological distance from opponents, see S. Marshall, *Men against Fire*; Gray, *Warriors*; Shalit, *Psychology*; Grossman, *On Killing*.

6. Fussell, *Wartime*, 115.

7. Cecil-Fronsman, *Common Whites*, 153 (first quotation); Thomas, *Confederacy as a Revolutionary Experience*, 18 (second and third quotations). For a discussion of how northern soldiers viewed Confederates and the South, see Reid Mitchell, *Civil War Soldiers*, 90–147. Some of the best analysis of southern frontier life can still be found in the classics: Cash, *Mind*, 3–28; Eaton, *History*; McCurry, *Masters*. I suspect that the familial authority McCurry finds in the established Low Country was as strong or stronger on the frontier.

8. Franklin, *Southern Odyssey*, xv. Franklin equated the trip to the "grand tour" of Europe: "Some southerners did make *the* grand tour of Europe, but a much larger number went to the North. In the preparations for the trip and in the reactions, during and after the experience, it seemed a satisfactory substitute for the longer journey" (1). Firebrands such as James Hammond and Robert Rhett spoke of countrymen above the Mason-Dixon Line from personal experience.

9. Yancey quoted in William Taylor, *Cavalier and Yankee*, 7.

10. Cash, *Mind*, 4. LeShan, *Psychology of War*, sees the development of abstractions for other people or nations as a common indicator of ensuing war.

11. Yancey quoted in William Taylor, *Cavalier and Yankee*, 7.

12. Foner, *Free Soil*, 313; Cash, *Mind*, 44; Franklin, *Militant South*, 24 ("agricultural frontier"), 14 ("fighters' fatherland"). For the moral undertones of the slavery debates, see Snay, *Gospel of Disunion*, 12–13, 24.

13. Faust, *James Henry Hammond*, 345–47. Hammond's speech is in *Congressional Globe*, 35th Cong., 1st sess., Appendix, 69–71. Newspapers throughout the South printed excerpts from the address, and according to Faust, "a subscription for twenty-five thousand copies of the address was raised almost at once" (*James Henry Hammond*, 347). The Georgian's editorial is quoted in Stampp, *Causes of the Civil War*, 210. Iverson's speech in *Congressional Globe*, 36th Cong., 2nd sess., 12.

14. Montague, *Disenchantment*, 162–63.

15. Dower, *War without Mercy*, 261. For different arguments about the pervasiveness of the Cavalier myth, see Bonner, "Roundheaded Cavaliers?"; Carmichael, *Last Generation*.

16. Chamberlayne, *Ham Chamberlayne*, 186.

17. Soldier quoted in Jimerson, *Private Civil War*, 127. For a similar opinion of the Army of the Potomac, see Harry Lewis to mother, April 6, 1864, Harry Lewis Papers, SHC.

18. At the Crater, one Rebel noted, "the negroes fought better than their white Yankee brethren" (Thomas Elder to Anna Fitzhugh [May] Elder, July 30, 1864, Thomas Claybrook Elder Papers, VHS). See also Milton Barrett to brother and sister, August 1, 1864, in Heller and Heller, *Confederacy*, 123; Edmund Fitzgerald Stone letter, n.d., VHS.

19. Kristen Smith, *Lines Are Drawn*, 86.

20. Ibid., 99. Volck also sketched Lincoln as Don Quixote with Butler as Sancho Panza. A deluded Lincoln proudly rides a worn-out horse, and a drunk Butler sits an equally worthless mule. A distant windmill marks the folly of their efforts.

21. Ibid., 93.

22. Civil War poetry and music exemplifies the way in which popular culture shaped soldiers' perspectives, yet military historians have seldom used these sources. Fahs's cultural study of wartime literature, *Imagined Civil War*, points the way. For the influences of music and the aural world in general on Civil War participants, see Mark Smith, *Listening*. For music in battle, see Hess, *Union Soldier*, 112. For a comparative look at Japanese war songs, see Dower, *War without Mercy*, 213–14.

23. "Call All! Call All!" and "Georgia," in *Songs and Ballads*, ed. Frank Moore, 31–33.

24. Frank Ticknor, "The Old Rifleman," in ibid., 119–20.

25. Stephen F. Hale to Governor Beriah Mogoffin, December 27, 1860, quoted in Dew, *Apostles of Disunion*, 95.

26. Charles Clark, address to citizens of Columbus, Mississippi, November 16, 1863, OR, ser. 4, 2:960–62; *Southern Confederacy*, February 2, 1864, p. 2.

27. Mother to Dunbar Affleck, May 21, 1864, Thomas Affleck Correspondence and Writings, LSU; Thomas J. Key Diary, April 10, 1864, in Cate, *Two Soldiers*, 70; Reuben Pierson to sister, August 11, 1863, in *Brothers*, 207; W. Harrison Daniel, *Southern Protestantism*, 39. Key uses "misceginator" in his December 7, 1864, entry (164). Democrats used the term *miscegenator* to demonize Republicans during the 1864 presidential campaign.

28. Ronald Lee, "Exploded Graces," 145–46.

29. Reid Mitchell, *Civil War Soldiers*, 24–25.

30. Charles Clark, address to citizens of Columbus, Mississippi, November 16, 1863, *OR*, ser. 4, 2:960–62.

31. Frank Moore, *Songs and Ballads*, 109–10.

32. St. George Tucker, "The Southern Cross," "Georgia," and "Call All! Call All!" (third quotation), all in *Songs and Ballads*, ed. Frank Moore, 15 (first quotation), 16 (second quotation), 30–33 (third quotation).

33. J. H. H., "Southern Song of Freedom"; De. G., "Justice Is Our Panoply"; James R. Randall, "Maryland, My Maryland"; A Rebel, "Manassas"; B, "Chivalrous C.S.A."; M. F. Bigney, "The Battle-Field of Manassas"; Anne Chambers Ketchum, "Battle-Call," all in *Songs and Ballads*, ed. Frank Moore, 66 (first quotation), 83 (second through sixth quotations), 72 (seventh quotation), 93 (eighth quotation), 97 (ninth quotation), 102 (tenth and eleventh quotations), 131 (twelfth quotation).

34. Ada Rose, "Nil Desperandum," in ibid., 158.

35. Samuel S. Meetze to sister, March 13, 1864, Confederate Papers, SHC; Albright Diary, March 1, 1865.

36. Moore, *Songs and Ballads*, 166–69. Perhaps the most remarkable atrocity song was James R. Randall's "At Fort Pillow" (in *War Poets*, ed. Hubner, 105–8). Randall justifies the Confederates' slaughter of hundreds of prisoners as retribution for numberless Federal offenses.

37. Kristen Smith, *Lines Are Drawn*, 101.

38. Ibid., 103, 76.

39. Regiments of former slaves fought in 1863, but most Confederate soldiers did not oppose them until 1864. Rebels' savagery toward African Americans in blue can be reconciled with their support for enlisting slaves in their own army because many Confederate soldiers voiced a greater commitment to independence and victory than to the institution of slavery.

40. Reuben Pierson to sister, August 11, 1863, in *Brothers*, 207; Green Berry Samuels to wife, August 21, 1863, in Spencer, Samuels, and Samuels, *Civil War Marriage*, 190.

41. Edwin Fay to wife, July 23, 1863 (first quotation), July 10, 1863 (second through fourth quotations), in *Infernal War*, 298, 295, 290; William Nugent to wife, August 27, 1863 (fifth through ninth quotations), September 25, 1863 (tenth and eleventh quotations), in *Nellie*, 128, 129, 138.

42. Davis Diary, October 6, 1864 (first quotation); Power, *Lee's Miserables*, 142–43; James Adams to parents, September 16, 1864, Israel L. Adams and Family Papers, LSU; Heartsill Diary, July 31, 1864 (third and fourth quotations), August 11, 1864 (fifth quotation), 211, 212.

43. Schivelbusch, *Culture of Defeat*, 61; Richard W. Waldrop to father, October 3, 1864, Richard Woolfolk Waldrop Papers, SHC.

44. Spencer Welch to wife, October 20, 1863, in *Surgeon's Letters*, 81–82; J. Kelly Bennette Diary and Letters, June 20, 1864, SHC.

45. Edgeworth Bird to wife, November 30, 1864 (first quotation), in *Granite Farm*, 218; Grant Taylor to wife, June 21, 1864 (second quotation), in *Cruel War*, 262; Charles Blackford to wife, June 18, 1864 (third quotation), in *Lee's Army*, 257; Elias Davis to

wife, July 27, 1864, Elias Davis Papers, SHC; James Ferdinand Izlar Diary, February 15, 1865, USC. Taylor's apprehension about the region was heightened by destruction he saw that corroborated with stories from Dalton.

46. Paul Higginbotham to brother, July 1, 1864 (first and second quotations), Higginbotham Papers; Charles Blackford to wife, July 11, 1864 (third and fourth quotations), in *Lee's Army*, 266; Walters Diary, July 8, 1864 (fifth and sixth quotations), 132; Albright Diary, June 16, 20, 1864. See also Power, *Lee's Miserables*, 117; Spencer Welch to wife, July 6, 1864, in *Surgeon's Letters*, 102. Sherman's treatment of Atlanta produced a greater uproar; see James Madison Brannock to wife, September 12, 1864, Brannock Papers; William E. Sloan Diary, July 28, 1864, CWC; James Adams to parents, September 16, 1864, Israel L. Adams and Family Papers, LSU; Thomas J. Key Diary, August 4, 1864, in Cate, *Two Soldiers*, 108.

47. Quoted in Schivelbusch, *Culture of Defeat*, 61; Sarah Conner to her sister, August 7, 1864, Conner Papers; William E. Sloan Diary, July 28, 1864, CWC.

48. Silver, *Confederate Morale*, 85–86; Reid Mitchell, *Civil War Soldiers*, 25–28; Stephen A. Jordan Diary, May 15, 1864, CWC. Both Americans and Japanese accused the other side of similar atrocities in the Pacific War (Dower, *War without Mercy*, 115–29). See also Wiley, *Life of Johnny Reb*, 311; *OR*, ser. 1, vol. 12, pt. 2, 202–3; vol. 20, pt. 1, 880; vol. 51, pt. 2, 329.

49. W. Harrison Daniel, *Southern Protestantism*, 40; John Cotton to wife, ca. November 1864, in *Yours till Death*, 120; Silver, *Confederate Morale*, 87; Malinda Taylor to Grant Taylor, September 2, 1864, in *Cruel War*, 280; Thomas J. Key Diary, September 23, 1864, in Cate, *Two Soldiers*, 138–39. Silver asserts that "the triple-edged combination of horrors at the North, atrocities of Northerners in the South, and the threat of overwhelming barbarism if the Confederacy failed, moved into high gear in the last two years of the war. Stories of desecrated churches, desolated homes, and outraged women became common" (*Confederate Morale*, 87). Escott concurs, "Southern churchmen responded warmly to Davis's reliance on religion and proved to be the staunchest propagandists for the Confederate cause. As the fortunes of the South declined in 1863, the preachers followed the president's lead in dwelling on Union atrocities and the horrors of life under the depraved Yankees" (*After Secession*, 184).

50. Ignatieff, *Warrior's Honor*, 176; *Southern Confederacy*, December 14, 1864, p. 2. Dower illuminates a similar relationship between atrocity myths and perceptions of the enemy in the Pacific War: "atrocities and war crimes played a major role in the propagation of racial and cultural stereotypes. The stereotypes preceded the atrocities, however, and had an independent existence apart from any specific event" (*War without Mercy*, 73).

51. McPherson, *For Cause and Comrades*, 149.

52. John Bratton to wife, July 9, 1864, John Bratton Papers, SHC; Richard W. Waldrop to mother, October 6, 1864, Richard Woolfolk Waldrop Papers, SHC; Green Berry Samuels to wife, August 21, 1863, in Spencer, Samuels, and Samuels, *Civil War Marriage*, 190; Sam R. Lockhart to mother, July 5, 1864, Confederate Papers, SHC.

53. Thomas Elder to wife, July 1, 1864 (first quotation), Thomas Claybrook Elder Papers, VHS; Walters Diary, July 9, (second quotation), August 4, 1864 (third quotation),

133, 141; Edgeworth Bird to wife, August 4, 1864 (fourth quotation), in *Granite Farm*, 180–81.

54. Edgeworth Bird to wife, August 28, 1864 (first quotation), August 4, 1864 (second quotation), in *Granite Farm*, 196, 181; John Doyle to Maggie Knighton, August 26, 1864, Josiah Knighton and Family Papers, LSU; Charlie DeNoon to parents, July 8, 1864, in Couture, *Charlie's Letters*, 226. For an example of the idea of Yankees stealing slaves, see Albright Diary, June 30, 1864.

55. Thomas J. Key Diary, December 7, 1864, in Cate, *Two Soldiers*, 164; James Brannock to wife, March 29, 1864, Brannock Papers; Berkeley Diary, September 23, 1864, 101; Wiley, *Life of Billy Yank*, 352–53 (fourth through sixth quotations).

56. William Nugent to wife, August 11, 1863, in *Nellie*, 125; Edmund Fitzgerald Stone to Samuel Marion Stone, n.d., Edmund Fitzgerald Stone Letter, VHS; James Madison Brannock to wife, March 29, 1864 (second quotation), Brannock Papers; James R. Randall, "At Fort Pillow," in *War Poets*, ed. Hubner, 108.

57. Paul Higginbotham to brother, August 1, 1864, Higginbotham Papers; Walters Diary, August 1, 1864, 140. Some Confederates were sickened by the massacres.

58. Samuel King Vann to Nancy Elizabeth Neel, August 17, 1864, in Vann, *"Most Lovely Lizzie,"* 41; Edgeworth Bird to wife, July 17, 1864, in *Granite Farm*, 176; Power, *Lee's Miserables*, 117. For a detailed description of the trenches around Petersburg, see Thomas John Moore to Thomas W. Hill, October 27, 1864, Thomas John Moore Papers, USC.

59. Walters Diary, August 2, 1864 (first quotation), 141; Thomas John Moore to Thomas W. Hill, October 27, 1864 (second quotation), Thomas John Moore Papers, USC; William I. Box to wife, October 21, 1864 (third quotation), Box Family Papers, USC; Fred Fleet to mother, August 19, 1864 (fourth quotation), in *Green Mount*, 333; Gray, *Warriors*, 138–39 (fifth quotation). For other accounts of fatigue in the trenches, see William Casey to cousin, July 20, 1864, William Casey to Jimmie Casey, June 30, 1864, both in William Thomas Casey Papers, VHS. The proximity of trench warfare caused both a standardization of hostility and regressions into tit-for-tat retaliation. Preservation of life and logic could trump aggression and hatred if both sides agreed to follow certain rules, such as curbing sharpshooters, allowing the retrieval of wounded, and giving pickets a safe passage at the start and finish of their shifts. Violations of these "rules" escalated hostilities. When Edmund Stone and his fellow skirmishers broke a truce and killed a number of unsuspecting black pickets, the Federals retaliated with an artillery barrage that night; see Edmund Fitzgerald Stone Letter, n.d., VHS.

60. Fussell, *Great War*, 77 (first quotation), 75 (second quotation). The dichotomies of war separate a soldier not only from the enemy but also from civilians, officers, and even his prewar self. For more on these polarities, see Linderman, *Embattled Courage*, 154. Linderman cautions scholars who compare trench warfare in the Civil War and World War I; however, both events shared the conditions stressed in this section: stark polarity, monotony, tactical deadlock, desensitization, and filth.

61. McPherson, *For Cause and Comrades*, 152; Thomas J. Newberry to father, November 19, 1863, in Enoch Mitchell, "Civil War Letters," 74. See also Jimerson, *Private Civil War*, 175.

62. Robert Stiles to Rosa Stiles, June 15, 1864, Robert Augustus Stiles Papers, VHS; William Casey to mother, February 14, 1864, William Thomas Casey Papers, VHS; Urban G. Owen to wife, June 2, 1864, in Enoch Mitchell, "Letters of a Confederate Surgeon," 169; Foster Diary, July 23, 1864, 115. For similar impressions of the enemy dead, see Walters, *Norfolk Blues*, 123, 140; *Surgeon's Letters*, 94–95, 98. Fussell, *Great War*, 77, also considers the impact of dead foes on soldiers' perceptions. Hiram Smith Williams, an engineer in the Army of Tennessee, expressed empathy for fallen enemy soldiers on a number of occasions: "Poor fellows! I would pity the untimely death of the bitterest foe I have on Earth" (Williams Diary, 32 [quotation], 33, 68). In contrast, when Edwin Fay helped bury enemy bodies, he "printed Abolitionist on a Oak Board and stuck it at his head for the Yanks to see if they should come after we left" (*Infernal War*, 180).

63. Urban G. Owen to wife, May 28, 1864 (first and second quotations), June 2, 1864, in Enoch Mitchell, "Letters of a Confederate Surgeon," 167, 169; Edwin Fay to wife, October 8, 1863, in *Infernal War*, 342.

64. Richard Launcelot Maury Diary, March 28, 1865, VHS; Edmund T. Eggleston Diary, November 28, 1864, in Noyes, "Excerpts," 354; Samuel Pickens Diary, November 15, 1864, in *Voices*, 325; Richard Stanford Webb to cousin, November 3, 1864, Webb Family Papers, SHC; David Crawford to mother, May 12, 1864, Crawford Family Letters, USC; Leonidas Polk to wife, June 9, 1864, Leonidas Lafayette Polk Papers, SHC; W. R. Redding to wife, n.d., W. R. Redding Papers, SHC. Creed Davis also used the word *specimen* when describing prisoners: "Some prisoners captured to day. Good specimens of the New England Yankees" (Davis Diary, June 4, 1864).

65. Albright Diary, August 19, August 26 (quotation), August 27, 1864; Abel Crawford to wife, June 21, 1864, CWC; Heartsill Diary, 199–206; James B. Jones Diary, October 7 (quotation), October 8–21, 1864, Jones Family Papers, SHC. Some writers on the subject of twentieth-century century warfare stress that encounters with prisoners often bridge the psychological distances belligerents create. As Gray puts it, "One opportunity the front-line soldier has to know the enemy as a human being is when he takes prisoners, and this is frequently a crucial experience for soldiers. The prisoner of war reveals to his opponent that he, too, cherishes life and that he has at least a minimal trust in your humanity, otherwise he would not be surrendering. The soldier who has taken, or himself been made, a prisoner of war will inevitably be a changed man and fighter. His foe has been demonstrated to be comprehensible and of the same stuff, at least outwardly, as he himself is made of" (*Warriors*, 137). Dower also contends that Japanese prisoners in the Pacific War revealed a level of humanity and cooperation that did not exist in American stereotypes of the enemy (*War without Mercy*, 60–71). My research seldom found similar instances in Confederate interactions with the enemy; for a rare example of such an occurrence, see Percy Nagel to mother, August 16, 1864, Percy Nagel Papers, 1852–64, USC.

66. Davis Diary, May 18, 1864; Reuben Pierson to David Pierson, May 22, 1864, in *Brothers*, 237; John Cotton to wife, June 9, 1864, in *Yours till Death*, 112; George Knox Miller to wife, July 1, 1864, George Knox Miller Papers, SHC; Abe G. Jones to mother, October 28, 1864, Jones Family Papers, SHC. See also Walters Diary, October 10, October 30, 1864, 162–63, 170; Power, *Lee's Miserables*, 77.

67. Wiley, *Life of Johnny Reb*, 314; George Binford to cousin, June 3, 1864, George C.

Binford Letters, VHS; George Knox Miller to wife, July 1, 1864, George Knox Miller Papers, SHC; Walters Diary, June 3, 1864, 122; Power, *Lee's Miserables*, 77–78. In numerous instances, Confederates complimented the enemy's valor or resolve; see, for example, Giles Buckner Cooke Diary, April 1, 1865, VHS; *Brothers*, 239; *Nellie*, 209–10.

68. Reuben Pierson to father, April 19, 1864, in *Brothers*, 233; William Nugent to wife, May 5, 1864, in *Nellie*, 175; Thomas J. Key Diary, May 1, 1864, in Cate, *Two Soldiers*, 78. See also Hugh W. Montgomery to A. W. Hyatt, May 25, 1864, Hyatt Papers. Montgomery admitted that northern financial trouble "opens a new theater of hope to a struggling people." Since all these accounts were written within weeks of each other, they likely were either responses to rumor or news from the North or wishful thinking that provided an alternative route to victory than the soon-to-commence spring campaigns.

69. Walters Diary, November 7, 1864, 172; William Nugent to wife, May 5, 1864, in *Nellie*, 175; Paul Higginbotham to brother, June 10, 1864, Higginbotham Papers. Visions of northern financial ruin also appeared in southern sermons; see Stephen Elliott, *Gideon's Water-Lappers*, 9.

70. Edwin H. Fay to wife, July 17, 1864, in *Infernal War*, 399.

71. Parents to Fred Fleet, June 12, 1864, in *Green Mount*, 332; Silver, *Confederate Morale*, 82–84, 90–91; William L. Nugent to wife, May 5, 1864, in *Nellie*, 174; Edgeworth Bird to Wilson Bird, January 17, 1865, in *Granite Farm*, 236–37; James Madison Brannock to wife, March 29, 1864, Brannock Papers; Charles Fenton James to Emma A. James, February 7, 1865, Charles Fenton James Letters, VHS. Brannock had a similar reaction after the fall of Atlanta; see Brannock to wife, September 12, 1864, Brannock Papers.

Chapter Three. Without a Murmur: Confederate Endurance and the Immediate War

1. Clausewitz, *On War*, 188–89.

2. Fussell, *Wartime*, 140–41.

3. I do not seek to valorize the men who persevered but rather to explain how their perceptions of the war encouraged them to further resistance and even provided some troops with hope of victory.

4. Davis Diary, November 8, 1864; Charles Blackford to Susan Leigh Blackford, August 10, 1864, in *Lee's Army*, 272; Edgeworth Bird to wife, January 17, 1864, in *Granite Farm*, 157; Thomas John Moore to Mr. Hill (overseer), August 1, 1864, Thomas John Moore Papers, USC; Lafayette Orr to mother, January 29, 1864, in *Campaigning*, 127–28. For Confederate standards of rations, see Hagerman, *American Civil War*, 252. The quality and quantity of rations fluctuated throughout the war.

5. R. E. Elliott to John A. Crawford, January 10, 1864, Crawford Family Letters, USC; Davis Diary, January 2, 1865 (fifth quotation), December 1, 1864 (sixth quotation), December 31, 1864 (seventh quotation); Percy Nagel to mother, June 22, 1864, Percy Nagel Papers, 1852–64, USC; George Knox Miller to wife, June 2, 1864, George Knox Miller Papers, SHC. For soldiers' justifications for foraging, see Junius Newport Bragg to wife, September 20, 1864, in Bragg, *Letters*, 249. Hardships could strengthen or erode comradeship. When rations were low in May 1864 and Hiram Williams "had two large

crackers left," he divided his food with a messmate who had nothing. "I cannot bear to see any of my friends with nothing to eat as long as I have any," Williams wrote in his diary. Williams's generosity backfired, however, because he was without food the following day and could find no one willing to supplement his scant supply of cornmeal. "It was the first time I had ever asked for anything to eat," he exclaimed, "and it will be the last" (Williams Diary, May 19, May 20, 1864, 75, 77).

6. Frank Adams to parents, January 19, 1865 (first and fifth quotations), Israel Adams and Family Papers, LSU; Charles Blackford to wife, January 24, 1864, in *Lee's Army*, 234; Green Berry Samuels to wife, November 7, 1863, in Spencer, Samuels, and Samuels, *Civil War Marriage*, 200; James Brannock to wife, October 21, 1864, Brannock Papers; Reuben Pierson to father, January 15, 1864, in *Brothers*, 224; Charles Andry to mother, September 21, 1864, Michel Thomassin Andry and Family Papers, LSU. Not all soldiers quietly accepted poor rations. On March 21, 1864, troops at Bristol, Tennessee, demanded more food and received an extra day's rations. This action only pacified the men for a week, however, and on April 2, 1864, a party charged the commissary, killing a lieutenant and wounding several others (William Montgomery Diary, March 22, April 3, 1864, in Montgomery, *Georgia Sharpshooter*, 45, 47; Milton Barrett to siblings, April 1, 1864, in Heller and Heller, *Confederacy*, 115–16). Scholars have identified these gender ideals and the pressures they cause in other wars. In their extensive study of American soldiers in World War II, Stouffer and colleagues note, "The code of masculinity . . . attached value and prestige to enduring danger and hardship, while the general orientation of social values toward the aim of fighting the war lent prestige to the persons most directly concerned with this aim" (*American Soldier*, 2:308).

7. Fred Fleet to parents, June 6, 1864, in *Green Mount*, 327; Edwin Leet to Sarah A. Leet, October 18, 1864, Edwin Leet Letters, 1864–65, LSU; Paul Higginbotham to brother, June 22, 1864, Higginbotham Papers; Grant Taylor to wife, February 20, 1864, in *Cruel War*, 224.

8. J. S. Gooch to uncle, February 1[?], 1864, Confederate Papers, SHC; Thomas Boatwright to wife, March 28, 1864, Thomas F. Boatwright Papers, SHC; Elias Davis to wife, August 13, 1864, Elias Davis Papers, SHC.

9. Charles Blackford to Susan Blackford, June 13, June 7, 1864, in *Lee's Army*, 255, 252; Paul Higginbotham to brother, July 1, 1864, Higginbotham Papers; James Brannock to wife, January 31, 1864, Brannock Papers; Marion Hill Fitzpatrick to wife, October 29, 1863, in Fitzpatrick, *Letters to Amanda*, 97. For more soldiers' reactions to Federal plunderers at their homes, see William Montgomery Diary, July 8, 1864, in Montgomery, *Georgia Sharpshooter*, 54; Joseph Richard Manson Diary, November 24, 1864, VHS; George Binford to cousin, March 2, 1864, George C. Binford Letters, VHS; Edgeworth Bird to Sallie Bird, September 22, 1864, in *Granite Farm*, 203.

10. Hess, *Union Soldier*, 65; Grant quoted in McPherson, *Battle Cry of Freedom*, 731.

11. Charles DeNoon to parents, May 28, 1864, in Couture, *Charlie's Letters*, 222; Davis Diary, June 4, 1864; Samuel McKittrick to Mary Stennis McKittrick, June 5, 1864, in Lewis, "Confederate Officer's Letters," 493–94; Theodore Honour to wife, May 24, 1864, Theodore A. Honour Papers, 1859–65, USC; Paul Higginbotham to brother, June 22, 1864, Higginbotham Papers.

12. Thomas Hampton to wife, June 26, 1864, August 10, 1864, Hampton Letters;

Williams Diary, November 13, 1864, 121; George Knox Miller to wife, May 20, 1864, George Knox Miller Papers, SHC; Lawrence Ross to wife, July 7, 1864, in Ross, *Personal Civil War Letters*, 64; McPherson, *Battle Cry of Freedom*, 734; Freeman, *Lee's Lieutenants*, 676–77.

13. Ross, *Personal Civil War Letters*, xi; Bates, *Texas Cavalry Officer's Civil War*, 327.

14. Williams Diary, February 20, 1864, 26–27; Spencer Welch to wife, May 7, 1864, in *Surgeon's Letters*, 94–95; Theodore Honour to wife, May 24, 1864, Theodore A. Honour Papers, 1859–65, USC; Grant Taylor to wife, June 16, 1864, in *Cruel War*, 259; *OR*, ser. 1, vol. 38, pt. 3, 848–50.

15. Berkeley Diary, June 3, June 4, 1864, 79–80.

16. Ibid. Berkeley suffered a similar experience in September 1864: "Today . . . at my gun, three men, one after the other, were shot down at my right hand. . . . I thought my time would certainly come next" (Berkeley Diary, September 19, 1864, 98).

17. Ibid., July 9, 1864, 86–87; Robert Stiles to mother, July 24, 1864, (first through third and sixth quotations), Robert Stiles to father, September 12, 1864, (fourth and fifth quotations), Robert Augustus Stiles Papers, VHS.

18. Samuel Vann to Nancy Elizabeth Neel, August 25, 1864, in Vann, *"Most Lovely Lizzie,"* 45, 47; Charles DeNoon to parents, May 28, 1864, in Couture, *Charlie's Letters*, 222; Berkeley Diary, September 19, (first through third quotations), September 24, 1864 (fourth quotation), 98, 102. For consolidation, see Lafayette Orr to mother, January 29, 1864, in *Campaigning*, 127–28; Charles James to Emma James, February 9, 1865, Charles Fenton James Letters, VHS; Thomas Hampton to wife, March 9, 1865, Hampton Letters.

19. Spencer Welch to wife, October 2, 1864, in *Surgeon's Letters*, 107; John Jackman Diary, October 2, October 3, 1864, in Jackman, *Diary*, 147; for details of Jackman's wound, see 140. Some soldiers expressed concern for the thinning of the ranks. In June 1864, Charles Blackford wrote, "I am very anxious about our lines here. Lee has so few men with which to keep them up that it will be hard to maintain them. He has no mobile reserve to shift about whenever an attack is made. All are in the main line, and that is thin. If these lines are broken Richmond falls, and with the fall of Richmond the war and the Confederacy come to an end" (Charles Blackford to wife, June 16, 1864, in *Lee's Army*, 256). Few soldiers expressed Blackford's objective view of numerical disparities.

20. Escott, *After Secession*, 150; *OR*, ser. 4, 2:944–52, 1024–49; Spencer Welch to wife, October 12, 1864, in *Surgeon's Letters*, 108–9. In World War II, American soldiers perpetuated the same hierarchy of military matters and combat personnel above civilian and rear echelon support; see Stouffer et al., *American Soldier*, 2:290–323.

21. Thomas Elder to wife, October 13, 1864 (first and second quotations), October 16, 1864 (third quotation), in Thomas Claybrook Elder Papers, VHS; Edgeworth Bird to Sallie Bird, October 18, 1864, in *Granite Farm*, 206; Davis Diary, October 21, 1864.

22. Power, *Lee's Miserables*, 226–27; Walters Diary, October 14 (first and second quotations), October 15, 1864 (third and fourth quotations), 164; Fred Fleet to mother, October 11, 1864 (fifth quotation), Fred Fleet to father, September 29, 1864 (sixth quotation), in *Green Mount*, 344, 341. See also Fletcher Brabham to Jube, November 25, 1864, Brabham Family Letters, USC; Henry Calvin Conner to wife, November 4, 1864, Conner Papers.

23. Thomas John Moore to Mr. Hill (overseer), August 1, 1864, Thomas John Moore Papers, USC; Williams Diary, June 24, (second quotation), May 1, 1864 (third quotation), 98, 54, 42–44; Walters Diary, December 25, 1864, 181; P. E. Retif to mother, September 26, 1864 (fifth quotation), P. E. Retif Letters, LSU. See also William Casey to mother, July 20, 1864, William Thomas Casey Papers, VHS; Rawleigh Downman to wife, January 30, 1865, Downman Family Papers, VHS.

24. Charles Blackford to Nannie Blackford, August 2, 1864, in *Lee's Army*, 270; Robert D. Trieves to Lizzie Brewer, May 14, 1864, Harman Dinwiddie Papers, VHS; Fred Fleet to Lou, November 26, 1864, in *Green Mount*, 348.

25. David Crawford to brother, September 29, 1864, Crawford Family Letters, USC; Theodore Honour to wife, June 14, 1864, Theodore A. Honour Papers, 1859–65, USC; Thomas Boatwright to wife, March 6, 1864, Thomas F. Boatwright Papers, SHC; Berkeley Diary, September 19, 1864, 98.

26. Clausewitz, *On War*, 189, 188.

27. James Drayton Nance to wife, January 1, 1864, James Drayton Nance Papers, USC; Henry Calvin Conner to wife, December 14, 1864, Conner Papers; Henry Armand London to father, January 26, 1865, Henry Armand London Diary and Letters, SHC.

28. For two women who remained fiercely loyal to the Confederacy, see Stone, *Brokenburn*; Dawson, *Sarah Morgan*.

29. Fletcher Brabham to Jube, October 26, 1864, Brabham Family Letters, USC; William Nugent to wife, August 30, 1863, in *Nellie*, 131; Thomas John Moore to Mr. Hill (overseer), August 1, 1864, Thomas John Moore Papers, USC.

30. Harry Lewis to mother, March 12, 1864, Harry Lewis Papers, SHC; Marion Hill Fitzpatrick to wife, January 1, 1865, in Fitzpatrick, *Letters to Amanda*, 194.

31. Hynes, *Soldiers' Tale*, 8; Clausewitz, *On War*, 187; soldier quoted in Royster, *Destructive War*, 187.

32. Fred Anderson, *People's Army*, 142–64.

33. Ever since Hannibal's Carthaginians smashed a Roman army at the battle of Cannae in 212 B.C., it has been a benchmark for the decisive battle. For more on how the concept of decisive battles first developed, see Hanson, *Western Way*. Royster identifies the prevalence of faith in a climactic battle during the Civil War: "Throughout the war Americans persisted in expecting one climactic battle that would decide the outcome and end the fighting. . . . In the last grand battle, they believed, the scale of effort would be so great, the killing so horrible, and the result so clear that the losers would concede defeat in the war, no matter what their remaining resources" (*Destructive War*, 254).

34. Shaara, *Killer Angels*, 356 (first quotation), 358 (second through fourth quotations). An example of the high-tide metaphor appears in McPherson's *Battle Cry of Freedom*: "In Pennsylvania the high tide of the Confederacy receded from Gettysburg" (636).

35. Jedediah Hotchkiss Diary, July 3, 1863, in Hotchkiss, *Make Me a Map*, 158; Robert Moore Diary, July 3 (third through fifth quotations), July 13, 1863 (sixth quotation), in Robert Moore, *Life*, 153, 156. McPherson argues that Lee's army exuded an "aura of invincibility" before Gettysburg (*Battle Cry of Freedom*, 647). My work contends that troops sustained this aura after the failed campaign. As this chapter shows, numerous rationalizations and misperceptions of the immediate war helped perpetuate this ethos.

36. Edgeworth Bird to wife, July 7 (first quotation), July 12, 1863 (second quotation),

in *Granite Farm*, 115, 122; Spencer Welch to wife, July 17, 1863, in *Surgeon's Letters*, 59; David Wyatt Aiken to wife, July 11, 1863, in Tapert, *Brothers' War*, 161. For Fredericksburg, see Rable, *Fredericksburg! Fredericksburg!* My analysis of the way in which Confederates assessed Gettysburg echoes Gallagher's argument in *Third Day*.

37. McPherson, *Battle Cry of Freedom*, 664; Edgeworth Bird to wife, July 9, 1863, in *Granite Farm*, 118; David Wyatt Aiken to wife, July 11, 1863, in Tapert, *Brothers' War*, 162; Reuben Pierson to father, ca. July 15, 1863 (sixth quotation), July 19, 1863 (seventh and eighth quotations), in *Brothers*, 203, 204.

38. Edgeworth Bird to wife, July 9 (first quotation), July 19, 1863 (second quotation), in *Granite Farm*, 118, 125; Spencer Welch to wife, August 2, 1863, in *Surgeon's Letters*, 69; Reuben Pierson to sister, August 11, 1863, in *Brothers*, 206–7.

39. Edgeworth Bird to wife, July 19, 1863, in *Granite Farm*, 125; Reuben Pierson to father, ca. July 15, 1863, in *Brothers*, 203; Tally Simpson to cousin, July 18, 1863, in Simpson, *Far, Far from Home*, 257–58.

40. Robert A. Moore Diary, August 15, August 24, 1863 (Humphreys quotations), in Robert Moore, *Life*, 161, 162.

41. Ulysses Grant, *Personal Memoirs*, 1:567; McPherson, *Battle Cry of Freedom*, 636–38; William Nugent to wife, July 8, 1863, in *Nellie*, 116.

42. William Nugent to wife, July 28, (first through fifth quotations), August 4 (sixth and seventh quotations), August 7 (eighth through eleventh quotations), August 15, 1863 (twelfth through fourteenth quotations) in *Nellie*, 116–17, 120–22, 126. Other Confederates echoed Nugent's conviction that a more vigorous war policy would reverse Rebel misfortunes. Many soldiers accused Pemberton, a Pennsylvanian, of treason. Georgia corporal A. P. Adamson thought, "Pemberton basely sold Vicksburg." Like Nugent, Adamson believed, "If we had all such Generals as Lee, Beauregard, Price, Breckenridge and Johnston, and such as Pemberton and Holmes dismissed, we could yet expect to be successful" (Augustus Pitt Adamson to sister, August 10, 1863, in Adamson, *Sojourns*, 173).

43. Spencer Welch to wife, January 16, 1864, in *Surgeon's Letters*, 86; George Binford to cousin, March 2, 1864, George C. Binford Letters, VHS; James Brannock to wife, March 20, 1864, Brannock Papers; William Nugent to wife, March 8, March 20, 1864, in *Nellie*, 157, 159, 163. See also Frank Batchelor to wife, April 24, 1864, in Batchelor, *Batchelor-Turner Letters*, 81.

44. Franklin Gaillard to Maria Porcher, March 27, 1864, Franklin Gaillard Letters, SHC; Elias Davis to wife, March 4 (fourth quotation), March 9, 1864 (fifth through seventh quotations), Elias Davis Papers, SHC; Robert P. Tutwiler to aunt, April 24, 1864, Mrs. Thomas Chalmers McCorvey Papers, SHC; Reuben Pierson to Mary Catherine Pierson, March 28, 1864, in *Brothers*, 230–31. Before the 1864 campaigns began, Lee was convinced that "if victorious, we have everything to hope for in the future. If defeated, nothing will be left for us to live for" (quoted in Dowdey, *Lee's Last Campaign*, 60). His all-or-nothing attitude appealed to battle-tested and war-weary troops. For a rare example of a Rebel who was not optimistic before the 1864 campaign commenced, see Charles Blackford to Susan Blackford, May 1, 1864, in *Lee's Army*, 242–43.

45. James Brannock to wife, January 31, 1864, Brannock Papers; Green Berry Samuels to wife, March 30, 1864, in Spencer, Samuels, and Samuels, *Civil War Marriage*, 210; Henry Calvin Conner to wife, April 4, 1864, Conner Papers.

46. Historians have not discussed how reviews affected soldiers' perceptions of their army. Larry Daniel begins his study of the Army of Tennessee with Johnston's review at Dalton, Georgia, in 1864, but uses the incident as a vignette to introduce the army's men and commanders rather than examines the event's significance (*Soldiering*, 1–10). For a detailed eyewitness account of a review, see David Crawford to mother, April 30, 1864, Crawford Family Letters, USC.

47. James Brannock to wife, January 31, 1864, Brannock Papers; Thomas Hampton to wife, February 14, 1864 (third and fourth quotations), January 31, 1864 (fifth quotation), Hampton Letters; Thomas J. Key Diary, April 19, 1864, in Cate, *Two Soldiers*, 72; Grant Taylor to wife, March 9, 1864, in *Cruel War*, 230–31; William Montgomery Diary, April 29, 1864, in Montgomery, *Georgia Sharpshooter*, 48. Not all soldiers liked reviews; some considered them needless marching; see Williams Diary, April 19, 1864, 48–49.

48. Thomas J. Key Diary, March 31 (first quotation), April 7, 1864 (second quotation), in Cate, *Two Soldiers*, 66, 68; Thomas Hampton to wife, April 8, 1864, in Hampton Letters; Lafayette Orr to brothers, April 30, 1864, in *Campaigning*, 135–36; Percy Nagel to mother, April 20, 1864, Percy Nagel Papers, 1852–64, USC; Fred Fleet to parents, June 6, 1864, in *Green Mount*, 327–28. Wiley briefly notes, "Sham battles were staged on grand and realistic scale to fire enthusiasm for spring campaigns" (*Life of Johnny Reb*, 132).

49. Power, *Lee's Miserables*, 2, 3; Robert P. Tutwiler to aunt, April 24, 1864, quoted in *Lee's Miserables*, 2; Elias Davis to sister-in-law, April 24, 1864, Elias Davis Papers, SHC.

50. Harry Lewis to mother, April 6, 1864, Harry Lewis Papers, SHC; Wiley, *Life of Johnny Reb*, 133; OR, ser. 1, 33:1144–45; Power, *Lee's Miserables*, 3; McPherson, *Battle Cry of Freedom*, 718–19. See also OR, ser. 1, vol. 32, pt. 2, 571–82.

51. Power, *Lee's Miserables*, 20–21.

52. Green Berry Samuels to wife, May 7, 1864, in Spencer, Samuels, and Samuels, *Civil War Marriage*, 216 (third quotation), 217 (fourth quotation). Power agrees that "on the whole, the officers and men of the army viewed the Wilderness as a resounding Confederate triumph" (*Lee's Miserables*, 24). See also Berkeley Diary, May 5, 1864, 73; Charles Blackford to Susan Blackford, May 5, May 6, 1864, in *Lee's Army*, 243–44, 244–45; William Montgomery Diary, May 6, 1864, in Montgomery, *Georgia Sharpshooter*, 48–49.

53. Livermore, *Numbers and Losses*, 112–13; McPherson, *Battle Cry of Freedom*, 732; Foote, *Civil War*, 223.

54. John Hampden Chamberlayne to mother, May 15, 1864, in Chamberlayne, *Ham Chamberlayne*, 220; Robert Stiles to mother, May 15, 1864 (second quotation), Robert Stiles to sister, May 20, 1864 (third and fourth quotations), in Robert Augustus Stiles Papers, VHS; David Crawford to mother, May 12, 1864, Crawford Family Letters, USC; Charles Blackford to wife, May 19, 1864, in *Lee's Army*, 245; Charles DeNoon to parents, May 15, 1864, in Couture, *Charlie's Letters*, 220–21; John Francis Shaffner to wife, May 25, 1864, Fries and Shaffner Papers, SHC; Abel H. Crawford to Dora, May 19, 1864, CWC.

55. James Tinkler to parents, May 15, 1864, James C. Tinkler Letters, USC; David Crawford to sister, May 16, 1864, Crawford Family Letters, USC; John Francis Shaffner to wife, May 25, 1864, Fries and Shaffner Papers, SHC.

56. J. J. Young to Edmund W. Jones, May 25, 1864, Edmund Walter Jones Papers,

SHC; Walters Diary, May 9, 1864, 115; Thomas Elder to wife, May 13, May 20, 1864, Thomas Claybrook Elder Papers, VHS; Robert Trieves to Lizzie Brewer, May 14, 1864, Harman Dinwiddie Papers, VHS.

57. Spencer Welch to wife, July 6, 1864, in *Surgeon's Letters*, 102–3; Paul Higginbotham to brother, August 1, 1864, Higginbotham Papers; John William McLure to wife, August 3, 1864, McLure Papers; Elias Davis to wife, August 13, 1864, Elias Davis Papers, SHC; James D. Albright Diary, July 30, 1864, VHS. Welch noted the difference in morale at home and at the front: "In the interior where there is no danger nearly everybody is whipped, and they should be ashamed of themselves."

58. Power, *Lee's Miserables*, 210–11; Thomas Goree to Robert Daniel Goree, December 18, 1864, in Goree, *Longstreet's Aide*, 139–40; Spencer Welch to wife, October 12, 1864, in *Surgeon's Letters*, 108; Fred Fleet to mother, September 8, 1864, in *Green Mount*, 338; Walters Diary, September 29, 1864, 158–59.

59. J. P. Cannon Diary, May 15, 1864, in Cannon, *Bloody Banners*, 66; McPherson, *Battle Cry of Freedom*, 744; Foote, *Civil War*, 318. Johnston's army started with about fifty thousand arms but soon gained another fifteen thousand from General Leonidas Polk.

60. George Binford to cousin, June 3, 1864, George C. Binford Letters, VHS. See also Benjamin Seaton Diary, May 11, May 12, 1864, in Seaton, *Bugle Softly Blows*, 50–51; James Brannock to wife, May 12, 1864, Brannock Papers.

61. Johnston quoted in Foote, *Civil War*, 340–41; John Jackman Diary, May 19, 1864, in Jackman, *Diary*, 127; James Brannock to wife, May 20, 1864 (attached to May 12, 1864 letter), Brannock Papers; McPherson, *Battle Cry of Freedom*, 747.

62. James Brannock to wife, May 20, 1864 (attached to May 12, 1864 letter), Brannock Papers; Williams Diary, May 20, 1864 (third quotation), 76; John Cotton to wife, May 21, 1864, in *Yours till Death*, 107; John Hagan to wife, May 18, 1864, in Wiley, "Confederate Letters," 272; Stephen A. Jordan Diary, May 19, 1864, CWC; George Knox Miller to wife, May 20, 1864, George Knox Miller Papers, SHC.

63. James Brannock to wife, May 20, 1864 (attached to May 12, 1864 letter), Brannock Papers; J. P. Cannon Diary, May 27, 1864, in Cannon, *Bloody Banners*, 69; Edmund T. Eggleston Diary, May 20, 1864, in Noyes, "Excerpts," 342; Robert Franklin Bunting to editor of the *Houston Tri-Weekly Telegraph*, June 11, 1864, Robert Franklin Bunting Papers, TSLA; McPherson, *Battle Cry of Freedom*, 747.

64. Foote, *Civil War*, 354; Foster Diary, May 17, 1864, 78; Thomas Hampton to wife, May 23, 1864, Hampton Letters; James Iredell Hall to parents, May 30, 1864, in Fleming, *Band of Brothers*, 102; J. P. Cannon Diary, June 1, 1864, in Cannon, *Bloody Banners*, 71. As in Virginia, both sides misperceived the enemy's numbers. One Confederate read in a northern newspaper "that they have one hundred and twenty thousand troops and estimate ours at ninety thousand, over estimating both" (Lee to Maggie Knighton, May 27, 1864, Josiah Knighton and Family Papers, LSU). He was correct.

65. George Binford to cousin, June 3, 1864, George C. Binford Letters, VHS; James Brannock to wife, May 21, 1864 (attached to May 12, 1864 letter), Brannock Papers; George Knox Miller to wife, June 1864 (fragment), George Knox Miller Papers, SHC.

66. John Cotton to wife, May 21, 1864, in *Yours till Death*, 106; Grant Taylor to wife, May 29, 1864, in *Cruel War*, 254; William Nugent to wife, June 9, 1864, in *Nellie*, 179–

80; Frank Batchelor to wife, June 30, 1864, in Batchelor, *Batchelor-Turner Letters*, 81. Cotton also thought that the Federals were suffering worse than the Rebels (John Cotton to wife, June 9, 1864, in *Yours till Death*, 112). Taylor repeated his claim that the enemy would be whipped in a general battle in Grant Taylor to Malinda Taylor, June 5, 1864, in *Cruel War*, 255. See also Thomas Hampton to wife, June 13, 1864, Hampton Letters.

67. McPherson, *Battle Cry of Freedom*, 749; Royster, *Destructive War*, 296–320.

68. J. Litton Bostick to mother, June 28, 1864, Bostick Family Papers, 1831–[1861–64]–1870, TSLA; Thomas Jefferson Newberry to father, June 29, 1864, in Enoch Mitchell, "Civil War Letters," 77; Samuel McKittrick to wife, June 28, 1864, in Lewis, "Confederate Officer's Letters," 494; George Knox Miller to wife, July 1, 1864, George Knox Miller Papers, SHC. See also William E. Sloan Diary, June 27, 1864, CWC; Edmund T. Eggleston Diary, June 28, 1864, in Noyes, "Excerpts," 345; James Iredell Hall to parents, July 8, 1864, in Fleming, *Band of Brothers*, 104.

69. John W. Cotton to wife, July 4, 1864, in *Yours till Death*, 115; Johnston quoted in Horn, *Army of Tennessee*, 339; James Brannock to wife, July 9, 1864, Brannock Papers; J. P. Cannon Diary, June 29, 1864, in Cannon, *Bloody Banners*, 79; J. Litton Bostick to mother, June 28, 1864, Bostick Family Papers, 1831–[1861–64]–1870, TSLA; Grant Taylor to wife, June 26, 1864, in *Cruel War*, 264; McPherson, *Battle Cry of Freedom*, 750. See also Lee to Maggie Knighton, July 9, 1864, Josiah Knighton and Family Papers, LSU; Grant Taylor to wife, July 3, 1864, in *Cruel War*, 265; James Bates to brother-in-law, July 8, 1864, in Bates, *Texas Cavalry Officer's Civil War*, 302–3.

70. Frank Batchelor to wife, June 30, 1864, in Batchelor, *Batchelor-Turner Letters*, 81; James Brannock to wife, July 9, 1864, Brannock Papers. See also Grant Taylor to wife, July 9, 1864, in *Cruel War*, 68; William Nugent to wife, July 6, 1864, in *Nellie*, 188; Lawrence Ross to wife, July 7, 1864, in Ross, *Personal Civil War Letters*, 64; J. P. Cannon Diary, July 9, 1864, in Cannon, *Bloody Banners*, 81.

71. George Knox Miller to wife, July 12, 1864, George Knox Miller Papers, SHC; Urban G. Owen to wife, July 16, 1864, in Enoch Mitchell, "Letters of a Confederate Surgeon," 171–72; John W. Hagan to wife, July 11, 1864, in Wiley, "Confederate Letters," 285.

72. Benjamin M. Seaton Diary, July 9, 1864, in Seaton, *Bugle Softly Blows*, 56; Williams Diary, July 4, 1864, 101; James C. Bates to mother and sister, July 8, 1864, in Bates, *Texas Cavalry Officer's Civil War*, 305; Thomas Hampton to wife, July 4, 1864, Hampton Letters; John W. Hagan to wife, July 4, 1864, in Wiley, "Confederate Letters," 282. See also Williams Diary, July 1, 1864, 100.

73. McPherson, *Battle Cry of Freedom*, 753; Foster Diary, July 18, 1864, 106–7; William Nugent to wife, August 8, 1864, in *Nellie*, 201–2. Hiram Williams also did not agree with Johnston's removal; see Williams Diary, July 18, 1864, 104.

74. Robert W. Banks to father, July 25, 1864, in Osborn, "Civil War Letters," 215; James Bates to sister, June 20, 1864, in Bates, *Texas Cavalry Officer's Civil War*, 299; Thomas Hampton to wife, July 19, 1864, Hampton Letters; James Brannock to wife, July 26, 1864, Brannock Papers.

75. McPherson, *Battle Cry of Freedom*, 754–55.

76. Williams Diary, July 22, 1864, 106; Robert W. Banks to father, July 25, 1864, in

Osborn, "Civil War Letters," 216; William Nugent to wife, July 26, August 8, 1864, in *Nellie*, 190, 196–97.

77. James Brannock to wife, July 26, 1864, Brannock Papers; Thomas Hampton to wife, July 27, August 10, 1864, in Hampton Letters; Benjamin Seaton Diary, August 3, 1864, in Seaton, *Bugle Softly Blows*, 57. For other optimistic reports of Hood's offensives, see James Bates Diary, July 23, July 30, 1864, in Bates, *Texas Cavalry Officer's Civil War*, 310, 311; John Cotton to wife, August 10, 1864, in *Yours till Death*, 117. McPherson has noted that Atlanta newspapers also heralded Hood's work as victories (*Battle Cry of Freedom*, 755).

78. Samuel King Vann to Nancy Elizabeth Neel, August 25, 1864, in Vann, *"Most Lovely Lizzie,"* 46; John Doyle to Maggie Knighton, August 26, 1864, Josiah Knighton and Family Papers, LSU.

79. Edmund T. Eggleston Diary, August 26, 1864, in Noyes, "Excerpts," 349; McPherson, *Battle Cry of Freedom*, 774.

80. William Nugent to wife, September 10, 1864, in *Nellie*, 206; Foster Diary, September 1, 1864, 129; Lawrence Ross to Dr. D. A. Tinsley, September 14, 1864, in Ross, *Personal Civil War Letters*, 68; Williams Diary, September 1, 1864, 110.

81. Foster Diary, September 1, 1864, 129; James Brannock to wife, September 12, 1864, Brannock Papers; James Bates to mother, September 19, 1864, in Bates, *Texas Cavalry Officer's Civil War*, 316; *Southern Confederacy*, September 17, 1864, p. 2.

82. Davis's speeches quoted in McPherson, *Battle Cry of Freedom*, 806–7. The troops received Davis with mixed emotions because many of them blamed him for removing Johnston and consequently losing Atlanta. As for Davis's analogy between Sherman's march through Georgia and Napoleon's retreat from Moscow, William Nugent retorted, "I'd rather witness it than hear 'talk' of it beforehand" (William Nugent to wife, September 26, 1864, in *Nellie*, 213). For other soldiers' opinions of Davis after the fall of Atlanta, see James Brannock to wife, September 12, 1864, Brannock Papers; Foster Diary, September 1, 1864, 129; Lafayette Orr to sister, Mary, October 5, 1864, in *Campaigning*, 147.

83. McPherson, *Battle Cry of Freedom*, 811.

84. John Cotton to wife, September 24, 1864, in *Yours till Death*, 118; James Bates to mother, October 10, 1864, in Bates, *Texas Cavalry Officer's Civil War*, 320; Foster Diary, October 2, October 7, 1864, 136.

85. Lafayette Orr to sister, November 9, 1864, in *Campaigning*, 148; James Brannock to wife, October 21, 1864, Brannock Papers; Foster Diary, October 14, 1864, 140. When the Rebels passed by Decatur and left it in Federal hands, the troops made excuses about why they had not liberated the heavily guarded town. See Lafayette Orr to sister, November 9, 1864, in *Campaigning*, 148; James Bates to mother, November 8, 1864, in Bates, *Texas Cavalry Officer's Civil War*, 327.

86. William Nugent to wife, November 14, 1864, in *Nellie*, 225; Foster Diary, November 21, 1864, 145.

87. Foote, *Civil War*, 663–64.

88. Ibid., 669; McPherson, *Battle Cry of Freedom*, 812–13.

89. Samuel Vann to Nancy Elizabeth Neel, December 6, 1864, in Vann, *"Most Lovely*

Lizzie," 63; Lafayette Orr to father, December 7, 1864, in *Campaigning*, 152. In his study of the Army of Tennessee, Larry Daniel accepts Confederates' positive descriptions of Franklin as their genuine beliefs (*Soldiering*, 149–50).

90. Samuel Vann to Nancy Elizabeth Neel, December 6, 1864, in Vann, *"Most Lovely Lizzie,"* 63; Robert Franklin Bunting to editor of the *Houston Tri-Weekly Telegraph*, December 7, 1864, Robert Franklin Bunting Papers, TSLA. The letter appeared in the newspaper's February 23, 1865, issue.

91. Henry McCall Holmes Diary, December 1, 1864 (first through third quotations), in Holmes, *Diary*, 23; Foster Diary, December 1, 1864, 150–51.

92. Foote, *Civil War*, 675–81.

93. McPherson, *Battle Cry of Freedom*, 814–15; Lafayette Orr to Henry Orr, January 4, 1865, in *Campaigning*, 154; Edmund T. Eggleston Diary, December 15, 1864, in Noyes, "Excerpts," 356.

94. Foote, *Civil War*, 704–5; McPherson, *Battle Cry of Freedom*, 815.

95. Schofield, *Forty-six Years*, 248; Foote, *Civil War*, 669, 675–81; McPherson, *Battle Cry of Freedom*, 812–15.

Chapter Four. Gray Grapevines: Rumors and the Distant War

1. Virgil, *Aeneid*, 101–2.

2. Samuel Horace Hawes Diary, October 18, 1864, VHS.

3. Stoler, " 'In Cold Blood,' " 153; Taussig, "Culture of Terror," 492.

4. S. A. Smith, "Talking Toads and Chinless Ghosts," 406.

5. Gallagher, *Third Day*, 1–30; *Richmond Dispatch*, July 13, 1863, quoted in Gallagher, *Third Day*, 4. Gallagher points out that some remote Confederates considered Gettysburg a disaster. James Barr was one of them; see James Barr to wife, July 21, 1863, in Barr, *Let Us Meet in Heaven*, 120.

6. Edwin Fay to wife, July 10, 1863, in *Infernal War*, 290.

7. Joshua Callaway to wife, July 8, 1863 (second quotation), in Callaway, *Civil War Letters*, 110; Edwin Fay to wife, July 10, 1863 (third and fourth quotations), in *Infernal War*, 290; Robert Moore Diary, July 12, 1863, in Robert Moore, *Life*, 156; Edgeworth Bird to wife, July 12, 1863 (fifth quotation), in *Granite Farm*, 122; Samuel Pickens Diary, July 16, 1863 (sixth quotation), in *Voices*, 188.

8. A. P. Adamson to father, August 28, 1863, A. P. Adamson to sister, August 30, 1863, in Adamson, *Sojourns*, 182, 183.

9. Jefferson Davis to Soldiers of the Confederate States, August 1, 1863, OR, ser. 4, 2:687–88. Soldiers praised Davis's speech. Alabamian Sam Pickens considered it "an excellent & able address." He wrote that Davis "is confident of our final success, & says victory is within our grasp if every one will be at his post & do his duty" (Samuel Pickens Diary, August 4, 1863, in *Voices*, 193). See also Robert Moore Diary, August 4, 1863, in Robert Moore, *Life*, 159–60.

10. Reuben Pierson to father, July 19, 1863, in *Brothers*, 204; Joshua Callaway to wife, July 11, 1863 (second and third quotations), July 19, 1863 (fourth quotation), in Callaway, *Civil War Letters*, 111–12, 115–16; Edwin Fay to wife, August 8, 1863 (fifth and sixth quotations), in *Infernal War*, 317. See also Edgeworth Bird to wife, July 19, 1863, in

Granite Farm, 125; A. P. Adamson to sister, August 10, 1863, in Adamson, *Sojourns*, 173; Marion Fitzpatrick to wife, July 16, 1863, in Fitzpatrick, *Letters to Amanda*, 78.

11. *OR*, ser. 4, 2:687; Edgeworth Bird to wife, August 15 (first and second quotations), August 18, 1863 (third quotation), in *Granite Farm*, 135, 145; Marion Fitzpatrick to wife, July 20, 1863 (fourth quotation), in Fitzpatrick, *Letters to Amanda*, 79; Reuben Pierson to father, July 19, 1863 (fifth and sixth quotations), in *Brothers*, 204; Spencer Welch to wife, July 17, 1863 (seventh and eighth quotations), in *Surgeon's Letters*, 60.

12. Marion Fitzpatrick to wife, July 20, 1863, in Fitzpatrick, *Letters to Amanda*, 79; Samuel Pickens Diary, September 3, 1863, in *Voices*, 197; William Nugent to wife, September 20, 1863, in *Nellie*, 135; Edwin Fay to wife, July 10, August 8, 1863 (seventh and eighth quotations), in *Infernal War*, 290, 316. A few soldiers recorded dread rumors after Vicksburg. William Nugent noticed, "Frequent rumors reach us of the advance of a force of Yankees; but we sit in our office perfectly quiet feeling that these canards are engendered in fevered brains, & are the result of fear." Nugent understood that "a story once set afloat increases in intensity; in compound ratio with the distance it travels" (William Nugent to wife, August 15, 1863, in *Nellie*, 126). Sam Pickens heard rumors that Charleston had fallen after Vicksburg. "It is a wild rumor that originated in the fear that that would be the case," he said (Samuel Pickens Diary, July 17, 1863, in *Voices*, 188).

13. Samuel Pickens Diary, September 24–26, 1863, in *Voices*, 201–2; Edwin Fay to wife, September 24, 1863, in *Infernal War*, 336; William Nugent to wife, September 25, 1863, in *Nellie*, 136.

14. William Nugent to wife, September 25, 1863, in *Nellie*, 137; Marion Fitzpatrick to wife, September 27, 1863, in Fitzpatrick, *Letters to Amanda*, 91; Edwin Fay to wife, October 2, 1863, *Infernal War*, 339; Samuel Pickens Diary, October 3, 1863, in *Voices*, 202–3.

15. Stephen Crane, *The Red Badge of Courage*, in Greenberg and Pronzini, *Treasury*, 69; Gallagher, *Confederate War*, 58. Of course, Crane was writing about the Union army in 1863, but throughout the war, both sides spread rumors before active campaigning resumed.

16. David Crawford to mother, May 12, 1864 (quotations), David Crawford to sister, May 16, 1864, Crawford Family Letters, USC; William Alexander Diary, June 19, 1864 (third and fourth quotations), William D. Alexander Papers, SHC; James Blackman Ligon to mother, June 30, 1864 (fifth and sixth quotations), James Blackman Ligon Letters, USC. Joseph Johnston's Army of Tennessee received "official" reports of Lee's victories during this period; see John Hagan to wife, June 5, 1864, in Wiley, "Confederate Letters," 274.

17. Henry Orr to father, July 10, 1864, in *Campaigning*, 142–43.

18. Albright Diary, July 24 (quotation), July 28, 1864; John W. McLure to wife, July 24, 1864, McLure Papers.

19. Allport and Postman, *Psychology of Rumor*, 167; Walter Benjamin, "The Storyteller," in *Illuminations*, 90. This hidden layer of meaning confirms rumors' value to historians. News is ephemeral, while stories are timeless and often reveal a culture's values, fears, and beliefs.

20. McPherson, *For Cause and Comrades*, 149.

21. Paul Higginbotham to brother, July 1, 1864 (first and second quotations), Higginbotham Papers; Charles Blackford to wife, July 11, 1864 (third and fourth quotations),

in *Lee's Army*, 266; Walters Diary, July 8, 1864 (fifth and sixth quotations), 132. See also Power, *Lee's Miserables*, 117; Spencer Welch to wife, July 6, 1864, in *Surgeon's Letters*, 102. Sherman's treatment of Atlanta produced a greater uproar; see James Madison Brannock to wife, September 12, 1864, Brannock Papers; James Adams to parents, September 16, 1864, Israel L. Adams and Family Papers, LSU; Thomas J. Key Diary, August 4, 1864, in Cate, *Two Soldiers*, 108.

22. Albright Diary, July 24, 1864.

23. Henry Orr to father, July 10, 1864, James Orr to mother, July 18, 1864, in *Campaigning*, 142, 144; James Bates to mother and sister, July 8, 1864, in Bates, *Texas Cavalry Officer's Civil War*, 305. For another soldier's report of the rumor that Grant had been killed, see John William McLure to wife, n.d., McLure Papers.

24. James Blackman Ligon to mother, June 30, 1864, James Blackman Ligon Letters, USC; Walters Diary, July 4, 1864, 131.

25. Richmond paper quoted in Hoehling, *Last Train*, 167, 251; John Jones, *Rebel War Clerk's Diary*, 259; John Trevillian to sister, July 23, 1864, England Family Papers, VHS; Henry Calvin Conner to wife, August 4, 1864, Conner Papers; Albright Diary, July 23, 1864.

26. William E. Sloan Diary, August 3, 1864 (first quotation), CWC; Stephen A. Jordan Diary, August 1, 1864 (second and third quotations), CWC; W. R. Redding to wife, August 14, 1864, W. R. Redding Papers, SHC; Edwin Fay to wife, August 22, 1864, in *Infernal War*, 402; Connelly, *Autumn of Glory*, 453.

27. Davis Diary, September 6, 1864; Heartsill Diary, September 12, October 18–19, 1864, 217 (quotation), 221.

28. Henry Chambers Diary, September 7, 1864, Henry Alexander Chambers Papers, 1832–1925, SHC; John W. Cotton to wife, September 24, 1864, in *Yours till Death*, 118; Albright Diary, October 1–2, 1864. Of course, not all Confederates accepted rumors of Hood's retaking Atlanta; see John McLure to wife, September 5, 1864, McLure Papers.

29. Walters Diary, October 4, 1864, 160; Spencer Welch to wife, October 25 (first quotation), October 2, 1864 (second quotation), in *Surgeon's Letters*, 110, 107; Thomas Elder to wife, September 11, 1864, Thomas Claybrook Elder Papers, VHS. See also Dunbar Affleck to mother, September 18, 1864, Thomas Affleck Correspondence and Writings, LSU.

30. Thomas Hampton to wife, December 5 (first quotation), December 18, December 19 (second quotation), Hampton Letters; Henry Calvin Conner to wife, December 6, 1864, Conner Papers; Samuel Pickens Diary, December 6, 1864, in *Voices*, 329.

31. Thomas Hampton to wife, December 26 (quotation), December 30, 1864, Hampton Letters. Distant Confederates often failed to acquire accurate reports of Sherman's March to the Sea. Shrouded in uncertainty, the campaign seemed to many Rebels a massive Union folly. They hoped that Confederate forces would shrink Sherman's army in countless engagements along the march and finally capture the remnants of the force. See Samuel Pickens Diary, December 4, December 6, 1864, in *Voices*, 329; Henry Chambers Diary, November 18, 1864, Henry Alexander Chambers Papers, 1832–1925, SHC. When bad news did arrive from Georgia, many Confederates dismissed it as Yankee propaganda. See unknown (perhaps Willis Washington) to friend, December 3, 1864, Box Family Papers, USC.

32. Hugh Montgomery to Arthur W. Hyatt, December 27, 1864, Hyatt Papers; Edward Crenshaw Diary, January 1, 1865, in Crenshaw, "Diary," 370. Some Confederates accepted the dire situation in the western theater; see Thomas Goree to Robert Daniel Goree, December 18, 1864, in Goree, *Longstreet's Aide*.

33. Reid Mitchell, *Civil War Soldiers*, 191. Recent important work on soldiers' morale includes McPherson, *For Cause and Comrades*; Gallagher, *Confederate War*; Berry, *All That Makes a Man*; Carmichael, *Last Generation*.

34. Henry Calvin Conner to wife, April 4, 1864, Conner Papers; Robert P. Tutwiler to aunt, April 24, 1864, Mrs. Thomas Chalmers McCorvey Papers, SHC.

35. Heartsill Diary, April 9, 1864, 200; Foote, *Civil War*, 46; Reuben Pierson to father, April 19, 1864, in *Brothers*, 233; Lafayette Orr to brothers, April 30, 1864, in *Campaigning*, 136; Thomas J. Key Diary, April 17, 1864, in Cate, *Two Soldiers*, 72. Within days of Taylor's victory near Mansfield, General Sterling Price also won a minor battle in the trans-Mississippi. Though Rebels celebrated these victories as a tandem of triumph, the combined Union casualties did not come close to the fourteen thousand figure spread through the Army of Tennessee. For soldiers' reactions to Price's success, see Benjamin Seaton Diary, April 10, 1864, in Seaton, *Bugle Softly Blows*, 49; Heartsill Diary, April 14, 1864, 200; Thomas Elder to wife, April 25, 1864, Thomas Claybrook Elder Papers, VHS.

36. Walters Diary, May 15–16, 1864, 118; Henry Beck Diary, May 15–16, 1864, in *Voices*, 269–70.

37. McPherson, *Battle Cry of Freedom*, 756–57; *Times* of London quoted in Foote, *Civil War*, 461.

38. Theodore Honour to wife, July 12, 1864, Theodore A. Honour Papers, 1859–65, USC; Paul Higginbotham to brother, July 10, July 14, 1864 (quotations), Higginbotham Papers.

39. Davis Diary, July 13, 1864; Thomas Moore to Mr. Hill (overseer), July 16, 1864, Thomas John Moore Papers, USC; Giles Buckner Cooke Diary, July 14, 1864, VHS; James Brannock to wife, July 17, 1864, Brannock Papers; James Orr to mother, July 18, 1864, in *Campaigning*, 143; Albright Diary, July 8, 1864; Urban G. Owen to wife, July 16, 1864, in Enoch Mitchell, "Letters of a Confederate Surgeon," 172. See also John L. Sheppard to father, July 11, 1864, Sheppard Family Papers, USC; Abe G. Jones to mother, July 15, 1864, Jones Family Papers, SHC; William E. Sloan Diary, July 15, 1864, CWC; Edward Crenshaw Diary, July 14, 1864, in Crenshaw, "Diary," 452.

40. McPherson, *Battle Cry of Freedom*, 757.

41. I rarely uncovered instances when soldiers admitted the strength of northern commitment and the health of the Federal economy. In January 1864, Edwin Fay speculated on the chance of a financial collapse on Wall Street and conceded that the enemy "have proved themselves far more able financiers than we" (Edwin Fay to wife, January 9, 1864, in *Infernal War*, 385). In September 1864, William Nugent wrote, "The spirit and unanimity still manifested by the North on the subject of the war is an unfavorable omen" (William Nugent to wife, September 26, 1864, in *Nellie*, 209–10). Considering the Confederacy's financial woes and internal strife, this dearth of accurate assessments of enemy strengths is remarkable.

42. Edwin Fay to wife, January 9, 1864, in *Infernal War*, 385; *New York Sunday Mercury* quoted in Nelson, *Bullets, Ballots, and Rhetoric*, 10; James Orr to mother, July 18,

1864, in *Campaigning*, 143; John McLure to wife, August 17 (fourth quotation), August 27, 1864 (fifth through seventh quotations), McLure Papers.

43. Junius Bragg to Anna Josephine Goddard, February 1, 1864, in Bragg, *Letters*, 203; Paul Higginbotham to brother, July 10, 1864, Higginbotham Papers; James D. Albright Diary, July 12, 1864, VHS; Grant Taylor to wife, December 29, 1864, in *Cruel War*, 319.

44. William Nugent to wife, July 26, 1864, in *Nellie*, 203; Edwin Fay to wife, July 17, 1864, in *Infernal War*, 399.

45. Theodore Honour to wife, August 30, 1864, Theodore A. Honour Papers, 1859–65, USC; John McLure to wife, August 31, 1864, McLure Papers; Thomas Elder to wife, August 29, 1864, Thomas Claybrook Elder Papers, VHS; Walters Diary, August 29, 1864, 149; Davis Diary, August 30, 1864. Nelson observes that "Confederate hopes for an immediate and favorable consummation of the war escalated to dizzy heights in August" (*Bullets, Ballots, and Rhetoric*, 85).

46. John McLure to wife, September 15, 1864, McLure Papers; David Crawford to mother, October 23, 1864, Crawford Family Letters, USC; William Nugent to wife, September 17 (sixth quotation), August 2, 1864 (seventh quotation), in *Nellie*, 206, 207–8, 193–94. See also James Brannock to wife, September 12, 1864, Brannock Papers; Peter Guerrant to uncle, October 9, 1864, Guerrant Family Papers, VHS; Charles Blackford to wife, June 16, 1864, in *Lee's Army*, 256.

47. James Brannock to wife, September 12, 1864, Brannock Papers; Stephen Elliott, "*Vain Is the Help of Man,*" 12; William Harris, *Lincoln's Last Months*, 23; Walters Diary, November 7, 1864, 172. Hugh Montgomery heard rumors that McClellan had won the election (Hugh Montgomery to Arthur W. Hyatt, November 19, 1864, Hyatt Papers).

48. Doggett, *War and Its Close*, 15.

49. Lawrence Ross to Lizzie Ross, March 19, 1864, in Ross, *Personal Civil War Letters*, 62; William Nugent to wife, March 20, 1864, in *Nellie*, 162; Thomas J. Key Diary, January 1, 1864, in Cate, *Two Soldiers*, 22; Henry Calvin Conner to wife, March 21, 1864, Conner Papers; *Southern Confederacy*, March 10, 1864, p. 1; Elias Davis to wife, April 7, 1864, Elias Davis Papers, SHC. Jared Sanders heard the same rumors in Louisiana (Jared Sanders to Bessie Sanders, January 16, 1864, Jared Y. Sanders and Family Papers, LSU). Junius Bragg thought that rumors of foreign intervention were lies started by the enemy: "They love to make us feel good once in a while, and it is really quite clever of them" (Junius Bragg to Anna Josephine Goddard, January 18, 1864, in Bragg, *Letters*, 62).

50. James Bivings to father, June 12, 1864, James Morris Bivings Papers, USC. See also Henry Calvin Conner to wife, July 28, 1864, Conner Papers. Patterns of gossip were not as apparent to Civil War participants as they are in hindsight. Rumors from all three categories plagued the Confederacy throughout the war. Nonetheless, this pattern appears in my evidence, suggesting that Rebel rumors changed over time.

51. John W. McLure to wife, August 22, 1864, McLure Papers. This is not to say that Rebels lost hope of winning on their own fronts. As previous chapters confirm, many troops sustained hopeful perceptions of their campaigns.

52. McPherson, *Battle Cry of Freedom*, 732–34, 741–42; Foote, *Civil War*, 295. According to Rosnow, a psychologist, four elements encourage the creation and diffusion of

rumors: the credibility of the report, its importance or relevance, the uncertainty of the times, and personal anxiety ("Rumor as Communication," 19–20). Confederate gossip scored well in all four areas.

53. Paludan, *People's Contest*, 246.

54. Hugh W. Montgomery to Arthur W. Hyatt, May 25, 1864, Hyatt Papers; Daniel Scully Diary, May 25, 1864, in Bergeron, "Captain Daniel Scully's Diary," 92–93. Even southern ministers commented on the poor state of northern finances; see Stephen Elliott, *Gideon's Water-Lappers*, 9.

55. William Alexander Diary, May 10, 1864, William D. Alexander Papers, SHC; Walters Diary, May 6, 1864, 113–14.

56. Walters Diary, May 6, 1864, 113–14. Vernon Scannell, a British soldier in World War II, offered a fine comparison in his memoirs when he discussed the rumors that flourished in camp while his unit waited to begin the Normandy invasion. According to Scannell, rumors flourished in an environment replete with "boredom, cold, exhaustion, squalor, lack of privacy, monotony, ugliness and a constant teasing anxiety about the future" (quoted in Fussell, *Wartime*, 41). See also Rosnow, "Rumor as Communication," 20; Shibutani, *Improvised News*, 39; Leed, *No Man's Land*, 128; Allport and Postman, *Psychology of Rumor*, 7–8, 31, 34.

57. Paul Higginbotham to brother, August 1, 1864, Higginbotham Papers; Shibutani, *Improvised News*, 17. For more on distance and rumors in wartime, see Fussell, *Wartime*, 38; Allport and Postman, *Psychology of Rumor*, 184. Social historians have stressed environment's significance in shaping rumor mills and oral cultures. Life within the domestic sphere, the slave quarters, and Parisian neighborhoods shaped women's gossip, talk of slave conspiracies, and rumors of revolution, respectively.

58. Daniel Scully Diary, May 25, 1864, in Bergeron, "Captain Daniel Scully's Diary," 92; Heartsill Diary, May 5, 1864, 202–3; Hugh Montgomery to Arthur Hyatt, October 14, 1864, Hyatt Papers. Of course, soldiers who suffered most from the effects of distance and a confined world were not prison guards but prisoners themselves. For examples of the ways in which rumors affected prisoners' perceptions of the war, see Hall, *Diary*.

59. Braudel, *Mediterranean*, 355, 369. For more on the history of distance, see McCusker, "Demise of Distance"; Nickles, *Under the Wire*.

60. Robert Moore Diary, July 12, 1863, in Robert Moore, *Life*, 156. Only a thorough study of the speed of Civil War news will yield useful measurements. These measurements require scores of documents from various armies to confirm when and how news arrived. Troops sometimes recorded when and how news arrived in their letters and diaries, providing scholars a circuit of Civil War communications—a veritable switchboard of news. Nonetheless, painstaking research is needed to describe this switchboard in detail.

61. James B. Jones Diary, June 21, 1864, July 16, 23, 1864, October 30, 1864, Jones Family Papers, SHC; Edmund T. Eggleston Diary, May 10, 1864, in Noyes, "Excerpts," 340; William Alexander Diary, July 26, 1864, William D. Alexander Papers, SHC; Samuel Pickens Diary, December 6, 1864, in *Voices*, 329; Henry Chambers Diary, October 17, 22, 1864, November 12, 1864, Henry Alexander Chambers Papers, 1832–1925, SHC; Thomas J. Key Diary, April 18, 1864, in Cate, *Two Soldiers*, 72; Daniel Scully Diary, May

25, 1864, in Bergeron, "Captain Daniel Scully's Diary," 92. In 1865, news traveled faster between the two armies (about two days in transit) because the Army of Tennessee was fighting in the Carolinas rather than in Georgia or Tennessee.

62. Albright Diary, May 7, 1864; James Barr to wife, September 3, 1864, in Barr, *Let Us Meet in Heaven*, 131.

63. Brayton Harris, *Blue and Gray*, x. Future research needs to examine more fully the link between Rebel rumors and Confederate newspapers.

64. Ibid.; Boorstin, *Americans*, 133.

65. Allport and Postman, *Psychology of Rumor*, 47, 188; Shibutani, *Improvised News*, 44; Brayton Harris, *Blue and Gray*, ix.

66. Shibutani, *Improvised News*, 44. Allport and Postman add that false reports of peace can also be explained by competing papers trying to be the first to print the big story (*Psychology of Rumor*, 8–9).

67. Risley, "Confederate Press Association," 225 (first quotation), 229, 230 (second quotation); Arnold, *Grant Wins the War*, 256–57.

68. Risley, "Confederate Press Association," 238 (first quotation), 235 (second quotation), 235 (third quotation).

69. McPherson, *Battle Cry of Freedom*, 808; Risley, "Confederate Press Association," 235.

70. Spencer Welch to wife, October 12, 1864, in *Surgeon's Letters*, 108; John McLure to wife, October 12, 1864, McLure Papers; William Alexander Diary, October 14, 1864, William D. Alexander Papers, SHC; David Crawford to mother, October 23, 1864, Crawford Family Letters, USC. Some Confederates were skeptical of these reports. Henry Chambers thought that "the news from Georgia is good if true" and questioned how Hood's army survived "in a country barren of supplies" (Henry Chambers Diary, October 19, 1864, Henry Alexander Chambers Papers, 1832–1925, SHC).

71. Berends, "'Wholesome Reading,'" 131 (first quotation), 149 (second through fifth quotations), 148 (sixth and seventh quotations). Berends's explanation for positive reporting in the religious military press resembles my argument here: "Since the Confederacy lost, the optimism and bravado may seem misplaced as if editors had held onto a cause long lost. This interpretation has driven some historians, but it is mistaken; for the writers of the [religious military press], such optimism was the logical conclusion to their whole message" (131–32).

72. Davis's May 2, 1864, address quoted in Jefferson Davis, *Papers*, 381, 382–83; James B. Jones Diary, October 5, 1864, Jones Family Papers, SHC; Davis's November 7, 1864, address quoted in Foote, *Civil War*, 624.

73. Silver, *Confederate Morale*, 90; Stephen Elliott, *Gideon's Water-Lappers*, 9.

74. Festinger, *Theory*, 198; Kuhn, *Structure*. For criticism of Festinger's theory, see Peter Lienhardt, "The Interpretation of Rumour," in *Studies*, ed. Beattie and Lienhardt, 105–31.

75. Grant Taylor to wife, December 29, 1864, in *Cruel War*, 319; Paul Higginbotham to brother, July 1, 1864, Higginbotham Papers; Henry Orr to father, July 10, 1864 (second quotation), in *Campaigning*, 142; Edwin Fay to wife, August 22, 1864 (third quotation), in *Infernal War*, 402; Lafayette Orr to brothers, April 30, 1864 (fourth quotation), in *Campaigning*, 136; Thomas Hampton to wife, December 18, 1864 (fifth quotation), Hamp-

ton Letters; Charles Blackford to wife, July 17, 1864, in *Lee's Army*, 267; Henry McCall Holmes Diary, September 25 (quotations), September 27, 1863, in Holmes, *Diary*, 19; William Nugent to wife, October 11, 1863, in *Nellie*, 139.

76. Hugh Montgomery to Arthur Hyatt, October 14, 1864, Hyatt Papers; Taussig, "Culture of Terror," 494.

77. Rosnow, "Psychology of Rumor," 585.

Chapter Five. The Face of Surrender: Diehard Rebels in 1865

1. Blair Burwell to wife, April 8, 1865, Burwell Family Papers, 1825–1976, VHS.

2. Schivelbusch, *Culture of Defeat*; Davies, *Rebel Angels*, 148–49; Collingwood, *Idea of History*, 317.

3. David Pierson to father, January 11, 1865, in *Brothers*, 222; Ham Chamberlayne to mother, January 20, 1865, in Chamberlayne, *Ham Chamberlayne*, 306; Edgeworth Bird to wife, January 17, 1865, in *Granite Farm*, 236–37; Edward Crenshaw Diary, January 10, 1865, in Crenshaw, "Diary," 372; J. M. Bonner to Arthur W. Hyatt, January 7, 1865, Hyatt Papers.

4. David Pierson to father, January 11, 1865, in *Brothers*, 222; John Cotton to unknown, January 20, 1865, in *Yours till Death*, 124–25; Berkeley Diary, January 29 (sixth quotation), January 8 (seventh through ninth quotations), February 10, 1865 (tenth and eleventh quotations), 117, 115, 118; Davis Diary, February 7 (twelfth quotation), February 5 (thirteenth through fifteenth quotations), February 16, 1865. Berkeley's comment regarding his hawkish cousin raises the issue of whether soldiers or civilians maintained high morale longer. Of course, diehards and pessimists existed in both groups. My research on soldiers shows that many of them found ways to sustain their faith in ultimate triumph throughout the war's final eighteen months. And I agree with Escott, *After Secession*, which stresses the prevalence of dissatisfaction and war weariness among civilians. For more gloomy soldiers, see John A. Johnson to Ella Arnold, January 3, 1865, John A. Johnson Letters, SHC; John M. Frank to Jefferson Hedrick, February 27, 1865, Frank Family Letters, SHC.

5. Grant Taylor to wife, January 4 (first quotation), January 24, 1865 (second quotation), in *Cruel War*, 321, 324. Historians have not adequately stressed this difference between troops who left the ranks but intended to return and men who deserted the army and its cause. Many soldiers reported that their comrades were absent without leave instead of assuming that they had deserted. See John Cotton to wife, January 9, 1865, in *Yours till Death*, 124; William L. Nugent to wife, January 26, 1865, in *Nellie*, 234.

6. Davis Diary, January 10, 1865; Peter Guerrant to unknown, January 10, 1865, Guerrant Family Papers, VHS; James Orr to Sammie Orr, January 26, 1865, in *Campaigning*, 155–56.

7. Charles Blackford to wife, March 24, 1865, in *Lee's Army*, 289–90; William James Griggs to cousin, [winter 1864–65], Griggs Family Papers, 1861–65, VHS.

8. Charles Fenton James to Emma James, February 13, 1865, Charles Fenton James Letters, VHS; Heartsill Diary, April 9 (quotation), April 24, 1865, 237, 239. Of course, troops who returned tardy from furloughs could have invented excuses for extending their liberty, and when James blamed civilians for the soldiers' actions, he was seeking

scapegoats. Many scholars, however, have commented that the Confederate populace seemed to ignore the war and its consequences as the end drew nearer. Extravagant balls and elaborate dinners pervaded Richmond's social scene during the war's final months.

9. George Marion Coiner to Kate, February 24, 1865, Coiner Family Papers, VHS; Reuben Pierson to father, ca. January 30, 1864, in *Brothers*, 226–27; Walters Diary, January 5, 1865, 185; Carter, *When the War Was Over*, 6; James M. Williams to wife, March 18, 1865, in James Williams, *From That Terrible Field*, 157, 179. Of course, executing troops for desertion late in the war failed to end the practice. For more criticism of deserters, see John Francis Shaffner to wife, January 20, 1865, Fries and Shaffner Papers, SHC; James B. Jones to grandmother, February 4, 1865, Jones Family Papers, SHC.

10. Foote, *Civil War*, 743; James Ferdinand Izlar Diary, January 15, 1865, USC; Henry London to father, January 26, 1865, Henry Armand London Diary and Letters, SHC; G. G. Young to brother, January 25, 1865, Young Family Papers, USC; John Francis Shaffner to wife, January 20, 1865, Fries and Shaffner Papers, SHC; Fred Fleet to father, January 23, 1865, in *Green Mount*, 357.

11. Charles Fenton James to Emma James, February 13, 1865, Charles Fenton James Letters, VHS; Edgeworth Bird to daughter, January 7, 1865, in *Granite Farm*, 231; Heartsill Diary, February 25, 1865, 231; Marion Fitzpatrick to wife, January 1, 1865, in Fitzpatrick, *Letters to Amanda*, 194; John Francis Shaffner to wife, January 20, 1865, Fries and Shaffner Papers, SHC. Later in January, Fitzpatrick counted "a large number [of comrades] who have resolved to die rather than submit to Yankee rule, and never; never give it up" (Marion Fitzpatrick to wife, January 7, 1865, in Fitzpatrick, *Letters to Amanda*, 196).

12. J. W. Hardie and Mrs. L. Hardie to Arthur W. Hyatt, January 11, 1865, Hyatt Papers.

13. Richard Launcelot Maury Diary, March 27, 1865, VHS.

14. Rumor of Sherman's defeat in Samuel Pickens Diary, February 28, 1865, in *Voices*, 357; Hugh Montgomery to Arthur W. Hyatt, February 1, 1865, Hyatt Papers.

15. Samuel Pickens Diary, January 19, 1865, in *Voices*, 346; Jared Y. Sanders to Bessie, January 16, 1865, Jared Y. Sanders and Family Papers, LSU; Hugh Montgomery to Arthur W. Hyatt, February 1, 1865, Hyatt Papers. As had been the case after the fall of Atlanta, many Confederates first denied the accuracy of bad news in 1865. In Louisiana, Edwin Fay wrote that "we get awful Yankee accounts down here but I do not begin to believe them (Edwin Fay to Sarah Shields Fay, January 7, 1865, in *Infernal War*, 411–12). Frank Adams similarly admitted, "We have been hearing very bad news but I am in hopes it is not true" (Frank Adams to sister, January 13, 1865, in Israel L. Adams and Family Papers, LSU).

16. William Nugent to wife, February 26, 1865, in *Nellie*, 234; Samuel Pickens Diary, January 24 (second quotation), January 25, 1865 (third quotation), in *Voices*, 348; John Cotton to unknown, January 27, 1865, *Yours till Death*, 127–28; Hugh Montgomery to Arthur W. Hyatt, January 24, 1865, Hyatt Papers. Nugent figured that the enemy's only remaining hope was "to starve us into submission." See also Henry Calvin Conner to wife, January 1865, Conner Papers; Thomas B. Hampton to wife, January 28, 1865, Hampton Letters. Not everyone believed these rumors. Robert Augustus Stiles dismissed them in a letter to his mother: "Do not rely to much on Peace rumors. Hunter, Stephens &

Judge Campbell have gone off somewhere, 'they say' Washington. Nothing will come of it I fear!" (Robert Augustus Stiles to mother, January 19, 1865, Robert Augustus Stiles Papers, VHS). James Brannock told his wife, "The people here and all along the route [of the Army of Tennessee through Mississippi] are excited on the subject of *peace*. Every body seems to think we are bound to have it. I hope and pray it may be so, but I am not very sanguine about it" (James Brannock to wife, February 8, 1865, Brannock Papers).

17. Lincoln quoted in McPherson, *Battle Cry of Freedom*, 823.

18. Charles Fenton James to Emma A. James, February 7, 1865, Charles Fenton James Letters, VHS; Thomas J. Key Diary, February 21, 1865, in Cate, *Two Soldiers*, 195; Ham Chamberlayne to mother, February 13, 1865, in Chamberlayne, *Ham Chamberlayne*, 308–9; Edward Crenshaw Diary, February 9, 1865, in Crenshaw, "Diary," 377; Davis Diary, February 3, 1865; John McLure to wife, February 6, 1865, McLure Papers. At the Richmond meeting, Confederate Secretary of State Judah Benjamin advocated arming the slaves and allowing the central government to take possession of all resources that could help the Confederacy gain independence.

19. James D. Albright Diary, February 4, 1865, VHS; Edwin Fay Diary, February 19, 1865, in *Infernal War*, 427; Thomas B. Hampton to wife, February 3, 1865, Hampton Letters; Heartsill Diary, March 10, 1865, 232; Richard Launcelot Maury Diary, February 5, 1865, VHS; William Robert Webb to mother, February 12, 1865, Webb Family Papers, SHC. See also James B. Jones to grandmother, February 16, 1865, James B. Jones to brother, February 19, 1865, both in Jones Family Papers, SHC; Albright Diary, February 6, 1865; Samuel Pickens Diary, February 8, 1865, in *Voices*, 348.

20. Davis Diary, February 8, 1865; John Francis Shaffner to wife, January 20, 1865, Fries and Shaffner Papers, SHC; John Bratton to wife, February 17, 1865, John Bratton Papers, SHC; George Marion Coiner to Kate, February 6, 1865, Coiner Family Papers, VHS; Edward Crenshaw Diary, February 5, 1865, in Crenshaw, "Diary," 376; John L. Sheppard to mother, February 7, 1865, Sheppard Family Papers, USC.

21. Davis quoted in McPherson, *Battle Cry of Freedom*, 824.

22. Levine, *Confederate Emancipation*; Dillard, "Independence or Slavery"; Durden, *Gray and the Black*.

23. Hugh Montgomery to Arthur Hyatt, February 1, 1865, Hyatt Papers.

24. Richard Launcelot Maury Diary, February 20 (first quotation), March 23, 1865 (second through sixth quotations), VHS; McPherson, *Battle Cry of Freedom*, 835.

25. Hugh Montgomery to Arthur W. Hyatt, January 24, 1865, Hyatt Papers; Thomas J. Key Diary, January 18, January 22, 1865, in Cate, *Two Soldiers*, 181–82; William Nugent to wife, January 26, 1865, in *Nellie*, 234; Fred Fleet to father, January 23, 1865, in *Green Mount*, 357; McPherson, *Battle Cry of Freedom*, 683. Civilians also transmitted these rumors to men in the ranks; see Anna J. Bragg to Junius Bragg, January 26, 1865, in Bragg, *Letters*, 265.

26. Heartsill Diary, February 16, 1865, 230; William Nugent to wife, January 26, 1865, in *Nellie*, 234–35; Charles Blackford to wife, March 8, 1865, in *Lee's Army*, 279; E. D. Cheatham to Arthur W. Hyatt, March 20, 1865, Hyatt Papers; Edward Crenshaw Diary, March 25, 1865, in Crenshaw, "Diary," 384; David Pierson to father, March 26, 1865, in *Brothers*, 254–55.

27. *Resolutions Adopted by the Staunton Artillery.*

28. *Resolutions Adopted by Bratton's Brigade*; *Resolutions Adopted by Company "H,"* *"I," and "K"*; *Resolutions Passed at a Meeting of the Fourteenth Virginia Infantry*; *Resolutions Adopted by Humphrey's Mississippi Brigade*; *Resolutions Passed at a Meeting of the Ninth Virginia Infantry*; Heartsill Diary, May 13, 1865, 233. Heartsill's resolutions, which also vowed to cross the Mississippi and aid eastern comrades in the struggle, were not unanimously adopted by his unit, the W. P. Rangers. Thirty men signed, and thirty-one refused, most likely because the resolutions were drafted only weeks before capitulation and because western troops were often unwilling to cross the river and fight in the East.

29. *Resolutions Adopted by McGowan's Brigade*; *Resolutions Adopted by Humphrey's Mississippi Brigade*; *Resolutions Passed at a Meeting of the Ninth Virginia Infantry*; *Resolutions Passed at a Meeting of the Fourteenth Virginia Infantry*; *Resolutions Adopted by the Officers and Men of the Fifty-seventh Virginia Regiment*; *Resolutions Adopted by Bratton's Brigade*. See also *Resolutions Adopted by Company "H," "I," and "K"*: "We ridicule, as absurd, the idea of reconstruction; for we believe re-union would subject us again to the government of that sectional majority which is confined to the abolition States, and which is alike a stranger to our institutions, feelings and habits of thought as a people, and foreign to our territory."

30. *Resolutions Adopted by McGowan's Brigade*; *Resolutions Adopted by the Officers and Men of the Fifty-seventh Virginia Regiment*.

31. *Resolutions Adopted by Humphrey's Mississippi Brigade*; *Resolutions Passed at a Meeting of the Ninth Virginia Infantry*; *Resolutions Adopted by the Officers and Men of the Fifty-seventh Virginia Regiment*; *Resolutions Adopted by Bratton's Brigade*; *Resolutions Passed at a Meeting of the Fourteenth Virginia Infantry*.

32. Charles Fenton James to Emma A. James, February 7 (first through third quotations), February 9, 1865 (fourth and fifth quotations), Charles Fenton James Letters, VHS; Edwin Fay Diary, March 4, 1865, in Cate, *Two Soldiers*, 199. The passion that resolutions exude reflected both the emotionally charged atmosphere in which the vows were drafted and the knowledge that they were written for the eyes of the country.

33. Fred Fleet to mother, February 2, 1865, in *Green Mount*, 359. These statements do not illuminate soldiers' mentalities as faithfully as diary entries and private letters, but they do reinforce the beliefs found in those more reliable sources.

34. J. W. Hardie and Mrs. L. Hardie to Arthur W. Hyatt, January 11, 1865, Hyatt Papers; Thomas B. Hampton to wife, February 26, 1865, Hampton Letters; James Ferdinand Izlar Diary, February 21, 1865, USC.

35. James T. Wallace Diary, March 10, 1865, SHC; Thomas J. Key Diary, March 10, 1865, in Cate, *Two Soldiers*, 200; Foote, *Civil War*, 823–24; Rawleigh Downman to wife, March 18, 1865, Downman Family Papers, VHS; Richard Launcelot Maury Diary, March 10, 1865, VHS. James Albright heralded the battle of Kinston as "glorious news" on the fast day (Albright Diary, March 10, 1865).

36. James Keith to wife, January 15, 1865, Keith Family Papers, 1831–1916, VHS; J. William Jones, *Christ in the Camp*, 353; Richard Stanford Webb to cousin, March 23, 1865, Webb Family Papers, SHC; Silver, *Confederate Morale*, 55; John Paris Diary, March 19, 1865, John Paris Papers, SHC; Richard Launcelot Maury Diary, March 28, 1865, VHS; Davis Diary, January 5, 1865; Robert Augustus Stiles to mother, January 19, 1865, Robert Augustus Stiles Papers, VHS.

37. Richard Launcelot Maury Diary, March 8 (first quotation), February 5 (second quotation), February 11 (third and fourth quotations), February 24 (fifth quotation), February 28 (sixth quotation), March 20, 1865 (seventh and eighth quotations), VHS.

38. Ibid., February 24 (first through third quotations), February 20 (fourth through seventh quotations), March 9, 1865 (ninth quotation), VHS.

39. Ibid., March 20 (first and second quotations), March 30, 1865 (third and fourth quotations), VHS; Livermore, *Numbers and Losses*, 135; McPherson, *Battle Cry of Freedom*, 830. For another contemporary account of Bentonville, see William Davenport Jones to father, March 18, 1865, Edmund Walter Jones Papers, SHC.

40. George Alexander Martin Diary, April 2–3, 1865, VHS; Cornelius Hart Carlton Diary, April 3, 1865, VHS; McPherson, *Battle Cry of Freedom*, 846; Foote, *Civil War*, 886–90.

41. Walters Diary, April 3, 1865, 219; Henry Chambers Diary, April 2, 1865, Henry Alexander Chambers Papers, 1832–1925, SHC. Evidence such as Chambers's reaction to Richmond's fall confirms that the Lost Cause legend predated defeat. The process of memorializing the Confederacy and its defenders started during the war.

42. Walters Diary, April 4 (first quotation), April 5 (second and third quotations), April 6, 1865 (fourth through sixth quotations), 219–21. For other diaries of the retreat to Appomattox, see Albright Diary; William D. Alexander Papers, SHC; Kena King Chapman Diary, SHC.

43. Raleigh Downman to wife, April 6, 1865, Downman Family Papers, VHS.

44. Cornelius Hart Carlton Diary, April, 4–8, 1865, VHS; Giles Buckner Cooke Diary, April 6, 1865, VHS; Lee quoted in McPherson, *Battle Cry of Freedom*, 848. See also James D. Albright Diary, April 6, 1865, VHS; David McIntosh Diary, April 6, 1865, David Gregg McIntosh Papers, VHS.

45. Giles Buckner Cooke Diary, April 8, 1865, VHS; Foote, *Civil War*, 929–39; Lee quoted in McPherson, *Battle Cry of Freedom*, 848.

46. Foote, *Civil War*, 951.

47. David McIntosh Diary, April 9, 1865, David Gregg McIntosh Papers, VHS; Ham Chamberlayne to brother and sister, April 12 (fifth and sixth quotations), Ham Chamberlayne to sister, April 21, 1865 (seventh quotation), Ham Chamberlayne to sister, June 2, 1865 (eighth and ninth quotations), in Chamberlayne, *Ham Chamberlayne*, 320–21, 325, 330. McIntosh's account, like most soldiers' diaries at the very end of the war, might have been written from memory when he returned home. It is impossible to know for certain, but his entries were written in the past tense at this point. Men such as McIntosh and Chamberlayne may have been posturing when they fled capitulation to continue the fight. They might have understood that the end had come and wanted to stake their claim as the last Rebels standing. This might explain the boastful tone of their writing. But it is just as likely that they could not bear surrendering. Moreover, it is difficult to believe that Chamberlayne rode all the way to Mississippi simply to prove his undying devotion to the cause.

48. James D. Albright Diary, n.d. [probably immediately after the war], VHS; Walters Diary, April 11, 1865, 226. See also John Bell Vincent Diary, April 10–12, 1865, VHS. Vincent went through the motions of stacking arms and receiving Federal rations, but he remained "in camp in suspense of what is our final destiny." Though Grant's terms allowed

them to go home, many Confederates feared that the Federal government would punish them.

49. Henry Chambers Diary, April 9, 1865, Henry Alexander Chambers Papers, 1832–1925, SHC.

50. Samuel Pickens Diary, April 11 (first and second quotations), April 12, 1865 (third and fourth quotations), in *Voices*, 370; Kena King Chapman Diary, April 10, 1865, SHC; Wyatt-Brown, *Shaping*, 234.

51. Joseph Bryan to John Randolph Bryan, April 6, 1865, Bryan Family Papers, 1774–1942, VHS; Mosby's address copied in Frederick Fillison Bowen Papers, VHS.

52. William Mebane Pollard Diary, April 10, 1865, CWC; William E. Sloan Diary, April 6, April 8, 1865 (quotations), CWC.

53. Foster Diary, April 10 (first quotation), April 16 (second and third quotations), April 20, 1865 (fourth quotation), 163–66.

54. Ibid., April 19 (first quotation), April 24 (second quotation), April 22, 1865 (third through fifth quotations), 165–67.

55. Edgeworth Bird to daughter, April 26, 1865, in *Granite Farm*, 247; George Mercer Diary, April 16, 1865, in Lane, *Times*, 252–53.

56. D. E. Huger Smith to mother, April 21, 1865 (first through third quotations), D. E. Huger Smith to grandmother, April 22, 1865, both in *Mason Smith Family Letters*, ed. Smith, Smith, and Childs, 197–98; William E. Sloan Diary, May 1, 1865, CWC.

57. Edwin Leet to Sarah Leet, April 26, 1865, Edwin Leet Letters, 1864–65, LSU; Charles Andry to father, April 24, 1865, Michel Thomassin Andry and Family Papers, LSU.

58. Louis Bringier to wife, April 23, 1865, Louis A. Bringier and Family Papers, LSU; David Pierson to father, April 27, 1865, in *Brothers*, 256–57.

59. Heartsill Diary, April 16, April 19 (first through fourth quotations), April 20, 1865 (fifth through eighth quotations), 238–39.

60. Ibid., May 7 (first quotation), May 13 (second quotation), May 7 (third quotation), May 11, 1865 (fourth and fifth quotations), 241–43; Jared Y. Sanders to Bessie Sanders, May 11, 1865, Jared Y. Sanders and Family Papers, LSU.

61. Heartsill Diary, April 23, 1865, 239; Junius Bragg to wife, April 23, 1865, in Bragg, *Letters*, 272; Edwin Fay to wife, May 5, 1865, in *Infernal War*, 442.

62. Foote, *Civil War*, 1019–21.

Conclusion. The Aftermath of Invincibility

1. Gilmore, a bandmaster in the Union army, wrote "When Johnny Comes Marching Home" in 1863. Like many Civil War songs, it was popular with both sides.

2. Wyatt-Brown, *Shaping*, 230–54; Carmichael, *Last Generation*, 179–211.

3. Giles Buckner Cooke Diary, April 13, 1865, VHS; Jared Sanders to Bessie, May 11, 1865, Jared Y. Sanders and Family Papers, LSU; Foster Diary, May 4, 1865, 174.

4. Junius Bragg to wife, May 20, 1865, in Bragg, *Letters*, 276; William H. Ellis Diary, April 10, 1865, LSU; John Jackman Diary, May 8, 1865, in Jackman, *Diary*, 168; Reid, *After the War*, 360.

5. Kena King Chapman Diary, April 16, April 19, 1865 (last quotation), SHC; David McIntosh Diary, April 23, 1865, David Gregg McIntosh Papers, VHS; Berkeley Diary, June 24, 1865, 144.

6. John Paris Diary, April 10, 1865, John Paris Papers, SHC; soldier and newspaper correspondent quoted in Carter, *When the War Was Over*, 12–13; Eliza Andrews Diary, May 3, 1865, in Andrews, *War-Time Journal*, 199. Many troops expressed entitlements to lesser degrees. Rebel diarists often noted whether homeowners gave them room and board for free or expected payment from the returning veterans. See, for example, William H. Ellis Diary, LSU.

7. Rolle, *Lost Cause*, 3–20. For more on Confederate exiles, see Hanna and Hanna, *Confederate Exiles*; Weaver, "Confederate Emigration"; Sutherland, "Exiles, Emigrants, and Sojourners."

8. Bennett, *Narrative*, 416; J. William Jones, *Christ in the Camp*, 353.

9. Goldfield, *Still Fighting*, 19.

10. Blight, *Race and Reunion*, 259; Early, *Memoir*, xiv (Gallagher's quotation), xxv, 71, 142; Faulkner, *Absalom, Absalom*, 11.

11. Berkeley Diary, April 26, 1865, 135; George Mercer Diary, August 8, 1865, in Lane, *Times*, 256; Henry Calvin Conner to mother, sisters, and brothers, August 11, 1865, Conner Papers; unknown to John Bratton, November 20, 1865, John Bratton Papers, USC.

12. Edmund Jones to editor, n.d. (first through third quotations), Edmund Jones, Memorial Day Address, Raleigh, North Carolina, May 11, 1896 (fourth and fifth quotations), Edmund Walter Jones Papers, SHC.

13. Charles Fenton James, Address to the Hollywood Memorial Association, May 30, 1901, Charles Fenton James Papers, SHC; John Shaffner, Memorial Day Speech, 1902, Fries and Shaffner Papers, SHC. For more on the connections between wartime identity and the postwar lives of white southerners, see Rubin, *Shattered Nation*.

14. Eleazar quoted in Ayers, *Promise*, 27.

15. Warren, *Legacy of the Civil War*, 15; Wilson, *Baptized in Blood*; Gaines Foster, *Ghosts*; Gallagher and Nolan, *Myth*; Poole, *Never Surrender*.

16. Woodward, *Burden*. Dower's work on the Pacific War and Japan's reaction to defeat offers promising contrasts to the Confederate experience; see Dower, *War without Mercy*; Dower, *Embracing Defeat*. In *Culture of Defeat*, German scholar Wolfgang Schivelbusch compares defeat in the American South, France after the Franco-Prussian War, and Germany after World War I. He argues, "Every society experiences defeat in its own way. But the varieties of response within vanquished nations—whether psychological, cultural, or political—conform to a recognizable set of patterns or archetypes that recur across time and national boundaries" (10). Schivelbusch devotes only four pages to the Civil War, however. Defeat and the members of the generation that coped with it cannot be understood until their war experiences and ethos are thoroughly examined.

17. Peter Gay, "Psychoanalysis and the Historian," in *Freud*, ed. Roth, 118; Ignatieff, *Warrior's Honor*, 51. Royster has shown that both Unionists and Confederates valued their cultures so highly that they "saw no need to weigh the costs of violence in the balance

against their purposes and interests." Certain of their own superiority, both sides sought "to triumph through inflicting and sustaining casualties so great as to overawe the enemy" (*Destructive War*, 256). For Freud's efforts to connect his work on the individual psyche to group mentality, see *Group Psychology*.

18. Ovid, *Metamorphoses of Ovid*, 53.

Selected Bibliography

MANUSCRIPTS

Center for American History, University of Texas at Austin

Confederate States of America Records
Cowan Family Papers
Edward Richardson Crockett Diary, 1864–65
Thomas B. Hampton Letters
William P. Head Papers, 1861–69
Demetria Ann Hill Collection
John W. Hill Correspondence, 1861–66
John B. Long Papers, 1858–88
David M. Ray Papers, 1859–79

Georgia Historical Society, Savannah

Battle-Adams Papers
John W. Bentley Papers
Charlton Family Papers
Clay Papers
S. D. Clements Letter, 1863
E. D. Fennell Papers
Gordon Family Papers
Hilton Papers
John J. Hogg Papers
William Lovett Papers
John McCorkle Papers
J. M. McNeel Letter
Robertson Papers
Joseph Frederick Waring Papers
Charlton H. Way Papers
Wayne-Stites-Anderson Papers

Hill Memorial Library, Louisiana State University, Baton Rouge

Israel L. Adams and Family Papers
Thomas Affleck Correspondence and Writings
Michel Thomassin Andry and Family Papers
Louis A. Bringier and Family Papers
William H. Ellis Diary
Arthur W. Hyatt Papers
J. G. Kilbourne and Family Papers
Josiah Knighton and Family Papers
Edwin Leet Letters, 1864–65
P. E. Retif Letters
Jared Y. Sanders and Family Papers
William H. Tamplin Letters

South Caroliniana Library, University of South Carolina, Columbia

James Morris Bivings Papers
Box Family Papers
Brabham Family Letters
Bratton Family Papers
John Bratton Papers
Henry Calvin Conner Papers
Crawford Family Letters
Dalton Family Papers
Theodore A. Honour Papers, 1859–65
James Ferdinand Izlar Diary, 1865
Jefferies Family Collection of Letters, 1861–65
James Blackman Ligon Letters
William Barr Lowrance Letters
McGraw Family Papers
McLure Family Papers, 1845–1922
Thomas John Moore Papers
Percy Nagel Papers, 1852–64
James Drayton Nance Letters
Sheppard Family Papers
Thomson Family Papers
James C. Tinkler Letters
Young Family Papers

Southern Historical Collection, University of North Carolina at Chapel Hill

James W. Albright Books
Isaac Alexander Papers
William D. Alexander Papers

Allen-Simpson Papers
Barkley Family Papers
J. Kelly Bennette Diary and Letters
Thomas F. Boatwright Papers
John Bratton Papers
Henry Alexander Chambers Papers, 1832–1925
Kena King Chapman Diary
Confederate Papers
James Conner Letters
Elias Davis Papers
Frank Family Letters
Fries and Shaffner Papers
Franklin Gaillard Letters
Charles Fenton James Papers
John A. Johnson Letters
Jones Family Papers
Edmund Walter Jones Papers
Harry Lewis Papers
Henry Armand London Diary and Letters
Mrs. Thomas Chalmers McCorvey Papers
George Knox Miller Papers
Leroy Moncure Nutt Papers
John Paris Papers
Patton Family Papers
Leonidas Lafayette Polk Papers
W. R. Redding Papers
Achilles James Tynes Papers
Richard Woolfolk Waldrop Papers
James T. Wallace Diary
Webb Family Papers

Tennessee State Library and Archives, Nashville

Betty Family Papers, 1835–1935
Bostick Family Papers, 1834–[1861–1864]–1870
Civil War Collections, Confederate and Federal
Hamilton-Williams Family Papers, 1850–1971

Virginia Historical Society, Richmond

James D. Albright Diary
George C. Binford Letters
Bland Family Papers
Bolling Family Papers, 1749–1956
Frederick Fillison Bowen Papers

James Madison Brannock Papers
Alexander Gustavus Brown Papers
Bryan Family Papers, 1774–1942
Burwell Family Papers, 1825–1976
Cornelius Hart Carlton Diary
William Thomas Casey Papers
Coiner Family Papers
Giles Buckner Cooke Diary, 1864–65
Cooke Family Papers, 1835–78
E. L. Cox Diary
Creed Thomas Davis Diary, May 4, 1864–February 20, 1865
Harman Dinwiddie Papers
Downman Family Papers
Thomas Claybrook Elder Papers
Francis Marion Ellett Papers
England Family Papers
Alexander Mason Evans Papers
Greene Family Papers
Griggs Family Papers, 1861–65
Guerrant Family Papers
Randolph Harrison Papers
Samuel Horace Hawes Diary
James Hays Papers
Paul M. Higginbotham Papers, 1862–82
Moses Drury Hoge Papers
Charles Fenton James Letters
Keith Family Papers, 1831–1916
Joseph Richard Manson Diary
George Alexander Martin Diary
Mason Family Papers, 1813–1943
Richard Launcelot Maury Diary
David Gregg McIntosh Papers
Miller Family Papers
William Young Mordecai Papers
John Baxter Moseley Diary
James Eldred Phillips Papers
J. E. Shuman Letter
Smith Family Papers
Joseph D. Stapp Letters
Stevenson Family Papers
Robert Augustus Stiles Papers
Edmund Fitzgerald Stone Letter
Franklin Stringfellow Papers, 1864–1951
James Alexander Turrentine Diary, 1865
John Bell Vincent Diary, 1864–65

PUBLISHED PRIMARY SOURCES

Adamson, A. P. *Sojourns of a Patriot: The Field and Prison Papers of an Unreconstructed Confederate*. Ed. Richard Bender Abell and Fay Adamson Gecik. Murfreesboro, Tenn.: Southern Heritage, 1998.

Anderson, John Q., comp. *Campaigning with Parsons' Texas Cavalry Brigade, CSA: The War Journals and Letters of the Four Orr Brothers, Twelfth Texas Cavalry Regiment*. Hillsboro, Tex.: Hill Junior College Press, 1967.

————. *A Texas Surgeon in the C.S.A.* Tuscaloosa, Ala.: Confederate, 1957.

Andrews, Eliza Frances. *The War-Time Journal of a Georgia Girl, 1864–1865*. Ed. Spencer Bidwell King Jr. Macon, Ga.: Ardivan, 1960.

Atkinson, Joseph M. *God, the Giver of Victory and Peace: A Thanksgiving Sermon, Delivered in the Presbyterian Church, September 18, 1862, Raleigh, N.C.* Raleigh, N.C.: n.p., 1862. Confederate Imprints Microfilm Series No. 4123.

Barr, James Michael. *Let Us Meet in Heaven: The Civil War Letters of James Michael Barr, Fifth South Carolina Cavalry*. Ed. Thomas D. Mays. Abilene, Tex.: McWhiney Foundation, 2000.

Batchelor, Benjamin Franklin. *Batchelor-Turner Letters, 1861–1864: Written by Two of Terry's Texas Rangers*. Ed. H. J. H. Rugeley. Austin, Tex.: Steck, 1961.

Bates, James C. *A Texas Cavalry Officer's Civil War: The Diary and Letters of James C. Bates*. Ed. Richard Lowe. Baton Rouge: Louisiana State University Press, 1999.

Bennett, William W. *A Narrative of the Great Revival Which Prevailed in the Southern Armies during the Late Civil War between the States of the Federal Union*. Philadelphia: Claxton, Remsen, and Haffelfinger, 1877.

Bergeron, Arthur W., Jr., ed. "Captain Daniel Scully's Diary of the Red River Campaign, 1864." *Military History of the West* 35 (2005): 77–98.

Berkeley, Henry Robinson. *Four Years in the Confederate Artillery: The Diary of Private Henry Robinson Berkeley*. Ed. William H. Runge. Chapel Hill: University of North Carolina Press, 1961.

Bettersworth, John K., ed. *Mississippi in the Confederacy: As They Saw It*. Baton Rouge: Louisiana State University Press, 1961.

Bird, Edgeworth. *The Granite Farm Letters: The Civil War Correspondence of Edgeworth and Sallie Bird*. Ed. John Rozier. Athens: University of Georgia Press, 1988.

Blackford, Susan Leigh, comp. *Letters from Lee's Army; or, Memoirs of Life in and out of the Army in Virginia during the War between the States*. Lincoln: University of Nebraska Press, 1998.

Blessington, J. P. *The Campaigns of Walker's Texas Division*. Austin, Tex.: Pemberton, 1968.

Bragg, Junius Newport. *Letters of a Confederate Surgeon, 1861–65*. Ed. Mrs. T. J. Gaughan. Camden, Ark.: Hurley, 1960.

Burgwyn, William Hyslop Sumner. *A Captain's War: The Letters and Diaries of William H. S. Burgwyn, 1861–1865*. Ed. Herbert M. Schiller. Shippensburg, Pa.: White Mane, 1994.

Burrows, J. L. *Nationality Insured! Notes of a Sermon Delivered at the First Baptist*

Church, Augusta, Ga., September 11th, 1864. Augusta, Ga.: n.p., 1864. Confederate
  Imprints Microfilm Series 4129.
Callaway, Joshua K. *The Civil War Letters of Joshua K. Callaway.* Ed. Judith Lee
  Hallock. Athens: University of Georgia Press, 1997.
Cannon, J. P. *Bloody Banners and Barefoot Boys: A History of the Twenty-seventh
  Regiment Alabama Infantry* CSA: *The Civil War Memoirs and Diary Entries of J. P.
  Cannon, M.D.* Comp. and ed. Noel Crowson and John V. Brogden. Shippensburg,
  Pa.: Burd Street, 1997.
Cate, Wirt Armistead, ed. *Two Soldiers: The Campaign Diaries of Thomas J. Key,
  C.S.A., December 7, 1863–May 17, 1865, and Robert J. Campbell, U.S.A., January 1,
  1864–July 21, 1864.* Chapel Hill: University of North Carolina Press, 1938.
Chamberlayne, John Hampden. *Ham Chamberlayne—Virginian: Letters and Papers of
  an Artillery Officer in the War for Southern Independence, 1861–1865.* Richmond,
  Va.: Dietz, 1932.
Chesebrough, David B., ed. *"God Ordained This War": Sermons on the Sectional
  Conflict, 1830–1865.* Columbia: University of South Carolina Press, 1991.
Cotton, John Weaver. *Yours till Death: Civil War Letters of John W. Cotton.* Ed. Lucille
  Griffith. Birmingham: University of Alabama Press, 1951.
Couture, Richard T. *Charlie's Letters: The Correspondence of Charles E. DeNoon.*
  Bolling Island Plantation, Va.: Couture, 1982.
Crenshaw, Edward. "Diary of Captain Edward Crenshaw, of the Confederate States
  Army." *Alabama Historical Review* 1 (Winter 1930): 438–52.
Cutrer, Thomas W., and T. Michael Parrish, eds. *Brothers in Gray: The Civil War
  Letters of the Pierson Family.* Baton Rouge: Louisiana State University Press,
  1997.
Davis, Jefferson. *The Papers of Jefferson Davis.* Vol. 10, October 1863–August 1864.
  Ed. Lynda Lasswell Crist, Kenneth H. Williams, and Peggy L. Dillard. Baton Rouge:
  Louisiana State University Press, 1999.
Dawson, Sarah Morgan. *The Civil War Diary of Sarah Morgan.* Ed. Charles East.
  Athens: University of Georgia Press, 1991.
Doggett, D. S. *The War and Its Close: A Discourse, Delivered at Centenary Church,
  Richmond, Va., Friday, April 8th, 1864 . . . on the Occasion of the National Fast.*
  Richmond, Va.: n.p., 1864. Confederate Imprints Microfilm Series 4137.
Dunaway, Thomas S. *A Sermon Delivered by Elder Thomas S. Dunaway, of Lancaster
  County, Virginia, before Coan Baptist Church.* Richmond, Va.: n.p., 1864.
  Confederate Imprints Microfilm Series 4138–2.
Early, Jubal A. *A Memoir of the Last Year of the War for Independence, in the
  Confederate States of America, Containing an Account of the Operations of His
  Commands in the Years 1864 and 1865.* Intro. Gary W. Gallagher. Columbia:
  University of South Carolina Press, 2001.
Elliott, Stephen. *Gideon's Water-Lappers: A Sermon Preached in Christ Church,
  Savannah.* Macon, Ga.: n.p., 1864. Confederate Imprints Microfilm Series 4143.
———. *"Vain Is the Help of Man."* Macon, Ga.: Burke, Boykin, 1864. Confederate
  Imprints Microfilm Series 4143.

Fay, Edwin Hedge. *This Infernal War: The Confederate Letters of Edwin H. Fay*. Ed. Bell I. Wiley. Austin: University of Texas Press, 1958.

Fitzpatrick, Marion Hill. *Letters to Amanda: The Civil War Letters of Marion Hill Fitzpatrick, Army of Northern Virginia*. Ed. Jeffrey C. Lowe and Sam Hodges. Macon, Ga.: Mercer University Press, 1998.

Fleet, Benjamin Robert. *Green Mount: A Virginia Plantation Family during the Civil War: Being the Journal of Benjamin Robert Fleet and Letters of His Family*. Ed. Betsy Fleet and John D. P. Fuller. Lexington: University of Kentucky Press, 1962.

Fleming, James R. *Band of Brothers: Company C, Ninth Tennessee Infantry*. Shippensburg, Pa.: White Mane, 1996.

Foster, Samuel T. *One of Cleburne's Command: The Civil War Reminiscences and Diary of Capt. Samuel T. Foster, Granbury's Texas Brigade, CSA*. Ed. Norman D. Brown. Austin: University of Texas Press, 1980.

Freemantle, Arthur James. *Three Months in the Southern States: April–June, 1863*. New York: Bradburn, 1864.

Goree, Thomas Jewett. *Longstreet's Aide: The Civil War Letters of Major Thomas J. Goree*. Ed. Thomas W. Cutrer. Charlottesville: University Press of Virginia, 1995.

Goyne, Minetta Altgelt. *Lone Star and Double Eagle: Civil War Letters of a German-Texas Family*. Fort Worth: Texas Christian University Press, 1982.

Grant, Ulysses S. *The Personal Memoirs of U. S. Grant*. 2 vols. New York: Webster, 1885–86.

Griscom, George L. *Fighting with Ross' Texas Cavalry Brigade, C.S.A.: The Diary of George L. Griscom, Adjutant, Ninth Texas Cavalry Regiment*. Ed. Homer L. Kerr. Hillsboro, Tex.: Hill Junior College Press, 1976.

Hall, James Edmond. *The Diary of a Confederate Soldier: James E. Hall*. Ed. Ruth Woods Dayton. Lewisburg, W.Va.: n.p., 1961.

Harwell, Richard Barksdale, ed. *A Confederate Diary of the Retreat from Petersburg, April 3–20, 1865*. Atlanta: Emory University Publications, 1953.

Heartsill, William Williston. *Fourteen Hundred and 91 Days in the Confederate Army*. Ed. Bell I. Wiley. Jackson, Tenn.: McCowat-Mercer, 1954.

Heller, J. Roderick, III, and Carolynn Ayers Heller, eds. *The Confederacy Is on Her Way up the Spout: Letters to South Carolina, 1861–1864*. Athens: University of Georgia Press, 1992.

Holmes, Henry McCall. *Diary of Henry McCall Holmes, Army of Tennessee, Assistant Surgeon, Florida Troops, with Related Letters, Documents, Etc*. Ed. Alester G. Holmes Jr. State College, Miss.: n.p., 1968.

Hotchkiss, Jedediah. *Make Me a Map of the Valley: The Civil War Journal of Stonewall Jackson's Topographer*. Ed. Archie P. McDonald. Dallas: Southern Methodist University Press, 1973.

Hubbs, G. Ward, ed. *Voices from Company D: Diaries by the Greensboro Guards, Fifth Alabama Infantry Regiment, Army of Northern Virginia*. Athens: University of Georgia Press, 2003.

Hubner, Charles W., ed. *War Poets of the South and Confederate Camp-Fire Songs*. Atlanta: Byrd, n.d.

Ingram, George W. *Civil War Letters of George W. and Martha F. Ingram, 1861–1865.* Comp. Henry L. Ingram. College Station: Texas A & M University, 1973.

Jackman, John S. *Diary of a Confederate Soldier: John S. Jackman of the Orphan Brigade.* Ed. William C. Davis. Columbia: University of South Carolina Press, 1990.

Jamison, Robert David. *Letters and Recollections of a Confederate Soldier, 1860–1865.* Comp. Henry Downs Jamison Jr. and Marguerite Jamison McTigue. Nashville, Tenn.: Jamison, 1964.

Jones, J. William. *Christ in the Camp.* Richmond: Johnson, 1887.

Jones, John B. *A Rebel War Clerk's Diary.* New York: Sagamore, 1958.

Jordan, Weymouth T., ed. "Mathew Andrew Dunn Letters." *Journal of Mississippi History* 1 (April 1939): 110–27.

Lane, Mills, ed. *Times That Prove People's Principles: Civil War in Georgia.* Savannah: Beehive Press, Library of Georgia, 1993.

Lee, J. Edward, and Ron Chepesiuk, eds. *South Carolina in the Civil War: The Confederate Experience in Letters and Diaries.* Jefferson, N.C.: McFarland, 2000.

Lewis, Donald W., ed. "A Confederate Officer's Letters on Sherman's March to Atlanta." *Georgia Historical Quarterly* 51 (December 1967): 491–94.

Marshall, Elizabeth H. "Watch on the Chattahoochee: A Civil War Letter." *Georgia Historical Quarterly* 43 (Winter 1959): 427–28.

McCollom, Albert O. *The War-Time Letters of Albert O. McCollom: Confederate Soldier.* Ed. Walter J. Lemke. Fayetteville, Ark.: Washington County Historical Society, 1961.

Melville, Herman. *Poems of Herman Melville.* Ed. Douglas Robillard. New Haven: Yale University Press, 1976.

Mitchell, Enoch L., ed. "The Civil War Letters of Thomas Jefferson Newberry." *Journal of Mississippi History* 10 (January 1948): 44–80.

———, ed. "Letters of a Confederate Surgeon in the Army of Tennessee to His Wife." *Tennessee Historical Quarterly* 4 (December 1945): 341–53; 5 (March 1946): 61–81; 5 (June 1946): 142–81.

Montgomery, William Rhadamanthus. *Georgia Sharpshooter: The Civil War Diary and Letters of William Rhadamanthus Montgomery, 1839–1906.* Ed. George F. Montgomery Jr. Macon, Ga.: Mercer University Press, 1997.

Moore, Frank, ed. *Songs and Ballads of the Southern People, 1861–1865.* New York: Appleton, 1886.

Moore, Robert A. *A Life for the Confederacy: As Recorded in the Pocket Diaries of Pvt. Robert A. Moore, Co. G, Seventeenth Mississippi Regiment, Confederate Guards, Holly Springs, Mississippi.* Ed. James W. Silver. Jackson, Tenn.: McCowat-Mercer, 1959.

Muir, Andrew F. "The Battle of Atlanta as Described by a Confederate Soldier." *Georgia Historical Quarterly* 42 (March 1958): 109–11.

Negri, Paul, ed. *Civil War Poetry: An Anthology.* Mineola, N.Y.: Dover, 1997.

Noyes, Edward. "Excerpts from the Civil War Diary of E. T. Eggleston." *Tennessee Historical Quarterly* 17 (December 1958): 336–58.

Nugent, William Lewis. *My Dear Nellie: The Civil War Letters of William L. Nugent to*

Eleanor Smith Nugent. Ed. William M. Cash and Lucy Somerville Howorth.
Jackson: University Press of Mississippi, 1977.

Osborn, George C., ed. "Civil War Letters of Robert W. Banks: Atlanta Campaign."
Georgia Historical Quarterly 27 (June 1943): 208–16.

Paxton, Elisha Franklin. *The Civil War Letters of General Frank "Bull" Paxton, CSA, a
Lieutenant of Lee and Jackson.* Ed. John Gallatin Paxton. Hillsboro, Tex.: Hill Junior
College Press, 1978.

Peddy, George Washington. *Saddle Bag and Spinning Wheel: Being the Civil War
Letters of George W. Peddy, M.D., and His Wife, Kate Featherston Peddy.* Ed.
George Peddy Cuttino. Macon, Ga.: Mercer University Press, 1981.

Poché, Felix Pierre. *A Louisiana Confederate: Diary of Felix Pierre Poché.* Ed. Edwin
C. Bearss. Natchitoches: Louisiana Studies Institute, Northwestern State University
of Louisiana, 1972.

Priest, John Michael, ed. *Stephen Elliot Welch of the Hampton Legion.* Shippensburg,
Pa.: Burd Street, 1994.

Rees, William. *A Sermon on Divine Providence, Delivered February 4th, 1863
(Thanksgiving Day), in the Methodist Church, at Austin.* Austin, Tex.: n.p., 1863.
Confederate Imprints Microfilm Series 4185–1.

Reid, Whitelaw. *After the War: A Southern Tour, May 1, 1865, to May 1, 1866.* New
York: Moore, Wilstach, and Baldwin, 1866.

Renfroe, J. J. D. *"The Battle Is God's": A Sermon Preached before Wilcox's Brigade.*
Richmond, Va.: n.p., 1863. Confederate Imprints Microfilm Series 4186.

Resolutions Adopted by Bratton's Brigade, South Carolina Volunteers. Richmond, Va.:
n.p., 1865.

*Resolutions Adopted by Company "H," "I," and "K," Thirteenth Virginia Infantry,
January 28, 1865.* Richmond, Va.: n.p., 1865.

*Resolutions Adopted by Humphrey's Mississippi Brigade, Army of Northern Virginia,
February 3, 1865.* Richmond, Va.: n.p., 1865.

Resolutions Adopted by McGowan's Brigade, South Carolina Volunteers. Richmond,
Va.: n.p., 1865.

Resolutions Adopted by the Officers and Men of the Fifty-seventh Virginia Regiment.
Richmond, Va.: n.p., 1865.

Resolutions Adopted by the Staunton Artillery, February 1st, 1865. Richmond, Va.:
n.p., 1865.

Resolutions Passed at a Meeting of the Fourteenth Virginia Infantry. Richmond: n.p.,
1865.

Resolutions Passed at a Meeting of the Ninth Virginia Infantry. Richmond, Va.: n.p.,
1865.

Ross, Lawrence Sullivan. *Personal Civil War Letters of General Lawrence Sullivan
Ross, with Other Letters.* Comp. Perry Wayne Shelton. Ed. Shelly Morrison. Austin,
Tex.: Morrison, 1994.

Schofield, John M. *Forty-six Years in the Army.* New York: Century, 1897.

Seaton, Benjamin M. *The Bugle Softly Blows: The Confederate Diary of Benjamin M.
Seaton.* Ed. Harold B. Simpson. Waco, Tex.: Texian, 1965.

Simpson, R. W. *Far, Far from Home: The Wartime Letters of Dick and Tally Simpson,*

Third South Carolina Volunteers. Ed. Guy R. Everson and Edward H. Simpson Jr. New York: Oxford University Press, 1994.

Smith, D. E. Huger, Alice R. Huger Smith, and Arney R. Childs, eds. *Mason Smith Family Letters, 1860–1868*. Columbia: University of South Carolina Press, 1950.

Smith, Kristen M., ed. *The Lines Are Drawn: Political Cartoons of Civil War*. Athens, Ga.: Hill Street, 1999.

Spencer, Carrie Esther, Bernard Samuels, and Walter Berry Samuels, eds. *A Civil War Marriage in Virginia: Reminiscences and Letters*. Boyce, Va.: Carr, 1956.

Stampp, Kenneth M., ed. *The Causes of the Civil War*. New York: Simon and Schuster, 1959.

Stanard, Beverly. *Letters of a New Market Cadet, Beverly Stanard*. Ed. John G. Barrett and Robert K. Turner Jr. Chapel Hill: University of North Carolina Press, 1961.

Stone, Kate. *Brokenburn: The Journal of Kate Stone, 1861–1868*. Ed. John Q. Anderson. Baton Rouge: Louisiana State University Press, 1972.

Swank, Walbrook D., comp. *Confederate Letters and Diaries, 1861–1865*. Shippensburg, Pa.: White Mane, 1988.

Tapert, Annette, ed. *The Brothers' War: Civil War Letters to Their Loved Ones from the Blue and Gray*. New York: Random House, 1988.

Taylor, Grant. *This Cruel War: The Civil War Letters of Grant and Malinda Taylor, 1862–1865*. Ed. Ann K. Blomquist and Robert A. Taylor. Macon, Ga.: Mercer University Press, 2000.

Taylor, Walter Herron. *Lee's Adjutant: The Wartime Letters of Colonel Walter Herron Taylor, 1862–1865*. Ed. R. Lockwood Tower and John S. Belmont. Columbia: University of South Carolina Press, 1995.

U.S. War Department. *The War of the Rebellion: The Official Records of the Union and Confederate Armies*. 70 vols. Washington, D.C.: U.S. Government Printing Office, 1880–1901.

Vann, Samuel King. *"Most Lovely Lizzie": Love Letters of a Young Confederate Soldier*. Ed. William Young Elliott. Birmingham, Ala.: n.p., 1958.

Walters, John. *Norfolk Blues: The Civil War Diary of the Norfolk Light Artillery Blues*. Ed. and intro. Kenneth Wiley. Shippensburg, Pa.: Burd Street, 1997.

Watson, James Monroe. *Confederate from East Texas: The Civil War Letters of James Monroe Watson*. Ed. Judy Watson McClure. Quanah, Tex.: Nortex, 1976.

Welch, Spencer Glasgow. *A Confederate Surgeon's Letters to His Wife*. Marietta, Ga.: Continental, 1954.

Wiley, Bell I., ed. "Confederate Letters of John W. Hagan." *Georgia Historical Quarterly* 38 (September 1954): 268–90.

Williams, Hiram Smith. *This War So Horrible: The Civil War Diary of Hiram Smith Williams*. Ed. Lewis N. Wynne and Robert A. Taylor. Tuscaloosa: University of Alabama Press, 1993.

Williams, James M. *From That Terrible Field: Civil War Letters of James M. Williams, Twenty-first Alabama Infantry Volunteers*. Ed. John Kent Folmar. University: University of Alabama Press, 1981.

SECONDARY SOURCES

Allport, Gordon W., and Leo Postman. *The Psychology of Rumor*. New York: Holt, 1947.

Anderson, Fred. *A People's Army: Massachusetts Soldiers and Society in the Seven Years' War*. Chapel Hill: University of North Carolina Press, 1984.

Andreopoulos, George J., and Harold E. Selesky, ed. *The Aftermath of Defeat: Societies, Armed Forces, and the Challenge of Recovery*. New Haven: Yale University Press, 1994.

Arnold, James R. *Grant Wins the War: Decision at Vicksburg*. New York: Wiley, 1997.

Ash, Stephen V. *When the Yankees Came: Conflict and Chaos in the Occupied South, 1861–1865*. Chapel Hill: University of North Carolina Press, 1995.

Auman, William T., and David D. Scarboro. "The Heroes of America in Civil War North Carolina." *North Carolina Historical Review* 58 (October 1981): 327–63.

Ayers, Edward L. *In the Presence of Mine Enemies: War in the Heart of America, 1859–1863*. New York: Norton, 2003.

———. *The Promise of the New South: Life after Reconstruction*. New York: Oxford University Press, 1992.

Ballard, Michael B. *A Long Shadow: Jefferson Davis and the Final Days of the Confederacy*. Jackson: University Press of Mississippi, 1986.

Baynes, John. *Morale: A Study of Men and Courage: The Second Scottish Rifles at the Battle of Neuve Chapelle, 1915*. New York: Praeger, 1967.

Beattie, J. H. M., and R. G. Lienhardt, eds. *Studies in Social Anthropology: Essays in Memory of E. E. Evans-Pritchard by His Former Oxford Colleagues*. Oxford: Clarendon, 1975.

Benjamin, Walter. *Illuminations*. Ed. Hannah Arendt. Trans. Harry Zohn. New York: Schocken, 1969.

Berends, Kurt. "'Wholesome Reading Purifies and Elevates the Man': The Religious Military Press in the Confederacy." In *Religion and the American Civil War*, ed. Randall M. Miller, Harry S. Stout, and Charles Reagan Wilson. New York: Oxford University Press, 1998.

Berens, John F. *Providence and Patriotism in Early America, 1640–1815*. Charlottesville: University Press of Virginia, 1978.

Berger, Peter L. *The Sacred Canopy: Elements of a Sociological Theory of Religion*. New York: Doubleday, 1967.

Beringer, Richard E., Herman Hattaway, Archer Jones, and William N. Still Jr. *Why the South Lost the Civil War*. Athens: University of Georgia Press, 1986.

Berry, Stephen W., II. *All That Makes a Man: Love and Ambition in the Civil War South*. Oxford: Oxford University Press, 2003.

Blair, William. *Virginia's Private War: Feeding Body and Soul in the Confederacy, 1861–1865*. New York: Oxford University Press, 1998.

Blight, David W. *Race and Reunion: The Civil War in American Memory*. Cambridge: Harvard University Press, 2001.

Boles, John B. *The Great Revival, 1787–1805: The Origins of the Southern Evangelical Mind*. Lexington: University Press of Kentucky, 1972.

———. *The Irony of Southern Religion*. New York: Lang, 1994.

Boles, John B., and Evelyn Thomas Nolen., eds. *Interpreting Southern History: Historiographical Essays in Honor of Sanford W. Higginbotham*. Baton Rouge: Louisiana State University Press, 1987.

Bonner, Robert B. "Roundheaded Cavaliers? The Context and Limits of a Confederate Racial Project." *Civil War History* 48 (March 2002): 34–59.

Boorstin, Daniel J. *The Americans: The National Experience*. New York: Random House, 1965.

Boritt, Gabor S., ed. *Why the Confederacy Lost*. New York: Oxford University Press, 1992.

Braudel, Fernand. *The Mediterranean and the Mediterranean World in the Age of Philip II*. Trans. Siân Reynolds. New York: Harper and Row, 1972.

Brugger, Robert J. "The Mind of the Old South: New Views." *Virginia Quarterly Review* 56 (Spring 1980): 277–95.

Burton, Orville Vernon. *In My Father's House Are Many Mansions: Family and Community in Edgefield, South Carolina*. Chapel Hill: University of North Carolina Press, 1985.

Campbell, Jacqueline Glass. *When Sherman Marched North from the Sea: Resistance on the Confederate Home Front*. Chapel Hill: University of North Carolina Press, 2003.

Canary, Robert H., and Henry Kozicki, eds. *The Writing of History: Literary Form and Historical Understanding*. Madison: University of Wisconsin Press, 1978.

Carmichael, Peter S. *The Last Generation: Young Virginians in Peace, War, and Reunion*. Chapel Hill: University of North Carolina Press, 2005.

———. *Lee's Young Artillerist: William R. J. Pegram*. Charlottesville: University Press of Virginia, 1995.

Carter, Dan T. *When the War Was Over: The Failure of Self-Reconstruction in the South, 1865–1867*. Baton Rouge: Louisiana State University Press, 1985.

Cash, W. J. *The Mind of the South*. New York: Knopf, 1941.

Cecil-Fronsman, Bill. *Common Whites: Class and Culture in Antebellum North Carolina*. Lexington: University Press of Kentucky, 1992.

Cherry, Conrad. *God's New Israel: Religious Interpretations of American Destiny*. Englewood Cliffs, N.J.: Prentice-Hall, 1971.

Clausewitz, Carl Von. *On War*. Trans. Michael Howard and Peter Paret. Princeton: Princeton University Press, 1976.

Collingwood, R. G.. *The Idea of History*. Ed. Jan van der Dussen. Oxford: Oxford University Press, 1994.

Connelly, Thomas Lawrence. *Autumn of Glory: The Army of Tennessee, 1862–1865*. Baton Rouge: Louisiana State University Press, 1971.

Daniel, Larry J. *Soldiering in the Army of Tennessee: A Portrait of Life in a Confederate Army*. Chapel Hill: University of North Carolina Press, 1991.

Daniel, W. Harrison. *Southern Protestantism in the Confederacy*. Bedford, Va.: Print Shop, 1989.

Davies, Robertson. *The Rebel Angels*. New York: Viking, 1982.

Davis, William C. *The Cause Lost: Myths and Realities of the Confederacy*. Lawrence: University Press of Kansas, 1996.

Dean, Eric T., Jr. *Shook over Hell: Post-Traumatic Stress, Vietnam, and the Civil War.* Cambridge: Harvard University Press, 1997.

Dew, Charles B. *Apostles of Disunion: Southern Secession Commissioners and the Causes of the Civil War.* Charlottesville: University Press of Virginia, 2001.

Dillard, Philip D. "Independence or Slavery: The Confederate Debate over Arming the Slaves." Ph.D. diss., Rice University, 1999.

Donald, David. "The Proslavery Argument Reconsidered." *Journal of Southern History* 37 (February 1971): 3–18.

———, ed. *Why the North Won the Civil War.* Baton Rouge: Louisiana State University Press, 1960.

Dowdey, Clifford. *Lee's Last Campaign: The Story of Lee and His Men against Grant—1864.* Boston: Little, Brown, 1960.

Dower, John W. *Embracing Defeat: Japan in the Wake of World War II.* New York: Norton, 1999.

———. *Japan in War and Peace: Selected Essays.* New York: New Press, 1993.

———. *War without Mercy: Race and Power in the Pacific War.* New York: Pantheon, 1986.

Durden, Robert F. *The Gray and the Black: The Confederate Debate on Emancipation.* Baton Rouge: Louisiana State University Press, 1972.

Eaton, Clement. *A History of the Old South.* New York: Macmillan, 1949.

Elliott, Emory. *Power and the Pulpit in Puritan New England.* Princeton: Princeton University Press, 1975.

Escott, Paul D. *After Secession: Jefferson Davis and the Failure of Confederate Nationalism.* Baton Rouge: Louisiana State University Press, 1978.

Fahs, Alice. *The Imagined Civil War: Popular Literature of the North and South, 1861–1865.* Chapel Hill: University of North Carolina Press, 2001.

Farmer, James Oscar, Jr. *The Metaphysical Confederacy: James Henley Thornwell and the Synthesis of Southern Values.* Macon, Ga.: Mercer University Press, 1986.

Faulkner, William. *Absalom, Absalom.* New York: Random House, 1936.

———. *Intruder in the Dust.* New York: Random House, 1948.

Faust, Drew Gilpin. "Christian Soldiers: The Meaning of Revivalism in the Confederate Army." *Journal of Southern History* 53 (February 1987): 63–90.

———. *The Creation of Confederate Nationalism: Ideology and Identity in the Civil War South.* Baton Rouge: Louisiana State University Press, 1988.

———. *James Henry Hammond and the Old South: A Design for Mastery.* Baton Rouge: Louisiana State University Press, 1982.

Festinger, Leon. *A Theory of Cognitive Dissonance.* Evanston, Ill.: Row, Peterson, 1957.

Fisher, Walter R. *Human Communication as Narration: Toward a Philosophy of Reason, Value, and Action.* Columbia: University of South Carolina Press, 1987.

Foner, Eric. *Free Soil, Free Labor, Free Men: The Ideology of the Republican Party before the Civil War.* New York: Oxford University Press, 1970.

Foote, Shelby. *The Civil War: A Narrative.* Vol. 3. New York: Random House, 1974.

Foster, Gaines M. *Ghosts of the Confederacy: Defeat, the Lost Cause, and the Emergence of the New South, 1865 to 1913.* New York: Oxford University Press, 1987.

Franklin, John Hope. *The Militant South, 1800–1861*. Cambridge: Harvard University Press, 1956.

———. *A Southern Odyssey: Travelers in the Antebellum North*. Baton Rouge: Louisiana State University Press, 1976.

Freeman, Douglas Southall. *Lee's Lieutenants: A Study in Command*. Vol. 3. New York: Scribner's, 1944.

Freud, Sigmund. *Group Psychology and the Analysis of the Ego*. Trans. James Strachey. London: Hogarth, 1949.

Fuller, Alexandra. *Don't Let's Go to the Dogs Tonight: An African Childhood*. New York: Random House, 2001.

Fussell, Paul. *The Great War and Modern Memory*. New York: Oxford University Press, 1975.

———. *Wartime: Understanding and Behavior in the Second World War*. New York: Oxford University Press, 1989.

Gallagher, Gary W. *The Confederate War: How Popular Will, Nationalism, and Military Strategy Could Not Stave Off Defeat*. Cambridge: Harvard University Press, 1997.

———, ed. *The Third Day at Gettysburg and Beyond*. Chapel Hill: University of North Carolina Press, 1994.

Gallagher, Gary W., and Alan T. Nolan, eds. *The Myth of the Lost Cause and Civil War History*. Bloomington: University of Indiana Press, 2000.

Gaston, Paul M. *The New South Creed: A Study in Southern Mythmaking*. New York: Knopf, 1970.

Genovese, Eugene. *A Consuming Fire: The Fall of the Confederacy in the Mind of the White Christian South*. Athens: University of Georgia Press, 1998.

———. *The Political Economy of Slavery: Studies in the Economy and Society of the Slave South*. New York: Pantheon, 1965.

———. *Roll, Jordan, Roll: The World the Slaves Made*. New York: Pantheon, 1974.

Goldfield, David. *Still Fighting the Civil War: The American South and Southern History*. Baton Rouge: Louisiana State University Press, 2004.

Grant, Susan-Mary. *North over South: Northern Nationalism and American Identity in the Antebellum Era*. Lawrence: University Press of Kansas, 2000.

Gray, J. Glenn. *The Warriors: Reflections on Men in Battle*. New York: Harcourt and Brace, 1957.

Greenberg, Martin H., and Bill Pronzini, eds. *A Treasury of Civil War Stories*. New York: Bonanza, 1985.

Gribben, William. *The Churches Militant: The War of 1812 and American Religion*. New Haven: Yale University Press, 1973.

Griffith, Paddy. *Battle Tactics of the Civil War*. New Haven: Yale University Press, 1989.

Grimsley, Mark. *The Hard Hand of War: Union Military Policy toward Southern Civilians, 1861–1865*. New York: Cambridge University Press, 1995.

Grimsley, Mark, and Brooks D. Simpson, eds. *The Collapse of the Confederacy*. Lincoln: University of Nebraska Press, 2001.

Grossman, Dave. *On Killing: The Psychological Cost of Learning to Kill in War and Society*. Boston: Little, Brown, 1995.

Hagerman, Edward. *The American Civil War and the Origins of Modern Warfare:*

Ideas, Organization, and Field Command. Bloomington: Indiana University Press, 1988.

Hale, Grace Elizabeth. *Making Whiteness: The Culture of Segregation in the South, 1890–1940.* New York: Pantheon, 1998.

Halttunen, Karen, and Lewis Perry, eds. *Moral Problems in American Life: New Perspectives on Cultural History.* Ithaca: Cornell University Press, 1998.

Hanna, Alfred Jackson, and Kathryn Abbey Hanna. *Confederate Exiles in Venezuela.* Tuscaloosa, Ala.: Confederate, 1960.

Hanson, Victor Davis. *The Western Way of War: Infantry Battle in Classical Greece.* New York: Knopf, 1989.

Harris, Brayton. *Blue and Gray in Black and White: Newspapers in the Civil War.* Washington, D.C.: Brassey, 1999.

Harris, William C. *Lincoln's Last Months.* Cambridge: Harvard University Press, 2004.

Harvey, Robert. *The Undefeated: The Rise, Fall, and Rise of Greater Japan.* London: Macmillan, 1994.

Hatch, Nathan O. *The Democratization of American Religion.* New Haven: Yale University Press, 1989.

Hattaway, Herman, and Archer Jones. *How the North Won: A Military History of the Civil War.* Urbana: University of Illinois Press, 1983.

Hess, Earl J. *Liberty, Virtue, and Progress: Northerners and Their War for the Union.* New York: New York University Press, 1988.

———. *The Union Soldier in Battle: Enduring the Ordeal of Combat.* Lawrence: University Press of Kansas, 1997.

Heyrman, Christine Leigh. *Southern Cross: The Beginnings of the Bible Belt.* Chapel Hill: University of North Carolina Press, 1997.

Hoehling, Adolph A. *Last Train from Atlanta.* New York: Yoseloff, 1958.

Horn, Stanley Fitzgerald. *The Army of Tennessee.* Norman: University of Oklahoma Press, 1941.

Hynes, Samuel. *The Soldiers' Tale: Bearing Witness to Modern War.* New York: Penguin, 1997.

Ignatieff, Michael. *The Warrior's Honor: Ethnic War and the Modern Conscience.* London: Chatto and Windus, 1998.

Jimerson, Randall C. *The Private Civil War: Popular Thought during the Sectional Conflict.* Baton Rouge: Louisiana State University Press, 1988.

Keegan, John. *The Face of Battle.* New York: Penguin, 1976.

Kuhn, Thomas. *The Structure of Scientific Revolutions.* Chicago: University of Chicago Press, 1962.

Lee, Ronald Glenn. "Exploded Graces: Providence and the Confederate Israel in Evangelical Southern Sermons, 1861–1865." Master's thesis, Rice University, 1990.

Leed, Eric J. *No Man's Land: Combat and Identity in World War I.* Cambridge: Cambridge University Press, 1979.

Lepore, Jill. *The Name of War: King Philip's War and the Origins of American Identity.* New York: Random House, 1998.

LeShan, Lawrence. *The Psychology of War: Comprehending Its Mystique and Its Madness.* Chicago: Noble, 1992.

Levine, Bruce. *Confederate Emancipation: Southern Plans to Free and Arm Slaves during the Civil War*. Oxford: Oxford University Press, 2006.

Linderman, Gerald F. *Embattled Courage: The Experience of Combat in the American Civil War*. New York: Free Press, 1987.

Livermore, Thomas L. *Numbers and Losses in the Civil War in America: 1861–65*. Bloomington: Indiana University Press, 1957.

Logue, Larry M. *To Appomattox and Beyond: The Civil War Soldier in War and Peace*. Chicago: Dee, 1996.

Luraghi, Raimondo. *The Rise and Fall of the Plantation South*. New York: Watts, 1978.

Lynn, John A. *The Bayonets of the Republic: Motivation and Tactics in the Army of Revolutionary France, 1791–94*. Urbana: University of Illinois Press, 1984.

Marshall, S. L. A. *Men against Fire: The Problem of Battle Command in Future War*. Washington, D.C.: Combat Forces Press and Morrow, 1947.

Maxwell, William. *So Long, See You Tomorrow*. New York: Random House, 1980.

McCardell, John. *The Idea of a Southern Nation: Southern Nationalists and Southern Nationalism, 1830–1860*. New York: Norton, 1979.

McCurry, Stephanie. *Masters of Small Worlds: Yeomen Households, Gender Relations, and the Political Culture of the Antebellum South Carolina Low Country*. New York: Oxford University Press, 1995.

McCusker, John J. "The Demise of Distance: The Business Press and the Origins of the Information Revolution in the Early Modern Atlantic World." *American Historical Review* 110 (April 2005): 294–321.

McKitrick, Eric L. *Andrew Johnson and Reconstruction*. Chicago: University of Chicago Press, 1960.

McPherson, James M. *Battle Cry of Freedom: The Civil War Era*. New York: Oxford University Press, 1988.

———. *Crossroads of Freedom: Antietam*. Oxford: Oxford University Press, 2002.

———. *For Cause and Comrades: Why Men Fought in the Civil War*. New York: Oxford University Press, 1997.

———. *What They Fought For, 1861–1865*. Baton Rouge: Louisiana State University Press, 1994.

McPherson, James M., and William J. Cooper Jr., eds. *Writing the Civil War: The Quest to Understand*. Columbia: University of South Carolina Press, 1998.

Miller, Randall M., Harry S. Stout, and Charles Reagan Wilson, eds. *Religion and the American Civil War*. New York: Oxford University Press, 1998.

Mitchell, Reid. *Civil War Soldiers*. New York: Penguin, 1988.

———. *The Vacant Chair: The Northern Soldier Leaves Home*. New York: Oxford University Press, 1993.

Montague, C. E. *Disenchantment*. London: Chatto and Windus, 1922.

Moran, Charles McMoran Wilson. *The Anatomy of Courage*. Boston: Houghton Mifflin, 1967.

Morgan, Edmund S. *American Slavery, American Freedom: The Ordeal of Colonial Virginia*. New York: Norton, 1975.

Nelson, Larry E. *Bullets, Ballots, and Rhetoric: Confederate Policy for the United States Presidential Contest of 1864*. University: University of Alabama Press, 1980.

Nickles, David Paul. *Under the Wire: How the Telegraph Changed Diplomacy*. Cambridge: Harvard University Press, 2003.

O'Brien, Michael, ed. *All Clever Men Who Make Their Way: Critical Discourse in the Old South*. Fayetteville: University of Arkansas Press, 1982.

Osterweis, Rollin G. *The Myth of the Lost Cause, 1865–1900*. Hamden, Conn.: Archon, 1973.

Ovid. *The Metamorphoses of Ovid*. Trans. David R. Slavitt. Baltimore: Johns Hopkins University Press, 1994.

Pakenham, Thomas. *The Boer War*. New York: Random House, 1979.

Paludan, Phillip Shaw. *A People's Contest: The Union and Civil War, 1861–1865*. Lawrence: University Press of Kansas, 1988.

Poole, W. Scott. *Never Surrender: Confederate Memory and Conservatism in the South Carolina Upcountry*. Athens: University of Georgia Press, 2004.

Power, J. Tracy. *Lee's Miserables: Life in the Army of Northern Virginia from the Wilderness to Appomattox*. Chapel Hill: University of North Carolina Press, 1998.

Rable, George C. *Fredericksburg! Fredericksburg!* Chapel Hill: University of North Carolina Press, 2002.

Risley, Ford. "The Confederate Press Association: Cooperative News Reporting of the War." *Civil War History* 47 (September 2001): 222–39.

Robertson, James I., Jr. *Soldiers Blue and Gray*. Columbia: University of South Carolina Press, 1988.

Rolle, Andrew F. *The Lost Cause: The Confederate Exodus to Mexico*. Norman: University of Oklahoma Press, 1965.

Rosnow, Ralph L. "Psychology of Rumor Reconsidered." *Psychological Bulletin* 87 (May 1980): 578–91.

———. "Rumor as Communication: A Contextualist Approach." *Journal of Communication* 38 (March 1988): 12–28.

Roth, Michael S., ed. *Freud: Conflict and Culture*. New York: Knopf, 1998.

Royster, Charles. *The Destructive War: William Tecumseh Sherman, Stonewall Jackson, and the Americans*. New York: Knopf, 1991.

———. *A Revolutionary People at War: The Continental Army and American Character, 1775–1783*. Chapel Hill: University of North Carolina Press, 1979.

Rubin, Anne Sarah. *A Shattered Nation: The Rise and Fall of the Confederacy, 1861–1868*. Chapel Hill: University of North Carolina Press, 2005.

Schivelbusch, Wolfgang. *The Culture of Defeat: On National Trauma, Mourning, and Recovery*. Trans. Jefferson Chase. New York: Metropolitan, 2003.

Schwartz, Regina M. *The Curse of Cain: The Violent Legacy of Monotheism*. Chicago: University of Chicago Press, 1997.

Schweiger, Beth Barton. *The Gospel Working Up: Progress and the Pulpit in Nineteenth-Century Virginia*. Oxford: Oxford University Press, 2000.

Shaara, Michael. *The Killer Angels*. New York: Random House, 1974.

Shalit, Ben. *The Psychology of Conflict and Combat*. New York: Praeger, 1988.

Shattuck, Gardiner H., Jr. *A Shield and Hiding Place: The Religious Life of the Civil War Armies*. Macon, Ga.: Mercer University Press, 1987.

Shibutani, Tamotsu. *Improvised News: A Sociological Study of Rumor*. Indianapolis: Bobbs-Merrill, 1966.

Shinn, Roger Lincoln. *Wars and Rumors of Wars*. Nashville: Abingdon, 1972.

Shy, John. *A People Numerous and Armed: Reflections on the Military Struggle for American Independence*. New York: Oxford University Press, 1976.

Silver, James W. *Confederate Morale and Church Propaganda*. Tuscaloosa, Ala.: Confederate, 1957.

Slotkin, Richard. *Regeneration through Violence: The Mythology of the American Frontier, 1600–1860*. Middletown, Conn.: Wesleyan University Press, 1973.

Smith, Mark M. *Listening to Nineteenth-Century America*. Chapel Hill: University of North Carolina Press, 2001.

Smith, S. A. "Talking Toads and Chinless Ghosts: The Politics of 'Superstitious' Rumors in the People's Republic of China, 1961–1965." *American Historical Review* 111 (April 2006): 405–27.

Snay, Mitchell. *Gospel of Disunion: Religion and Separatism in the Antebellum South*. Cambridge: Cambridge University Press, 1993.

Stampp, Kenneth M. *The Peculiar Institution: Slavery in the Ante-Bellum South*. New York: Knopf, 1956.

Starr, Louis M. *Bohemian Brigade: Civil War Newsmen in Action*. New York: Knopf, 1954.

Stoler, Ann Laura. " 'In Cold Blood': Hierarchies of Credibility and the Politics of Colonial Narratives." *Representations* 37 (Winter 1992): 151–89.

Stouffer, Samuel A., Arthur A. Lumsdaine, Marion Harper Lumsdaine, Robin M. Williams Jr., M. Brewster Smith, Irving L. Janis, Shirley A. Star, and Leonard S. Cottrell Jr. *The American Soldier*. 4 vols. Princeton: Princeton University Press, 1949.

Stowell, Daniel W. *Rebuilding Zion: The Religious Reconstruction of the South, 1863–1877*. New York: Oxford University Press, 1998.

Sutherland, Donald E. "Exiles, Emigrants, and Sojourners: The Post–Civil War Confederate Exodus in Perspective." *Civil War History* 31 (September 1985): 237–56.

Taussig, Michael. "Culture of Terror—Space of Death: Roger Casement's Putumayo Report and the Explanation of Torture." *Comparative Studies in Society and History* 26 (July 1984): 467–97.

Taylor, William A. *Cavalier and Yankee: The Old South and the American National Character*. New York: Braziller, 1961.

Thomas, Emory M. *The Confederacy as a Revolutionary Experience*. Englewood Cliffs, N.J.: Prentice-Hall, 1971.

———. *The Confederate Nation, 1861–1865*. New York: Harper and Row, 1979.

Tuveson, Ernest Lee. *Redeemer Nation: The Idea of America's Millennial Role*. Chicago: University of Chicago Press, 1968.

Verhey, Jeffrey. *The Spirit of 1914: Militarism, Myth, and Mobilization in Germany*. Cambridge: Cambridge University Press, 2000.

Virgil. *The Aeneid*. Trans. Robert Fitzgerald. New York: Random House, 1981.

Warren, Robert Penn. *The Legacy of the Civil War: Meditations on the Centennial.* New York: Random House, 1961.

Watson, Bruce Allen. *When Soldiers Quit: Studies in Military Disintegration.* Westport, Conn.: Praeger, 1997.

Weaver, Blanche H. C. "Confederate Emigration to Brazil." *Journal of Southern History* 27 (February 1961): 33–53.

Wecter, Dixon. *When Johnny Comes Marching Home.* New York: Houghton Mifflin, 1944.

White, Luise. *Speaking with Vampires: Rumor and History in Colonial Africa.* Berkeley: University of California Press, 2000.

Wiley, Bell I. *The Life of Billy Yank: The Common Soldier of the Union.* Indianapolis: Bobbs-Merrill, 1951.

———. *The Life of Johnny Reb: The Common Soldier of the Confederacy.* Indianapolis: Bobbs-Merrill, 1943.

Wilson, Charles Reagan. *Baptized in Blood: The Religion of the Lost Cause, 1865–1920.* Athens: University of Georgia Press, 1980.

Woodward, C. Vann. *American Counterpoint: Slavery and Racism in the North-South Dialogue.* Boston: Little, Brown, 1964.

———. *The Burden of Southern History.* Baton Rouge: Louisiana State University Press, 1960.

Woodworth, Steven E. *While God Is Marching On: The Religious World of Civil War Soldiers.* Lawrence: University Press of Kansas, 2001.

Wyatt-Brown, Bertram. *The Shaping of Southern Culture: Honor, Grace, and War, 1760s–1890s.* Chapel Hill: University of North Carolina Press, 2001.

———. *Southern Honor: Ethics and Behavior in the Old South.* Oxford: Oxford University Press, 1982.

Index

Alabama, 52

Albright, James W.: on Confederate religion, 26; on the enemy, 63, 71; reacts to defeat, 170; reacts to Hampton Roads peace conference, 156; spreads rumors, 101, 122, 125, 129

American Revolution, 14, 40, 44, 47, 54; Confederate comparisons to, 31, 142, 161, 183

Appomattox, Va., 91, 178, 180, 183; campaign, 5, 167–69; Lee's surrender at, 169–71. *See also* surrender

Army of Northern Virginia, 5, 6, 86, 138, 156; during Appomattox campaign, 167–69; black Union troops and, 67; crime within, 181; after Gettysburg, 92–94; invincible aura of, 1–2, 18, 76, 98–99, 121, 162, 210n35; learns of Fort Fisher's fall, 153; learns of Vicksburg's fall, 119; morale of, 96; during Overland campaign, 24, 99–101; reacts to enemy atrocities, 61, 123; religious revivals in, 27–28, 165; surrenders, 169; veteran character of, 76. *See also* Lee, Robert E.; *and individual battle names*

Army of Tennessee, 6, 28, 99, 141; during Atlanta campaign, 102–9; morale of, 95; reacts to enemy atrocities, 62; reacts to Lee's surrender, 171–

73; returns to Tennessee, 111–14; surrenders, 173; veteran character of, 76. *See also individual battle names*

Army of the Potomac, 47, 53, 86, 99, 134

Atlanta, Ga., 3, 35, 69, 128, 150; campaign for, 29, 68, 70, 76, 91, 102–9; distant view of, 64, 123–24, 135, 138; fall of, 2, 33, 109–10, 124–26, 133–34; inaccurate reporting about, 141–42; presidential campaign and, 131; Union treatment of, 61–63, 204n46, 217n21

atrocities, 143, 177, 179; compared to other wars, 204n50; complicate surrender, 170; historical memory of, 183; intensify enemy stereotypes, 61, 64–67, 204n49; in military unit resolutions, 160; in music, 56–57

attrition, 35–36, 77, 83–85, 88

Beauregard, P. G. T., 98, 125, 128, 211n42; rumors about, 135, 136

Berkeley, Henry Robinson, 87; at Cold Harbor, 83–84; on defeat, 183–84; on gloom, 149; sees Richmond's burnt district, 180

Bird, Edgeworth, 78; on Confederate religion, 23; expresses culture of invincibility, 120; on gloom, 149, 153; on manpower shortages, 85–86; on rations, 78; reacts to defeat, 173; reacts to Gettysburg, 92–94; on retaliation, 66

Grant, Ulysses S. (*continued*)
captures Vicksburg, 94; Confederates
underestimate, 70, 86, 96–97, 99–101,
142, 166; rumors about, 71, 119,
121–23, 128, 141, 142, 174
Great Awakening, 11
Great Revival of 1801–1805, 13
guerrilla warfare, 6, 56–57

Hampton, Thomas, 107, 151–52; on
Confederate religion, 21, 23, 25;
estimates casualties, 104; on fatigue,
82; on the military situation, 108,
164; reacts to Hampton Roads
peace conference, 156; sees sham
battle, 97–98; spreads rumors,
126
Hampton, Wade, 135–36
Hampton Roads peace conference,
155–58
Heartsill, William W., 71, 151–53, 156;
on Confederate religion, 24–25; on
the military situation, 159; reacts to
Atlanta, 124–25; reacts to defeat,
174–75; records rumors, 136–37
Higginbotham, Paul, 63, 136; anxious
about home front, 80–81; at the Crater,
67, 101; on fatigue, 82; spreads rumors,
128, 130, 144
home front, 80–81, 96, 193; religion and,
22–23; rumors and, 118, 121, 133;
soldiers' anxiety over, 39, 64; soldiers'
separation from, 88–90, 178
honor, southern, 28, 40, 44–45, 55;
Cavalier Myth and, 46; Lost Cause
and, 181; military spirit and, 76, 89,
113, 152, 187; postwar defiance and,
182; at war's end, 156, 167, 173–74
Hood, John Bell, 82–83, 103; as
commander of Army of Tennessee,
107–14, 148–49; rumors about,
124–26, 134, 138, 141–42, 154. *See
also* Army of Tennessee
Hooker, Joseph, 47, 118
hunger, 19, 36, 78, 83. *See also* rations

Jackson, Thomas "Stonewall," 52, 197n33
Johnston, Joseph E., 83, 102–6, 109, 123,
176; censors news, 141; removed from
command, 107, 108, 124, 149, 215n82;
returns to command, 166; reviews
troops, 97; rumors about, 119, 125, 137,
166, 174; surrenders, 172–73; troops'
confidence in, 23, 76, 106–7, 211n42

Kennesaw Mountain, battle of, 72, 90,
105–6, 123

Lee, Robert E., 3, 99, 127–28; addresses
desertion, 151; assaults fail on Sundays,
26; Confederate faith in, 27, 90, 121,
123, 127; defensive strategy of, 83;
promoted to command all armies,
165–66; reviews troops, 97; sickness of,
82; surrenders, 169. *See also* Army of
Northern Virginia
Lincoln, Abraham, 52, 120, 159;
assassinated, 174; caricatures of, 47–
51, 57–60, 202n20; at Hampton Roads
conference, 155–56; presidential
campaign of 1864 and, 129–32;
prisoner exchange system and, 67,
130; reelected, 134, 150, 163; southern
clergymen criticize, 18
Longstreet, James, 28, 91, 96, 151
Lost Cause, the, 14, 167, 174, 181–86;
Confederate origins of, 2, 3, 8, 227n41

Mansfield, Battle of, 24, 71, 90, 127,
219n35
March to the Sea, 30, 65, 88, 111, 141,
150, 218n31. *See also* Sherman,
William Tecumseh
masculinity, 3, 126, 208n6; challenged by
the enemy, 55–57, 179; encourages
endurance, 77, 79, 187; and noncombatants, 85; patriotic appeals to, 37–38.
See also warrior's code
McClellan, George B., 47, 70; and
presidential campaign, 71, 72, 131–32,
220n47; at Seven Days' Battles, 17, 21

religion, Confederate: antebellum roots of, 11–15; atheism and, 16; clergy and, 18–20, 37–38, 204n49; fast days and, 17, 18, 26–29, 36, 38, 164, 198n38, 198n43; God's favor and, 9–10, 15–20, 23–26, 36–40; impact of, 10; national sin and, 32–33; popular Scriptures of, 10, 15, 18, 25, 31, 38, 39, 54; theodicy and, 30–36, 199n47; typologies and, 15, 18, 20–21; wartime revivals of, 27–30, 35–36, 154, 165, 197n38. *See also* Providence

religious military press, 20, 54, 142, 200n62, 222n71

Resaca, Ga., 111; battle of, 23, 102

revenge. *See* vengeance

reviews, military: Confederate, 28, 29, 94, 97–98, 212n46; Federal, 178

Richmond, Va., 6, 31, 35, 128; black Confederates in, 158; civilian morale within, 155–56, 166, 224n8; defense of, 69, 73, 76, 100–101, 209n19; destruction in, 180; evacuation of, 5, 40, 142, 167–68, 171; manpower deficiencies around, 85–86, 98; newspapers of, 56, 118, 124, 141, 157; rumors about, 71, 97, 122–23, 137, 141–42, 172, 174–75; Seven Days' Battles for, 17, 52, 86; symbolic value of, 109, 135. *See also* Confederate government

rumors, 3, 7, 8; after Atlanta's fall, 124–26; causes of, 135–45, 220n52, 220n56; credibility of, 134–35; of Europe, 121, 132–34, 158–59, 172, 175, 220n49; of Grant's death, 122–23; historical value of, 116–17, 126–27, 145–46, 217n19; about the home front, 64, 80, 88, 217n12; of military victory, 101, 120–24, 126, 141–42, 174; from minor theaters, 127–29, 154; of northern collapse, 73–74, 100, 120, 128, 129–32; of peace, 121, 155–56, 159, 174, 179, 224n16; proliferate in 1865, 154, 176

Schofield, John M., 76, 112–15, 164

secession, 41, 45–46; postwar explanations for, 185; religion and, 194n4; wartime rumors of, 129–33, 145

Seven Days' Battles, 20–21, 52, 198n38

sham battles, 29, 98, 212n48

Shelby, Jo, 181

Shenandoah Valley, 86, 101, 127, 138; destruction of, 39, 61, 160, 180

Sheridan, Philip H., 61, 86, 180

Sherman, William Tecumseh, 33, 35, 111; during Atlanta campaign, 102–9, 123–27; captures Atlanta, 109; during Carolinas campaign, 149, 166, 175; embodies barbaric enemy, 53, 61–64; during March to the Sea, 150–51; negotiates surrender of the Army of Tennessee, 172; rumors about, 141–42, 174. *See also* March to the Sea

slavery, 19, 156, 172; Confederate defeat and, 36, 117, 182, 188; Confederate emancipation and, 155, 158, 203n39; Confederate fears of subjugation and, 55, 57, 153, 160–62; culture of invincibility and, 4, 6, 188; diehards' postwar views of, 185; national sin and, 32–33, 196n21; religion and, 11, 13–14; sectionalism and, 42–43, 44, 201n2. *See also* subjugation

Smith, Kirby, 127, 175–76

Spotsylvania Court House, battle of, 21, 72, 99, 100, 127; rumors of, 121, 123, 136, 138

stereotypes, enemy. *See* enemy stereotypes

Stuart, J. E. B., 52

subjugation, 119, 156; Confederate fears of, 57, 64, 74, 119, 175, 179; postwar resistance against, 182. *See also* slavery

surrender, 148, 173–74; at Appomattox Court House, 169–71; Confederates opposed to, 56, 74, 85, 155–56, 172–73; culture of invincibility after, 7–8, 178–86; at Durham Station, 173; of the trans-Mississippi, 176; at Vicksburg, 94–95, 119–20

Taylor, Grant, 64, 105; on desertion, 150; on military situation, 104, 214n66; spreads rumors, 144

Taylor, Richard, 121

telegraphy, 116, 118, 119, 137–41, 143

Thomas, George, 111, 126, 142, 154

Timrod, Henry, 17–18

Trans-Mississippi Department, 6, 101, 138, 152; misinformation within, 124, 136–37, 158–59; rumors about, 120, 127–28, 133, 219n35; surrender of, 175–76

trench warfare, 33, 205n60; desertion from, 80; enemy stereotypes and, 67–69, 73, 205n59; fatigue of, 81–82; inflated casualty figures of, 100, 137; religious revivals within, 35, 176; rumors within, 101–2, 123, 125, 131, 134–36

vengeance, 3, 69, 127, 162; encourages rumors, 123; God as instrument of, 37, 62, 65; against the home front, 88, 129; intensifies enemy stereotypes, 41, 56–57, 64–67

Vicksburg, Miss., 30, 67, 96, 182; distant view of, 118–19, 137–38; enemy stereotypes after, 53, 61; fall of, 94–95, 120, 211n42; inaccurate reporting about, 125, 141; as a major turning point, 76, 94; religious revivals after, 27, 31, 34; rumors about, 119–21, 122, 137, 217n12

Volck, Adalbert Johann, 47, 49, 57, 58, 202n20

Walters, John, 86, 100, 167–68, 170; on desertion, 152; on the enemy, 67–68, 72–73; on gloom, 87; on the presidential campaign, 131–32; records rumors, 127–28, 135–36; on retaliation, 65–66

war correspondents, 139–40

warrior's code, 79, 107, 208n6. *See also* masculinity

war weariness, 77, 119–20, 129, 150, 223n4

Welch, Spencer Glasgow, 62, 83; on manpower shortage, 85; on the military situation, 95, 97, 101, 125; reacts to Gettysburg, 92–93; spreads rumors, 141–42

Wilderness, Battle of the, 23, 39, 72, 81, 83; distant rumors of, 121, 123; participants' view of, 99–100, 212n52; rumors spread within, 135–36

Yancey, William L., 43–44

CPSIA information can be obtained
at www.ICGtesting.com
Printed in the USA
LVHW090058201120
672187LV00003B/54